Pro iOS Design and Development

HTML5, CSS3, and JavaScript with Safari

Andrea Picchi

Apress®

Pro iOS Web Design and Development: HTML5, CSS3, and JavaScript with Safari

Copyright © 2011 by Andrea Picchi

ISBN-13 (pbk): 978-1-4302-3246-9

ISBN-13 (electronic): 978-1-4302-3247-6

Trademarked names, logos, and images may appear in this book. Rather than use a trademark symbol with every occurrence of a trademarked name, logo, or image we use the names, logos, and images only in an editorial fashion and to the benefit of the trademark owner, with no intention of infringement of the trademark.

The use in this publication of trade names, trademarks, service marks, and similar terms, even if they are not identified as such, is not to be taken as an expression of opinion as to whether or not they are subject to proprietary rights.

President and Publisher: Paul Manning
Lead Editor: Steve Anglin
Development Editor: Matthew Moodie
Technical Reviewer: Daniel Paterson
Editorial Board: Steve Anglin, Mark Beckner, Ewan Buckingham, Gary Cornell, Morgan Engel, Jonathan Gennick, Jonathan Hassell, Robert Hutchinson, Michelle Lowman, James Markham, Matthew Moodie, Jeff Olson, Jeffrey Pepper, Douglas Pundick, Ben Renow-Clarke, Dominic Shakeshaft, Gwenan Spearing, Matt Wade, Tom Welsh
Coordinating Editor: Adam Heath
Copy Editor: Ginny Munroe
Compositor: MacPS, LLC
Indexer: BIM Indexing & Proofreading Servies
Artist: SPi Global
Cover Designer: Anna Ishchenko

Distributed to the book trade worldwide by Springer Science+Business Media, LLC., 233 Spring Street, 6th Floor, New York, NY 10013. Phone 1-800-SPRINGER, fax (201) 348-4505, e-mail orders-ny@springer-sbm.com, or visit www.springeronline.com.

For information on translations, please e-mail rights@apress.com, or visit www.apress.com.

Apress and friends of ED books may be purchased in bulk for academic, corporate, or promotional use. eBook versions and licenses are also available for most titles. For more information, reference our Special Bulk Sales–eBook Licensing web page at www.apress.com/bulk-sales.

The source code for this book is available to readers at www.apress.com. You will need to answer questions pertaining to this book in order to successfully download the code.

To my parents, Gianni and Carla, for their endless support.

To my fiancée and "Mia Principessa," Simona, source of strength, love, and will.

—Andrea Picchi

Contents at a Glance

Contents

About the Author

With a background in psychology (University of Padova) and computer science (University of Pisa), **Andrea Picchi** started designing WebApps for the new Apple device in 2007 when the first iPhone was launched on the market. After the first release of the Apple SDK in 2008, he started developing Native Apps using Objective-C.

He also worked with the SimBin Development Team AB on the videogame RACE07—The Official WTCC Game project—and supported the group's iPhone iUI Developers, iPhoneWebDev and iPhone Application Development course at Stanford University.

In recent years, Andrea Picchi has spoken at many important conferences around Europe, twice at the WhyMCA Mobile Developer Conference with a talk on "The Cognitive Paradigm of Touch-Screen Devices" and another on "A Cognitive Approach to the User-Centered Design for Mobile Design and Development." He also spoke at IASummit with a speech on "Cognitive Design and Optimization of Touch-Screen Interfaces" and at UXConference with a speech on "Cognitive Optimization of Mobile Touch Contexts."

In 2011 he also started to teach "iOS WebApps" in a course also available on iTunesU and "Mobile Device Development" in a first-level Master, both organized by the Computer Science Department of the University of Pisa.

Today, as a mobile project manager, his priority has been to implement a cognitive approach to touch-screen interface design in both mobile and ubiquitous computing contexts. He also continues his work designing and developing for iOS with both the web model (using HTML5, CSS3, JavaScript) and SDK model (using Cocoa-Touch in Objective-C).

About the Technical Reviewer

 **Daniel Paterson** has a master's degree in comparative literature, and he penned a memoir on integrating literary theory into fictional works, taking novels by Umberto Eco, Milan Kundera, and David Lodge as examples. After his university years, Daniel entered web development and joined Newsweb/Lagardère Active in April 2009. Passionate about the Web as about many other things, he enjoys every opportunity to work on interesting projects and to develop his skills.

Acknowledgments

This book could not have been written without the fine folks at Apress.

Steve Anglin, who started everything rolling by contacting me and offering this great opportunity. Thanks, Steve. Adam Heath, who managed the project, and Kelly Moritz, who organized my schedule and deadlines. The development editor, Matthew Moodie, and the technical reviewer, Daniel Paterson, who drew on their experience to show me how to turn something good into something great.

A very special thanks to Carl Willat and Clay Andres.

Carl Willat worked with me on the project from day one. Carl read and reviewed everything I wrote in this book and helped me to explain all my ideas in more elegant and correct form.

Clay Andres's unique combination of charisma, deep knowledge, and professionalism inspires everyone around him. Clay is able to look beyond ordinary ways of thinking and see the shortest path for bringing a project to success. I can't image a better editorial director for any author.

Finally, thanks to my parents, Gianni and Carla, for their endless support and to my fiancée, Simona, for faithfully supporting me in all the bad and good moments and for being the center of everything that has value in my life.

—Andrea Picchi

Preface

"A journey of a thousand miles begins with a single step . . ."

—Lao-Tzu

Mobile Device Evolution

These are exciting times for those who live and work with technology every day, whether they are young people who have been using technology since birth, or, like many others, have had to adapt to it.

It is an exciting moment because in recent years there is no other example of technology that has changed our lives so dramatically as has the evolution of the mobile device.

Since in knowing the past you'll be more prepared to understand the present and help create the future, in this book we'll precede our discussion of how to get there with a short history of smartphones, with our beloved iPhone or iPad in hand.

Humble Beginnings: The Early Mobile Web

Everything started in 1908, when Nathan B. Stubblefield of Murray, Kentucky was issued the first US patent for a wireless telephone.

Forty years later, the zero generation (0G) of mobile telephones was introduced. Mostly used as car phones, they were meant to connect mobile users in cars to the fixed public telephone network.

The zero generation was not officially categorized as mobile device technology since it did not support the automatic change of channel frequency during calls (Handover), which would allow the user to move from one cell (the present-day radio base station covered area) to another.

Figure 1. *The zerogeneration: Mobile car phone (1960s)*

In the 1960s, a new full-duplex VHF/UHF radio system launched by Bell Systems, and subsequently improved by AT&T, called "Improved Mobile Telephone Service" (IMTS), brought many improvements, such as direct dialing rather than connection through an operator, and higher bandwidth.

The first-generation (1G) *cellular systems*, developed between the late 1960s and the early 1970s, were analog, and still based on IMTS technology. The systems were "cellular" because coverage areas were split into smaller hexagonal areas called "cells," each of which were served by a low-power transmitter and receiver.

> **NOTE:** A cellular system is a radio network made up of a number of radio cells, each served by at least one fixed-location transceiver (device that is both a transmitter and receiver) known as a base station. These cells cover different areas and combine to provide radio transmission over a wider range than that of one cell.
>
> The simple structure of the cellular *mobile-radio network* consists of the following:
>
> ▨ PSTN: Public switched telephone network
>
> ▨ HLR: Home location register
>
> ▨ MSC: Mobile switching center
>
> ▨ VLR: Visitor location register
>
> ▨ RBS: Radio base station

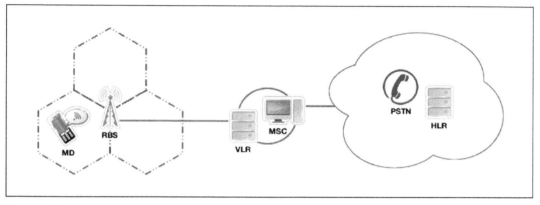

Figure 2. *The common (and simple) PCS (Personal Communication Service) network architecture*

The 1G analog systems for mobile communications saw two key improvements during 1070s: the invention of the *microprocessor*, and the digitization of the control link between the mobile phone and the cell site.

> **NOTE:** A microprocessor incorporates most or all of the functions of a computer's central processing unit (CPU) on a single integrated circuit (IC or microchip).

In 1973 Dr. Martin Cooper at Motorola invented the first modern portable handset. Legend has it that his first call was to his rival Joel Engel, head of research at Bell Labs, giving him the news about how the competition between them had turned out.

The first commercial handheld cellular phone was launched by Motorola only ten years later in 1983 and called DynaTAC. This brick-like phone had a weight of 28 ounces (0.8Kg) and a price of "only" $4,000.

> **HISTORICAL NOTE:** Martin Cooper, the inventor of world's first cellular phone, the Motorola DynaTAC, first had the idea from watching Captain James T. Kirk talk over his communicator in the famous *Star Trek* TV series in the 1960s.
>
> In today's world, talking on the go seems normal, but back in the early 1960s when Star Trek was first aired, most people's phones worked only with cords.

Expanding Mobile's Reach: GSM Device

The second generation (2G) ofdigital cellular systems was first developed at the end of the 1980s. These systems digitized not only the control link but also the voice signal.

The new systems provided better quality and higher capacity at a lower cost to consumers. GSM (Global System for Mobile Communication, originally Groupe Special Mobile) was the first commercially operated digital system using *TDMA protocol* (time division multiple access) for its channel access method.

NOTE: A channel access method allows several terminals connected to the same multi-point transmission medium to transmit over and receive to share its capacity.

Fundamental forms of *channel access schemes* are as follows:

▨ FDMA: Frequency division multiple access

▨ TDMA: Time division multiple access

▨ CDMA: Code division multiple access

▨ SDMA: Space division multiple access

GSM networks pioneered low-cost implementation of the "Short Message Service" (SMS), also known as text messaging, which has since been supported on other mobile phone standards as well. The new GSM standard also includes a worldwide emergency telephone number feature. This three-digit number is localized, and some countries have a different emergency number for each of their various emergency services. A few common numbers are 112, 999, and 911.

In the 1990s, along with the new way of transmitting information, a new generation of small 100–200g handheld devices started replacing the brick-sized phones. This change was made possible thanks to technological advancements that included smaller batteries and more energy-efficient electronics. The 1990s were the glory years of Motorola, Inc. and its famous MicroTAC phone, which was released in 1989 and remained a status symbol for almost a decade.

In 1997, the GSM system was extended with a packet data capability by the new GPRS (general packet radio service), and again in 1999 with a higher-speed data transmission protocol called EDGE (Enhanced Data Rates for GSM Evolution). Those two new versions of GSM protocol were called 2.5G and 2.75G networks, respectively.

In the same year, Nokia launched 7110, the first terminal with *WAP* (Wireless Application Protocol), which for the first time permitted Internet access directly from the phone. "A small step for a protocol but a giant leap for mankind."

NOTE: WAP 1.0 standard, released in 1998, describes a complete software stack for mobile Internet access. Nokia was also a co-founding member of the WAP standard.

A WAP browser provides all the basic service of a computer-based web browser but is simplified to operate within the restrictions of a mobile phone. Users can connect to WAP sites written in or dynamically converted to WML (Wireless Markup Language) and access them via the WAP browser.

After having released its first phone in 1992 (the Nokia 1011), in the 2000s Nokia took control of the mobile devices market from Motorola and, with 1.2 billion phones in use and more than 806 different devices made and sold, still leads it today.

Figure 3. *The 2G generation: GSM devices (1990s)*

Another Step Forward: UMTS Device

The third-generation (3G) systems promised faster communications services, including voice, fax, and Internet anytime and anywhere, with seamless global roaming. 3G technologies were an answer to the International Telecommunications Union's IMT-2000 specification and were originally supposed to be a single, unified, worldwide standard, but in practice the 3G world has been split into three camps: *UMTS*, *CDMA2000*, and *TD-SCDMA*.

> **NOTE:** The UMTS standards are as follows:
>
> ■ **UMTS:** Based on W-CDMA technology, it is the solution generally preferred by countries using GSM, centered in Europe. UMTS is managed by the 3GPP organization also responsible for GSM, GPRS, and EDGE.
>
> ■ **CDMA2000:** This is an outgrowth of the earlier 2G CDMA standard IS-95. CDMA2000's primary proponents are outside the GSM zone in the Americas, Japan, and Korea. It is managed by 3GPP2, which is separate and independent from UMTS's 3GPP.
>
> ■ **TD-SCDMA:** This technology is being developed in the People's Republic of China by the companies Datang and Siemens.

The first (pre-commercial) *3G network* was developed in Japan in 2001 and supported 144 Kbits of bandwidth with high-speed movement (e.g., vehicles), 384 Kbits (e.g., on campus), and 2 Mbits for stationary use (e.g., in-building).

NOTE: 3G systems are intended to provide a global mobility with a wide range of services including telephony, paging, messaging, Internet, and broadband data. The simple structure of the *3G network* consists of the following:

IP: IP-based network
PSTN: Public switched telephone network
CN: Core network
UTRAN: UMTS Terrestrail Radio Access Network
VLR: Visitor location register

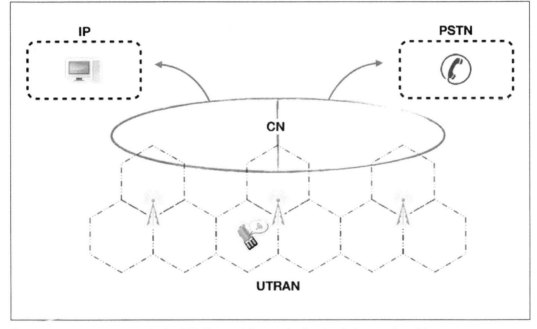

Figure 4. *The common (and simple) PCS (Personal Communication Service) network architecture*

The last evolution of 3G protocol is the HSDPA (high speed downlink packet access), developed in 2005 and called 3.5G. 3.5G is a packet-based protocol data service in W-CDMA downlink with data transmission up to 8–10 Mbits.

Expanding Mobile Capabilities: Smartphones

The first *smartphone* was called Simon and was designed by IBM in 1992 and shown as a concept product that year at COMODEX (Computer Dealer's Exhibition), the computer industry trade show held in Las Vegas.

Simon was released to the public in 1993 and sold by BellSouth. Besides being a mobile phone, it also contained a calendar, address book, world clock, calculator, notepad, games, and mail and fax capabilities.

The next attempt was in 1996 by Nokia, with itsmobile device called "Communicator." This distinctive palmtop computer-style smartphone was the result of a collaborative effort with

Hewlett-Packard, combining an early successful and expansive HP personal digital assistant (PDA) with Nokia's bestselling phone around that time. The Nokia 9000 Communicator was the first true smartphone, with an operating system called GEOS 3.0.

The Ericsson R380, released in 2000, was the first phone sold as a "smartphone" and the world's first touch-screen phone. The R380 had the usual PDA functions and a large touch-screen combined with an innovative flip so it could also be used as normal phone. It was also the first commercially available Symbian OS (5.0) phone. However, it could not run native third-party applications.

Figure 5. *The 3G generation: Smartphones (2000s)*

NOTE: There is no industry standard definition of a smartphone, but we can see it as a "mobile phone offering advanced capabilities that runs complete operating system software providing a standardized interface and platform for application developers."

Source: SmartphoneAppsPedia

In 2002, Handspring released the Palm OS Treo smartphone, utilizing a full keyboard that combined wireless web browsing, e-mail, calendar, and contact organizer with mobile third-party applications that could be downloaded or synced with a computer.

Also in 2002, RIM released the BlackBerry, which was the first smartphone optimized for wireless e-mail use. By December 2009, it had achieved a total customer base of 32 million subscribers.

Redefining Mobile's Reach: The Next-Generation Protocols

The fourth-generation (4G) system is a successor to 3G and aims to provide a wide range of data rates up to ultra-broadband (gigabit speed) Internet access to mobile as well as stationary users. The name of this new project is LTE (Long Term Evolution) and is a set of enhancements to the UMTS (Universal Mobile Telecommunications Systems) architecture.

The LTE specification provides downlink peak rates of at least 100 Mbits and an uplink of at least 50 Mbits with a RTT (round-trip time) of less than 10 ms.

But beyond these numbers, the most important point of the LTE draft is the "Persuasive Network" that describes an amorphous, and at present entirely hypothetical concept, where the user can be simultaneously connected to several wireless access technologies and can seamlessly move between them (vertical handoff). The access technologies can be Wi-Fi, UMTS, EDGE, or any other future access technology.

> **NOTE:** Vertical handoff refers to a network node changing the type of connectivity it uses to access a supporting infrastructure, usually to support node mobility.

The 4G network will be based on OFDM (orthogonal frequency division multiplexing) protocol and will probably use smart antennas.

> **NOTE:** Smart antennas are antenna arrays with smart signal processing algorithms used to identify spatial signal signatures such as the direction of arrival (DOA) of the signal and use them to track and locate the antenna beam on the mobile device.

The Mobile WiMAX (IEEE 802.16) mobile broadband access standard is also branded 4G and offers peak data rates of 128 Mbits downlink and 56 Mbits uplink.

Advanced Human-Device Interaction: Touch-Screen Devices

On June 29, 2007, when the first iPhone was introduced at "MacWorld Conference and Expo" by Apple, the mobile market changed irreversibly. Increasing numbers of handsets with touch screens have started to appear on the market following the lead set by Apple's iPhone.

The touch screen has gained popularity and become more common on handsets, helping to make the handsets more intuitive, pleasant, and efficient to use.

Handsets with intuitive user interface allowed quick and easy access to various applications and services.Alternatively many smartphones and high-end handsets with useful and innovative features have been commercial failures simply because their user interface was too complex and difficult for convenient use.

> **NOTE:** A touch screen is an electronic visual display that can detect the presence and location of a touch (typically a finger or a pen) within the display area.
>
> There are a few types of touch-screen technologies:
>
> ■ Capacitive (used on iPhone)
>
> ■ Resistive
>
> ■ Surface acoustic wave
>
> ■ Strain gauge
>
> ■ Optical imaging
>
> ■ Dispersive signal technology
>
> ■ Acoustic pulse recognition
>
> ■ Coded LCD on bidirectional screen

On November 11, 2008, HTC produced the "Touch HD," a device with a much larger screen than its predecessors. This device, like all other HTC devices, runs Windows Mobile and the HTC proprietary user interface TouchFLO 3D.

On June 6, 2009, Palm released its Palm Pre, a smartphone with a multi-touch screen and a sliding QWERTY keyboard based on webOS, the new Linux-based operating system from Palm.

> **HISTORICAL NOTE:** The QWERTY keyboard layout was devised and created in the early 1870s by Christopher Latham Sholes (1819–1890), a newspaper editor and printer who lived in Milwaukee, Wisconsin. This layout takes its name from the first six characters at the left of the keyboard's top row.
>
> Source: Wikipedia

On January 5, 2010, Google launched its "Nexus One," a smartphone with touch-screen technology based on Android OS, Google's open source mobile operating system. As with the Apple iPhone, the large capacitive touch screen is capable of handling multi-touch gestures.

Unfortunately for competing brands, Apple's real secret was not just the touch screen, as many people thought, but what the iPhone was capable of achieving through touch-screen technology: a brand new user interface experience.

I say "unfortunately" because although any brand can make use of the latest advanced "projected capacitive" technology, not every brand has an operating system like iOS, for implementing all the services and killer applications that help make an iOS device unique.

That's why, from an operative system point of view, Apple is at least a few years ahead of all other competitors, and that's why one good development team, the people from Google, focused first of all on developing itsAndroid OS and then later the Nexus Series smartphone.

> **NOTE:** Later in this book, we will analyze how this technology changed the paradigm used for building every user interface dedicated to the mobile world. Fornow the key idea to remember is that the more complex the structure you need to implement, the simpler must be the interface design with which the user interacts.

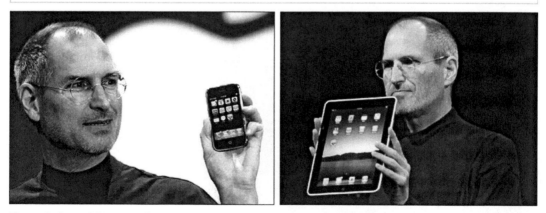

Figure 6. *Steve Jobs presenting the iPhone (2007) and introducing the iPad (2010)*

On January 27, 2010, Apple launched the iPad to fill the gap between the iPhone and the MacBook. Apple iPad runs iOS 3.2 (called iPhone OS at the time), with a resolution of 1024x768 pixels and offers new native applications optimized for this new environment.

The iPad's screen is composed of a single piece of multi-touch glass, with no up or down, left or right. There is no single orientation, and therefore it can be positioned to fit the user's needs. That's really the big thing behind the Apple iPad, and that's why, if with the Apple iPhone we were able to achieve a new device experience, with the iPad we will be able to bring this experience to thousands of potential users who, until now, had never thought about a having a "computer" in their lives.

> **READING NOTE:** If you want to analyze how multi-touch technology will impact the desktop computer's future and how our lives will probably change in accordance with this revolution, jump to last chapter.

I like to think of the iPad as the Wii of the mobile ecosystem. The Nintendo Wii was criticized by the hardcore gamers, but what they didn't realize was that the Nintendo Wii was meant for everyone but them.

> **CITATION:** "We all want things to be simpler, and now here is a simple thing. I think it will be a huge success."
>
> Steve Wozniak, co-founder of Apple, Inc.

On June 7, 2010, Apple lunched the latest version of the iPhone, called iPhone 4, and everything changed again. The iPhone 4 runs the fourth generation of the iPhone OS firmware, released initially on June 21, 2010 and renamed iOS 4. The new smartphone from Apple introduced FaceTime, the video calling feature, HD video recording, and Multitasking, where the user can use multiple applications at the same time.

> **NOTE:** Multitasking and iOS5 run only on iPhone 4 S, iPhone 4, iPhone 3G S,iPad, and iPad2. The last firmware version for the iPhone 2G is 3.1.3, released on February 2, 2010, and for iPhone 3G it is 4.2.1, released on November 2010.

The iPhone 4 S and iPhone 4 have a 960 x 640 resolution based on the new retina display developed by Apple with 326 ppi. It's called retina display because is beyond the retina capability of perceive no more than 300 ppi.

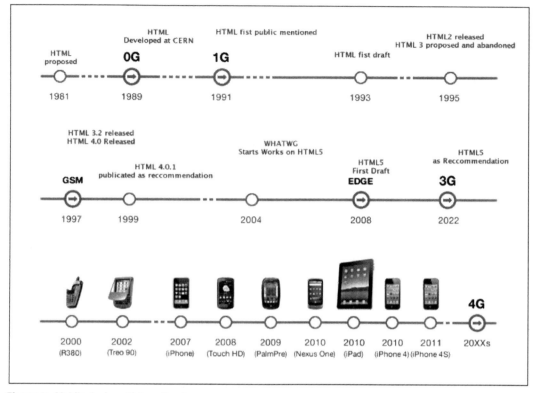

Figure 7. *Mobile devices history timeline*

For this reason, thanks also to touch-screen technology, the future is full of opportunities for those who want to design and develop for iPhone and, even more, for iPad.

Introduction

"The only true voyage of discovery . . .would be not to visit strange lands but to possess other eyes . . ."

—Marcel Proust

Who Needs This Book

This book is for a designer and/or a developer whowants to start designing or developing iOS user interfaces or iOS WebApps (iPhone, iPod Touch, and iPad).

This book is writtenwith simplicity in mind, and the goal is to bring you along in the entire process involved in designing and developing for Apple's mobile devices, implementing a real use case called "The Store."

You will design and develop using web standards like HTML5, CSS3, and JavaScript, and you will not need any of those skills for reading this book.We will use HTML5 and CSS3 from the basics.We will provide a JavaScript crash course and will also use a JavaScript Framework for making things easier and faster.

What You Will Learn from This Book

We split this book into three logical parts in order to achieve a better learning-oriented path.

In **Part One**, we will introduce the foundations of designing and developing for the mobile web and then how to transcend them.

In **Chapter 1**,"Think Mobile Touch," you will learn how to think in a mobile-oriented way, learning the mobile device's evolution, analyzing Apple's unique style.

In **Chapter 2**,"Agile Project Building for iOS Devices," you will learn how to implement a mobile information architecture through steps from the basic strategies to sketching and prototyping. We will also show a systemic approach to iOS mobile design, introducing first the content-out approach and then the page models and user-interface models, including the new inverted approach used with the iPad. You will also see accessibility and usability in Apple devices.

In **Chapter 3**,"Web Development for iOS Devices," you will learn how to use the web standards and some useful tools for developing your iOS WebApp fasterand more easily. You will be introduced to the framework that we will use in our case study, and, analyzing both NativeApps and WebApps, you will see the differences between a web development model using web standards and the SDK development model using Cocoa Touch and Objective-C. You will also see the different levels of approach to designing and developing a WebApp.

> **NOTE:** This book is focused on design and development for iOS, using web standards like HTML5, CSS3, and JavaScript; therefore we will not use Cocoa Touch Framework or the Object-C language in any of the projects of this book.

In **Part Two**, we will go deep into designing for iPhone and iPad, analyzing methodologies, best practices, and some useful tools for speeding up your workflow.

In **Chapter 4**, "User Interface Design for iOS Devices," you will start the real iOS user interface design process for mobile, working with both iPhone and iPad devices, also introducing the concepts behind a cognitive approach to the iOS user interface design process. You will be introduced to the concepts of positive-negative and active-passive interface; you will see the laws of perception, the color phycology, and how to use the most common reading patterns in iOS design. In the end, we will analyze the single elements of the iPhone and iPad user interface.

In **Chapter 5**, "iPhone UI Design: Think Simple," you will go deep intothe iPhone user interface design process, and you will learn the concepts and rules of this particular way to design user interfaces. You will see how to start from the sketch phase, using pen and paper, and go to the design phase, using Adobe Fireworks, analyzing every single graphic element of our use case user interface.

In **Chapter 6**, "iPad UI Design: Think Inverted," you will go deep intothe iPad user interface design, and you will learn the concepts and rules of this particular way to design user interfaces. You will be introduced to the invert-simplicity concept, and you'll see how to prioritize, shape, and group the iPad user interface elements. You will see the simplicity-complexity paradox keypoints, and you will see how to start from the sketch phase, using pen and paper, and go to the design phase, using Adobe Fireworks, analyzing every single graphic element of our use case user interface.

In **Part Three**, we will start to extend the web standards development for both iOS devices, iPhone and iPad.

In **Chapter 7**, "Web Standards for WebKit: Maximizing Mobile Safari," we will start comparing the iPhone and the iPad, and we will present pros and cons of hybrid and dedicated webpages. We will approach the web standards like HTML5, presenting the re-defined tags from HTML4 and the brand new ones like <canvas>, <video>, and <audio>, using these tags for adding features to our WebApp use case. We will approach CSS3 with all the new Level 3 properties, and JavaScript with a real crash course analyzing also the BOM (Browser Object Model) and the DOM (Document Object Model).

In **Chapter 8**, "Native iOS Environment Development," you will learn how to develop a WebApp, emulating the iOS environment from thevisual fundamentals, like going into full-screen mode, adding a springboard icon, or interacting with iOS services like the map, phone, SMS, or e-mail applications. You will be introduced to the touch event and gesture interaction in iOS devices, also seeing some examples of custom touch event handlers, including the orientation change event. In the end of the chapter, you will see how to expand the iOS Web Framework used for our use case.

In **Chapter 9**, "Native iOS Design Implementation," we will work over the web concept and the code behind the iOS webpages. You will learn how to emulate the native iPhone interface, watching the code that, step by step, implements every single user interface element in your WebApp, or how to simulate the new iPad interface. In both cases, we will finish with a real case study.

In **Chapter 10**, "Optimizing iOS WebApp," we will introduce how to optimize our WebApp or mobile webpage and all our assets used in our environment. You will learn how to optimize your WebApp performance minimizing bandwidth usage, how to optimize your WebApp code using web standards best practices, and how to compress your WebApp. You will also learn how to optimize the usability of your WebApp, addressing the most common usability problems that could affect your users. You will learn how to make your WebApp available offline, using the new HTML5 cache manifest feature, and in the last part of the chapter you will see how to use the new mobile SEO tools from Google and how to design your WebApp in a search engine–oriented way.

In **Chapter 11**, "Testing iOS WebApps," you will see the web development lifecycle, and you will learn how to test your WebApp or mobile webpage for iPhone or iPad using an agile approach. We will show how to choose the right test in order to save your budget, how to organize your test with Unified Modeling Language (UML), and how to evaluate your test's resultsin the right way. The chapter will end with some real examples.

In **Part Four**, we will examine the future of mobile web-based devices, how this revolution will change our daily lives, and how this technology will impact the future of desktop computers.

In **Chapter 12**, "Maximizing the Market for iOS WebApps," we will show how to maximize the market for iOS WebApps. You will learn how to promote your WebApp using different approaches like beta testers. You will see how to submit your WebApp to the Apple WebApp Portal and to other third-party portals and how to use the virality of social networks toreach all your potential users. In the last part of the chapter, you will see some tools for monetizing your WebApp.

In **Chapter 13**, "Looking Beyond the Mobile Web to Ubiquitous Computing," we will look behind the mobile web, discussing the explosion of mobile devices and wireless communications. We will also analyze the next-generation usability with multi-touch-screen technology, how the future will change for desktop computers, and how it will change our daily lives.

Where Will the Journey Through This Book Take You?

Reading this book, you will master the entire design and development flow; you will have a complete overview ofthe entire workflow involved in design and development for iOS in the real world; you will know exactly "what to do and how to do it" as a designer and/or developer.

This book will give you a mobile-oriented mentality, a solid knowledge of Apple's mobile device features, and the knowledge of all web standards involved in the design and development process.

Mastering the concepts and techniques used in this book, you will takeyour first step as a designer and developer, and, at the end of this journey, you will be ready to start your own first mobile project on iOS.

How Will You Get Started and Then How Will You Use What You've Learned?

The structure of this book is extremely learning-oriented because the entire book's structure is based on the real workflow used in design and development for iOS and implemented in this book on a real use case called "The Store."

Reading each chapter, you will go through this workflow, and, besides learning the web standards, the specific techniques, the tools, and everything else you need for design and development, you will experience learning the real workflow path used in every mobile-oriented project.

## Chapter 1

Think Mobile Touch

"A small step for man, one giant leap for mankind..."

—Neil Armstrong

These are exciting times for those who live and work with technology every day, whether they are young people who have used technology all their lives or they are like those who have adapted to it. These are exciting times because in recent years, no other example of technology has changed our lives so dramatically as the evolution of the mobile device.

In this book, you see how the mobile revolution has changed the way we develop applications and how touch screen technology brings new variables to the table. First, you learn how to use new touch design techniques to design a touch-based user interface. Then, you learn how to adapt the same touch-based design principles to the specific needs of the iPhone and iPad. We base our project on an agile version of the standard Information Architecture process for optimizing both user and single-developer (or small team) needs.

After the design phase, you learn how to implement the design in the development phase and how to use web standards and WebKit-based frameworks to achieve the project goals.

As a final step in the process, you learn how to test a mobile touch application and how to evaluate tests in a user-centered way before releasing the application through the Apple WebApp portal or other third-party portals.

Why the Mobile Web?

A mobile market exists, it's growing day by day, and it's a revolution that impacts our way of life like few others. The question is, "Why should we invest time and resources in this market?"

From Desktop to Mobile

The history of computing has had five main cycles according to Morgan Stanley (shown in Figure 1–1): mainframe computing (1960s), micro computing (1970s), personal computing (1980s), desktop Internet computing (1990s), and mobile Internet computing (2000s). Looking at the mobile Internet computing era, you can identify the reasons for this evolution.

Figure 1–1. *Technology cycles in computing history*

First, the new touch screen technology increases the interface's usability while reducing the frustration of mobile web browsing. Second is the incredible evolution of social networks such as Facebook and Twitter. Third are the new VoIP services that stand as attractive alternatives to traditional 2G and 3G cellular communication, which has been the new cheap data plans local ISPs have offered in the last few years.

The iPhone is at the center of this process because it catalyzed these three factors (also pioneering some of them) and as you can see from Figure 1–2, it has gained and maintained its dominant position on the market month after month. This is another good reason for starting to design and develop for the iPhone and iPad today. The time invested learning a language such as Objective-C (for native applications) or web standards (for web applications) is surely worth the effort in a short period of time.

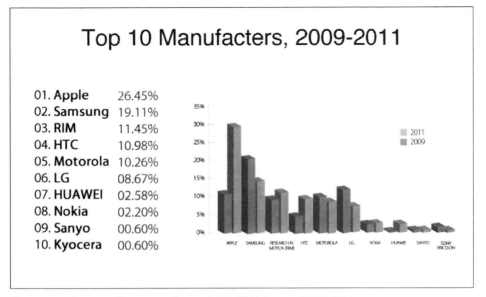

Figure 1-2. *Top manufactures on the market in 2011 (source: MobileMix)*

The nonstop evolution of mobile devices will, in the near future, involve some interactions that push the mobile ecosystem to optimize some of its services and present them as standard features for all devices while introducing other new services such as the ones in the following:

Augmented Reality

The mobile device can "browse" Reality using information from services over the Web.

Mobile Device as Wallet

We can make safe payments from our devices, transforming an ordinary smartphone into a debit or credit card. MCommerce also becomes more common.

TV on the Go

Mobile users get broad access to traditional and mobile-oriented content created by professional companies and ordinary users.

"Smart" Mobile Networks

This enables mobile phones to automatically connect to all available access points located in the user's nearby area.

Global Positioning Services

The user's position is automatically updated and exported for use by private and public applications.

Internet in Your Pocket

Today, you can browse the Internet with just a few touch screen devices on the market, but in the future, even "mass-production" mobile phones will come with HTML browsers.

Improved Ergonomics and Usability

Most users know that to run an application or enter inputs on a "mass-production" device, it's necessary to perform a lot of clicks on the phone keypad. In the near future, many such devices will be equipped with touch screen technology.

Mobile Market

Over 4 billion people own or have access to a mobile device today. Of those, almost 50 percent have access to the web through a mobile device and that number grows with each passing year.

Today, six major mobile operating systems are on the market:

- iOS
- Symbian OS
- Android
- RIM OS
- Windows Phone 7
- WebOS

You can see the different percentages of each OS worldwide in Figure 1–3.

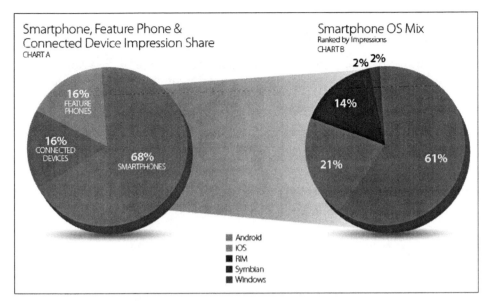

Figure 1–3. *Operating system share in 2011 (source: MobileMix).*

According to these percentages, the first good reason to start to design and develop for mobile devices today is that the market is large and there are more work opportunities than those in the desktop market.

With a mobile market that has become so greatly expanded, today more people access the web via mobile devices than with desktop computers. For services such as email, RSS, or social networks, the disparity between mobile Internet access and desktop Internet access is even larger. Today, these three services, shown in recent MobileMix reports, are the most used on mobile devices. ("Sixty percent of U.S. traffic came from WiFi-capable devices, and the iPhone is used more on WiFi than other smartphones." May, 2011 Report, page 17.) Speaking for myself, I can hardly imagine going to work every day without the ability to access RSS feeds and emails on my iPhone.

Why Mobile Now?

With the growth path evident in the evolution of mobile devices, you get the final reason to invest time in developing Apple devices. The reason is that those types of services are unavailable on nontouch screen devices and on some non-Apple devices that do have touch screens.

Today is the right moment to jump on board the train of mobile device development, because the center of our (computer) activities is definitely moving from the inside of our house to inside our pocket.

A Mobile-Oriented Approach

Design and development for mobile devices requires a small change of paradigm; technologies involved are different, user interfaces are different, and even environmental conditions are different because most of the time, your applications and services are used outdoors and not in a quiet and comfortable room.

Despite that, the only suggestion that you always need to keep in mind is common and obvious: Try to walk in the shoes of mobile users and everything will be fine.

In Part II of this book, we work with iPhone and iPad; for now, we show you some general points to remember in approaching the mobile-oriented paradigm for touch devices.

Mobile-Oriented Guidelines

To work with the issues that mobile site design presents and to get a result that is as user-friendly and useful as your standard site, some creative problem-solving skills are required, including:

- Understanding the hardware and software available
- Giving the user the feeling of visiting the standard site
- Giving the user the option to visit the standard site
- Designing for both portrait and landscape views
- Including only important content from your standard site
- Prioritizing your content for a linear user experience
- Optimizing your navigation for fingers
- Optimizing your code to reduce bandwidth usage
- Minimizing the use of images to reduce bandwidth usage
- Ensuring your redirects work properly
- Testing, testing, and testing!

Your goal as designer and developer is to build **One Web,** where the same information is available and optimized for different devices, as detailed in Figure 1–4.

ONE WEB DEFINED

The W3C defines the concept of One Web as follows:

"One Web means making, as far as is reasonable, the same information and services available to users irrespective of the device they are using. However, it does not mean that exactly the same information is available in exactly the same representation across all devices. The context of mobile use, device capability variations, bandwidth issues, and mobile network capabilities all affect the representation. Furthermore, some services and information are more suitable for and targeted at particular user contexts."

From "W3C Mobile Web Best Practice 1.0," Chapter 3.1

In accordance with the W3C standards, don't be afraid to offer different versions of your content, because the content's role is to bring a message to the users; for this reason, focus on offering the same (optimized) message and not necessarily the exact same content.

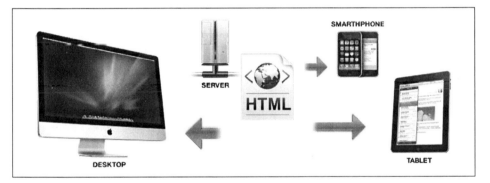

Figure 1–4. *The one-web paradigm visually*

This concept is the same one used in cross-browser design; unfortunately, many designers still believe that designing a cross-browser website means achieving the same website look in all of the existing browsers.

From a content-out point of view (and not only from that standpoint), the cross-browser design's primary function is to make the same message available through different browsers.

NOTE: We explain in depth the content-out approach in Chapter 2.

Apple's Mobile Hardware

One of the key points that you in this book is that "the hardware is not as important; the user experience is the real killer application." Despite that, having a deep knowledge of the hardware you use in your project is fundamental and required for designing and developing quality works.

Often people ask for guidance in designing a web site or a web application to be compatible with different models of the same device and the answer is always the same: If you design a web site, optimize your work for the oldest device because a website is a general resource and you need to guarantee to the users the availability of its functions.

If you design an iOS web application, you need to guarantee that a set of functions is available from the oldest device to the newest one and that a subset of those functions is optimized only for the newest device. A reasonable ratio might be 30 percent to 70 percent with 70 percent of functions made available to all device models.

Summary

This chapter showed how and with which technologies computing has gone through four generations. It also showed how devices that run iOS on top of their advanced capabilities are the best solution for both native and web developers.

This chapter described a general approach to the mobile-oriented paradigm and some basic principles for working around the issues that mobile web site and web application design present.

You were introduced to some killer services based on touch-screen devices and saw how almost all of them are used on the go. In addition, you saw how designers and developers need to approach this new type of mobile context to optimize the mobile user experience.

## Chapter 2

Agile Project Building for iOS Devices

"...the thing that has struck me the most is the difference between how we think people use the web site and how they actually use them."

—Steve Krug

The Mobile Strategy and Information Architecture Processes are two of the most important variables in the project flow. With these processes, you build the foundation of a web site or web application. Everything that follows is built on top of what you create at that stage.

For that reason, this chapter covers many fundamental details of these important processes, first defining a mobile strategy and then showing how to implement the Information Architecture Process.

Next, you will learn the three main steps in the Information Architecture process and how to adapt these steps in designing an iOS web application. I will discuss the "golden rules" of this approach and how usability and accessibility interact with each other in the process.

In the last part of this chapter, I will examine the iPhone and iPad design models and analyze their user interface elements.

Implementing a Mobile Information Architecture

Along our journey through this book, you will follow a visual flow (see Figure 2–1) so that you'll have a clear idea of where we are at any given point and how we'll get to where we're trying to go. The first step in the mobile project flow is the analysis phase. In this phase, you'll define your mobile strategy. The bigger your project is, the more important this first step will be. Planning a sound mobile strategy can mitigate the project's major risks.

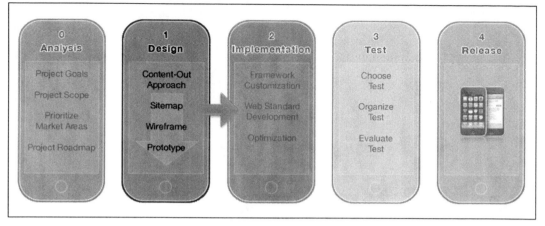

Figure 2–1. *Mobile Project Flow - Step 1.1: Information Architecture*

After the first step of analysis, you are ready to begin the Information Architecture Process. Your role is to interpret content for the mobile context. In the Mobile Information Architecture Process, you need to discover the kinds of information or service you want to deliver or offer, matching this information to the needs of the users. This process involves determining the appropriate metadata structure to use according to the environment of each user.

The user's immediate environment is the main difference between a mobile and desktop context, where user-information interaction is always the same and never changes.

> **NOTE:** As you'll see, working with mobile applications isn't that different from working with desktop projects. I'll go through the process to make sure you see the whole picture.

What Is Information Architecture and Why Is It Important?

Information Architecture (also known as IA) is the foundation of every project, and according to Richard Saul Wurman (from the AIA (American Institute of Architects) National Conference, 1976) we can define the information architect as follows:

- The individual who organizes the patterns inherent in data, making complex information clear.

- A person who creates the structure or map of information that allows others to find their personal path to knowledge.

- A member of the emerging 21st century professional occupation that addresses the needs of the age, focusing upon clarity, human understanding, and the science of the organization of information.

Success is not guaranteed just because your new web site or web application has great-looking visual design or offers the newest services on the market, because a well-engineered product can still fail if it has poor Information Architecture. From desktop to mobile, Information Architecture is one of the most underestimated steps in almost every project.

In using the Mobile Information Architecture, we will define not only how our information will be structured, but also how users will interact with it in a specific environment.

Information Architecture is not a fixed process; it can be adapted from context to context, optimizing the ratio between effort and achievements. The following is my personal view on this process, presented in 9 phases.

The Nine Phases of Information Architecture

The full Information Architecture process is composed of nine phases:

- Information research (IR),
- Information management (IM),
- Content architecture (CA),
- Experience design (XD),
- User experience (UX),
- Information design (ID),
- Usability engineering (UE),
- Interaction design (ID), and
- Human – computer interaction (HCI).

After the first IR (information research) phase, moving clockwise around the circle (see Figure 2–2) from IM (information management) through to HCI (human – computer interaction), the relative depth of detail increases.

In the IM phase, consultants concern themselves with very little detail, instead taking in the big picture.

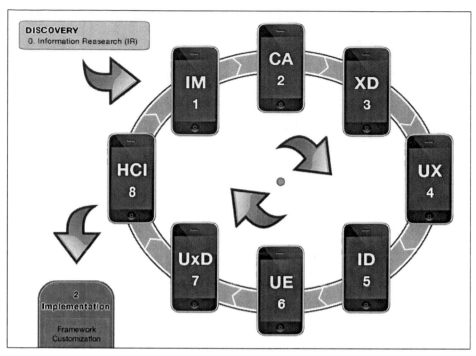

Figure 2–2. *Information Architecture Process: from design to implementation*

Obviously in this process there is room for iteration (as in most modern development methodologies), but generally the level of detail progresses as time moves forward.

Now it's time to see the nine phases in detail.

Information Research (IR)

This is the first step, where the collecting of information starts. It's a crucial phase, because future decisions will be made using the following information:

- Techniques used,
- Market analysis,
- Competitor comparison,
- Output documents, and
- Project requirements.

Information Management (IM)

This is the strategic part of the process. The purpose of this activity is to plan the overall approach an organization will take towards managing the information. The Information management approach involves

- Techniques used,
- Brainstorming,
- Process diagrams,
- Flowcharts,
- Roadmaps,
- Information management strategies,
- Output documents,
- Information management specifications, and
- Mobile strategies.

Content Architecture (CA)

This is where you design, at a fairly broad level, the content that will be found within a web site or application and how it will be structured and organized. To do this, you may rely on

- Techniques used,
- Content-out approach,
- Semantic markups,
- Site maps,
- Mind maps,
- Blueprints,
- Grey box wireframes,
- Swimlane charts,
- Electronic prototypes,
- Output documents, and
- Content specifications.

Experience Design (XD)

This takes a broader view of design beyond that of the asset and considers the total experience a user will have. The process involves the following:

- Techniques used,
- Integrated marketing campaigns,
  - Multichannel strategy,
  - Customer lifecycle plan,

- Customer relationship management strategies,
- Flowcharts,
- Site map, and
- Output documents,
  - Experience design specification.

User Experience (UX)

This is where you design the way a web site's or an application's content is organized in accordance with different user contexts:

- Techniques used,
- Wireframes,
- Paper prototypes,
- Electronic prototypes,
- Output documents,
- User experience specification, etc.

Information Design (ID)

This is the practice of designing how information is conveyed, either in textual or graphic terms:

- Techniques used,
- Paper prototypes,
- Page templates,
- Wireframes,
- Output documents,
- Information design specification, to name a few.

Usability Engineering (UE)

This is focused on engineering the user experience, typically through design patterns.

DEFINITION: Design Pattern

"A reusable solution to a commonly occurring problem within a given context.
A design pattern is not a finished design that can be transformed directly into code. It is a description or template for how to solve a problem that can be used in many different situations."
(Wikipedia)

If we apply an iterative process, UE could also make use of research conducted at the HCI level to solve usability problems. The focus, after all, is much more about the following nuts and bolts of the interface than about aesthetics:

- Outcomes and artifacts,
- Detailed wireframes,
- Paper prototypes,
- Electronic prototypes,
- Flowcharts,
- Output documents, and
- Usability engineering specification.

Interaction Design (ID)

This is the phase where you start designing a user interface that enables the user to interact with the site or application. The following are tools that can be used to improve Interaction Design:

- Outcomes and artifacts
- Storyboards
- Interaction sequence diagrams
- Interactive prototypes
- State diagrams
- Output documents
- Interaction design specifications

Human – Computer Interaction (HCI)

This is the most detailed activity, concerned with the science and mechanics of how users interact with computer systems or mobile devices.

- Outcomes and artifacts

- Task analysis
- User scenarios
- Electronic prototypes
- Output documents
- Human – computer interaction specification

An Agile and Optimized Information Architecture Process for iOS Design and Development

The Apple app store paradigm gives many individual developers the opportunity to work alone on their apps, or at least grouped in small teams. In my experience, a single designer or a small development team working on small or medium projects doesn't need to follow and strictly apply all the phases defined in the Information Architecture Process. Of course, all of the principles in the IA process are important, but you can group them into a few activities, saving work time without losing efficiency.

I truly believe in agile processes, and an agile and optimized Information Architecture Process for iPhone and iPad is the best way to ensure balance between working time and results.

In your iPhone and iPad optimized project flow, the Information Architecture involves the following phases.

1. Information Research (IR)

   Used technique: competitor comparison

2. Information Management (IM)

   Used technique: brainstorming, flowchart, roadmap

3. Content Architecture (CA)

   Used technique: content-out, site map, mind maps, GB wireframes

4. Experience Design (XD)

   Used technique: flowchart, site map, GB wireframes

5. User Experience (UX)

   Used technique: wireframes, paper prototypes

6. Information Design (ID)

   Used technique: wireframes, paper prototypes, page templates

7. Usability Engineering (UE)

   Used technique: paper prototypes, electronic prototypes, flowchart

8.   Interaction Design (ID)

Used technique: interaction sequence diagrams

9.   Human – Computer Interaction (HCI)

Used technique: electronic prototypes

> **NOTE:** The Agile Process has a feedback request to all members of the team at the end of each step. You can omit this request only if you are working as a freelancer. However, you shouldn't forget it when work in a team.

As you can see, you used common techniques in the IA process for more than one single activity, because the best way to create a good balance between work time and results is to follow two principles:

- Choose the most agile and optimized techniques for mobile contexts.
  For example, in the (4th) UX phase, use paper prototypes instead of electronic prototypes.

- Use the most common techniques in the flow.
  For example, by using paper prototypes you can "reuse" your artifact for the (4th) UX, (5th) ID, and (6th) UE phases.

> **NOTE:** By "reuse" I don't mean that you'll use exactly the same artifact from one process for another, because when moving forward in the IA process, the detail level of your artifact increases.
>
> Reusing the same artifact means starting from the original one and developing it to cause the artifact to evolve, and using this artifact evolution in the following step in the project flow, thus avoiding the cost of implementing and using a new technique for each step of the process.

At this point, you have seen the entire Information Architecture Process. Now, you also know how to modify this process in order to optimize your working time in small- and medium-sized projects. Now, let me show all of this visually.

The flow depicted in Figure 2–3 visually shows where to apply IA technique reuse in the Information Architecture Process.

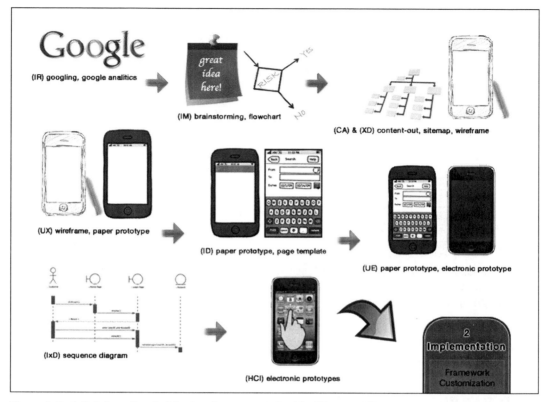

Figure 2–3. *Agile Information Architecture Process optimized for iPhone and iPad design*

Just to be clear, the agile process is usually the better choice, especially for a big project, but here, the key point is that in small and medium projects we don't need to design and develop our products following the entire IA flow.

Overview of the Three Main Processes in Information Architecture

The nine Information Architecture phases are included in the three main processes (as shown in Figure 2–4):

- ▨ Discovery,
- ▨ Analysis, and
- ▨ Architecture.

The discovery process is where you start to collect information about the web site or the application's market context. This process includes the IR phase.

The analysis process is where you start to work with the collected information by planning the right approach to developing a mobile strategy. The analysis process includes the Information Management (IM) phase.

The architecture process is where the design work is done. The architecture process includes the Experience Design (XD), Content Architecture (CA), User Experience (UX), Information Design (ID), Usability Engineering (UE), Interaction Design (ID), and Human – Computer Interaction (HCI) phases.

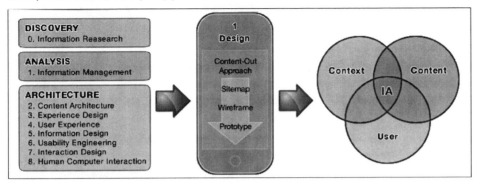

Figure 2–4. *The three processes in the Information Architecture framework*

As you can see so far, mobile Information Architecture isn't that different from how you might design the architecture of a desktop project. I have added only one point: the user context.

The user context (as shown in Figure 2–5) is a filter that changes the user experience.

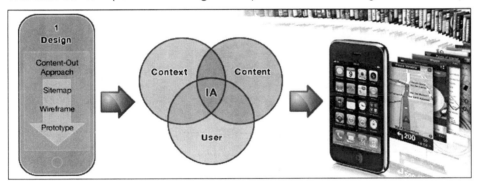

Figure 2–5. *Information Architecture framework: content, context, and user*

Imagine lying down on your sofa to read the latest feeds from your RSS reader in peace and quiet, and think about what that feels like. Now, imagine the same experience in the subway or, even worse, on a crowded bus at 7:30 in the morning.

In picturing these scenarios, you can understand that a user's experience changes dramatically when the context for the experience changes.

> **EXAMPLE:** The same context can have difference instances.
>
> - Context: "Reading RSS Feeds"
> - Context instances: Sofa RSS Reading, Walking RSS Reading, Subway RSS Reading, and Bus RSS Reading

For this reason, modeling the context instances with care is a key factor in our project. Making a mistake and forgetting a specific instance can cost "1" in the analysis phase, but the same mistake will cost "10" in the design phase and "100" in the development phase.

Forgetting an instance's context results is a relatively small mistake in the analysis phase, because we can always take a pen and add an entry to our context instances checklist. Designing a user interface using incomplete information from the analysis phase means designing an interface that might never match all the users' needs. Starting the development phase based on a badly designed interface means releasing services that some users will never be able to take advantage of. The error costs in the Information Architecture Process can be seen in Figure 2–6.

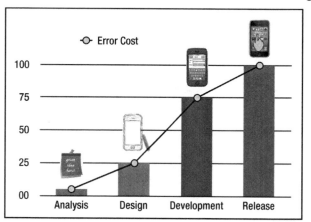

Figure 2–6. *Error costs in the Information Architecture Process*

For this reason, once you have gone further in your project flow, things change. If you need to step back in the project flow in order to handle a mistake in your Information Architecture, the entire project flow will be affected by deadlines and time horizons; perhaps even business goals will change during the delay.

Now, you can see how to optimize the working time spent in each IA phase, using an agile and optimized version of this process.

Abiding by the Golden Rules of Mobile Strategy

Mobile is a different medium and is governed by a different set of rules. But, once you have defined an agile Information Architecture Process, you can start to approach the general architectural case abiding by some golden rules.

Understand Users and Their Needs

Try to understand who the users are, what they are looking for from the web site or web application, and where they will be physically located when they use it.

Design with Mobility in Mind

I have already discussed context instances, understanding that context is crucial when creating any mobile product. Predicting user contexts could be difficult, because it is impossible to anticipate all possible circumstances that could affect the user experience.

Targeting mobile users ensures that your product can be used anywhere and at any time. Once you have the application's goals clearly in mind, try to picture all possible application scenarios, and then interview potential users about their usual mobile application contexts.

Don't Convert, Create

Simply porting a desktop web site or web application to a mobile device is a big mistake. We must create a new product rather than reimagine it for the small screen. Creating, rather than converting, experiences specifically for mobile devices enables users to get information both faster and in a more friendly fashion.

Keep It Simple

If there is a rule we must never forget, it's this one: iPhone and iPad are intelligent computers, but people want to use them in a simple way. People use Apple mobile devices (often) while they are doing something else like walking, talking, listening to music or speech, driving (please, don't do that!), and so on. A human being's cognitive resources are limited, and if we use a part of those resources during some other functional activity, we won't be able to manage complex structures like a typical desktop user interface at the same time. Following this principle, the more straightforward your application is, the better the mobile experience of your users will be. If you understand this key point, you also begin to appreciate Apple's decision to use iOS instead of a full version of OSX on the iPad.

Content-Out Approach

Web sites are created to deliver information. In the early days of the web, design played no part in a web site's existence. Today, we still see content as the most important part of a web site or web application, and everything must start from here (as shown in Figure 2–7).

The content-out approach is a ground-up approach where the content shows the designer how the final layout should be. The designers use the content to set the boundary of their possibilities and make the whole process easier and faster.

Figure 2–7. *HTML W3C compliant markup (left) and its semantic markup implementation (right) on the* Wall Street Journal *and* New York Times *web sites*

The content-out approach is closely related to semantic markup. The objective of this technique is to mark up the structure of the web content using the appropriate semantic elements. The elements are used according to their meaning, not because of the way they appear visually.

From top to bottom, this is a generic hierarchy of semantic meanings.

1. Navigation (main)

2. Branding area

3. Content main

4. Supplementary content

5. Navigation (supplementary)

6. Site information

> **NOTE:** The semantic approach is part of the "Web Content Accessibility Guidelines 2.0"
> (WCAG20) published by the W3C "Web Accessibility Initiative" (WAI) to support the development
> of more accessible web content.

Here are some steps that we use each time we employ the content-out approach.

1. Define the content.

2. Convert the content to HTML5.

3. Use semantic markup to set content hierarchies.

4. Use gray box wireframe to allocate layout space and proportion.

5. Design and style the layout.

In other words, in constructing the webpage, all content must be produced and converted to HTML5 before any markup, wireframe, or CSS3 styling takes place. Once you have put all our content into an unstyled webpage, you're free to go ahead in the process and think about which kind of design might best fit your content.

Representing an Information Architecture with a Site Map

Once you accomplish the information research and information management phases, and build the foundation of your project with the content-out approach, you are ready to represent the information and work on the content architecture and experience design phases, as show in Figure 2–8.

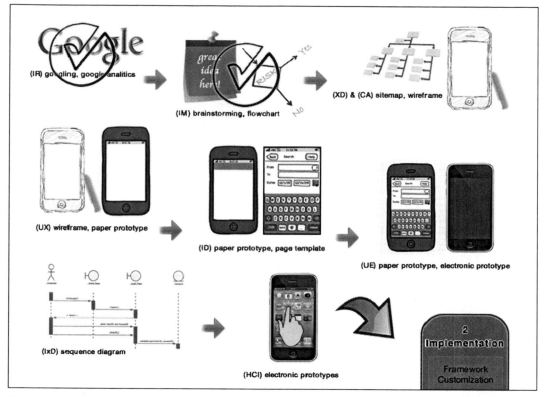

Figure 2–8. *Agile Information Architecture Process at phases 3 and 4: representing Information Architecture*

After defining the content with a content-out approach, the first item we use to define our mobile Information Architecture is the site map. It visually represents how all our content is connected and provides a clear path of how the user will travel through the informational space.

Mobile site maps are not dissimilar from site maps used on the web, but there is an important difference, as we see next.

Limited Chances for Mistakes

Information architects are always debating about which is the best choice—site maps that are wide or deep. Like everything else in computer science, this choice is never black and white.

> **NOTE:** Content architecture is where you start to insert the content in place, showing how it's organized. The best tool for organizing your content will be the wireframe, but all content you insert in the wireframe will be the implementation of what you represented previously on the site map.

On a desktop site map, you might decide to choose either a wide or a deep site map in order to answer a specific web site need, as show in Figure 2–9. In a mobile site map, you have only one choice: the wide site map. This occurs because the user experience is totally different from that of the desktop, and everything should be reachable in 2 to 4 linear taps.

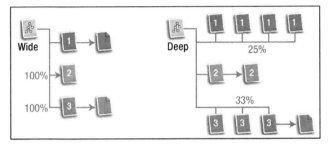

Figure 2–9. *Visual comparison between wide (the structure on the left) and deep site (the structure on the right) map*

Imagine using your iPhone to browse a page with the structures represented in Figure 2–10, in which both structures have three links in the primary level of navigation. By browsing the wide structure and choosing link number 1, you have a 100% chance of choosing the right path for our information. By browsing the deep structure and choosing link number 3, you have only a 33% chance of choosing the right path, and your chance drops to 25% if you choose link number 1.

Now, picture how many links you might face in a typical web site. How much risk is there of the user making a wrong choice? If users sitting at their desktop computer go down the wrong path, in a glance they can see how to return to the primary navigation level. But with an iPhone, this is not the right way to find peace in your (binary) life.

In this phase, you build the foundation of user experience by testing, at a very basic level, which kinds of interactions the user will have with the web site or web application.

> **NOTE:** We can define *interaction* in user experience as a kind of action that occurs between a human and a human interface every time the human uses the interface in order to achieve a goal or get a resource.

By working on the content architecture representing your site map structure, you also start to work (even if indirectly) on the user experience.

Provide Orientation Showing the Navigation Path

Providing orientation in the mobile user experience is a key factor, and for this reason it's important to keep in mind that we need to show on every page both its page title and navigation path. With a two-level structure and a tabbed navigation menu, we can omit the navigation path, because in this case both page title and navigation path provide the same information. Using a tab-based interface, we need to highlight the tab of the current page, exactly the way it's done, for example, on YouTube's video page.).

> **NOTE:** Showing the navigation path in a page means showing a certain site map path, from point A to point B. If you prefer, you can look at a navigation path as a single site map instance.

A mobile user has a limited amount of cognitive resources available for browsing and can easily experience a lost-in-space feeling. If our user interface is not based on tabs, we can use breadcrumbs to achieve the same goal and avoid user frustration.

If we have a wide site map, we can insert a few tabs in the interface or insert a drop-down menu. This kind of menu is handled very well by the iPhone and iPad, even when it contains a long list of options. In Figure 2–10, we have two good examples of tab navigation and drop-down menu: Google and *The New York Times*.

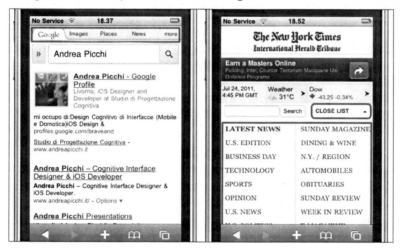

Figure 2–10. *Good examples of a tabbed menu and a drop-down menu: Google and The New York Times*

Sketching an Information Architecture with Wireframes

The site map showed how content is organized in the informational space. Now, it's time to work on user experience using your second information architecture tool: wireframes. Currently, you are phase four of the agile Information Architecture Process, as show in Figure 2–11.

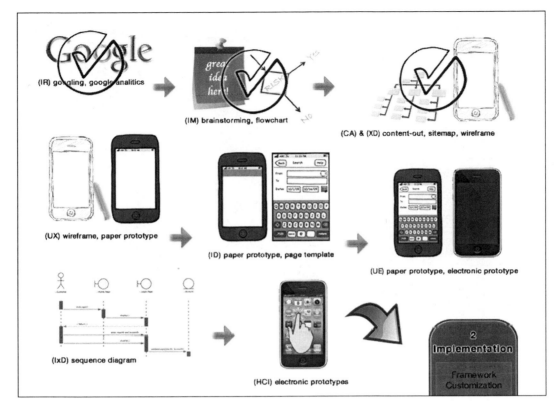

Figure 2–11. *Agile Information Architecture Process at phase 4: sketching Information Architecture*

Using wireframes, you lay out information on the page, making information space tangible. Working with wireframes provides a visual for the site map and defines how the user will interact with the experience.

The first approach is to sketch the wireframe structure with some freehand drawing, as can be seen in Figure 2–12. I believe in designing freehand, even more so when I need to create something, because the creative process is closely related to manual activity.

Figure 2–12. *A handmade tool for drawing an iPhone or iPod wireframe (Image Cultured Code)*

Once your idea becomes more tangible, you can use a printed sheet for redesigning the structure in a more detailed way.

I find wireframes to be the most valuable information deliverable, because they clearly communicate the layout idea and because you can reuse part of those deliverables for the next phase in the project flow: prototypes.

The only shortcoming that wireframes have is their inability to communicate complex structures; this is where prototypes come in.

Visualizing Interactions Through Prototypes

Prototyping might sound redundant or time-consuming, and many developers prefer to jump in and start coding things, but as mentioned before, prototypes come into play because after having wireframed a structure, you need to work on details.

With prototypes, you are at phases 5, 6, 7, and 8 (see Figure 2–13) where you can enter the information design, usability engineering, interaction design, and human – computer interaction phases.

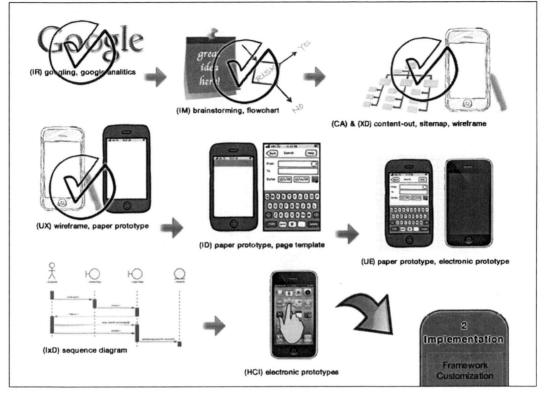

Figure 2–13. *Agile Information Architecture Process at phases 5, 6, 7, and 8: visualizing Information Architecture*

Working on your prototype also mitigates many of the major risks in the design phases, and in the end saves you time and money.

Prototypes (paper and electronic) are also the fastest possible way to design, iterate, and discuss concepts as a group. Once a prototype has been created, there is a solid foundation (even in a sketch form) that can be discussed, and which brings the concept to life.

A typical prototyping iteration path in a development team is

1. Sketch out your ideas,

2. Present to team,

3. Critique with team,

4. Bring it to life, and

5. Go back to step 1 (to iterate the process).

If you design a web site, you use the wireframe structure for producing the page templates.

Continuing in your agile approach to design and development, you see two ways of working with prototypes: paper and electronic.

Paper Prototype

The basic level is the paper prototype (pictured in Figure 2–14), which we can produce on printed-out wireframes by using stencil tools to design an accurate user interface, or even sketch the structure freehand with pen and paper.

Figure 2–14. *A paper prototype tool compared with a real iPhone*

The paper prototype is also useful in the test phase. Using it gives you the chance to reuse your work in the usability tests phase. You will see this technique more in depth in Chapter 11.

Electronic Prototype

The next level is the electronic prototype. With this tool, you can analyze how the prototyped structure behaves. With the electronic prototype, you simulate the human – interface interaction and have valid feedback before you code it.

A good solution is to use a lightweight structure based on HTML5, CSS, and JavaScript filled with temporary content and data. Loading this prototyped structure into your device produces the nearest possible experience of the final product, because you can see how much content will be displayed on the screen. Working with a remote file and a server with an electronic prototype, you can also start to deal with loading times and network latency. Electronic prototypes are also important for continuing your work on usability in the phase called usability engineering, in which you use more detailed prototypes as a base.

Electronic prototypes are also useful as support for the human – computer interaction phase where, using interaction sequence diagrams, you work on human – machine interaction and interaction design.

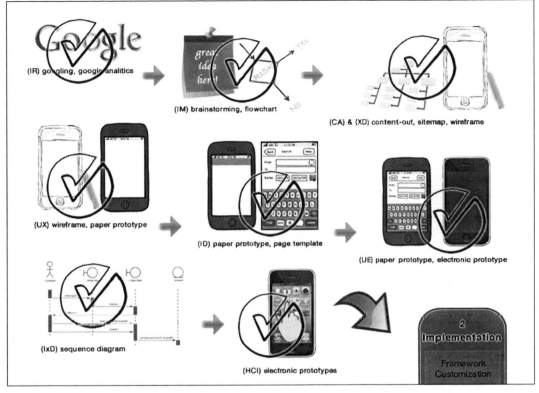

Figure 2–15. *A completed agile Information Architecture Process*

In Chapter 3, I present the framework for building web sites and web applications for iPhone and iPad. Once you understand the framework structure, you'll be able to define a template for speeding up the electronic prototype's implementation phase.

Systematic Approach to Mobile Design

As you saw in the mobile information process, the best way to achieve a goal is to set a path from where you are in comparison to where the goal is. In the design phase, there are no nine phases named as in the IA process, but there is still a systematic approach in order to stay focused on the path and optimize the entire workflow.

There are two important stages when working on your design: its accessibility and its usability. Accessibility and usability are closely related to each other, but the more important consideration is giving all users access to your web site or web application, followed by designing and optimizing its usability.

Accessibility in Apple Devices

According to W3C, web accessibility refers to the practice of making web sites and web applications accessible to people of all levels of ability. There is an overlap between MWBP (Mobile Web Best Practice) and WBP (Web Best Practice), because in most cases they have similar obstacles and similar solutions. Two of the most important needs that mobile web accessibility aims to address are visual and audio needs.

> **NOTE:** On December 11, 2008, the WAI (Web Accessibility Initiative) released WCAG 2.0 as a recommendation. WCAG consists of a set of guidelines on making content accessible, primarily for disabled users, but also for all user devices, including highly limited ones such as mobile phones and smartphones.

Addressing (at least) video and audio needs will make your web site or web application accessible to most of your potential users, as can be seen in Figure 2–16. But unfortunately, this is not always easy to achieve and sometimes even many well-known and successful products have at least some lack of accessibility.

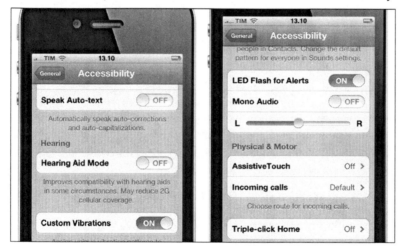

Figure 2–16. *Three accessibility services: Zoom (left), VoiceOver (center), and White on Black (right)*

The W3C WCAG 2.0 provides guidelines to make your web site or web application more accessible. Unfortunately, WCAG was not written with touch screen devices in mind, but most concepts behind the following points are reasonably applicable to both the iPhone and iPad.

- Use standard technologies properly.

- Provide a finger-friendly navigation structure.

- Provide orientation information on every web page.

- Provide control of font size.

- Provide good contrast among text, images, and background.

- Provide a high-contrast version of the web page.

- Provide a spoken version of the web page, as seen in Figure 2–17.

The iPhone and iPad have some new features that make them accessible for disabled users. For example, disabled users are not forced to remember long keyboard combinations to find what they are looking for: to select and open an item, users need to tap or double-tap it. In order for users to benefit from such features, designers and developers must know those features in order to optimize content and services.

VoiceOver

This feature makes your iPhone or iPad the first gesture-based screen reader that enables the user to physically interact with items on the screen. VoiceOver works with the iPhone and iPad's touch screens to let the user interact directly with objects on the screen. This makes it possible for users with impaired vision to access content and orient themselves on the site map.

Figure 2–17. *Accessibility features: VoiceOver*

VoiceOver is a device feature, independent from your web site or web application, that lets you benefit without any special effort on your part; however, good user interface design practices must be applied in order to avoid creating a frustrating navigation experience for the user. Soon, you will examine good user interface practices.

Voice Control

In addition to gestures, you can use voice commands to play music or make phone calls. All you need to do is press and hold the home button, listen for the audio prompt, and speak the name from the address book or the name of the artist from the iTunes playlist.

Zoom

With this function, seen in Figure 2.18, the user can magnify the entire Spotlight or Unlock screen, or any other screen application either native or purchased.

Figure 2–18. *Accessibility features: the Zoom*

Once enabled, one double-tap with three fingers instantly zooms in and out 200%, and the user can double-tap and drag three fingers to dynamically adjust the magnification between 100% and 500%.

White on Black

Users that prefer high contrast can use this option to change the display to white on black, as shown in Figure 2–19. This reverse polarity effect works in all applications including Home, Unlock, and Spotlight.

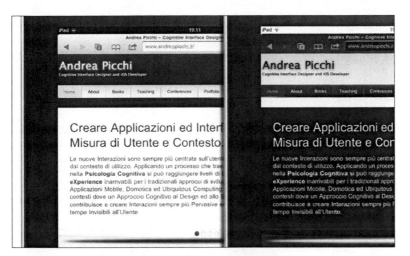

Figure 2–19. *Accessibility features: the White on Black*

The iPhone and iPad color menus are perfect for this kind of color inversion, but if you use insufficient color contrast for your web site or web application, the result won't be satisfactory. Use a color palette with sufficient contrast when designing the user interface in order to prevent this side effect.

Captioning

Both the iPhone and iPad support the playback of open captions, closed captions, and subtitling. Captions appear on the onscreen just like the closed captions that the user can see on TV. You can create your own using the appropriate tool.

Audible, Visible, and Vibrating Alerts

These options deliver both audible and visual alerts to the user. The user can set these alerts for phone calls, new text messages, new and sent e-mails, and calendar events.

Accessibility Software Features

From iOS5 on, Apple has introduced several significant advancements to accessibility in iOS devices. These new features make it easier for people with mobility, hearing, vision, or cognitive disabilities to get the most from their iOS devices. First, a new way to add certain features has been added, letting the user recall them quickly by touching a specific point on the touch-screen. Using this new menu, the user can access some setting functions and even get immediately back to the dashboard, bypassing the Home Button.

One relevant feature is the use of LED Flash and customizable vibration on incoming calls. When someone calls an iPhone, the LED Flash turns on and the custom vibration starts. A new Assistive Touch feature enables the user to customize gestures as macro shortcuts. Apple has also added a Speak Selection feature with an adjustable Speaking Rate slider for vocalizing text selections. Even older features have been improved, such as the VoiceOver that now includes custom element labeling.

Usability in iOS Devices

According to usability guru Jakob Nielsen, "usability is a Quality Attribute that assesses how easy interfaces are to use." Although accessibility mainly affects a subset of users, usability affects 100% of your users.

Careful and thoughtful work in information research can mitigate potential usability problems such as the one shown in Figure 2–20. In 2008, an interesting study on iPhone usability from Create with Context called "How People Really Use the iPhone" showed how hard it is sometimes for designers and developers to predict user behavior.

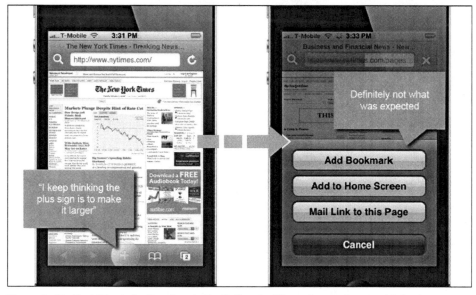

Figure 2–20. *Usability study: How People Really Use the iPhone (Image: Create with Context).*

Create with Context's study arrived at eight general rules for iPhone design and development, which now can also be applied to the iPad. Those rules are as follows:

- Take advantage of learned behavior.

   "Oh, this works just like the calendar"

- Avoid interaction inconsistencies.

   "This is weird, cancel is usually over there"

- Provide a clear conceptual link across widgets.

   "This button must be related to that box, since they're next to each other"

- Put space between action widgets.

  "Oh man, I didn't mean to send that SMS!"

- Plan for accidental overswiping.

  "I keep accidentally changing to a different screen"

- Don't rely exclusively on multi-touch.

  "It's hard to do this while I'm holding something in the other hand"

- Provide visual feedback for taps.

  "Did it hit that button? I'm not sure"

- Provide interaction affordances.

  "It's obvious that you're supposed to swipe left-and-right"

NOTE: A complete presentation of the study is available on Slideshare at

`http://www.slideshare.net/createwithcontext/how-people-really-use-the-iphone-presentation`.

For a downloadable PDF, visit
`http://www.createwithcontext.com/how-people-really-use-the-iphone.html`.

These problems are both fundamental to product usability and difficult to prevent at the same time, because the more you master something, the less you are able to put yourself in a newbie's shoes. That's one reason why great professors are so rare.

When to Work on Usability

So far, you have seen how important accessibility and usability are in your project in order to provide a good level of user experience to the widest possible range of users. Here, the most important question is this: when should you work on usability?

I can identify a few critical moments when working carefully on usability can improve the global perceived quality of your project. These points are the following:

1. **Before Starting the Project**

   You need to collect information about your competitors and see how they have solved specific application problems to achieve the project goals.

   You need to understand the user application contexts and figure out how you can optimize them.

2. **Before Starting to Design**

If you adapt a desktop web site or a web application, you need to decide what to keep (because it works in a mobile context) and what to discard (because it doesn't) from the web page structure. Create a site map to test and analyze the web site or web application content structure.

3. **In the Design Phase**

   Prioritize all web page contents.

   Represent the site map using a wireframe, paper prototype, and an electronic prototype.

4. **In the Test Phase**

   Use the prototypes to test the level of user experience.

You can see how the usability principles are applied in many phases of the project flow. In the following chapter, I will introduce a checklist that can help you to achieve a high level of user experience in your projects.

Differences Between iPhone and iPad Usability

The iPhone and the iPad run iOS, and they share the same navigation paradigm, but their use of different displays with differently sized elements changes the user's perception of the user interface to some degree, with resulting changes in usability and quality of user experience.

This brings us to the subject of iPad read-tap font asymmetry. On every iPhone web site or web application, if a font is too small to be read it is also too small to be touched.

> **NOTE:** Here, when I say "fonts," I refer to all the font-based structures such as navigation bars, side menus, forms, simple paragraphs, and so on.

In the iPad world, this doesn't happen in every context. Sometimes a font is big enough to be read but too small to be touched. In this case, we say that fonts are not finger-friendly. In this book, you see how to handle this situation using CSS3 style sheets.

From the standpoint of usability, this sets an important boundary between what works on the iPhone and what works on the iPad. Another important difference is the absence of the bottom bar in the iPad viewport.

Without the bottom bar, the quality of user experience is decreased, because that part of the navigation structure is missing. The user can work around this situation, tapping the Status Bar to quickly slide up to the top of the page and access the navigation structure in the Safari Bar. Unfortunately, not all users know this iOS feature, and too often they struggle trying to slide up to the top when looking for the navigation structure.

These are the two main points to remember when you contextualize your iPhone and iPad web pages. In the next section, you will see where and when in the project flow you need to apply your usability principles.

Mobile Accessibility and Usability Checklist

The following is a general list of accessibility and usability items to look for when designing a project.

Accessibility

- Reasonable site load time
- Adequate text-to-background contrast
- Easy-to-read font size/spacing
- Sparing use of extra JavaScript
- Alt tags for images
- Custom not-found/404 page
- Optimized print style sheet
- Optimized native device service integration
- Optimized layout for different iPhone models
- Optimized layout for both portrait and landscape
- Optimized images for both portrait and landscape
- Provided link to standard site

Usability: Navigation

- Main navigation easily identifiable
- Navigation labels clear and concise
- Reasonable number of buttons/links
- Company logo linked to home page
- Finger-friendly links and icons
- Consistent and easy-to-identify links
- Highlighted current location
- Back button in the page header
- Descriptive in-text links
- Customized spotlight screen icon

- Return of relevant error messages
- Easy-to-access site search

Usability: Content

- Wide site content map structure
- Negative space in the page design
- Clear visual page hierarchy
- Prioritized content
- Critical content above the fold
- Explanatory HTML page titles
- Major headings clear and descriptive
- Style and colors consistent
- Text emphasis sparingly used
- URLs meaningful and user-friendly

It's important that in your next project, starting from this general list, you contextualize your own usability checklist based on what is most important for your project.

iPhone Page Model

The iPhone page model refers to the fundamental building block of each iPhone's page. Every web site, web application, and even native application is based on this concept, and all iPhone content has a linear structure in one column.

Using the page model, the iPhone supports both portrait and landscape orientation in 320Í480 and 480Í320, at 163 ppi (pixels per inch) for the iPhone 2G, 3G, and 3GS, and in 640Í960 and 960Í640 at 326 ppi for the iPhone 4. Each orientation has its advantages; generally speaking, the portrait orientation is better for lists, whereas the landscape orientation makes most content easier to read.

The page model is the conceptual structure shared by the web site or web application contents and is shown by the screen inside a zone called the *visible area*, as seen in Figure 2–21.

The iPhone page model is based on five sections.

- Branding area
- Navigation (main)
- Content
- Navigation (sub)
- Site information

> **NOTE:** Within native applications (developed using Objective-C and Apple SDK) and web applications that simulate the native iPhone user interface, the branding area and navigation sections are often merged into a single header with no navigation.

Each time the user interacts with a link, a new page is loaded inside the visible area of the screen (visible area is analyzed in the next section, "iPhone User Interface"), and the old page is completely replaced. This happens in both portrait and landscape view.

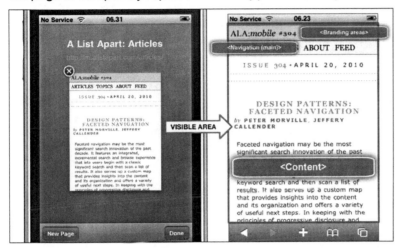

Figure 2–21. *The iPhone page model in thumbnail (left) and full-screen view (right) with semantic markup*

The iPhone structure page is also persistent, meaning that it preserves its structure and doesn't change when the user switches from portrait to landscape orientation. This concept might sound rather obvious, but as you will see when I analyze the iPad Block Model, it isn't a fixed rule.

Now that we understand the iPhone page model, it's time to analyze its user interface.

iPhone User Interface

The iPhone user interface is an iconographic and touch-based software that works on a capacitive touch-screen display. This interface is composed of two logical parts.

- Native user interface (NUI)
- Visible area

The NUI and the visible area together take the entire available screen area. From top to bottom, the iPhone screen area is composed of four different parts.

- Status Bar (part of NUI)
- URL Bar (part of NUI)

- Visible area

- Bottom Bar (part of NUI)

The NUI consists of all those elements that appear at either the top or the bottom of an iPhone page. There are different types of NUI used on the various native or web applications, but for the Mobile Safari Web Browser, there are just three, as summarized in Table 2–1.

Table 2–1. *Elements and Functionalities of the iPhone's Native User Interface*

NUI Element	Functionality	Size in Pixel
Status Bar	Displays overall iPhone status: network connectivity, battery charge, and current time	Portrait: 20px Landscape: 20px
URL Bar	Displays the web page title and major web functions: the URL bar, search field, and reload button	Portrait: 60px Landscape: 60px
Bottom Bar	Displays web page navigation functions: back and forward, bookmark button, and tab navigator	Portrait: 44px Landscape: 32px

The Status Bar and the URL Bar don't change their sizes when switching between portrait and landscape modes, but the Bottom Bar changes from 44px in the portrait mode to 32px in the landscape mode, as shown in Figure 2–22. This means that the available visible area doesn't have a fixed size.

As previously mentioned, every iPhone's page is shown inside a zone of the screen called the visible area. The visible area doesn't take 100% of the available screen, because the NUI takes away 124px in portrait view and 112px in landscape view.

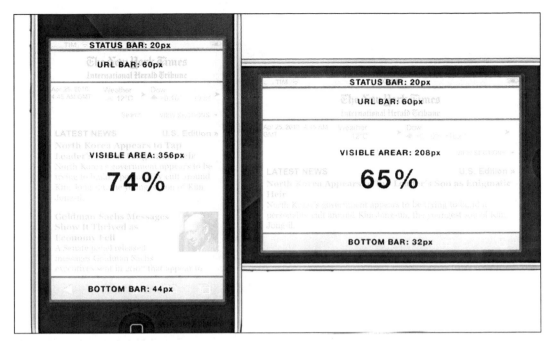

Figure 2–22. *Amount of visible area available in portrait and landscape view with URL Bar*

NOTE: On the iPhone, the user can always choose to show the Debug Console underneath the location bar, stealing 50 pixels from the visible area.

This fact is important because depending on an iPhone's orientation, we have different amounts of screen real estate available to us. The iPhone 4's display area, despite the higher resolution of its Retina Display, will have the same proportions and relative sizes between user interface elements like the Status Bar, the URL Bar, and the Bottom Bar. From the user point of view, besides having a screen with better definition and increased readability, nothing will change in the way he or she interacts with the iPhone 4. In Figure 2–23, we can see the dramatically improved clarity and sharpness delivered by the new Retina Display.

Figure 2–23. *The resolution delivered by the Retina Display*

Table 2–2 shows the percentages of 3.5 inches of available screen in each orientation for all iPhone models.

Table 2–2. *Amount of iPhone Available Screen Real Estate in Both Portrait and Landscape View*

Mode	Visible Area with URL	Visible Area without URL
Portrait	74%	87%
Landscape	65%	84%

iPad Block Model

iPad content is structured over a block model concept. The entire page is no longer the building block of the content; the concept is based on blocks inside the content page. On the iPhone, information is shown linearly, whereas iPad content is based mainly on a few different variations of a two-column layout.

The iPhone and iPad support two types of orientation, but both portrait in 768x1024 and landscape in 1024x768 (both at 132 ppi) are somewhat less defined compared with the 163 ppi of the old iPhone's display and the 328 ppi of the new Retina Display of the iPhone 4. Just as with the iPhone, each orientation has its advantages, but this time not in terms of space, because the amount of screen real estate available is enough for doing almost everything easily, using either view.

The exciting new thing about the iPad is that the double orientation option and the new screen resolution give us the capability to design two kinds of layouts. We can have two layouts optimized for their screen resolutions with the possibility to add or remove assets in each design.

Exactly as in 2007, when the first iPhone came out, a good example and an implicit guideline comes directly from Apple designers. In Figure 2–27, we can see how the native Note application uses the Block Model to present two different kinds of layouts. The user in landscape view interacts with a two blocks-based layout where he or she can view a to-do list in the left block and the selected to-do list entry in the right and main block.

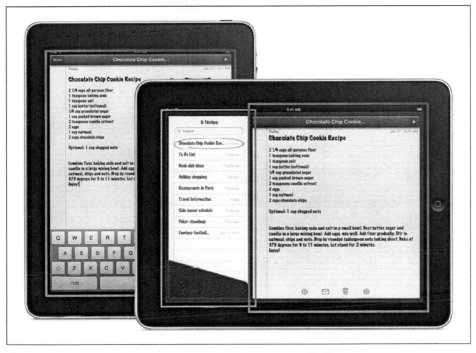

Figure 2–24. *An example of a two block model application: Note for iPad*

As introduced in the previous section, the iPad information structure is not strictly persistent as with the iPhone. As we have seen so far, this is not a problem, but an exciting opportunity for us.

> **NOTE:** In this case, the two blocks are in two columns, but this equality is not true all the time. In other cases, the added or removed block (in portrait or landscape orientation) could be a supplementary navigation, some kind of call-to-action button, or some other useful thing.

Looking at the Note application, we can see that the missing block in the portrait view contains some useful information the user might need, even when he or she is in the portrait view. For this reason, it is always a good practice to provide access to this block, even when it is not displayed in a given orientation.

Once again, Apple designers have provided us with a simple solution: using a pop-up menu, accessible by a button in the header's application. Consequently, we can access this part of the information without needing to change orientation, as shown in Figure 2–25. The block model used, like with the iPhone, is shown inside the visible area.

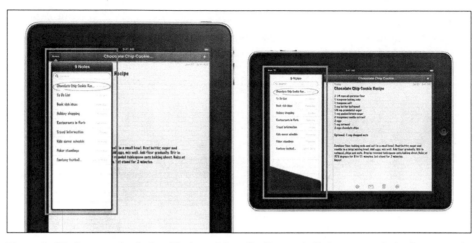

Figure 2–25. *An example of a two block model application: portrait view access to landscape content*

The iPad block model is also based on the same five sections:

- Branding area,
- Navigation (main),
- Content,
- Navigation (sub), and
- Site information.

When a user interacts with a link, the kind of behavior we have is more similar to what we see when interacting with a desktop page. Because the iPad supports a native resolution of 768x1024 or 1024x768, most designers don't feel the necessity to design and develop a specific structure optimized for this device.

In the developer community, we talk quite a lot about how to optimize web pages, and for the new Apple devices, we see guidelines on how to implement HTML5 markup or use HTML5 video player instead of the Adobe Flash player.

A web site invariably needs a completely different version of itself in order to be fully compatible with the iPhone, but with a few code modifications, you can turn your web content into content totally compliant with the iPad. The problem is that web sites designed for mouse navigation could be a bad experience for a mobile user who has vision issues or slightly larger than average fingers, as seen in Figure 2–26.

At this point, we can only rely on the zoom function offered by Mobile Safari in order to have an enjoyable experience, but for me, this is not the best way to show how designers can be creative and with their ideas improve the user's daily life.

Figure 2–26. *Official* TIME *web site: having an iPad-ready web site doesn't mean that we did the job right*

Now that I have discussed the iPad block model, you're ready to analyze its user interface.

iPad User Interface

The iPad runs the same operating system as the iPhone (iOS); therefore, we have pretty much the same user interface look and feel. The iPad user interface is still composed of two logical parts, but with a difference in the following.

- Native User Interface (NUI)
- Visible area

Once again, the NUI and the visible area together take up the entire available screen area, but this time from top to bottom. The iPad's screen area is composed of three different parts.

- Status Bar (part of NUI)
- URL Bar (part of NUI)
- Visible area

> **NOTE:** Some native applications like YouTube or iTunes use a Bottom Bar, as we saw in the iOS UI. This Bottom Bar is 48px height and is used to offer advanced options to the user.

The NUI consists of all those elements that appear at either the top or the bottom of an iPhone page. As designers and developers for Apple devices, we are interested in the Safari Web Browser Interface because our web site and web application will be rendered inside this application.

Even on the iPad, we have different types of NUI used on the various native or web applications, but for the Mobile Safari Web Browser, there are just two (the third is optional), as summarized in Table 2–3.

Table 2–3. *Elements and Functionality of the iPad's Native User Interface*

NUI Element	Functionality	Size in Pixel
Status Bar	Displays overall iPhone status: network connectivity, battery charge, and current time	Portrait: 20px Landscape: 20px
URL Bar	Displays the web page title and major web functions: the URL bar, search field, and reload button	Portrait: 44px Landscape: 44px
Bottom Bar	Displays application advanced options: Most Viewed (YouTube), Playlists (iTunes), and so on	Portrait: 48px Landscape: 48px

The visible area still doesn't take 100% of the available screen, because the NUI takes away 66px in both portrait and landscape view. The result is that with the URL Bar, we have 94% of the visible area available in portrait view and 92% available in landscape view. Without the URL Bar, we reach almost 100% of total screen availability; we have 98% in portrait and 97% in landscape orientation.

> **NOTE:** On the iPad, the user can always choose to show the Bookmarks Bar underneath the location bar, stealing 28 pixels from the visible area.

Compared with the iPhone we can note a significant relative increase in available visible area in both orientations, as can be seen in Figure 2–27.

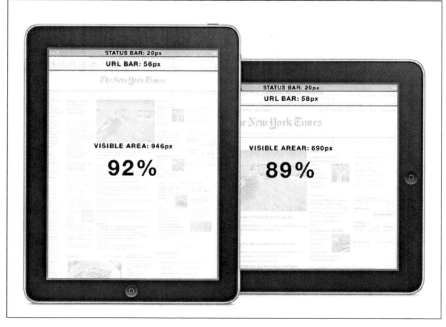

Figure 2–27. *Amount of visible area available in portrait and landscape view with the URL Bar*

With a 9.7-inch display and almost 100% of the available screen real estate, we have room to improve the mobile user experience dramatically and offer a degree of interaction never seen before. Table 2–4 shows the percentages of available screen.

Table 2–4. *Amount of iPad Available Screen Real Estate in Both Portrait and Landscape View*

Mode	Visible Area with URL	Visible Area without URL
Portrait	94%	98%
Landscape	92%	97%

Tools for Apple Mobile Design

Tools used in this chapter are both purchased and freeware. This list shows some of these useful tools that you can take advantage of for designing your next web site or web application.

Table 2–5. *Some Tools for Designing iPhone and iPad Web Sites and Web Applications*

Name	Scope	Type	Operating System
Timeline 3D	Roadmap	Application	OSX
XMind	Mind Map, Site Map	Application	OSX – Win - Linux
OmniGraffle	Site Map, Wireframe	Software	OSX - iOS
Cacoo	Site Map, Wireframe, UML	Web App	OSX – Win - Linux
App SketchBook	Wireframe	Tool	- - -
iPhone UI Stencil	Wireframe	Tool	- - -
iPad UI Stencil	Wireframe	Tool	- - -
iPhone GUI PSD	Wireframe	Image	OSX – Win - Linux
iPad GUI PSD	Wireframe	Image	OSX – Win - Linux
Balsamic Mockup	Wireframe	Application	OSX – Win - Linux
iPhone Mockup	Wireframe	Web App	OSX – Win - Linux
Prototyping for iPhone	Electronic Prototype	Firework PlugIn	OSX - Win
iPlotz	Electronic Prototype	Web App	OSX – Win - Linux
LiveView	Electronic Prototype	Application	OSX - iOS

Summary

In this chapter, you started your journey as a mobile designer and developer. Beginning with the Information Architecture Process and its nine steps, I illustrated which tools are best for each step of the process, defining an agile variation of the typical, and more complex, IA process.

I presented accessibility in Apple device design, and you saw how and with what hardware and software features you can address accessibility problems.

In the last part of the chapter, I discussed iPhone and iPad usability, showing how to deal with it, and I provided a usability checklist for controlling the project before jumping to the implementation phase. I also presented the iPhone and iPad user interface and the paradigms for its content: the iPhone page model and the iPad block model.

At the end, I provided a list of tools used in this chapter to help the designer in his or her next mobile project.

## Chapter 3

Web Development for iOS Devices

"...You've got everything you need if you know how to write apps using the most modern web standards...
...so developers, we think we ve got a very sweet story for you. YOU can begin building your iPhone apps today... "

—Steve Jobs

The Web Development process involves many technologies and many principles, and for that reason, this chapter will introduce many subjects and will be—I'm afraid—quite long.

In the first part, we will present the concept of frameworks, explaining how they're generally structured. Then we will introduce two Frameworks for developing a WebApp on iOS devices.

First we will look at four different approaches to WebApps and then go over the differences between a Mobile Web Site and a WebApp. We will also explain the differences between a WebApp and a Native Application and will show the pros and cons of the Web Development Model.

In the middle part of the chapter, we will present one of the core arguments of the book, namely Web Standards. We will introduce the new tags of HTML5 and the new properties of CSS3, and then we will cover the best practices of JavaScript.

In the last part of this chapter, we will analyze the browser support of Safari Mobile and WebKit Engine and we will introduce a fundamental concept that relates to any type of touch development process: a finger is not a mouse.

We will explore some development tools for Safari, and because it's important that a developer have a clear idea of the possibilities offered by both web and native development processes, we'll introduce the SDK (Native) Development Model.

Web Development Tools

Many tools are available to help make web development projects quicker and more productive. In addition to a handy text editor like Espresso (shown in Figure 3–1) with Smart Snippets, Code Folding and Code Sense functions, you will find plenty of tools, utilities, and frameworks that can greatly increase development speed, reduce debugging and testing time, and improve the quality of your output.

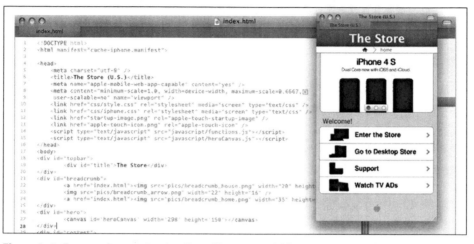

Figure 3–1. *Espresso is a good web editor with many useful features, such as LivePreview.*

The tools listed in Table 3–30, at the end of this chapter, consist of a variety of utilities, optimizers, and testing and debugging tools aimed at helping us create web sites and WebApps more efficiently.

The most important tool for a web developer is the framework that he will use as the foundation of the project, so let's analyze some useful iPhone and iPad frameworks.

Development Frameworks

As mentioned in "iPad Block Model" in Chapter 2, the tendency in iPad design is to use the desktop approach, relying on the iPad's capability of rendering these kinds of pages perfectly.

For this reason we have very little choice of iPad frameworks available on the net (e.g., JQuery Mobile, Sencha Touch). If we want to develop for the iPhone the story is completely different. These days we have many iPhone frameworks available that we can download for free from the internet.

For our purposes we will use one of the best frameworks available for developing a web site or a WebApp for iPhone: the iWebKit Framework.

What is a Framework and How is it Structured?

A framework in computer programming is an abstraction that allows common code that provides generic functionally to be overridden or customized by user code to provide more specific functionality.

A framework has these specific features:

■ **Control**

The overall program's flow of control is not dictated by the caller, but by the framework.

■ **Behavior**

A framework has a default behavior. This default behavior must be a useful behavior and not a series of no-ops (No Operation Performed).

■ **Extensibility**

A framework is extendible by the user through selective overriding or customized by user code that provides specific functionality.

■ **Modifiability**

The framework code is not allowed to be modified. The user can extend the framework, but not modify its code.

In our context, a **WebApp framework** is software that is designed to support the development of dynamic web sites or WebApps. This kind of framework aims to alleviate the overhead associated with common activities performed in web development, and to promote code reuse.

The frameworks proposed share the same structure and provide 3 kinds of resources:

■ **HTML Templates (page-name.html)**

The HTML templates are presented as examples; all we need to do is use these as our starting point and customize those pages according to our particular needs.

■ **CSS File (file-name.css)**

The CSS file defines the page, Apple native-like layout and all the Tags used in the HTML pages.

■ **JavaScript File (file-name.js)**

The JavaScript file defines the native-like behavior used in all HTML pages

The changes from one framework to another will be the project (documents) structure, how the files are organized, and the CSS class names or the JavaScript function names that we use. Apart from that, they're all functionally identical in terms of end-user interaction.

> **NOTE:** We can achieve the same final result with different frameworks. It's a good idea to work with the framework that offers the "best" features for our development requirements.

Now it's time to see what those frameworks have to offer.

iWebKit 5 Framework for iPhone

The iWebKit Framework 5.04 (Figure 3–2) divides the user interface (UI) into different `<div>` elements for the top bar, the content area, the footer, and other block elements. Assigning a specific id to the `<div>` we can classify it as a specific type of user interface element.

Figure 3–2. *The iWebKit for the iPhone Homepage*

Linking the Framework Elements

In order to link the framework elements, we need to insert into the HTML document head a link from the page to the CSS and JavaScript files.

```
<meta content="yes" name="apple-mobile-web-app-capable" />
<meta content="minimum-scale=1.0, width=device-width, maximum-scale=0.6667,
 user-scalable=no" name="viewport" />
<link href="css/style.css" rel="stylesheet" type="text/css" />
<script src="javascript/functions.js" type="text/javascript" language="JavaScript" >
</script>
```

UI Element: Header Bar

The Content Bar serves as a container for the page title. Usually at either side of this region we have one or more back or navigation buttons. This region is defined using:

```
<div id="topbar"></div>
```

Inside the Header Bar we will add a Title:

```
<div id="topbar">
        <div id="title">iWebKit 5 Demo</div>
</div>
```

Then we add a navigation button:

```
<div id="topbar">
        <div id="title">iWebKit 5 Demo</div>
        <div id="leftbutton">
                <a href="http://iwebkit.net" class="noeffect">PC Site</a>
        </div>
</div>
```

The id="leftbutton" specifies a single left button to include on the header bar. We can also include a right button on the right side of the header bar using id="rightbutton".

Alternatively, we can add multiple navigation buttons to the header using either <div id="leftnav"></div> or <div id="rightnav"></div>. Multiple buttons enable us to achieve a visual navigation path, just like a clickable breadcrumb trail in a desktop web site.

For example, notice the navigations in the header for the page shown below in Figure 3–3. We can choose to step back to the last visited page (the "Forms" page) or to jump back to the homepage (the house icon).

Figure 3–3. *The iWebKit Framework: Header Bar (left) and Navigation-Path (right)*

It is also important to offer a button that can take the user to the desktop version of our web site (see Figure 3–3, left). This is because a fundamental step in our Mobile Information Architecture was to prioritize and select the content as a subset of the original desktop version. In other words, sometimes the user can't access all of the information that can be found in the desktop version of the web site using the mobile app.

Below the Header bar, we can also add a supplemental navigation tribar, using `<div id="tributton"></div>`.

```
<div id="tributton">
    <div class="links">
        <a id="pressed" href="#">Home</a>
        <a href="changelog.html">Changelog</a>
        <a href="about.html">About</a>
    </div>
</div>
```

UI Element: Content Region

The Content Region serves as a container for all of the content elements of a page. This region is defined using:

```
<div id="content"></div>
```

All of the page content will be placed inside this kind of content wrapper, as shown in Figure 3–4.

Figure 3–4. *The iWebKit Framework: The Content Region (left) and the Gray Title (right)*

UI Element: Content Box Container

The Content Box serves as a container for the content. Usually, on top of this region, we have a Title that is defined using a `<span>` and both elements are defined using:

```
<span class="graytitle">Features</span>
```

The class `graytitle` defines the title with the typical iOS embossed style, and just below this tag we have the Content Box container defined using:

```
<ul class="pageitem"></ul>
```

Inside this `pageitem` container we can define many different types of elements, each with its own style defined inside a CSS class or id.

UI Element: Text Box

With the textbox class, we define a box for the text, often used as a page's description.

```
<li class="textbox"></div>
```

In Figure 3–5, we can see how the textbox contains two other elements, a Text Box Header and a Description.

Figure 3–5. *The IWebKit Framework: The Content Box Container (left) and the Text Box Header and Description (right)*

UI Element: Text Box Header and Description

Inside the textbox, we can define any kind of standard HTML content, but in this case we use a framework class to add a header using:

```
<span class="header">Discover iWebKit 5</span>
```

Then, we can add a paragraph of description:

```
<li class="textbox">
      <span class="header">Discover iWebKit 5</span>
      <p>Welcome to this demo. please &quot;touch&quot; around to discover
 iWebKit&apos;s features!</p>
</li>
```

UI Element: Menu Items

The Menu Items are the main components of our user interface. Now we will define a setting-like menu, which is defined using:

```
<li class="menu">
      <a href="technology.html">
              <img alt="list" src="thumbs/plugin.png" />
              <span class="name">The Technologies</span>
              <span class="arrow"></span>
```

```
        </a>
</li>
```

Each row is composed of a list element `<li class="menu"></li>` that contains a link element `<a></a>` that wraps three other tags: an image on the left `<img />`, a text `<span class="name"></span>`, and an icon on the right `<span class="arrow"></span>`.

If we want to add more links (rows), we need to add other blocks like those described above.

UI Element: Footer

A footer, as shown in Figure 3–6, can be useful for adding any relevant information about the site, in this case about the framework. The footer is defined using:

```
<div id="footer">
        <a href="http://iwebkit.net">Powered by iWebKit</a>
</div>
```

Figure 3–6. *The iWebKit Framework: The bottom part of its Homepage and the App Store List Page*

So far, we have analyzed the iWebKit homepage and its structure. This framework, as shown in Figure 3–7, offers many other page styles, including:

- Classic List
- App Store List
- iTunes Classic List
- iTunes Music List
- iPod List

Even with all of these options, the approach is always the same: open the code, analyze it, and then start customizing it following your project requirements. We can start to use a framework without knowing it, by using the source code.

Figure 3-7. *The iWebKit Framework: The other Page List Styles and the App Store List Page*

What follows is an exercise to help you get to know the iWebKit Framework.

EXPLORING THE IWEBKIT FRAMEWORK

Here is an exercise that will increase your knowledge of every framework style or page element that you might encounter. The following are guidelines, showing step by step what you need to do in this exercise.

1. Download the iWebKit Framework from: http://iwebkit.net/

2. Open the file "applist.html" in your favorite development IDE.

3. Open a preview of the page "applist.html" in Mobile Safari using your Device

4. Start by inserting Comments in the code explaining the characteristic of each tag. If you need an example, have a look back to the paragraph above where I introduced the iWebKit Homepage.

5. Try to Add, Remove, or Customize Framework Elements.

Repeat this exercise for all the other page styles in the iWebKit framework. Once you have finished this exercise, you will have completed the first step of preparing yourself to start using and customizing the framework.

The preceding is really just an introduction to the iWebKit structure; we will see how to use this framework in detail from Chapter 8 ("Creating WebApps: Mobile Application Development") on.

Mobile Web Site

A mobile iPhone or iPad web site is one designed specifically for Apple devices and should not be confused with viewing a site made for desktop browsers on a mobile browser. These kinds of web sites are characterized by the typical style of the iOS environment.

As we have seen earlier, in the Information Architecture section of this book, the content is never the same between desktop and mobile versions. In most cases, a mobile web site offers a subset of the main content, and in a prioritized way. But first let's see how the mobile market has evolved.

The mobile web before Apple's devices was like the Web of ten years earlier: slow, expensive to use, and not much to look at.

> **NOTE:** In computing, resolution independence is the concept whereby elements on a computer screen can be drawn at sizes independent from the pixel grid.

We can presume some general pros and cons of a mobile web site, as follows:

PROS

- Created with the same Web Standards used for the Desktop Version
- Easy to Maintain and Publish
- Offers an Extra Level of User Experience (Device Core-Features Interaction)
- Offers Services on the Go

CONS

- Offered Content is Limited
- Loads slowly, due to Network Latency

Mobile Applications

A mobile iPhone or iPad WebApp is a one that does not need to be downloaded from the App Store and installed on the device. Using HTML, CSS, and JavaScript, WebApps are able to provide a native-like application experience to the end user while running inside the Mobile Safari browser. Figure 3–8 shows two well-known WebApps: MobileMe and GoogleLatitude.

> **NOTE:** From now on in this book, I will use the word *native* to refer to real native applications for iOS and the term *native-like* to mean our WebApp that's built to emulate the (real) native user interface for iOS.

A WebApp with a native application-like experience offers a different paradigm. This real-time paradigm is based on touches that perform an action within the current view. As we will see in the next section, "Four Different Approaches to WebApp," this is a level

4 (Native-Like) experience and represents the highest level of user experience possible on this kind of device. This experience is very different from the desktop one, which is based on page metaphors in which a click equals a refresh of the content in view.

Figure 3–8. *Two Famous WebApps: MobileMe from Apple (left) and Google Latitude from Google (right)*

By using WebKit, the iPhone (and to an even greater extent the iPad) can render WebApps that have not been optimized for mobile devices in a perfectly usable way, including DHTML- and Ajax-powered content.

For this reason, we now see that the majority of usage of the mobile web is coming from devices with better browsers (typically WebKit Engine based Browsers), in some markets by a factor of 7:1.

Before looking at the pros and cons of WebApp, we need to examine the Web Development Model (WDM).

Web Development Model

The Web Development Model (WDM) is used to develop iPhone and iPad (web) applications using web standards like HTML, CSS and JavaScript.

Web Development Model: Pros and Cons

As we saw in Chapter 2, different projects have different requirements. Some applications are a better fit with the web development model (WDM) than are others. Knowing the pros and cons will help us make the right decision about which path might be more appropriate.

Many things have changed since 2008 when the first SDK was released and the WebApp vs. Native App battle began. Today, in 2011, following the latest version of

HTML and CSS and the recent worldwide network upgrades, things are markedly different.

Although differences between Native Apps and WebApps still exist, the tea leaves seem to show that in the future this gap will be narrowed to some extent. In May 2010, at the I/O Developer Conference, Google announced that soon Android-based WebApps will have access to local hardware capabilities (motion sensor, camera and Google's voice recognition). To me, this fact suggests that once Android WebApps are able to access hardware features, iOS WebApps will not wait very long to follow the same path and fill this last gap between WebApps and Native Apps

While we're waiting for this exciting day, we meanwhile need to make a thorough study of our project in order to clearly understand its needs and be able to choose the right approach in order to achieve the project's goals.

Essentially, a WebApp is a better option when:

1. We need to update our content frequently.

2. We don't need any of the Apple Store features.

3. We don't need especially fast graphic performance.

4. We are not dependent on native functionality.

5. We are not dependent on running our app in the background.

6. We are not dependent on sending (push) notifications.

If our application is not a Game, doesn't need the Camera, GPS, Accelerometer, Multimedia sound/graphics, heavy videos, or complete offline access, then it's probably a good idea to write a WebApp. An example of a good WebApp is the Gmail WebApp for iPad shown in Figure 3–9.

Native applications are certainly supposed to be faster because we can define our caching strategies, our network services, and our event/threading model. Native applications are also under control of the user, who decides what to install, update, and uninstall. The only part that involves networking is the process of getting the installation package. WebApps are instead under control of the server, which could eventually go off-line, in which case updates would have to be initiated and implemented by the application's creator.

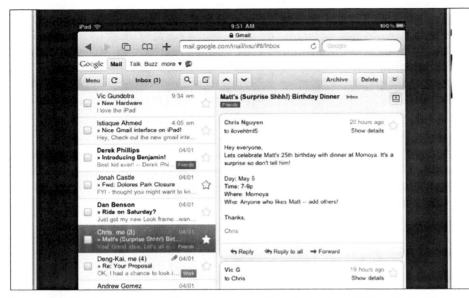

Figure 3–9. *Google provides us with a good example of how to develop a WebApp for the iPad.*

Native applications also get access to the camera, GPS (not just a single geolocation as in a WebApp), and other cool hardware features like the accelerometer. They can also preserve and access data in their own local data storage, and are even able to use SQLite, access data from another application, and allow complete offline access to their contents.

Native applications are also featured on the iTunes App Store page, providing a lot of free traffic, promotion, and income.

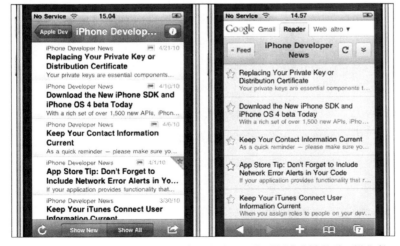

Figure 3–10. *Google Reader: Comparison between the MobileRSS Native UI (left) and the Google Web UI (right)*

On the other hand, the speed of the JavaScript engine in Safari has greatly improved, and we are now able to write WebApps that have the same performance as a native application, at least in most cases. Using the HTML caching system we can also provide offline access to the data of our WebApp. In Figure 3–10, we can see how we can achieve a native-like user experience with the Google Reader WebApp. Figure 3–10 also shows a comparison between the native app MobileRSS and the native-like app Google Reader.

If our application is not a game, doesn't need the camera, GPS, accelerometer, multimedia sound/graphics, heavy videos, or complete offline access, then it's probably a good idea to write a WebApp. Now, we can resume our previous discussion, compiling two easy-to-read lists with some important pros and cons of WebApps, which we will go on to discuss further.

Some **pros** of WebApps are:

- Objective-C skills are not required
- Apple development program subscription is not required
- Developing on a Mac running OSX is not required
- Web standards skills are reusable in other development areas
- Development life cycle is fast
- Bug fixing is in real time
- An enterprise WebApp doesn't require an enterprise license
- A WebApps don't require Download and Installation
- WebApps are accessible to Apple and non-Apple devices
- WebApps will run on every device (mobile or desktop) with a browser
- WebApps are packable in native app with tools like PhoneGap
- We don't have to share our revenue with Apple

Some **cons** of WebApps are:

- In some heavy contexts, WebApps are slower than native apps
- Some sophisticated UI effects are difficult to achieve
- Data stored in the file systems are not accessible
- Some hardware features are not accessible
- A personal payment system is required if we want to charge for the app

Some of these points are very relevant. I love Objective-C, I enjoy programming and I like the native approach paradigm, but in using the WDM, many creative web designers and developers will be able to reuse their (web standards) skills and start to work on iPhone and iPad in no time.

Being able to fix a bug in a timely fashion will also be an important advantage. With the WDM, fixing a bug is matter of days, sometimes hours, and we just need to fix the bug and upload the fix to the server. Every time we fix a bug in our native application, a new Approval Process from Apple begins. This process is out of the developer's control, and can sometimes be stressful. In Chapter 12, we will see how to partially remedy that problem, but in the general case this issue will still stand.

Another important "pro" to discuss is that, from a developer perspective, building WebApps instead of native ones provides the opportunity to produce cross-platform applications.

I know what you're thinking: Who cares about cross platform development? I'm not here to tell you to develop for Android or WebOS (although perhaps considering those devices in the Information Architecture Process might not be such a crazy idea), but I will suggest that developing a project with a high level of portability is a goal whose value you might not want to underestimate. In developing an iOS WebApp, you will be able to create the same WebApp for Android or WebOS with minimal modifications to your code.

Today, cross platform development doesn't only mean developing for different brands. With the old iPhone with its 480x320 pixel resolution at 163 ppi, the new iPhone 4 and iPhone 4 S with 960x640 pixel high resolution at 326 ppi, the iPad with 1024l768 pixel resolution at 132 ppi and the new iPod line, we have to be able to handle many different devices with similar services and operating systems.

> **NOTE:** Remember that, with the 4th Generation of iPhones, we have two different screen resolutions: 640x960 at 326 ppi for the new iPhone 4 and iPhone 4 S , and 320x480 at 163 ppi for the old models. We also have 2 different firmware histories: both the iPhone 2G and 3G run the old iPhone OS 3.1.3 (or earlier) and the iPhone 3G S, the iPhone 4 and iPhone 4 S and the iPad run the latest iOS firmware available; furthermore, multitasking is available only from iOS 4 on.

These devices must be considered differently, because their hardware is different, their performances are different, and the services each offers are different. What we have is a pseudo cross-platform scenario, which I call the **"Inside Cross-Platform"** context. Every year, a new iPhone model is introduced, and from now on, every year a new iPad model will be announced, and so it's better to be ready to develop with an inside cross-platform approach, because what we've seen so far is only the beginning.

A final and very relevant pro is that a WebApp can be packed as a native app with an open source tool like PhoneGap. You can have the best of both worlds in this way: writing a WebApp and then also producing a native application from it.

Four Different Approaches to a WebApp

When we develop a web site for a WebApp that can run in a browser, we can choose from four different approaches. All of these 4 kinds of WebApps are written using the same web standards, such as HTML4, HTML4, CSS2, CSS3, and JavaScript (version 1.6 and some features from 1.7 and 1.8), but the quality of the user experience offered is different for each level.

Level 1: Compatible

This is the ground-level approach to development and aims to provide a fully compatible structure with all of Apple's mobile devices. This kind of structure is marked up using HTML4 and CSS2 and is based on blocks, in order to be easily navigable and zoomable, as shown in Figure 3–11. Nevertheless, it's still too desktop-oriented for mobile users.

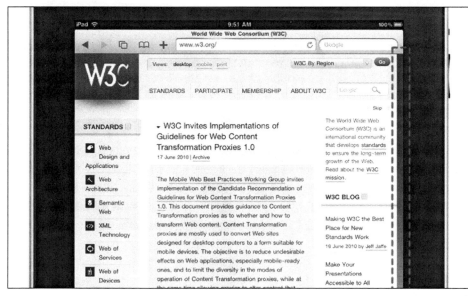

Figure 3–11. *A Compatible Web site: The Official W3C Web site doesn't have an Optimized Layout for iPad.*

This level of approach also has to avoid non-supported technologies like Flash, Java, and other plug-ins, and really doesn't do anything specifically aimed at iPhone or iPad users. The main goal here is to make sure that no barriers are placed to prevent a satisfactory browsing experience.

Every online W3C standard WebApp that doesn't use non-supported technologies is in this first category.

Level 2: Optimized

The second level of support for Apple devices is meant to provide a basic level of mobile user experience. This means that the layout is still desktop-oriented and although the web site or WebApp is marked up using HTML5, CSS3, and offers user interaction using JavaScript, it uses them in a very basic way, and won't support the latest features offered by the WebKit browsing engine. Neither does it provide any hardware interaction like GPS geolocation, or one touch SMS and phone calls. Figure 3–12 shows an example of an optimized WebApp.

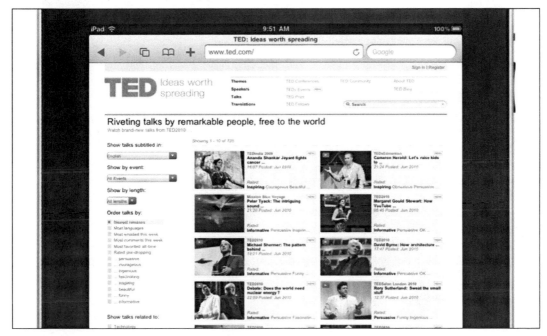

Figure 3–12. *An Optimized Web site: The TED Web site uses the HTML <video> tag in its Pages.*

Every web site or WebApp should be in this category at least, particularly if there is an active redirect to a dedicated or native resource. The iPad-ready web sites promoted on the official Apple web site are in this second category.

Level 3: Dedicated

The main difference in this third level of support is the tailored viewport dimension. This is the first step into a real mobile user experience. However, although these web sites and WebApps are tailored for iPhone or iPad viewing, they do not seek to emulate the native iOS user interface. Figure 3–13 shows an example of a dedicated WebApp.

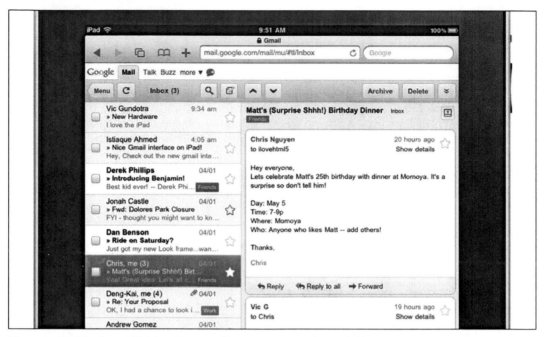

Figure 3–13. *A Dedicated WebApp: The use of Spaces in the Gmail page is iPad Oriented.*

These sites and applications are marked up using HTML5, CSS3, and offer user interaction through JavaScript, but use these standards in a very basic way without supporting the latest features offered by the WebKit browsing engine, and without offering hardware interaction like GPS geolocation, or one touch SMS and phone calls.

In this third level of approach, we have all the iPhone and iPad dedicated (mobile) versions of a WebApp.

Level 4: Native-Like

The native-like approach provides the highest level of mobile user experience and aims to emulate the native iOS user interface, providing a direct integration with device services, including Phone, Messages, Mail, Contacts, Maps, and geolocation service through GPS or GSM triangulation. Figure 3–14 shows an example of a native-like WebApp.

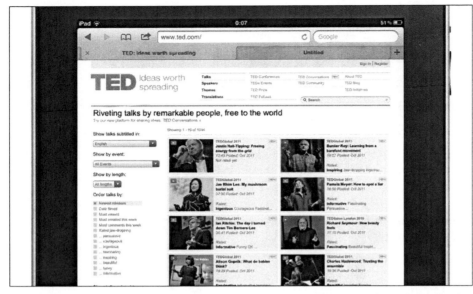

Figure 3–14. *A Native-Like WebApp: The Apple Store Use Case (re)Designed using a Native-like Structure*

It is important to consider and evaluate which of these degrees of development approach we want to utilize in the Information Architecture Process, in order to be consistent in the project and with the client's needs.

WebApp and Native App: What Makes the Difference for the User

Developing a WebApp that runs on Mobile Safari has some basic differences from one that runs as a native application. So far, we have seen these differences from a development prospective.

The next question is: are there any tangible differences for the end-user? How will the user experience change when the mobile user relies on a WebApp?

User Interface (UI)

As we saw in Chapter 2, the web and native application user interface consists of two parts: the native user interface (NUI) and the visible area.

Generally speaking, the Native User Interface changes as it goes from native to WebApps. It is composed of the following modules:

- **WebApp**

    Status Bar

    URL Bar (Mobile Safari)

Header Bar

Bottom Bar (not available on iPad)

■ **Native Application**

Status Bar

Header Bar

Bottom Bar

When rendering our WebApp inside Mobile Safari, we have to deal with an added bar between the Status and the Header Bar, as shown in Figure 3–15. We can work around this difference using meta tags and we achieve the exact look and feel of a native application.

Figure 3–15. *From WebApp to Native-Like Look and Feel: Gmail on iPhone.*

You will see how to emulate the native application look and feel in Chapter 8. The bottom part of the NUI also changes from native to WebApp and is composed of:

■ **WebApp**

Application Options and Features Bar

■ **Native Application**

Mobile Safari Bottom Bar

This is an unsolvable problem, because we can't hide it through meta tags. What we can do is to place a footer on top of it, but this practice will steal more pixels from the visible area and this is not recommended in most cases.

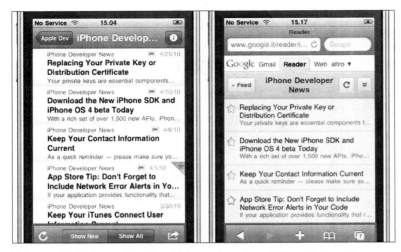

Figure 3–16. *Native and WebApp UI Comparison: Two Different Bottom Bars*

Personally, I don't consider this last point to be a real problem. Having the Mobile Safari Bottom Bar visible, as shown in Figure 3–16, makes sense to me. Since we use Mobile Safari as the natural environment for our applications, from a semantic perspective it's like having a native bottom bar.

User Experience (UX)

User experience is a broad topic and pervades many areas of our web (and native) applications. On top of that, we can identify a major area where those differences between native and WebApps are remarkable: the application controls.

In a native application, the user can change many of his application's settings and in this way have some sort of control over the user experience. In mathematical terms, he can define a few subsets of the user experience. This is impossible in a WebApp because, apart creating option pages that emulate the look and feel of native option pages, the only options we can interact with are the Mobile Safari Settings. Those settings will not modify the user experience, because the browser and the WebApp are two different entities. In other words, the settings you can change in Mobile Safari are not the WebApp's settings.

Figure 3–17. *Native and WebApp UI Comparison: Two Different Ways to Present an Application's Options*

A good example of a workaround for this problem is given to us by the Google Interface, which presents a subset of useful options using a dropdown menu, as shown in Figure 3–17. This example of good design doesn't really solve the problem, but it does considerably improve the user experience.

Another tangible difference is that the WebApp needs to be opened after we have opened the browser. The launching operation is divided into two steps: opening the browser, and opening the WebApp.

For this problem, we can use the ability of iOS to create a Springboard Icon that links to our WebApp, which we can launch using just one tap, exactly as we do with every other native application. We cover this point in Chapter 8.

Human Computer Interaction (HCI)

The user has a more responsive (human computer) interaction with a native compiled application than with a Safari-based WebApp. This is true for two reasons:

- Interpretive nature of web scripting
- Network dependence of WebApp

However, in spite of technological constraints, we can perform an optimization phase in order to achieve acceptable performance. Some of these techniques will be covered in Chapter 10.

In Table 3–1, we can see another instance of **intra-platform**, because we have to deal with three kinds of network protocols implemented on different hardware: four different versions of the iPhone, one version of the iPad, and one version of the iPod Touch.

Table 3–1. *Network Protocols Implemented in Apple's Mobile Devices*

Network Name	Network Protocol	Network Bandwidth
Wi-Fi	811.11	54 Mbps
3G	UMTS	Up to 7.2 Mbps
2G	EDGE	70-135 Kbps, 200 Kbps burst

Next, we will introduce web standards, the new features available with HTML and CSS, and JavaScript best practices.

Web Standards: HTML, CSS, and JavaScript

In this book, we will assume that you already know the basics of HTML, CSS, and JavaScript. We will approach HTML, CSS and JavaScript in an Apple device oriented way in Chapter 7, but in this book we will not be covering the basics of web standards. The reason is that it will be impossible to cover all of those three (very important) topics from their basics and keep the focus on and achieve our main goal: presenting the basics of how to design and develop for iPhone and iPad.

> **NOTE:** If you need to approach HTML and CSS foundations, a good book to look at is "Beginning HTML with CSS and XHTML" from Apress.
>
> If you need to approach JavaScript and DOM foundations, a good book to look at is "Beginning JavaScript with DOM Scripting and Ajax: From Novice to Professional" Christian Heilmann (Apress 2006).

However, before we get to Chapter 7, what we'll explore now is the role of those web standards in the development phase and how we'll use these newly introduced features for our purposes. In the meantime, if you need to go back-to-basics with web standards, find a good book and fill in any gaps in your missing knowledge.

Figure 3–18. *iPhone and iPad WebApp based on 3 Web Standards: HTML, CSS and JavaScript*

In the following pages, you will find two tables, one with the new tags in HTML, and one with all the <video> tag attributes, to use as a small standard reference.

As shown in Figure 3–18, HTML, CSS and JavaScript are used to achieve the following goals:

- HTML: Page structure (in semantic terms)

- CSS: Page presentation (in aesthetic terms)

- JavaScript: Page behavior (in user-interaction terms)

HTML: Introducing the New Features

HTML is designed to be the successor to HTML4 and aims to improve interoperability and reduce development costs by making precise rules on how to handle all HTML elements, and how to recover from errors.

Behind that, HTML also allows developers to create cross-platform design through expressing the content more semantically. An example is the group of new tags like <header>, <nav>, <section>, <aside>, and <footer> that make the content more machine-readable and therefore make it easier for the mobile browser and search engine to treat content properly.

Some of the new features in HTML are also functions for embedding audio, video, graphic, client-side data storage, and interactive documents. Five of the most exciting features introduced with HTML are:

- **Web Workers**

  Allows hyper-threading for web browser (supported from iOS5). Separate background threads are used to do processing without affecting the performance of a webpage. This is an important feature when we develop WebApps and (often) when we rely on heavy script to perform functions.

- **Video Element**

  Embed video without having to rely on third-party (often proprietary) plugins or codecs (which are not available on Apple mobile devices). Now embedding and manipulating a video is as easy as embedding and controlling an image.

- **Canvas**

  Allows us to render graphics and images on the fly. In certain situations in our mobile context, saving bandwidth by using a canvas instead of an image is extremely advantageous.

■ **Application Caches**

Gives the ability to store a WebApp locally and access it without having to connect to the internet. This is a giant step forward for anyone who develops WebApps, because now he has a valid alternative to native applications.

■ **Geolocation**

This API defines location information with a high-level interface (GPS) associated with the device hosting the API. This is another great feature, because previously only native applications could interact with cool hardware features like GPS (even if only for a single geolocation service).Is important to remark that the semantic nature of HTML requires an in-depth understanding of the precise meaning of each tag. We can go deeper on this important point by reading the official HTML Reference on the W3C web site.

> **NOTE:** The official W3C HTML Elements Reference is available at:
> `http://dev.w3.org/HTML/html-author/#the-elements`

In Table 3–2, I've listed alphabetically all the new tags in HTML. These tags will be added to the old, supported, and non-deprecated tags from HTML4. HTML is still a work in progress; you can see the full reference going to the official webpage at: `www.w3.org/TR/HTML/`.

Table 3–2. *New Tags in HTML (Ordered Alphabetically)*

Name	Device
`<article>`	Defines an Article
`<aside>`	Defines Content Aside from the Page Content
`<audio>`	Defines Audio Content
`<canvas>`	Defines Graphics
`<command>`	Defines a Command Button
`<datalist>`	Defines a Dropdown List
`<details>`	Defines Details of an Element
`<embed>`	Defines External Interactive Content or Plug-in
`<figcaption>`	Defines the Caption of a Figure Element
`<figure>`	Defines a Group of Media Content, and its Captions

Name	Device
`<footer>`	Defines a Footer for a Section or Page
`<header>`	Defines a Header for a Section or Page
`<hgroup>`	Defines Information about a Section in a Document
`<keygen>`	Defines a Generated Key in a Form
`<mark>`	Defines Marked Text
`<meter>`	Defines Measurement within a Predefined Range
`<nav>`	Defines Navigation Links
`<output>`	Defines some Types of Output
`<progress>`	Defines progress of a Task of any kind
`<rp>`	Used in Ruby Annotation for the Benefit of Browsers that don't Support Ruby Annotation
`<rt>`	Defines Explanation to Ruby Annotation
`<ruby>`	Defines Ruby Annotation
`<section>`	Defines a Section
`<source>`	Defines a Media Resource
`<summary>`	Defines the Header of a "detail" Element
`<time>`	Defines a date/time
`<video>`	Defines a Video

The new <video> tag is by far the most famous tag in whole HTML list because of the well-known controversy between Apple and Adobe about Flash technology support. An example is shown in Figure 3–19.

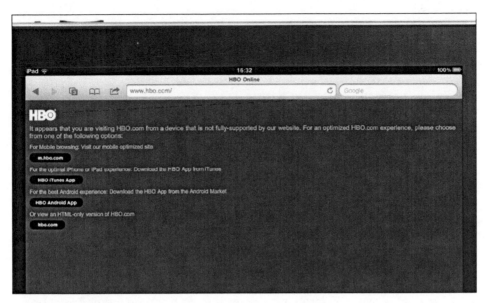

Figure 3–19. *The HBO Web site: The iOS does not support Adobe Flash Technology and instead embraces the HTML Video Standard.*

Today, if we want to insert video compatible with any of Apple's devices, we need to use this tag. For this reason, in Table 3–7, we show each `<video>` attribute with its related description.

Table 3–3. *Video Tags Attributes in HTML (Ordered Alphabetically)*

Attribute	Description
autoplay	When set to true, the video plays as soon as it buffered
controls	If set to true, the user is shown playback controls
end	Defines the endpoint of a video. if it's not defined, the video plays to the end.
height	Defines the height of the video player
loopend	Defines the ending point of a loop
loopstart	Defines the starting point of a loop
playcount	Defines the number of times a video clip is played. default value is set to 1
poster	Defines the URL of a "poster image" to show before the video begin to play
src	Defines the URL of the video

Attribute	Description
start	Defines the startpoint of a video. if it's not defined, the video starts from the beginning
width	Defines the width of the video player

The HTML code is:

```
<video src="videos/name-of-the-video.mov" controls="true"É
 poster="images/video-preview.jpg" width="300" height="200" />
```

Developing for desktop using HTML also brings a compatibility issue to browsing support, but in our context (Apple mobile devices) this problem doesn't exist, because Mobile Safari supports all the new tags and features from the last HTML draft. We will consider the entire HTML standard in a more detailed way in Chapter 7.

CSS 3: Introducing the New Features

The old CSS2 specification was too large and complex to be updated in one big chunk, so it has been broken down into smaller pieces from the World Wide Web Consortium (W3C). Some modules included are:

- The Box Model
- Multi-Column Layout
- Background and Borders
- Lists Module
- Text Effects
- Hyperlink Presentation
- Speech Module

NOTE: CSS is still a "work in progress" project, and you can have a better look over the complete list of modules at: www.w3.org/Style/CSS/current-work.

The main impact of CSS is the ability to use new selectors and properties in order to achieve new design features such as animation or gradients, and to achieve current design features in a much easier way.

Now we will see some of the most common properties that will be found in every framework that we'll use in designing and developing for the iPhone and iPad. Knowing these properties will be useful in Chapter 8 when we expand our frameworks.

NOTE: Until all the CSS modules reach recommended status, every browser vendor has the faculty to decide how to implement those properties. For this reason, a proprietary prefix is placed in front of every property.

The point of vendor-specific prefixes is to let other rendering engines know that the property can be safely ignored without creating an error, and at the same time let the developer know that those properties are experimental and not fully supported, even if planned by the W3C.

Once CSS has been completely defined, supported, and officially becomes a Web Standard, all these prefixes will be removed.

An example is:

```
border-radius: 3px;
-webkit-border-radius: 3px; (WebKit-based Browser implementation)
-moz-border-radius: 3px; (Gecko-based Browser implementation)
```

Safari (and other webkit based browsers) have supported `border-radius` with the -webkit-prefix since version 3 (no longer needed from version 5 onward).

At present, when working with desktop web sites and WebApps, we need to specify the same property several times, at least once for each of the most common browsers, in order to achieve a minimum level of CSS property accessibility.

NOTE: In our Apple devices context, the only thing we need to do is take care of WebKit CSS implementation, because we will only use WebKit-based browsers like Safari.

Border Radius

Achieving rounded borders using CSS2 coding can be tricky, and as we well know, iOS has rounded borders everywhere. Numerous methods available, but none is terribly straightforward. This requires us to use additional markup and to create individual images for each border.

Using CSS, creating a rounded border is incredibly fast and easy. As shown in the Table 3–4, we can apply this property to all corners or to individual corners, and width and color are easily altered.

The CSS syntax is:

```
-webkit-border-radius: <length>;
```

Table 3–4. *Border Radius Property in CSS.*

Name	border-radius
Value:	[length	percentage]
Initial:	[0]
Applies to:	all elements
inherited:	no
Percentages:	N/A
Media:	Visual
Computed Value:	as specified

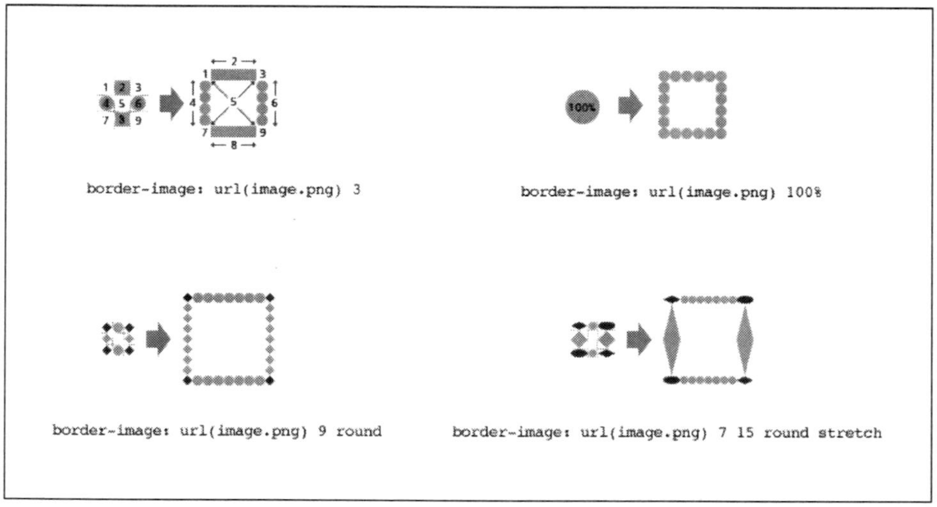

Figure 3–20. *Examples of Rounded Border Property in CSS (images Christian Krammer).*

Border Images

Border images are one of the most useful additions—take note that all of the big buttons that slide in from the bottom on the iPhone can also be designed with this property. CSS has the ability to repeat or stretch a border image as you choose, as shown in Table 3–5 and Figure 3–21.

The CSS syntax is:

```
-webkit-border-image: <source> <slice> <width> <outset> <repeat>;
```

Table 3–5. *Border Image Property in CSS.*

Name	border-image
Value:	[none | length] [number | percentage] [length | percentage | number | auto] [length | percentage] [stretch | repeat | round]
Initial:	[none] [100%] [1] [0] [stretch]
Applies to:	all elements
inherited:	no
Percentages:	N/A
Media:	Visual
Computed Value:	as specified

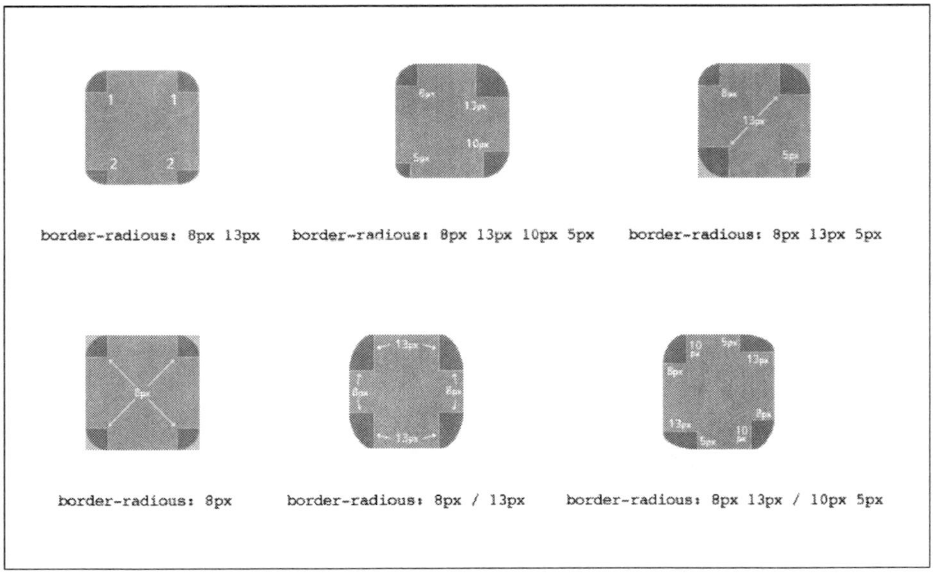

Figure 3–21. *Examples of Border Image Property in CSS (images Christian Krammer).*

Gradients

A gradient is a browser-generated image specified entirely in CSS, which consists of smooth fades between several colors. Gradients are specified using the -webkit-gradient function and can be passed in place of an image URL. There are two types of gradients, linear and radial. You can specify multiple in-between color values, called color stops, and the gradient function interpolates the color values between them.

The function you use to create a color stop is called color-stop. You pass this function as a parameter to the -webkit-gradient function to specify the start, intermediate, and end colors in both a linear and a radial gradient. The colors between the specified color stops are interpolated, as shown in Table 3.6 and Figure 3–22.

The CSS syntax is:

```
-webkit-gradient ( <gradient-line> <color-stop> <color-stop> <color-stop> );
-webkit-gradient ( <gradient-line> <color-stop> <color-stop> <color-stop> );
```

Table 3–6. *Gradient Property in CSS.*

Name	gradient()
Value:	[gradient-line] [color-stop] [color-stop] [color-stop]
Initial:	[top] [transparent] [transparent] [transparent]
Applies to:	all elements
inherited:	no
Percentages:	N/A
Media:	Visual
Computed Value:	as specified
Name	color-stop()
Value:	[color] [length | percentage]
Initial:	[transparent] [0%]

Name	gradient()
Applies to:	all elements
inherited:	no
Percentages:	N/A
Media:	Visual
Percentages:	N/A
Media:	Visual

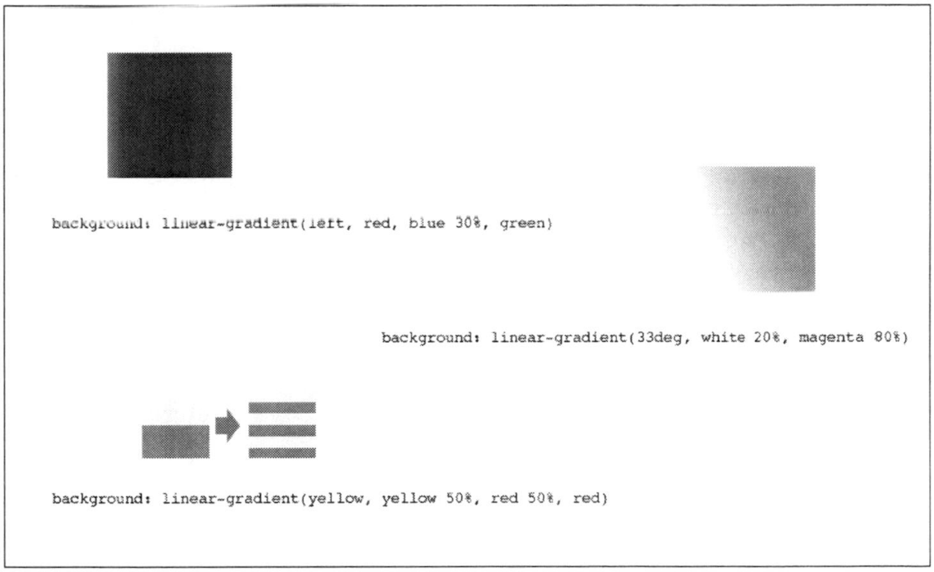

Figure 3–22. *Examples of Gradient Property in CSS (images Christian Krammer).*

Box Sizing

The new Box Model is one of the most extensive areas of the CSS draft. This box sizing aspect allows you to define certain elements to fit an area in a certain way. If, for some reason, we want to design a two-column bordered box in our user interface and place the two boxes side by side, it can be achieved using this model. This forces the browser to render the box with the specified width and height, and place the border and padding inside the box.

The box size property in CSS is shown in Table 3–7 and the CSS syntax is:

```
-webkit-box-sizing: <box-sizing value>;
```

Table 3–7. *Box Size Property in CSS.*

Name	box-sizing
Value:	[content-box | border-box | inherit]
Initial:	[content-box]
Applies to:	all elements
inherited:	no
Percentages:	N/A
Media:	Visual
Computed Value:	as specified

Box Shadow

Adding a box shadow was difficult with CSS2; usually we needed to use additional markup. While I wait to switch to a full CSS web site in the near future, for the time being I have personally added an additional <div> to my web site in order to add a paper-shadow-effect to the main content. The CSS alternative is more elegant and clean.

The box shadow property in CSS is shown in Table 3–8 and the CSS syntax is:

```
-webkit-box-shadow: <offset-x> <offeset-y> <blur radius> <color>;
```

Table 3–8. *Box Shadow Property in CSS.*

Name	box-shadow
Value:	[offset] [offset] [offset } [color]
Initial:	[0] [0] [0] [transparent]
Applies to:	all elements
inherited:	no
Percentages:	N/A
Media:	Visual
Computed Value:	as specified

Figure 3–23 shows an example of the box shadow property in CSS.

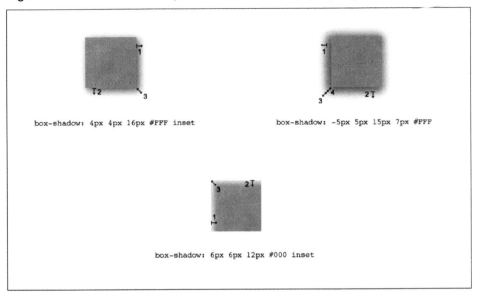

Figure 3–23. *Examples of Box Shadow Property in CSS (images Christian Krammer).*

Outline

Setting an element outline is already available in CSS2, but in CSS includes the ability to offset the outline away from its element, by a value that we define. It differs from a border in two ways:

- Outlines do not take up space
- Outlines may be non-rectangular

NOTE: All Outline Shapes are rectangular, but an outline can be an agglomeration of rectangle.

The outline property in CSS is shown in Table 3–9 and the CSS code is:

```
outline: <width> <style> <color>;
outline-offset: <offset>;
```

Table 3–9. *Outline Property in CSS.*

Name	outline
Value:	[width | inherit] [auto | style | inherit] [color | invert | inherit]
Initial:	[medium] [none] [invert]
Applies to:	all elements
inherited:	no
Percentages:	N/A
Media:	Visual
Computed Value:	as specified

Background Size

Before CSS, background size was determined by the actual size of the image used. This new CSS property makes it possible to specify the needed size of the background image in terms of percentage or pixels. When emulating the iOS user interface, we always try to use CSS properties instead of images wherever possible.

In any case, the background-size property, where it is needed, will allow us to re-use images in several different contexts and also expand a background to fill an area more accurately.

The background size property in CSS is shown in Table 3–10 and the CSS syntax is:

```
-webkit-background-size: <length-x> <length-y>;
```

Table 3–10. *Background Size Property in CSS.*

Name	background-size
Value:	[auto | length | percentage]
Initial:	[auto]
Applies to:	all elements
inherited:	no
Percentages:	N/A
Media:	Visual
Computed Value:	as specified

Figure 3–24 shows examples of the background size property in CSS.

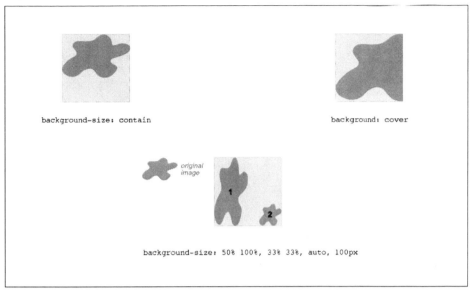

Figure 3–24. *Examples of Background Size Property in CSS (Images Christian Krammer).*

Background Origin

CSS also allows us to specify how the position of a background is calculated, as shown in Table 3–11. This allows great flexibility in terms of placing a background image.

The CSS syntax is:

```
background-origin: <origin-value>;
```

Table 3–11. *Background Origin Property in CSS.*

Name	background-origin
Value:	[content-box	border-box	padding-box]
Initial:	[padding-box]
Applies to:	all elements
inherited:	no
Percentages:	N/A
Media:	Visual
Computed Value:	as specified

Figure 3–25 shows examples of the background origin property in CSS.

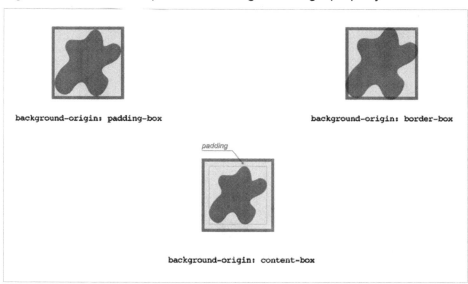

Figure 3–25. *Examples of Background Origin Property in CSS (images Christian Krammer).*

Multiple Backgrounds

The new ability to use multiple backgrounds is a great time saver, and allows us to achieve effects that previously required more than one <div>. The Multiple Background property, combined with the background size gives us a powerful tool in order to reduce the gap between a native UI look-and-feel and our emulated (web) user interface.

The multiple background property in CSS is shown in Table 3–12 and the CSS code is:

background: <source-1> <position> <repeat>, <source-n> <position> <repeat>;

Table 3–12. *Multiple Backgrounds Property in CSS.*

Name	background
Value:	[image | none] [length | percentage] [repeat | no-repeat]
Initial:	[none] [0% 0%] [repeat]
Applies to:	all elements
inherited:	no

Name	background
Percentages:	N/A
Media:	Visual
Computed Value:	as specified

Figure 3–26 shows examples of the multiple background property in CSS.

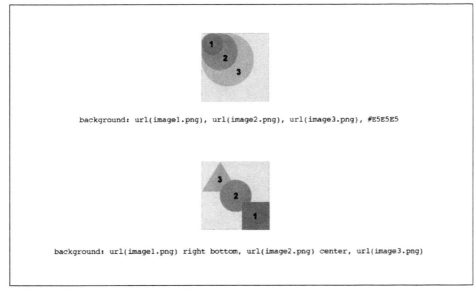

Figure 3–26. *Examples of (Multiple) Background Property in CSS (images Christian Krammer).*

Text Shadow

Text shadow is a fundamental CSS property for who want to emulate the native iOS user interface. Almost all the text in iOS is embossed and personally I find it very readable.

The text shadow property in CSS is shown in Table 3–13 and the CSS code is:

```
-webkit-text-shadow: <offset-x> <offeset-y> <blur radius> <color>;
```

Table 3-13. *Text Shadow Property in CSS.*

Name	text-shadow
Value:	[image | none] [length | percentage] [repeat | no-repeat]
Initial:	[none] [0% 0%] [repeat]
Applies to:	all elements
inherited:	no
Percentages:	N/A
Media:	Visual
Computed Value:	as specified

Examples of the text shadow property are shown in Figure 3-27.

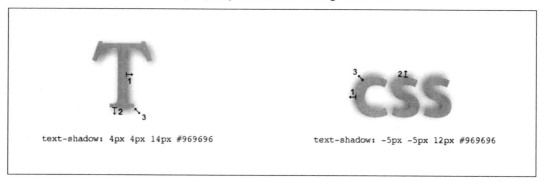

text-shadow: 4px 4px 14px #969696   text-shadow: -5px -5px 12px #969696

Figure 3-27. *Examples of Text Shadow Property in CSS (images Christian Krammer).*

Text Overflow

Text overflow is another fundamental property involved in iOS native user interface emulation. The ellipsis in a menu title indicates that the menu allows more than a simple tap-see-result action (e.g., Choose a Network...) but often in the iPhone environment, the title overflows the Header Bar, even more often if we use buttons on the left and right of this bar to help the user better navigate the content.

In this case, the text overflow Text Overflow property allows us to clip the text with some nice ellipses ("...") as a visual hint to the user that the text has been clipped. With the iPad, this problem no longer exists because of the larger screen.

The text overflow property is shown in Table 3-14 and the CSS syntax is:

```
text-shadow: <overflow-value>;
```

Table 3–14. *Text Overflow Property in CSS.*

Name	text-overflow
Value:	[clip | ellipsis | ellipsis-word | inherit]
Initial:	[clip]
Applies to:	all block-level elements
inherited:	no
Percentages:	N/A
Media:	Visual
Computed Value:	as specified

Word Wrapping

With CSS2, if a word is too long to fit within one line of an area, it expands outside. This is not a very common occurrence, but happens from time to time. The new word wrapping ability, shown in Table 3–15, allows us to force the text to wrap, even if it means splitting it mid-word.

Table 3–15. *Word Wrapping Property in CSS.*

Name	word-wrap
Value:	[normal | break-word]
Initial:	[normal]
Applies to:	all elements
inherited:	yes
Percentages:	N/A
Media:	Visual
Computed Value:	as specified

IMAGINE CSS

The CSS syntax is:

```
word-wrap: <wrap-value>;
```

The CSS code is:

```
word-wrap: break-word;
```

Web Fonts

This new property will be a revolutionary change for web design, but for those of us who need to work with the native iOS user interface, this property is not that useful. because we have Helvetica in the Safari Font Stack. Using the web font property could mean downloading potentially heavy files and having some strange logos to represent textually.

The web font property in CSS is shown in Table 3–16 and the CSS syntax is:

`@font-face { <font-family>; <source>; }`

Table 3–16. *Web Font Property in CSS.*

Name	@font-face
Value:	[family-name]
Initial:	[N/A]
Applies to:	all font face and font family
inherited:	no
Percentages:	N/A
Media:	Visual
Computed Value:	N/A

Tap Highlight

In the touch screen device paradigm, the hover status as we know it in the desktop user experience doesn't exist, but with this useful WebKit extension we can highlight a link or a JavaScript-clickable element. The alpha channel is also supported.

The tap highlight property in CSS is shown in Table 3–17 and the CSS syntax is:

`-webkit-tap-highlight-color: <color>;`

Table 3–17. *Tap Highlight Property in CSS.*

Name	tap-highlight-color
Value:	[color]
Initial:	[rgba(0,0,0,0)]
Applies to:	link, JavaScript clickable elements
inherited:	yes
Percentages:	N/A
Media:	Visual
Computed Value:	as specified

Multiple Columns

The multi column property is much more exciting from a desktop perspective, because the iPhone and iPad user interface doesn't use multi column layout very often. In some cases, this property can still be useful for achieving some nice content presentation. This property allows us to specify into how many columns our text should be split, and how they should appear.

There are four properties that relate to the multiple column layout in CSS that allow us to set the number of columns, width, amount of gap separating each column, and the border between each. The 4 properties are:

- column-count
- column-width
- column-gap
- column-rule

The multiple columns property in CSS is shown in Table 3–18 and the CSS syntax is:

```
.twoColumnLayout { <number of column> <width> <gap> <rule> }
```

Table 3–18. *Multiple Columns Property in CSS.*

Name	column-span
Value:	[integer | auto] [length | auto] [length | normal] [color]
Initial:	[auto] [auto] [normal] [same as for 'color' in CSS21]
Applies to:	non-replaced block-level elements (except table elements), table cells, inline block elements
inherited:	no
Percentages:	N/A
Media:	Visual
Computed Value:	the absolute length

Spanning Columns

This property is used in case we want an element to span more than one column; usually we use it for headings, tables or images.

The span column property in CSS is shown in Table 3–19 and the CSS syntax is:

```
column-span: <number-of-column>;
```

Table 3–19. *Span Column Property in CSS.*

Name	column-span
Value:	[1	all]
Initial:	[1]
Applies to:	static, non-floating elements
inherited:	no
Percentages:	N/A
Media:	Visual
Computed Value:	as specified

Transitions

The transition property can be used to spread a CSS property value modification such as height, width, or color over time. Not all properties can be animated with a transition, but all the important properties for iPhone and iPad development are in the list.

The first value refers to the property being transitioned, the second value controls the duration, and the third controls the type of transition.

The transitions property in CSS is shown in Table 3–20 and the CSS syntax is:

```
-webkit-transition: <property> <time> <function>;
```

Table 3–20. *Transition Property in CSS.*

Name	transition
Value:	[none	all	property] [time] [ease	linear	ease-in	ease-out	ease-in-out	cubic-bezier]

Name	transition
Initial:	[all] [0] [ease]
Applies to:	all elements, :before and :after pseudo elements
inherited:	no
Percentages:	N/A
Media:	Visual
Computed Value:	as specified

Figure 3–28 shows examples of the transition property in CSS.

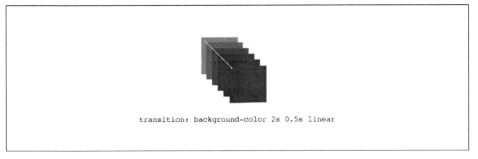

transition: background-color 2s 0.5s linear

Figure 3–28. *Examples of Transition Property in CSS (images Christian Krammer).*

Transforms

Transforms are used for modifying the geometry of objects through mathematical operations. This property is fundamental for emulating some of the typical iOS effects between pages, and it is useful for creating interesting visual effects and animations.

In the transform property, a list of transform functions will be used as values, and is applied in the order provided. Exactly as they are for the other CSS values, the individual transform functions are separated by white space.

The transform property works together with the transform-origin property to set the point of origin from where the transition takes place.

Available transform functions are:

- **matrix(number, number, number, number, number, number)**
  specifies a 2D transformation in the form of a transformation matrix of six values. matrix(a,b,c,d,e,f) is equivalent to applying the transformation matrix [a b c d e f].

- **translate(translate-value, translate-value)** specifies a 2D translation by the vector [tx, ty], where tx is the first translation-value parameter and ty is the optional second translation-value parameter. If ty is not provided, ty has zero as a value.

- **translateX(translation-value)** specifies a translation by the given amount in the X direction.

- **translateY(translation-value)** specifies a translation by the given amount in the Y direction.

- **scale(number, number)** specifies a 2D scale operation by the [sx,sy] scaling vector described by the 2 parameters. If the second parameter is not provided, it is takes a value equal to the first.

- **scaleX(number)** specifies a scale operation using the [sx,1] scaling vector, where sx is given as the parameter.

- **scaleY(number)** specifies a scale operation using the [1,sy] scaling vector, where sy is given as the parameter.

- **rotate(angle)** specifies a 2D rotation by the angle specified in the parameter about the origin of the element, as defined by the transform-origin property.

- **skew(angle, angle)** specifies a skew transformation along the X and Y axes. The first angle parameter specifies the skew on the X axis. The second angle parameter specifies the skew on the Y axis. If the second parameter is not given then a value of 0 is used for the Y angle (e.g., no skew on the Y axis).

- **skewX(angle)** specifies a skew transformation along the X axis by the given angle.

- **skewY(angle)** specifies a skew transformation along the Y axis by the given angle.

The transform property in CSS is shown in Table 3–21 and the CSS syntax is:

```
-webkit-transition: <transform function> <type of effect>;
-webkit-transition-origin: <transform origin>;
```

Table 3–21. *Transform Property in CSS.*

Name	Transform
Value:	[none | transform function | transform function]
Initial:	[none]
Applies to:	block-level and inline-level elements
inherited:	no

Name	Transform
Percentages:	Refer the size of the element's box
Media:	Visual
Computed Value:	as specified
Name	transform-origin
Value:	[percentage | length | left | center | right]
Initial:	[50% 50%]
Applies to:	block-level and inline-level elements
inherited:	no
Percentages:	Refer the size of the element's box
Media:	Visual
Computed Value:	for length the absolute value, otherwise a percentage

Figure 3–29 shows examples of the transform property in CSS.

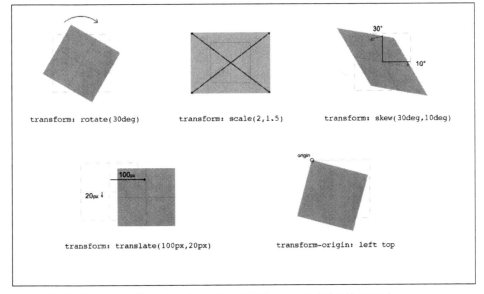

Figure 3–29. *Examples of Transform Property in CSS (images Christian Krammer).*

Animation

Animation, similar to transition, modifies properties over time. Using the transition property, we achieve a one-way effect from one value to another. This kind of property is useful for emulating iOS page transitions or creating Flash-Like animations.

Using the animation property, we can provide any number of intermediate values that are not necessarily linear, achieving fairly complex animations. These intermediate values are called keyframes and are the foundation of all animation processes.

> **NOTE:** A key frame in animation and filmmaking is a drawing that defines the starting and ending points of any smooth transition. They are called "frames" because their position in time is measured in frames on a strip of film. A sequence of keyframes defines which images the viewer will see, whereas the position of the keyframes on the film, video, or animation timeline defines the timing of the movement.

The animation property in CSS is shown in Table 3–22 and the CSS syntax is:

```
animation-name: <name>;
animation-duration: <time>;
animation-iteration-count: <integer>;
animation-timing-function: <function>;
@keyframes <name> {
        from {
                left: <start-x>;
                top: <start-y>;
        }
        to {
                left: <destination-x>;
                top: <destination-y>;
        }
}
```

Table 3–22. *Animation Property in CSS.*

Name	transform
Value:	[animation-name] [animation-duration] [animation-timing-function] [animation-delay] [animation-iteration-count] [animation-direction]
Initial:	see individual properties
Applies to:	block-level and inline-level elements
inherited:	no

Name	transform
Percentages:	N/A
Media:	Visual
Computed Value:	as specified

In our frameworks, the JavaScript takes care of the user interface's behavior, but the animation property offers a valid alternative in many other situations. This property is also the most complex of all CSS modules. For this reason, we will analyze all its properties in detail. More details are shown in Table 3–23.

Table 3–23. Further Details of *Animation Property in CSS.*

Name	animation-name
Value:	[none	name]
Initial:	{ none }
Applies to:	block-level and inline-level elements
inherited:	no
Percentages:	N/A
Media:	Visual
Computed Value:	as specified
Name	animation-duration
Value:	[time]
Initial:	[0]
Applies to:	block-level and inline-level elements
inherited:	no
Percentages:	N/A
Media:	Visual
Computed Value:	as specified

Name	animation-timing-function
Value:	[ease | linear | ease-in | ease-out | ease-in-out | cubic-bezier]
Initial:	[ease]
Applies to:	block-level and inline-level elements
inherited:	no
Percentages:	N/A
Media:	Visual
Computed Value:	as specified
Name	**animation-iteration-count**
Value:	[infinite | integer |
Initial:	{ 1]
Applies to:	block-level and inline-level elements
inherited:	no
Percentages:	N/A
Media:	Visual
Computed Value:	as specified
Name	**animation-direction**
Value:	[normal | alternate]
Initial:	[normal]
Applies to:	block-level and inline-level elements
inherited:	no
Percentages:	N/A
Media:	Visual
Computed Value:	as specified

Name	animation-play-state
Value:	[running | pause]
Initial:	[running]
Applies to:	block-level and inline-level elements
inherited:	no
Percentages:	N/A
Media:	Visual
Computed Value:	as specified
Name	**animation-delay**
Value:	[time]
Initial:	[0]
Applies to:	block-level and inline-level elements
inherited:	no
Percentages:	N/A
Media:	Visual
Computed Value:	as specified

Keyframes

Keyframes are used to specify the values for animating properties at various points during the animation. The keyframes specify the behavior of one cycle of the animation; the animation may iterate one or more times.

Keyframes are specified using a specialized CSS at-rule. A @keyframes rule consists of the keyword @keyframes, followed by the identifier animation-name that gives a name for the animation, followed by a set of style rules.

The CSS grammar for the keyframes rule is:

```
keyframes-rule: '@keyframes' IDENT '{' keyframes-blocks '}';
keyframes-blocks: [ keyframe-selectors block ] ;
keyframe-selectors: [ 'from' | 'to' | PERCENTAGE ] [ ',' [ 'from' | 'to' |E
  PERCENTAGE ] ];
```

The example below will produce an animation that moves an element from (0, 0) to (100px, 100px) over five seconds and repeats itself nine times (for a total of ten iterations). Note that we didn't use all the properties listed above because we didn't need them to achieve this particular effect.

Reflections

No other CSS property is so typically Apple-style as is the reflection property. Reflection is used on every product presentation in the Apple store and combined with the use of negative space, it is a valuable tool for achieving nice clean design.

> **NOTE:** Negative space, in art, is the space around and between the subject(s) of an image. Negative space may be most evident when the space around a subject, and not the subject itself, forms an interesting or artistically relevant shape, and such space is occasionally used to artistic effect as the "real" subject of an image. The use of negative space is a key element of artistic composition and visual design.

The box-reflection property is composed of 3 arguments or values in order to achieve the final effect. The first argument sets the direction of the reflection. The second argument specifies the offset of the reflection. The third argument is a mask applied to the reflection and passed using a property called gradient. Details are shown in Table 3–24.

The CSS syntax is:

```
-webkit-box-reflect: <direction> <offset> <mask-box-image>;
```

Table 3–24. *Reflection Property in CSS.*

Name	box-reflect
Value:	[above | below | left | right] [offset] [gradient()]
Initial:	none
Applies to:	all images
inherited:	no
Percentages:	N/A
Media:	Visual
Computed Value:	as specified

Name	gradient
Value:	[gradient()] [from()] [color-stop()]
Initial:	none
Applies to:	all images
inherited:	no
Percentages:	N/A
Media:	Visual
Computed Value:	as specified

JavaScript: Introducing Best Practices.

Browser-based development is the predominant platform for JavaScript, and usually it's executed in the context of a webpage. One of the considerations when writing JavaScript for iPhone or iPad is the abysmal performance offered by these devices, as illustrated in Figure 3–30.

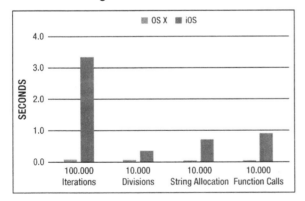

Figure 3–30. *JavaScript Performance Comparison between Mac OS X (left) and iOS (right)*

In these cases, following best practices for high-performance code becomes even more important. The following will present some best practice principles that will help us to develop a cleaner and faster code in our iPhone and iPad web sites and WebApps.

Make the Code Understandable

This first point is pretty easy to explain: choose easy to understand and short names for variables and functions. Is always a good practice to describe a value with your variable or function name.

Do Not Use Global Variables

Using global variables is usually a terrible idea because we run the risk of our code being overwritten by any other JavaScript that is added to the page after ours.

Use a Strict Coding Style

We must always use valid code. In general, browsers are very forgiving JavaScript parsers, but using a lax coding style will hurt us when we shift to another environment or hand our project over to another developer. The JavaScript Validator will help us achieve validity.

> **NOTE:** In difference to HTML and CSS, W3C doesn't offer any official Validator Service for our JavaScript code, fortunately Douglas Crockford, the founder of JSON and JSmin, has created JSLint a JavaScript Verifier.
> JSLint is available at: www.jslint.com/

Comment the Code as Much as Needed

It's important to remember that no matter how good your code is, still it never explains itself. When commenting our code, it's also important to avoid "line comment". Using /* */ is much safer, because it doesn't cause errors when a line break is removed.

Do Not Use Mixed Technologies

We can use JavaScript in many contexts, such as calculation, conversion, access outside resources (Ajax), and to define the behavior of an interface (event handling). For anything else, it's a good idea to stick with the technology we already have to do the job.

A good example would be if we were to try to change the presentation using JavaScript. That's really a bad approach, because people shouldn't have to change the JavaScript code to change a presentation's look-and-feel. All of the frameworks we'll be using put this principle into practice. It lets us use many customized user interface components without writing a single line of JavaScript code.

Use Shortcut Notation

Using shortcut notation, we can keep our code snappy and easier to read, once we become familiar enough with it.

Modularize the Code

Keeping the code modularized and specialized is always a time saving practice for a developer. Especially when we are beginners we have a tendency to write single functions to achieve all of our (behavior) goals. Unfortunately, as we start extending our code, we face the risk of writing the same code in several functions. In order to avoid this, it is important to write smaller, generic helper functions that fulfill one specific task.

Allow Progressive Enhancement

In writing our code, we must use JavaScript only to achieve specific behaviors. In any other cases we must use other web standards like HTML and CSS. The point here is to avoid a lot of JavaScript-dependent code. Developing in this way we will provide progressive enhancement and a first level of optimization, because DOM generation is slow and expansive.

> **DEFINITION:** Progressive enhancement is a strategy for web design that emphasizes accessibility... Progressive enhancement uses web technologies in a layered fashion that allows everyone to access the basic content and functionality of a web page, more advanced browser software or more experience an enhanced version of the page.
> —(source Wikipedia)

Allow for Maintenance and Customization

All of the things that are likely to change in our code should not be scattered throughout the code. A good practice is to put these bits of code into a configuration object and make it public, so that maintenance and customization will be easier to achieve.

Do Not Code Heavy Nesting Loops

Nesting loops inside of loops is always a bad idea, because it means taking care of several iterator variables. We can achieve the same result in a cleaner way using specialized tool methods.

Optimize the Loops

In JavaScript, loops can get terribly slow, most of the time because of bad coding. A good guideline is to always keep computation-heavy code outside of loops.

Make a Minimum Use of DOM

As we previously said, DOM generation is slow and expansive, so it is important to remember not to abuse it, or to overuse and scatter it about instead of using group operations.

Always Test Any Element

We can't simply trust any data that come in. An example of how to avoid this is to test data that get into our function as to its format using typeof, or to test availability of DOM elements before altering or using them.

Use JavaScript only to Add Behaviors

While writing our JavaScript code, it is hard keep track of the quality of the HTML we produce. We know in any case that JavaScript aims to implement behaviors in our web site or WebApp, and for this reason, if we find ourselves creating lots of HTML in JavaScript, we might be doing something wrong.

Develop Code for Humans First

As good practice, at certain points in the development process we always optimize our code. Is important to remember that live code is done for machines, and development code is done for humans, so we don't want to optimize prematurely and punish ourselves or the other developers who have to take over from us.

Browser Support for Standards: WebKit and Safari

When developing web sites or WebApps for the iPhone and iPad, the browser represents the foundation of all our projects. The Apple browser was developed over the WebKit browser engine, and uses web standards like:

- HTML, HTML4, XHTML, XHTML-MP
- CSS, CSS2
- JavaScript
- AJAX
- SVG
- Other technologies for text, video, audio, etc.

Think of Safari as being like your best friend (and maybe it is, since you will spend more time in front of this browser than with all your real friends): the better you know it, the less you will have problems with it.

Both Safari and Mobile Safari are based on the same WebKit browser engine and both support the full CSS2 specifications, passing the CSS Acid3 Test with a 100% score (see Figure 3–31). Both browsers also support almost all of the new CSS specifications, and personally I assume that all my iPhone or iPad web sites and WebApp support all CSS specifications, because all of the useful properties for development are supported. Safari also introduced some new WebKit properties like CSS -webkit-reflection, and -webkit-tap-highlight-color that we hope will be included in the CSS specification soon.

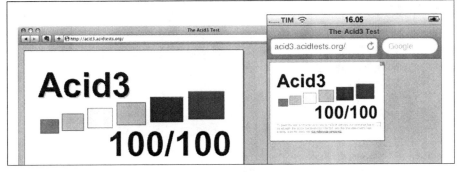

Figure 3–31. *Acid3 Test on Safari (left) and on Mobile Safari (right)*

The most famous behavior difference between Safari and Mobile Safari is the position: fixed issue (supported only from iOS5 on). This may become a problem when we want to insert some kind of UI element, like a fixed footer (or header), in the bottom (or upper) part or our web site or WebApp. In this case, if the user scrolls up and down the page so does the UI element.

In order to understand what and why this happens, we need to remember that what we see on the iPhone (and in some cases on the iPad) is just a viewport into the full HTML page.

> **NOTE:** The *viewport* area in a desktop context is the visible portion of a 2D area, which is larger than the visualization screen.

It's like having an open book in front of us, and in our hands a piece of paper with a square hole of 320x416 pixels cut out of the middle. Once we've laid the paper down onto the book's page surface, if we want to read the page we need to move the 320x416 square hole (the viewport) around and position it over the words we want to read. This is exactly what the Mobile Safari viewport does, and as we flick and scroll, we are moving the viewport around while the web site behind it stays static. The Figure 3–32 below, shows exactly this principle.

Figure 3–32. *Comparison between iOS and OS X Viewport dimensions.*

Therefore, the CSS property is valid and working. Because the viewport is moving rather than the page, the element appears to move. We have several methods for fixing this problem and we will see various ways to do it in Chapter 8.

The Mobile Safari browser is a Class A browser, meaning that it is comparable to a desktop-grade browser. In this section we saw how important is that a browser provide support for web standards, in the next section we will see the iOS limitation and constraints and what this does mean for a Web Developer.

iOS Limitation and Constraints

Since the iPhone and the iPad are mobile devices, they must obviously have constraints, and since nothing is infinite in this world (mathematical infinity apart), they've obviously got to have some limitations.

In the end, I always react positively to limitations and constraints, even if in the beginning sometimes they can make me upset, nervous, or even angry. I still remember the day when I realized that the old iOS firmware (called iPhone OS) didn't allow any multi-tasking features for native and third party applications, and it's probably better to forget what passed through my mind in those brief moments.

Our role as human beings and developers is to turn limitations and constraints into opportunities, giving value to everything that comes into our lives and everything that crosses our paths.

What we have facing us today are some hardware and software limitations and constraints. Table 3–28 shows the most important of these.

Table 3–28. *iPhone and iPad Limitation and Constraints*

Software Resource	Limitation
Opened Pages in Mobile Safari	8
Downloaded Resource over 3G	20MB
Non-Streamed Media Files	10MB
JavaScript Stack and Object Allocation	10MB
JavaScript Execution Limit	5 Seconds for each Top-Level Entry Point
PDF, Word, Excel Documents	30MB
PNG, GIF, TIFF Images	8MB
JPEG Images	128MB
Animated GIF	2MB
Technology Area	**Technology Not Supported**
Web Technology	Flash Media Based, Java Applet
Mobile Technology	WML
HTML	input type="file", Tooltip
CSS	hover, position: fixed
Bookmark Icon	.ico file
JavaScript Event	Several Mouse-Related Events
JavaScript Commands	showModalDialog(), print()
Security	DSA Keys, Diffie-Hellman Protocol, Self-Signed Certificates, Custom x.509 Certificates

As we can see from the second part of the table, in many cases the non-supported technologies are not fundamental, and in other cases we have great substitutions or nice workarounds; so let's think positive!

An example of how to redesign the user experience following the touch screen paradigm is the following. Imagine we're browsing from our desktop a webpage, and we're going to click on link in a menu. A dropdown menu with a few options is generated, and hovering over these options causes a description for that item to appear in an info box nearby. Clicking on the link takes us to another page.

This kind of user experience doesn't exist on the iPhone or iPad, because the CSS hover property is not supported.

What we can do is design an interface optimized for iPhone or iPad and let the info box appear when the link is tapped for the first time, and activate the link when the user makes a second tap, taking him to the desired page. A WebKit extension called tap-highlight-color can also used to cause the tapped element to be all or partially obscured by a color.

In the next paragraph, we will see how important is for a design to also provide support for the first line of user interface: the fingers.

A Finger is not a Mouse: The Importance of being Finger-Friendly

The first thing we need to master as iPhone or iPad developers (but also as general touch-devices developers), is that a finger is not a mouse. This is important to keep in mind for several reasons.

When we browse a webpage with our mouse, we move a pointer over the page. The pointer is just few pixels wide and just one or two pixels wide at the top. Looking at it from a **finger perspective**, we can have a tiny user with thin fingers, and a big user with fat fingers. Most users will be in the middle, but almost all will be unable to use their finger to tap a typical link from a desktop webpage. It doesn't matter what kind of link we are talking about it, a **finger un-friendly** link is unacceptable in any kind of touch design, as shown in Figure 3–33.

Figure 3–33. *Links are Completely Finger Un-Friendly without using the Zoom Function.*

Now, I can hear you saying, Thank God we have the Zoom! You are right, but our golden rule regarding mobile UX is that everything should be easily accessible with a minimal number of actions. On touch devices, we must design links with a minimum height of 30px. With a link height 30px, and the use of the right amount of non-touchable space between links, you can assume that almost all of your users will be able to tap the link and use the interface.

Another important aspect is that finger input does not always correspond to mouse input. A mouse has a left and a right button, a scroll in the middle, and it can move quickly to any place the user wants to go.

Many developers have said that the point here is to support all of the possible mouse-events in order to increase the touch user experience. I totally disagree. For me, the point is to design a user experience from zero, forget about the classic mouse user experience, and move forward without even a glance backward.

In Table 3–29, we display which gestures to implement for an optimized touch user experience, and how they change according to different contexts: web site, WebApp, and native application.

Table 3–29. *Finger Gestures and Mouse Events Comparison in Web site, WebApp, and Native App*

Gesture	Result	Web site	WebApp	Native App
Tap	Equivalent to a Left Click*	Yes	Yes	Yes
Double-Tap	Zoom and Center a Block of Content	Yes	No	No
Flick	Scroll the Page	Yes	Yes	Yes
Pinch Open	Zoom In on Content	Yes	No	No
Pinch Out	Zoom Out on Content	Yes	No	No
Touch & Hold 1	Copy, Cut, and Paste	Yes	Yes	Yes
Touch & Hold 2	Display an Info Bubble	Yes	Yes	No
Touch & Hold 3	Equivalent to a Right Click*	No	No	Yes

*Comparison use a (more common) Right-Hand Mouse Configuration

We also have several mouse interactions that have no gesture event equivalents on an iPhone or iPad, and some others that just belong to the past because they are not interesting in a touch screen paradigm. These interactions include:

- Hover Effects
- Hover-Generated Content
- Drag Window Applications
- A Few Click-Based Interactions

Inside Progressive Enhancement

Progressive enhancement is a practice of using layered techniques to allow anyone to access our content, regardless of his capabilities. Some techniques are related to communication while others focus on interaction.

To adopt a **progressive enhancement paradigm,** we just need to start from a content-out approach, as we saw in Chapter 2. Starting from the basic layer of marking up our text with a content-out approach using **HTML**, we add an extra layer for the presentation using **CSS**, and a final layer for the behavior using **JavaScript**.

This approach is part of the web standards best-practices that we need to apply, but when we're developing for Apple devices it's not enough to guarantee the final results. In this context, we have other variables to handle in order to provide a **graceful degradation** of our user experience. That's where inside progressive enhancement enters the scene, as shown in Figure 3–34.

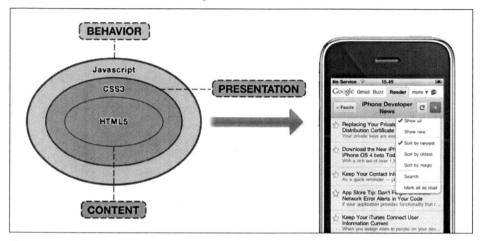

Figure 3–34. *Progressive Enhancement Paradigm on Web Site and WebApp*

As we saw in the section about pro and cons of a WebApp and what makes the difference between native and WebApp, the problem to consider is the inside cross-platform instance. Here, our main goal is to let the user experience gently degrade from the last iPhone or iPad available on the market to its first ancestor (iPhone 2G and iPad 3G).

A useful guideline for providing inside progressive enhancement is composed of the following points:

- Have a **Device Plan**: know which device model will be your primary target.

- Plan **Different Versions** of the same WebApp if you want to reach different kinds of devices like the iPhone/iPod and iPad, and then optimize separately each single user experience.

- Develop a **Common Denominator** between all supported devices in order to share a basic (and common) level of user experience. Visualize how to achieve different versions from the same Content-Out code in order to **optimize each user experience**.

- Use Web Standards in a **Semantic Way**, and mark up the content with HTML using a **Content-Out approach**. Begin to work on this first level of page usability before adding any CSS style.

- Use **CSS** to add a presentation Layer.

- Use **JavaScript** to provide User Interaction.

- Use **Usability Tests** in all phases of Information Architecture and Development to ensure that the user experience improves incrementally despite hardware differences

Developer Resources and Tools for Safari

The new version of Safari brings some new development features. These features are not available on Mobile Safari, but if we need to work on specific tasks like JavaScript debugging, or monitoring the assets activity, we can always use the desktop version for iPhone and iPad projects.

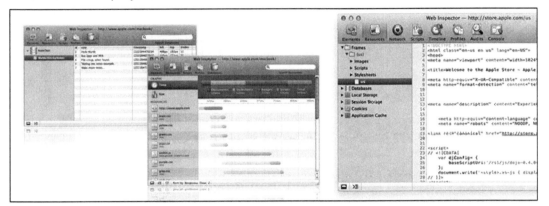

Figure 3–35. *Safari Development Tools: Databases (left), JavaScript Debugger (center), Resources (right).*

We can access all of the developer tools in Safari 5 from the menu bar by turning on the Develop menu in the Advanced pane of Safari preferences, as shown in Figure 3–35. In this way, we will have one-click access to all of the developer features.

Web Inspector

The Web Inspector is the Developer Tools command center where a Web Developer can easily access every available tool. All of the features that you will see in the next paragraph are accessible via Web Inspector.

Elements

With this tool, we can access the webpage's structure. With Elements Pane, we can also make changes to DOM and CSS code and see immediately a preview of changes.

Resources

With this tool, we can access the application's resource, thereby allowing us to view and modify local data and SQL database information. We can also have information on accessed domains.

Network

With this tool, we can monitor how resources are loaded over the network and we can deal with any sort of loading delay issue.

Script

With this tool, we can examine our JavaScript code and debugging at run-time. This tool also provides information over all of the resources used by our JavaScript code.

Timeline

With this code, we have a window over the interaction timeline of our WebApp. We can see how a webpage has been loaded and rendered.

Developer Tools for Mobile Safari

Mobile Safari has an integrated Debug Console, shown in Figure 3–36. It is not like working with the desktop version of this browser, but it can be useful for checking errors in our web site or WebApp.

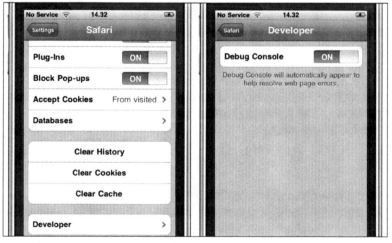

Figure 3–36. *The Mobile Safari Debug Console*

To activate this function, you need to go in the Settings page, enter the Safari page settings and choose Developer. In the developer page, toggle on the option Debug

Console. Once activated, the Debug Console will display a (limited) list of console messages.

SDK Development Model

In 2002, Apple launched Mac OS X, and at that time it made a complete suite of application development tools available to every user of the Macintosh. Since the appearance of OS X version 10.3, called Panther, those tools have been presented as parts of an integrated development environment called Xcode. All OS X applications such as Safari, iTunes, Mail, or iChat are developed by Apple using the same Xcode tool.

In this section, we will give a brief introduction to this paradigm and its components, because even if this book is about web development models, it's good for a developer to have a 360-degree perspective on the Apple development world.

Apple's Objective-C, Cocoa Touch, and Xtools Model

The Xtools IDE, Cocoa Touch Framework, and the Objective-C language comprise the trinity of every iOS developer. Everything starts from here.

Xcode IDE

When we talk about Xtools, in 99% of situations we're referring to the Xcode IDE, to the Interface builder, and to the iPhone/iPad Simulator.

Xcode is an IDE. With this tool, we can also manage all of our testing devices, and automatically package into iPhone/iPad applications with the proper certificates, and install applications on the iPhone/iPad itself.

The remote debugger function can also connect to the device in real-time, managing breakpoints as the application is controlled on the device and providing a good tool for real-time testing.

The iPhone/iPad Simulator

The iPhone/iPad simulator runs our application in much the same way as an actual iPhone/iPad device. This tool is every developer's best friend in the first phase of testing. Using the iPhone/iPad simulator, we can even simulate the touch gestures by using a mouse, and we can also provide a good resource for creating a video tutorial for our application.

Objective-C Language

Objective-C is an object-oriented language with a dynamic class system built as a superset over the standard C language. This language is built on top of Cocoa (Mac OS X) and Cocoa Touch (iOS) frameworks.

Objective-C also introduced a garbage collector optimized for multi-core Macs, but as iOS developers, we can forget about this feature because, on iOS, we must manually optimize our memory usage .

Cocoa Touch Framework

The Cocoa Touch framework drives all of the iOS applications and shares many proven patterns found on the Mac, but it is built with a special focus on touch-based interfaces and optimization.

The Cocoa Touch framework is composed of the following parts:

- Foundation framework
- UIKit framework
- Collection of frameworks

Foundation Framework

The Foundation framework is a layer that abstracts many of the underlying operative system elements, such as primitive types, bundle management, file operations, and networking, from the user interface objects in UIKit that we'll introduce next. This framework is the gateway to everything not explicitly part of the user interface, and defines a base layer of Objective-C classes.

In addition to providing a set of useful primitive object classes, it introduces several paradigms that define functionality not covered by the Objective-C language. The Foundation framework is designed with these goals in mind:

- Provide a small set of basic utility classes
- Make software development easier by introducing consistent conventions for things such as deallocation
- Support Unicode strings, object persistence, and object distribution.
- Provide a level of OS independence to enhance portability

The Foundation framework includes the **root object class**, classes representing basic data types such as strings and byte arrays, collection classes for storing other objects, classes representing system information such as dates, and classes representing communication ports.

This framework introduces several paradigms to avoid confusion in common situations, and to introduce a level of consistency across class hierarchies.

UIKit Framework

Mac OSX programmers use a framework called AppKit that supplies all of the windows, buttons, menus, graphics contexts, and event handling mechanisms that have come to define the OS X experience. The Cocoa Touch equivalent is called UIKit. The UIKit framework provides the classes needed to construct and manage an application's user interface for iPhone, iPad, and iPod Touch. It provides an application object, event handling, drawing model, windows, views, and controls specifically designed for a touch screen interface.

In addition to UIKit, the Cocoa Touch **collection of frameworks** includes everything needed to create world-class iPhone and iPad applications, from 3D graphics to professional audio, to networking, and even special device access APIs to control the camera, or to get location information from the GPS hardware.

Examples of those frameworks include:

- **Audio and Video**
    - Core Audio
    - OpenAL
    - Media Library
    - AV Foundation
- **Graphic and Animation**
    - Core Animation
    - OpenGL ES
    - Quartz 2D
- **Data Management**
    - Core Data
    - SQLite
- **Networking and Internet**
    - Bonjour
    - WebKit
    - BSD Socket

Cocoa Touch is built upon the **Model-View-Controller paradigm** and includes powerful Objective-C frameworks that perform entire tasks in just a few lines of code, while providing the foundational C-language APIs to give direct access to the system when needed.

> **NOTE:** The Model–View–Controller (MVC) is a software architectural pattern used in software engineering. The pattern isolates "domain logic" (the application logic for the user) from input and presentation (GUI), permitting independent development, testing, and maintenance of each.

The SDK Development Life Cycle

When we develop with the SDK development model, the life cycle is basically the same. What changes is just that we have a startup phase where we need to sign up for the Apple development program and a final phase where we submit our application to Apple for the approval process.

In Figure 3–37, we represent the three phases: design, implementation, and testing, under the common name of "Build", but the process structure is the same we see in Chapter 2.

The life cycle also shows how the last step changes, because the native application will go into the iTunes App Store, and not online as all WebApps do.

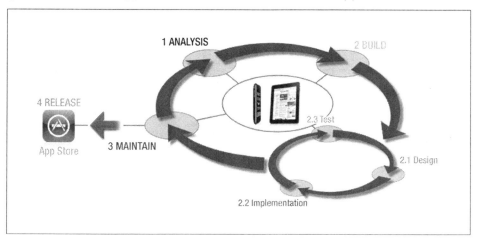

Figure 3–37. *SDK Development Model Life Cycle*

We will not be going further into Objective-C, Cocoa Touch, and Xtools, because this book is focused on designing and developing WebApps using web standards.

Hi, I'm a Mac

I want to end this chapter by sharing with you the words of **Steve Jobs** at WWDC 2007 about web development for the iPhone using Web Standards. I know that if Steve Jobs said something, it was always going to be self-servingly pro-Apple, but I also feel that many of his quotations are very inspiring.

> *"...the full Safari engine is inside of iPhone. And so, you can write amazing Web 2.0 and Ajax Apps that look exactly and behave exactly like apps on the iPhone..."*

> *"...they can make a call, can send email, they can even look up a location on Google Maps..."*

> *"...you've got everything you need if you know how to write apps using the most modern web standards..."*

> *"...so developers, we think we've got a very sweet story for you. YOU can begin building your iPhone apps today..."*

Tools and Frameworks for Apple Mobile Development

Tools used in this chapter are both freeware and paid. Table 3–30 lists some of those useful tools that you can use for designing your next web site or WebApp.

Table 3–30. *Frameworks and Tools Used for Develop iPhone and iPad Web sites and WebApps*

Name	Type	URL	Target Device
iWebKit	Framework	snippetspace.com/	iOS
Sencha Touch	Framework	http://www.sencha.com/	iOS, Android, ...
JQuery Mobile	Framework	http://jquerymobile.com/	iOS, Android, ...
PhoneGap	Framework	www.phonegap.com/	iOS, Android, ...

Name	Type	URL	Operative System
Espresso	Web Editor	macrabbit.com/espresso/	OSX
CSS Edit	CSS Editor	macrabbit.com/cssedit/	OSX
BBedit	Code Editor	barebones.com/products/bbedit/	OSX
Taco	Web Editor	www.tacosw.com	OSX
Aqua(E)macs	Editor	aquamacs.org	OSX
GNU Emacs	Code Editor	gnu.org/software/emacs/	OSX – Win - Linux
Notepad++	Code Editor	notepad-plus-plus.org/	Win

Name	Type	URL	Operative System
HTML	Validator	validator.w3.org/	OSX – Win – Linux
CSS	Validator	jigsaw.w3.org/css-validator/	OSX – Win – Linux
JavaScript	Validator	www.jslint.com/	OSX – Win – Linux

Summary

In this chapter, we introduced the concepts behind frameworks and we saw how a framework approach and structure in the development phase gives useful building blocks to the developer.

In the second part, we examined the web development model, its pros and cons, and four different ways to approach WebApp development. We also analyzed what makes the difference for the user of a WebApp, comparing native and WebApp user (and developer) experiences. Webkit and Safari were introduced, and we presented the typical device limitations and constraints and introduced the inside cross-platform concept.

In the third and last part of this chapter, we looked at the SDK development model, introducing Xtools, Objective-C and the Cocoa Touch framework. By illustrating the native application life cycle, we also saw how the use of other open source tools like PhoneGap allows us to develop a native application starting from a WebApp that was developed using web standards.

User Interface Design for iOS Devices

"Simplicity is the ultimate sophistication"

—Leonardo da Vinci

The user interface design phase is one of the most important stages of your entire project. The user interface is the foundation of everything in your WebApp: content, functions, and all types of services are all accessed through the elements that compose your user interface.

In this chapter, we define what an interface is inside a touch-screen ecosystem. We explore the concept of positive and negative space as it comes into play in the user interface design phase and see how the rule of perceptions helps us to conceptualize our interface design in our minds.

We discuss color psychology theory, suggesting how you can combine colors in an effective and pleasing way, and look at how colors affect the user's mood. Then we examine user reading patterns and see how you can influence them with your interface design.

In the last part of this chapter, we examine the user interface design process through all its phases and then we implement it in three different projects: one compatible with iPad, one with a native-like structure specific to iPad, and one with a native-like structure only for the iPhone.

User Interface Design

Most designers place simplicity above all else, and so do we. We value simple things, because they easily do all the things we need and none of the things we don't. Simplicity is harmonious. Leonardo da Vinci is quoted as saying, "simplicity is the ultimate sophistication." You should always keep this quote in mind when you sit in front of your computer to design your user interfaces. To be simple is to be elegant.

Over the years, we have seen how Apple style has changed, evolving its own interpretation of "simplicity,". In Figure 4–1, you can see how the surrounding world has been influenced by this style.

Figure 4–1. *Different brand, same style: Apple (left) and Palm (right).*

Palm is a big company that has changed the way of marketing its brand following the path blazed by Apple. Even the most recent ads of other companies, like Microsoft, are inspired by this way of thinking. Simplicity is quickly becoming the foundation of the new technology revolution, which is based on a touch-screen display.

Having completed the Analysis phase in step 0 of our project flow, we pass to the Design phase in step 1. In this phase, we start to work on our interface. As we can see from Figure 4–2, the user interface design is a sub-step of the entire Design phase and everything that is designed and approved in this phase is developed in the next phase of the project flow called "Implementation."

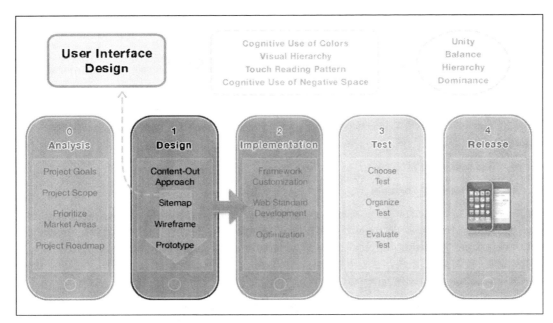

Figure 4–2. *The user interface design phase in the project flow context*

The user interface design process that is examined in this chapter is based on *simplicity.* After introducing some important subjects, such as negative and positive space, active and passive space, the theory behind color psychology, and reading patterns, we discuss how to go from the first step of compatibility, the compatible WebApp, to the full compatible native-like approach.

Before we start, we need to introduce an important new concept: what does the word "interface" really mean in the touch-screen ecosystem? Let's take a look at that now.

What Is an Interface?

As designers, you are familiar with the concept of *user interface,* but there are many kinds of interfaces all around us. Anytime we have an object we want to control or interact with, there is some kind of *interface* between this object and ourselves. The interface gives us a simple method to achieve our goal.

DEFINITION: Interface
Point of Interaction between two systems.

> **DEFINITION:** User interface
> Visual part of a computer application or operating system through which a user interacts with a computer or software.

With a device like the iPhone or the iPad, we have two kinds of interfaces, as shown in Figure 4–3:

- **Software interface**

- **Hardware interface**

iOS offers us some different software interfaces, and each different iPhone view has its own particular type. An address book style view uses the typical list approach interface with edge-to-edge links, the About Us style view might use a rounded rectangle approach.

Figure 4–3. *The types of iPhone's interfaces: software interface (left) and hardware interface (right).*

Beneath the software interfaces, we have a more primitive layer of interaction offered by the hardware interfaces. These software and hardware interfaces enable the user to interact with every aspect of the device. Using the hardware interface shown in Table 4–1, you can adjust the mic and speaker volume, turn the device on and off, and, with the touch-screen, use all the software interfaces offered by the operating system.

Table 4–1. *Two Examples of Hardware Interface Interaction.*

Goal	Interface	Feedback
Adjust the volume up or down	External buttons	Pop up box
Put in sleep mode the display	External button	Click FX

When we use any kind of mobile software on iOS devices, we also use the touch screen to perform the interaction. The display in our touch-screen context is also a hardware interface. This is an important point because it leads us straight to a new kind of paradigm that we have never seen before with the classic desktop or with the old mobile phone approach: everything is an interface.

Everything Is an Interface

What do we mean by this? With these words, we refer to iOS, in which every part in your software becomes an interface because of its touch-screen capabilities. In this chapter, we see how to design every WebApp part that is technically touchable and not just the "classic interface" used in the past by the desktop paradigm.

Using the touch screen, you can zoom, pinch, scroll, and do other gestural movements. These gestures enable the user to interact with all objects contained in the entire viewport—in other words, with all visible parts of our WebApp. Figure 4–4 shows how, with a touch-screen device, even the content must be treated as an interface, which is a passive interface in this case.

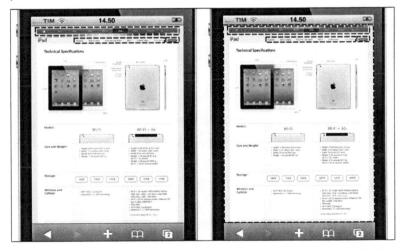

Figure 4–4. *The kind of iPhone's interfaces: active interface (left) and passive interface (right).*

In the classic navigation paradigm, when you use a mouse (or a stick in older mobile phones), you typically point to or choose only linkable parts of a WebApp. Nobody attempts to click in a *dead-zone* with the expectation that some action will occur.

> **NOTE:** The word *dead-zone* refers to a non-clickable zone inside the layout. Because it's non-clickable, a dead-zone part of a layout doesn't offer any level of interaction to the user.

Once you have understood this important concept, you can appreciate that every part of your interface, and every part of your WebApp, needs to be designed with care.

From now on, we will use *active interface* for the touchable or clickable part of our interface, and we will use *passive interface* for the merely touchable (zoomable) parts of our layout. Remember that the active interface is based on software capability (links) and the passive interface is based on hardware capability (touch-screen display). In Figure 4–4, you can see the active and passive interfaces in an iPhone and iPad "compatible" website.

As designers, being aware of this concept dramatically improves your design skills and raises the level of user experience offered by your project.

The new touch paradigm also changes the requirements of your interfaces and layouts, so the question now is, how should you design your touch interface and layout with this in mind?

Your touch interface and layout design is based on:

■ **A Cognitive Use of Colors**

Moods obtained using color reinforces the brand message.

■ **A New Visual Hierarchy**

Prioritizing interfaces and layouts, optimizing for touch-screen devices.

■ **A New Touch-Screen Reading Pattern Structure**

Optimizing the touch-screen UX in both native-like and compatible projects.

■ **A Cognitive Use of Passive and Active Negative Space**

Both active and negative spaces are based on the laws of perception.

Now that you know the tools to use, the question is, "What do you want to achieve using these tools?"

In designing your interface and layout, you should strive for:

■ **Unity**
Create harmony between the interface and the layout elements.

■ **Balance**
Create a visual equilibrium using the interface and the layout elements.

■ **Hierarchy**
Prioritize the interface and the layout elements.

■ **Dominance**
Create focal points on the interface and the layout elements.

All of these are important to understand as concepts. But being aware of them, recognizing them, and using them in your design is another matter altogether and requires practice.

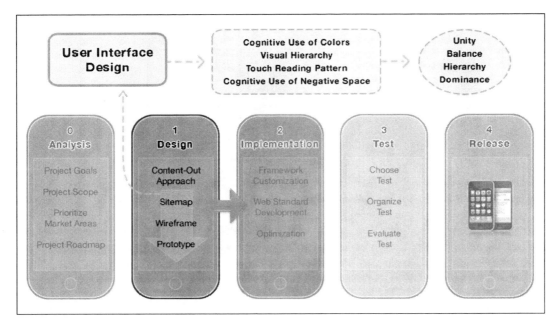

Figure 4–5. *The tools and the goals in the user interface design phase.*

First, we introduce a fundamental concept for this new touch paradigm: the negative space concept. You see how this simple idea completely changes your design style, and how closely related it is to the touch-screen paradigm.

The Rules of Perception in User Interface Design

The rules of perception are fundamental for every kind of designer. These rules are the filters that are used for interactions in life and are the foundation of our experiences. The role of these rules is to interpret and integrate single stimulus from the external environment into a single continuative form.

When designing interfaces for your Apple device, it is important to be aware of these rules in order to achieve specific goals with your design. Sometimes, you may want to transmit passion, energy, simplicity, or just be minimalist. The rules of perception help you to achieve better results in terms of quality and make the whole process even easier.

The Law of Proximity states that proximal elements in the perceptive field are perceived as a single entity. You can use this rule to create semantically–based groups or entities to the design.

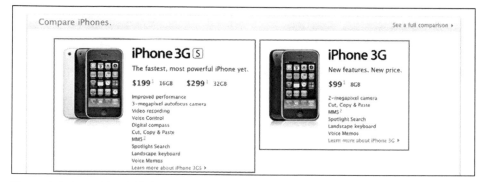

Figure 4–6. *Law of Proximity in two-column design.*

The Law of Similarity states that similar elements in the perceptive field are perceived as part of the same entity based on its geometry, color, or dimension. You can use this rule to create consistency in design between non-proximal elements.

Figure 4–7. *Law of Similarity in Site menu and in product details.*

The Law of Continuity states that continual elements in the perceptive field are perceived as joined into a single entity with a pattern and a direction. You can use this rule to create and add visual patterns and connections to the design.

Figure 4–8. *Law of Continuity in cover flow design.*

The Law of Closure states that some kinds of elements in the perceptive field are perceived as a certain form, even if some visual information is missing. We can use this rule to create visual forms or elements into design where physically it is not possible. In Figure 4–9, you can see how almost all corners are physically opened (red circles in Figure 4–9), but the mind, using the Law of Closure, fills this information gap and perceives continuative lines (and forms).

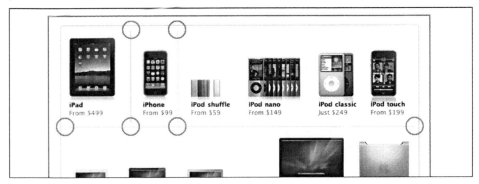

Figure 4–9. *Law of Closure in layout page design.*

The Law of Common Fate states that elements with the same direction in the perceptive field are perceived as a single moving entity. You can use this rule to create movement and add direction to the design.

Figure 4–10. *Law of Common Fate in spotlight design.*

The Law of Figure Ground Relationship states that Elements in the perceptive field are perceived as the union of its form with its background. You can use this rule to create connection between single elements, create dominance, and add contrast into design.

Figure 4–11. *Law of Figure Ground Relationship in logo design.*

The Law of Past Experience states that elements in the perceptive field are perceived in accordance with our past experience and its meanings. Past experience is stored in long-term memory and current experience is compared to already stored information. An example is shown in Figure 4–12. The word is not complete but, according to the Law of Past Experience, you are able to determine that the correct word is "iPhone4." You can use this rule to optimize every kind of visual perception related with the design and its user experience.

Figure 4–12. *Law of Past Experience in logo design*

Negative Space

In Chapter 3, we began to understand why space in your interface and layout is such an important consideration. Users perform actions using their fingers and need more physical space in order to interact with your interfaces in a comfortable way.

In addition, as you learned in the previous section, consider that every figure you see is in relationship with a ground. To us as designers, this means that every part of our interface or layout is in close relationship with the space around it. Working with this space, you can dramatically change the emotional effect on the user and change the level of user experience.

For our purposes, *negative space*, also known as whitespace, can be generally defined as the area of a certain page or interface not occupied by content. For a designer, negative space is the space between specific items on the page and does not have to be white or solid in color; it might contain gradients, patterns, or background objects.

DEFINITION: Negative space

The space around and between the subject or subjects of an image. The negative space might be most evident when the surrounding space, and not the subject itself, forms an interesting or artistically relevant shape. The use of negative space is a key element of artistic composition.

Designing a webpage or a user interface involves taking diverse objects and arranging them in a logical, functional, and attractive manner. The key concept to remember is that the attractiveness of your interface goes well beyond the design elements you use; you must also take into account the aesthetic quality of the negative space surrounding those elements.

The physical space occupied by each element is in relation to all the other items on the page. This physical space has its own rules. These rules, from the simple to the complex, depend on context. They all share the same key-point: they are subject to the influence of negative space.

Figure 4–13. *An example of perfect use of negative space in logo design (image Richard Fonteneau).*

The first thing you need to learn is how to see negative space in your interface or layout. What you must do is retrain your brain to look not only at the content, but also at the inverse of the content. If you think of an element as the combination of an item and the space around the item itself, your brain, using a process called the *Law of Figure Ground*, combines both the item and the negative space around it in order to represent the element.

Even though you are now familiar with the concept behind negative space, deciding on the right amount of negative space for your design requires a great deal on visual sensitivity and skill. Basically, the right amount of negative space is dictated by three factors:

- **Mood You Want to Obtain**
  (a portfolio website needs more space than an online magazine)

- **Quantity of Information to Be Delivered**
  (because negative space is expensive)

- **Medium You Are Designing for**
  (iPhone, iPad, desktop PC, Printer, and so on, might require different amounts)

Before understanding how to manipulate negative space, you need to consider the two kinds that might be important in our design:

- **Active Negative Space**
  (Used to lead the viewer from one element to another)

- **Passive Negative Space**
  (Used for creating balance, harmony, and breathing room)

Now, we offer some approaches to help make use of this powerful tool easier.

Passive Negative Space

This kind of negative space is important for obtaining certain moods and to reinforce the message behind your brand. In Figure 4–14, you can see the large amount of passive negative space used on the Apple website. Apple makes extensive use of this technique in order to promote and spread its brand in just the right way. At this point, it's important to remember that effective use of negative space is not just a matter of quantity but one of proper utilization. Sometimes it will be a good idea to add more space, and at other times you will want to eat up some of the empty space in your design.

Figure 4–14. *The use of passive negative space on the official Apple website.*

In order to improve your interface and layout design in this example, you need to analyze the current amount and appropriateness of negative space, and then decide which areas have too much of it and which areas have too little. In the case of the Apple website (Figure 4–14), you can see how lots of solid passive negative space can create a classy, elegant, and upscale vibe.

What else can you achieve with passive negative space?

Create Separate Groups of Content

You can use passive negative space to separate different groups or areas of information, less space to separate similar groups, and more space to separate groups that are more different. You also create sub-grouping by the way you configure the quantity of space you use.

Typically, this technique uses both a margin and a padding value on the elements. In Figure 4–15, you can see how the right amount of passive negative space creates separate groups of content, where each piece of content is composed of an image and a textual description.

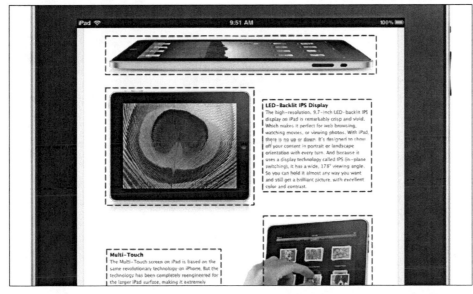

Figure 4–15. *The use of negative space to create groups of content and eliminate visual tension.*

Eliminate Visual Tension

When a shape is not balanced with other shapes, it suffers aesthetically and the user's cognitive reaction to this unbalanced relationship is a visual tension. Look at Figure 4–16 (and compare it with Figure 4–15) and pay attention where your eyes automatically go when you look at these shapes.

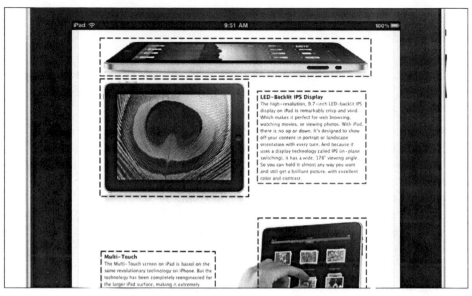

Figure 4–16. *An example of visual tension between two groups of content.*

Your eyes probably automatically went in the upper-left part of Figure 4–9 where the unbalanced relationship between two groups of content creates a visual tension.

You can use passive negative space to give some rest to the eyes and eliminate visual tension. Typically, this technique uses a margin value between layout elements. You can see an example of how to create separate groups of content in Figure 4–16.

Spotlight an Element

You can use passive negative space to spotlight an important element of your interface or layout. A classic example is placing the logo far from the navigation bar (or vice-versa). In this way, you give the element the space it needs to be noticed by the user.

With these techniques, a margin value is typically used between the spotlighted element and the rest of the element's design.

Figure 4–17. *The use of negative space to spotlight an element and create dominance.*

Create Dominance

You can use the passive negative space to create element dominance inside your interface or layout. Generally, you achieve element dominance using negative space combined with other techniques, but a nice and easy trick to achieve it is to let an element eat another element's negative space. An element that does this tends to stand out, and this technique works even more effectively if the layout or interface elements are equally spaced.

Typically, this technique uses a negative margin value between the dominant element and the adjacent elements. You can achieve the same visual effect without using any margin value and working on the element's perspective and position, as shown in Figure 4–18.

Figure 4–18. *A graphic way to achieve element rominance by eating negative space*

Improve Reading Experience and Understanding

You can use passive negative space to improve the user's reading experience and understanding on-the-go. When the user attempts to operate a mobile device on-the-go, he/she is always struggling to understand its content because of the circumstances and distractions of the busy real world. Achieving the goal of a good reading experience and user comprehension is equally important on both the iPhone and the iPad, but, because its screen is so much smaller, it is especially important to maintain a high quality user experience on the iPhone.

Typically, this technique manipulates not only the size of the characters, but also passive negative space through the use of line-height, word-space, and letter-space value between words and characters. In Figure 4–19, you can see how the use of the line-height property increases readability of the text and gives you more breathing room in the layout.

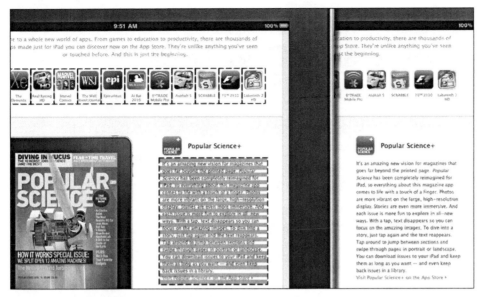

Figure 4–19. *Finger-friendly icons and well-spaced paragraphs.*

Offer a High Level of User Experience

You can use passive negative space to design touch-friendly interfaces and layouts. In your WebApp, everything is an interface, and because a finger needs more room than a mouse pointer does, the negative space plays a fundamental role. The worst enemy of every interface is the feeling of frustration generated by a non-touch friendly design. This problem is more common in a compatible WebApp than it is in a native-like one, because the framework used for a native-like, interface-based project guarantees a comfortable navigation to the user.

Typically, this technique uses a line-height value for the main content part and a margin value between the groups of elements composing an interface. In Figure 4–11, you can see how the icons are extremely finger friendly for a compatible website. The whole highlighted zone is touchable, and the element has a width of 73px and a line-height of 1.5em. With this kind of structure, it's actually hard to tap in the wrong place.

Active Negative Space

Once you have defined your content using passive negative space, it's time to define a navigation path for the user using active negative space. Active negative space is important for grabbing the attention of and guiding the user in his journey through the content of your WebApp.

By predicting the navigation path of your user, you are able to optimize the content and therefore the user experience. In Figure 4–20, you can see how, in the Apple website, the bold style is used to direct attention to critical points of the content. In this case, the active negative space is the space created by the bold style—in other words, the space that the bold style adds around all the bold characters.

Figure 4–20. *The use of negative space and positive space (dashed rectangle) in the official Apple Website.*

The active negative space shape creates a path inside the content. In Figure 4–20, you have three different linear paths (from left to right) where the user is free to jump from one to another but always inside the "swim-lines" shaped by the bold characters.

In the final analysis, you can add more room to your composition (interface or layout) to better emphasize or structure the content, and create some sort of path navigation for the user.

A pre-requisite for the active negative space is correct use of the passive negative space, because, if the content complexity is too great, it will be impossible for the user's cognitive process to create any kind of navigation path inside the content. In these cases, the mind is unable to isolate any kind of pattern for deciding how to read the content because of the high level of background noise.

Color Psychology

The psychology of color is a complex subject in design theory. The colors you use in your interfaces and layouts significantly impact how the user will perceive your WebApp.

> **NOTE:** As you read in Chapter 2, colors are also fundamental if you want to guarantee a high level of accessibility to your WebApp. When you choose your palette, you must keep this point in mind as much as your brand message.

This book does not cover this aspect in depth, but in order to design simple and effective interfaces, you need to know how to reinforce your message using this powerful tool.

Color can be described in three ways:

- **By its name**
- **By its purity**
- **By its light/dark value**

According to this three-way scheme, some of the terms that are used to describe colors are:

- **Hue**
  The actual color of an object. Green is a hue, as are red, yellow, blue, purple, and so on.

- **Intensity**
  The brightness or dullness of a color. Adding white or black to a color lowers its intensity. An intense and highly saturated color has a high chroma.

- **Saturation**
  The degree of purity of a hue. Pure hues are highly saturated. When gray is added the color becomes desaturated.

- **Chroma**
  The purity of a hue in relation to gray. When there is no shade of gray in a color, a color has a high chroma. Adding shades of gray to a hue reduces its chroma.

- **Luminance**
  The measure of the amount of light reflected from a color. Adding white to a hue makes it lighter and increases its value or luminance. Consequently, adding black makes it darker and lowers the value or luminance.

- **Tone**
  The result of adding gray to a hue. Shades and tints are tones at the extremes.

- **Shade**
  The result of adding black to a hue to produce a darker hue.

- **Tint**
  The result of adding white to a hue to produce a lighter hue.

In Figure 4–21, you can observe the Munsell color scheme and see how value, hue, and chroma work together.

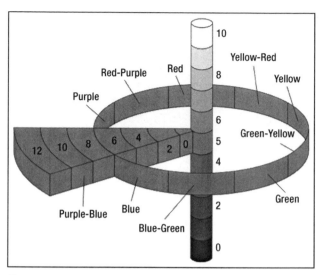

Figure 4–21. *The Munsell color scheme (image Jacobolus).*

HISTORICAL NOTE: Albert Henry Munsell (1858-1918) was an American painter, teacher of art, and the inventor of the Munsell color system, an early attempt at creating an accurate system for numerically describing colors.

The colors are typically presented using a wheel where they are divided into two basic groups:

- **Warm colors**
  Red, orange, yellow

- **Cool colors**
  Blue, purple, green

Warm colors evoke emotions ranging from feelings of warmth, comfort, and coziness, to anger and aggression. As a rule, cool colors are described as calm and tranquil but can also be associated with sadness or indifference.

Using colors as triggers, you can guide the user in his/her experience, directing his/her attention and creating a visual (reading) path through your content.

How Colors Affect User Mood

It is important to remember that color meanings have their roots in human history, and this means that some meanings are shared by all people in the world, and others are typical of certain cultures and might change over the years.

Despite some differences in color meanings from one culture to another, there are many common factors shared by colors. The most important factor for us is that the user's reaction to color is instantaneous, unconscious, and directly affects his moods. In the following, we present the meaning of all the basic colors in order to help you choose the right one when designing your user interface.

Blue

This color is seen as trustworthy, dependable, and committed. Blue is the color of the sky and the ocean, and is perceived as a constant of our lives. It invokes rest and causes the body to produce chemicals that are calming. Despite that, not all blues are serene and sedate; electric or brilliant blue becomes dynamic and dramatic.

Blue is the least gender-specific color, having equal appeal to both men and women.

The physical and mental effects are as follows:

- Stimulates calm
- Stimulates cooling
- Encourages and aids intuition

Green

This color occupies more space in the spectrum visible to the human eye. Green is the most pervasive color in the natural world, and natural greens, from forest to lime, are seen as tranquil and refreshing, with a natural balance of cool and warm (blue and yellow) undertones.

The physical and mental effects are as follows:

- Promotes relaxation
- Stimulates smoothing
- Offers a sense of renewal, self-control, and harmony

Yellow

This color shines with optimism, enlightenment, and happiness. Shades of golden yellow carry a positive sense and, in general, optimism, energy, and creativity.

The physical and mental effects are as follows:

- Stimulates mental activity
- Stimulates memory
- Encourages communication

Red

This color has more personal association than any other color. Red is recognized as a stimulant and exciting. The amount of this color directly influences the level of energy perceived. Red draws attention and a keen use of this color as an accent can immediately focus attention on a particular element.

The physical and mental effects are as follows:

- Stimulates energy
- Increases enthusiasm
- Encourages action and confidence
- Offers a sense of protection from fears and anxiety

Orange

This color is a relative of red and is more controversial than any other color in the spectrum. Orange can bring both positive and negative associations and generally elicits a stronger "love it" or "hate it" response from people. Fun and flamboyant orange radiates warmth and energy, and some tones, such as terra cotta, have a broad appeal.

The physical and mental effects are as follows:

- Stimulates creativity
- Stimulates activity and enthusiasm
- Encourages socialization

Purple

This color embodies the balance of red stimulation and blue calm. This dichotomy can cause unrest or uneasiness unless the undertone is clearly defined. At which point, the purple takes on the characteristic of its undertone. Purple gives a sense of mystical and royal qualities, and is often recognized as creative and eccentric.

The physical and mental effects are as follows:

- Stimulates calm
- Encourages creativity
- Offers a sense of spirituality

Brown

This color says stability, reliability, and approachability. Brown is the color of the earth and is associated with all things natural or organic.

The physical and mental effects are as follows:

- Evokes stability
- Gives a feeling of wholesomeness
- Offers a sense of orderliness

White

This color projects purity, cleanliness, and neutrality. White is also related to cleanliness and safety through its association with bright light.

The physical and mental effects are as follows:

- Stimulates and aids mental clarity
- Enables fresh beginnings
- Encourages us to clear clutter or obstacles
- Evokes purification of thoughts or actions

Gray

This color is timeless, practical, and solid. Gray is the color of intellect, knowledge, and wisdom and can mix well with any color, but an overuse can bring a feeling of loss or depression. If used in silver undertones, this color can be associated with a smart and strong character.

The physical and mental effects are as follows:

- Evokes traditionalism and seriousness
- Gives a feeling of expectancy
- Offers a sense of intelligence and wisdom

Black

This color is authoritative and powerful. Black can evoke strong emotions and its overuse can be overwhelming.

The physical and mental effects are as follows:

- Evokes a sense of potential and possibility
- Gives a feeling of inconspicuousness
- Offers a sense of mystery and formality

When you design an interface for a website or a web application, it is important to analyze every possible task that the user might want to do when interacting with your user interface. Some tasks work best in a certain environment, whereas others are better accomplished in a totally different one. One example of this might be an online shopping cart, where using too much black in your interface might inadvertantly create an ominous feeling of mystery, potentially increasing the percentage of check-out aborts by your users. In Table 4–2, we have a summary of some of the emotions and feelings associated with colors.

Table 4–2. *Major Emotion and Feeling Related to Colors.*

Color	Emotions / Feelings
Blue	Depth, stability, professionalism, loyalty, reliability, honor, trust
Green	Durability, reliability, safety, honesty, optimism, harmony, freshness, relaxing
Yellow	Comfort, liveliness, intellect, happiness, energy
Red	Strength, boldness, excitement, determination, desire, courage, enthusiasm
Orange	Enthusiasm, cheerfulness, affordability, stimulation, creativity
Purple	Nobility, luxury, mystery, royalty, elegance, magic
Brown	Endurance, confident, casual, reassuring, earthy
White	Cleanliness, purity, newness, peace, innocence, simplicity, freshness
Gray	Conservatism, traditionalism, intelligence, seriousness, wisdom
Black	Power, elegance, sophistication, formality, strength, mystery

How to Combine the Colors

Once you know the meaning of each color, the obvious question is how do you choose the right colors for your design? The simple answer is that you should always choose one or more colors that reinforce the design message, but what happens if you want to create a palette for your design based on several colors? How can you put together more than one color?

We have three types of patterns to help us create a palette for your design.

Monochromatic Color Scheme

This pattern uses a single color in varying shades (see Figure 4–20). The result is a soothing and pleasing palette that is pleasing to the eye, especially in the blue or green hues.

Analogous Color Scheme

This pattern uses colors that are adjacent to each other on the color wheel.

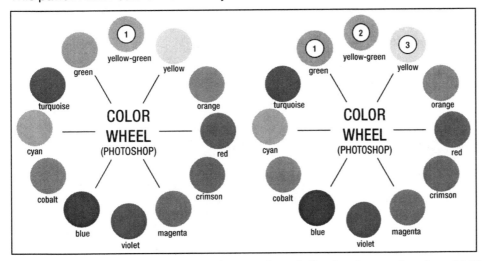

Figure 4–22. *An example of a monochromatic color scheme (left) and analogous color scheme (right).*

Complementary Color Scheme

This pattern uses high contrast colors selected from opposite positions on the color wheel (see Figure 4–21). The result is to put together a warm color with a cool color in a way that's pleasing to the eye.

Split Complementary Color Scheme

This pattern uses one color and then two more colors that are adjacent to the complement of the initial color.

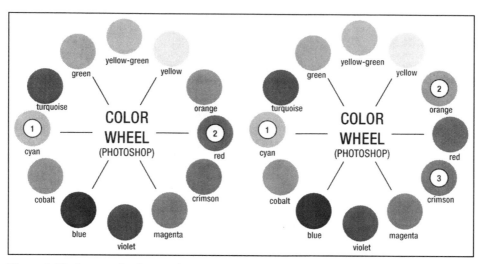

Figure 4–23. *An example of a complementary color scheme (left) and split complementary color scheme (right),*

Triadic Color Scheme

This pattern uses three colors equally spaced from each other around the color wheel (see Figure 4–22). The result is a harmonious color scheme.

Tetradic Color Scheme

This pattern uses colors at the corner of a rectangle inscribed on the color wheel.

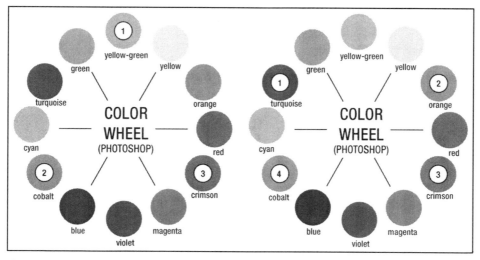

Figure 4–24. *An example of a triadic color scheme (left) and tetradic color scheme (right).*

Using these six patterns, you can create many palettes based on various kinds of colors. In Figure 4–24, you can see an example of how to choose colors following the triple and complementary color scheme.

At the end of this chapter, we suggest some tools for choosing or generating colors for your palette. However, it's always important to remember what meaning is behind a certain color. In order to be coherent with the brand of your WebApp, you need to choose the right colors.

The Interface Hierarchy

The primary role of your active interface is to create a connection between different parts of your content, and, for the passive interface, to give a general structure to your overall content. Beyond that, both active and passive interfaces have a more important role: to guide the user.

Interfaces guide the user through your content. Your interface must also be prioritized because the different parts of your content are prioritized, too. Directing the user through your content is an important goal to keep in mind when you design your user interfaces.

The prioritized content you use for an iPad native-like version Is a proper subset of your desktop content and the prioritized content you use for a native-like iPhone version is a proper subset of your iPad content and desktop.

When we introduced the concept of Mobile Information Architecture, you saw how important it is to prioritize content in a mobile device. But how do you prioritize your interfaces when implementing a visual hierarchy?

> **NOTE:** A visual hierarchy is used in page design to help the viewer process information. Visual hierarchy is the order in which most people see and identify your content's elements.

Besides the use of active and negative space previously introduced in this chapter, you will now learn wjat other tools can help you implement a visual hierarchy in your active and passive interfaces.

You can create a hierarchy in your design by adjusting the visual weight of your elements. More visual weight is generally seen as more important and more easily noticed by the user, and less visual weight is seen as less important.

- **Size**
  Larger elements carry more weight and focus the user's attention.

- **Color**
  Some colors are perceived as having more weight than others. Red seems to be the heaviest, whereas yellow seems to be the lightest.

■ **Density**
Increasing the number of elements in a certain space gives more weight to that space.

■ **Value**
A darker object has more weight than a lighter object. The reason why red is perceived as the heaviest color is still unknown.

■ **Negative Space**
Using the Law of Perception, you can create many levels of hierarchy.

As you can see from Figure 4–26, hierarchy helps to give order to your active and passive interfaces. Hierarchy priority interfaces with and aids in communication. In Figure 4–26, you can see how much heavier the reading experience is with the hierarchy on the right. This creates extra demands on the user's cognitive resources and results in a less satisfactory user experience.

Figure 4–25 *Differences between good content hierarchy (left) and bad content hierarchy (right).*

Creating our hierarchy should begin with thoughtful consideration of the page's goal. Only when you intellectically decide on the hierarchy of uour page should you attempt to visually design that hierarchy.

Reading Patterns

The first time we run a usability test on a WebApp, we always receive the results with a surprised face. The fact is the reality that the user reading pattern is totally different from what you expected when you were designing your interface.

In reality, the phrase "reading pattern" is appropriate because users don't actually read pages, they scan them. They skim them looking for words or phrases that catch their eye. Now the question is: why do users do this? We can suggest several answers.

■ **User Is Usually in a Hurry**

The user browsing the web is motivated by the desire to save time, because he knows that the answer is somewhere nearby and his objective is just to discover where he needs to look.

■ **User Knows He/She Doesn't Need to Read Everything**

The user knows that most of time he/she will be interested in only a portion of the content offered by a page. For this reason, the user will only look for relevant bits of content and ignore all other parts that he/she deem as irrelevant.

■ **User Has Learned to Scan Using Other Media in the Past**

The user, in past experiences with magazines, newspapers, or books, has learned to scan content in order to find the parts they they're interested in.

> **NOTE:** Reading patterns vary according to the different reading-directions adopted by different cultures. It is important to remember that what we discuss in this section applies only to right-to-left reading cultures.

Despite the fact that users scan content instead of reading it, in the world of left-to-right readers, we can still isolate some reading patterns. These patterns are highly influenced by images that appear in the content but the interesting thing here is that, instead of using a micro or macro linear pattern, the user tends to read using an "F" or a "Z" pattern on our WebApp. This means that we have two different major approaches to content, both based on conventions that the user has adopted during 10 or 20 years or more of content browsing.

Users have been trained to pay attention to certain spots because that's where the most important information usually resides. For this reason, it is important to remember that if we deviate from these conventional patterns in designing our interfaces, we do so at our peril.

The Z-Shaped Pattern

The Z reading pattern is the typical pattern that comes to mind when we think about reading web content. Typically, we start from the left-top position where the logo is situated, and then drop down to the content's first paragraph, where we start the Z movement.

If the user is satisfied with the content after he reads the first line of the paragraph, he will continue reading and jump to the next line of the same paragraph.

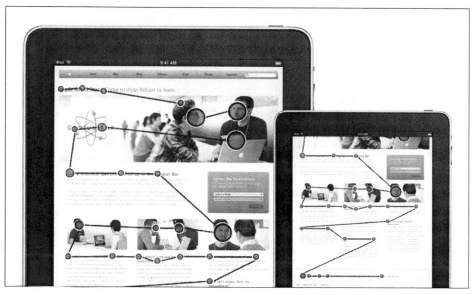

Figure 4–26. *The Z-shaped pattern in the Apple Genius Bar page.*

The story changes when, after having read the first line of the paragraph, the user decides that the content is not what he was looking for. In this case, the user will jump directly to the first line of the next paragraph or the next portion of content.

This changes the height of each Z sub-pattern and the number of Z sub-patterns that compose the overall Z reading pattern. In Figure 4–27, we can see how the Z pattern changes depending on whether the user is interested in the first line of a paragraph.

Implications of the Z-Shaped Pattern

The Z pattern is closely related to the classic reading pattern from hard-copy newspapers, magazines, or journals, and shares the same implications:

■ **User Can Jump from One Paragraph to Another**

If the user is not interested in the first line of the paragraph, he will jump to the first line of the next paragraph or the next group of content.

■ **User Will Always Look in the Left-Bottom Part of the Pattern**

The designer can be assured that the user will look at a certain part of the content, and he can make use of this information by placing some important call-to-action buttons in this zone.

The Z pattern is more common in non-expert users or more generally when a user finds interesting content. Despite the fact that it's generally not the most common pattern, it's important to keep it in mind because the user will tend to switch to this kind of pattern every time he/she finds an interesting bit of content. This means that a user can start with a different pattern and then switch to a Z pattern before returning again to the original one.

The F-Shaped Pattern

The F reading pattern is typically composed of two horizontal stripes followed by a vertical stripe. The F can also stand for fast, because this is the typical pattern used by a user in a hurry-mode.

This pattern is composed of three eye movements:

1. The user reads in a horizontal movement across the upper part of the content area. This element forms the F's top bar.

2. The user then moves down the page a bit and begins to read across in a shorter second horizontal movement. This element forms the F's lower bar.

3. The user scans the content's left side in a vertical movement. This element forms the F's vertical stem.

In this mode, the user's reading patterns are not always composed of exactly three parts and are not always like the letter F, but we can easily recognize the pattern even in its different variations.

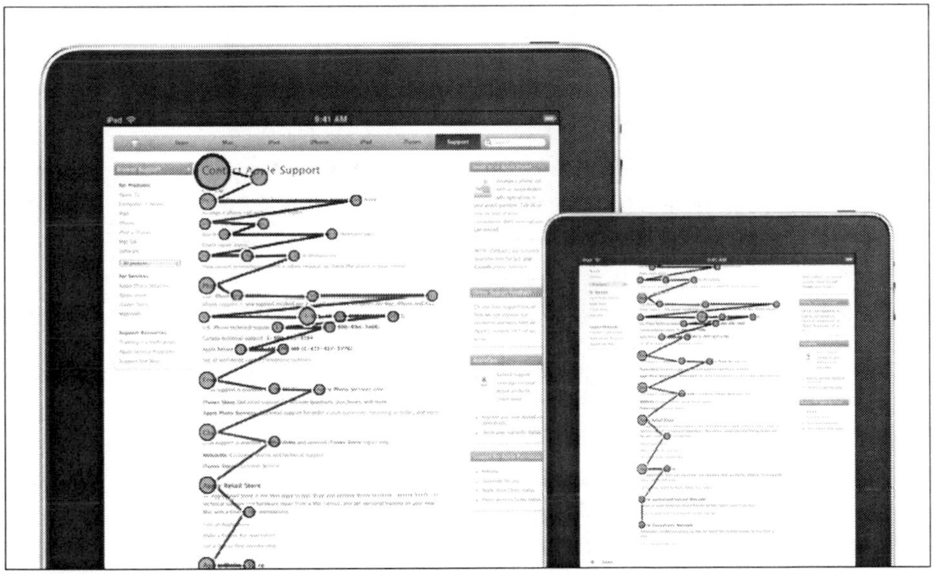

Figure 4–27. *The F-shaped pattern in the Apple Support page.*

Anyone familiar with object-oriented programming can see that the F reading pattern is like the super-class and that different user behaviors are like different implementations of the super class.

Implications of the F-Shaped Pattern

The implications of the F pattern show how important it is to follow a guideline in the design phase in order to optimize the user experience. These implications are as follows:

- **User Won't Read the Content thoroughly in a Word-by-Word Manner**

  Exhaustive reading is rare, especially during Internet research. Some users might read a larger portion of your contents but most won't.

- **Most Important Information Must Be Stated in the First Two Paragraphs**

  That's the only way to have some hope that the user will actually read the content. Reading more of the first paragraph probably will drive the user deeper into the content.

- **Begin Paragraphs with Information-Carrying Words**

  This is because the stem of the "F" pattern will have less chance of grabbing the user's attention than will the top bar. In this part of the pattern, the user reads only the first words of the paragraph.

- **Insert the Most Important Links of the User Interface on the Left Side**

  The F pattern decreases the user attention from left-to-right; links on the far right part of the user interface are less likely to be noticed.

An important factor concerning the F reading pattern is that it might also be influenced by the browsing context. If a user looks for something that contains numbers, a price for example, the F pattern could be transformed in an "E" or a "Comb" pattern.

Images in Reading Patterns

Images are a powerful tool of web design. By using the correct image, you can explain a concept or evoke a feeling and so improve the level of user experience and the likelihood of passing the right message to the user.

A tool can be used in either one of two ways, one good and the other bad. Using the wrong image can waste space in your layout, confusing the user, and breaking his reading pattern without a constructive purpose.

What can really catch the user's attention and draw him to an image? According to the latest research from the Norman Nielsen Group, the images users choose to look at have the following characteristics:

- **High Contrast and High Quality**
  Crisp and colorful.

- **Cropped rather than Overlay Reduced**
  When necessary fit a small space.

- **Easy to Interpret and Almost Iconic**
  When are not excessively detailed.

- **Highly Related to the Content**
  To the content of the page.

- **Possess Magnetic Features**
  When an image is full of charisma.

Magnetic features are important in an image, but what kind of image is a magnetic one? Magnetic images include the following:

- Approachable and Smiling Faces

- People Looking at the Camera

- Sexual Anatomy

- Appetizing Food

- Clear Instruction or Information

- Shape Dynamism

In choosing your images, you also need to know what kind of images users ignore. These kinds of images have the following characteristics:

- Low Contrast and Low Quality

- Cold, Fake, or Too Polished

- Busy for the Space

- Generic, or Obvious Stock Art People or Objects

- Not Related to the Content

- Boring

When you use bad images in your layout, the user perceives them as obstacles in his/her journey through the content. They alter the user's reading pattern, absorb an extra amount of their cognitive resources, and generally decrease the quality of his/her experience.

Influencing the Reading Pattern

The rules about the reading pattern are general ones that are applicable to the majority of situations. The interesting thing is that, in some cases, we can influence the reading pattern using some strong visual hierarchy.

In Figure 4–29, we can see how, in some cases, a strong visual hierarchy can disrupt the user focus and break the "F" or "Z" pattern rule. In this example, everything is intentionally designed to optimize the brand message without compromising the user's reading experience.

The strong visual hierarchy guides the user from the page title, through the image, to the spotlighted page sub-title, and, in the end, to the sub-section of the website. These kinds of design techniques are important for anyone who wants to bring their design skills to the next level, because they can make the difference between a good design and a professional one.

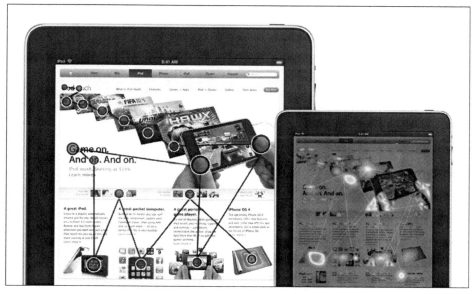

Figure 4–28. *The eye-tracking test (left) and the corresponded heat map (right).*

As we can see in Figure 4–29 (right), eye-tracking tests are often represented with a heat map. A heat map is a graphical representation of data where the values taken by a variable in a two dimensional table are represented as colors. A heat map adds the third dimension to the eye-tracking test table representing large values with red colors and smaller values with blue colors.

There is also another side of the coin. As *Stan Lee* has written "with great power there must also come—great responsibility." This is true because, if a designer is not aware of these rules, he will risk unwittingly altering the reading pattern and compromising the interface hierarchy by incorporating non-essential information on the page. In other words, visitors might leave the page before finding what they were looking for, because they might think it isn't present in the content.

HISTORICAL NOTE: Stan Lee is an American writer, editor, and memoirist, who introduced complex, naturalistic characters, and a thoroughly shared universe into superhero comic books.

> **DEFINITION:** A shared universe is a fictional universe to which more then one writer contributes. (source Wikipedia)

As the final point of this section, we want to point out that these days the user doesn't have an optimized reading pattern for touch-screen devices, at least not for devices with anything bigger than iPhone's 3.5-inch display. The iPad's 9.7-inch display will change the user's browsing habits in the next few years, and so will Safari Mobile's capability to break the vertically–oriented reading flow, which enables the user to jump from one point to another using a double-touch, or by zooming and pinching on the content. This tendency will probably create a new tablet reading flow composed of many micro F and Z reading patterns.

As designers and developers, you need to pay attention to collecting as much feedback as possible. Nowadays, the user is the only source of reliable information for establishing a new approach to designing the next generation of touch-screen user experience.

Reading Pattern Guideline

So far, we have presented the F and Z paths, the most common user reading patterns. We saw how, in some cases, it can be useful to change these patterns in order to achieve specific goals.

Eye-tracking studies have revealed valuable information about how people read and interact with websites and web applications. What we can learn from these studies are some tactics to optimize our interfaces.

These tactics are summarized as follows:

- **Logo in the Top-Left Positions Works Best**

  As we saw in the first part of this section, the user has been trained over the years to look in the upper left part of a page for specific kinds of information, such as brand logos. Only famous brands, well–known throughout the world and recognized immediately by the user, have the option to break this rule.

- **Tagline under the Logo Improves General Page Understanding**

  This is related to the previous point. When the user looks at the logo, a tagline underneath gives him a better understanding of the logo and a better chance of understanding the content, and there will be less likelihood of his leaving the page.

- **Navigation at the Top of the Page Works Best**

  As primary navigation, a horizontal navigation bar works better than a vertical one on the side.

■ **Headline Must Grab Attention in Less than 1 Second**

You need to grab the user attention in a fast way and get to the point instantly.

■ **Headlines Draw User's Eyes before Pictures Do**

If you use a strong headline, you can dominate any other influence, even from images. In Figure 4–27, you can see how the headline "iPod Touch" has been reduced to a light weight compared with the image in order to avoid interfering with it.

■ **Pure Reading Patterns Are Appropriate Only "Above the Fold"**

Today, scrolling a page is not the source of frustration and confusion that it was in the 90s. Now, with a touch-screen device, the user is able to scroll down a page faster than he/she ever could with a mouse. This means that reading patterns "below the fold" have become much more unpredictable. If your design works because of certain eye movement patterns on the part of the user, you must be sure that every important element of your design is in the first visible part of your WebApp where the user "reads" using a higher degree of focus on the content.

■ **User Often Scans Only the First Few Words of a Headline**

This means that long headlines don't work well. In these cases, the user scans the first few words before deciding whether to continue reading. For this reason, it's important to front-load the headlines with the most interesting and provocative words.

■ **People Scan the Left Side of a List of Headlines**

This is related to the previous point. When presented with a list of headlines or links, the user will scan down the left side of the list, looking at the first couple of words, to find something he/she is interested in. The user will not necessarily read each line from beginning to end. For the same reason we discussed before, you need to insert the most mind-catching words up front.

■ **Bigger Font Size Improves the User Experience**

If the user is not forced to zoom in and out, his/her level of frustration decreases and, inversely proportionally, the user experience is improved. Implementing this approach with an iPhone is not always possible but when designing an iPad-compatible WebApp, this is an important requirement to remember.

■ **Short Paragraphs Encourage Reading**

Big blocks of type look imposing and difficult to read. For this reason, it's better to organize the content into a flow of ideas rather than large, distinct paragraphs.

- **More Negative Space Between Paragraph Helps to Focus User Attention**

  If a user is searching for something in your content, having "enough" space between paragraphs will suggest a landing point, emphasizing the first line of the following paragraph.

- **Multimedia Works Better than Text for Unfamiliar or Conceptual Information**

  Or to put it another way, "one picture is worth a thousand words." Reading relies on people having some understanding of the subject. The more unfamiliar a user is with a subject, the faster and more easily he/she will understand it if you use a multimedia message instead of text.

- **Call-to-Action Buttons at the End of the Reading Pattern Work Best**

  The natural position for a call-to-action button is at the end of a reading pattern. The button could be placed at the end of the content and/or at the end of a single paragraph.

- **Strong Visual Hierarchy can Influence User Reading Pattern**

  By adding some weight and dynamics with an image or a headline, we can change the structure of a reading pattern.

Most of these tactics work in both a desktop and mouse context and a touch-screen and finger context because the user is not a variable but a constant in this equation. What is a variable are the hardware interfaces that the user uses to interact with the software interfaces. In the next paragraphs, we will see how this slightly changes the user experience in certain cases.

It is also important, where possible, to continue to design using these conventions and habits in order to offer a smooth transition between a desktop PC–user experience and the new touch-screen user experience. The passage of time and natural human evolution do the rest. Now, we are ready to look at the user interface design process.

The User Interface Design Process

This process involves some steps that you have already seen in Chapter 2. You start the process by planning the interface. You sketch its structure and study the level and type of interaction that happen between the user and the interface. You create the aesthetic of the interface, and finally produce a deliverable for the development phase. If you remember the Information Architecture Process presented in the Chapter 2, you will go smoothly through the following phases.

Research

The research phase is too often misunderstood and overlooked; sometimes because we are working with a small budget and sometimes just because it is less tangible than other phases in the process.

Despite that, the fact is that without good research, you can't truly understand the requirements of your interface, or have an idea of what your competitors in the market have done before. Even worse, you won't have a clear idea of what will be the level and type of interaction you want from your interface.

As you previously saw in Chapter 2, the information that is collected in this phase is fundamentally important for the final result, and an error at this point dramatically impacts the entire process.

Structure

Designing the structure of our interfaces, you need to consider two cases:

- **Active Interface**
  Interface based on active links—for example, Navigation Bar

- **Passive Interface**
  Interface based on passive negative space—for example, page layout

You start by designing the passive interfaces using the negative space concept to choose which layout areas will be filled with a portion of your content and which will be left blank. As you now know, negative areas are important in our layout for cognitive and interactive reasons.

Once you define the negative and positive space of your layout, you start designing the active interface and sketching its content structure. The tools upi use are a flow chart and then a site map to plan the active interface's content.

In keeping with our content-out approach, once you have a clear idea about the interface's content, you start to organize its visual structure. The visual structure is sketched using wireframes and paper prototypes.

Aesthetic

Once you know the structure of your interfaces, you can take a deep breath and keeping in mind the rules of perception, enjoy the next step: designing the interface's aesthetic. This is usually the most satisfying part of the process for every designer. For this step, you use your preferred graphic design program. In the following section, we assume that you're going to use Adobe Fireworks, but the choice is up to you. It's important to remember that working on the aesthetic part of our interfaces means working on both design style and typography.

Interaction

Once the interfaces are structured and designed to your aesthetic satisfaction, you need to work on their interaction with the user. For this phase, use sequence diagrams for developing the use-cases, and electronic prototypes to test them in a real environment. If you need to develop a simple use-case for your interfaces that doesn't have a complex context, and you just want to have an idea of "what the user will do," you can use use-case diagrams, saving both time and effort. Working on the interface's interaction means working on navigation elements, form elements, audio and video elements, and passive interfaces based on negative space.

Deliverables

When the artistic part of your interaction design work is finished, you need to produce deliverables for the next phase of development. To accomplish this last step of the process, you work on the design composition, electronic prototype, and style guide.

Design Composition

Design composition is the artwork that shows the entire interface, composed of active and passive interfaces. This deliverable is also used to show the client the project's status because it serves as a picture of what will eventually be your WebApp.

Electronic Prototypes

An electronic prototypes is an interactive version of our design based on HTML5, CSS3, and Javascript. We have several frameworks available on the Internet that can help us to develop our electronic prototype without wasting much time. In the last paragraph of this chapter, you will find the tools used in the interface design process.

Style Guides

By designing style guides, you ensure that the brand will be carried through the next phase of development. Style guides are like page templates where the designer shows how certain sections of the design can be applied to a page, regardless of the variable content.

If you are an independent designer and developer working by yourself, you can skip some of these deliverables, such as design composition or electronic prototypes, but we still suggest that you produce some style guides just in case you ever need to go back to your project at some point in the future. Style guides help you avoid mistakes that might happen because you forget the message, the style, or other details of your project.

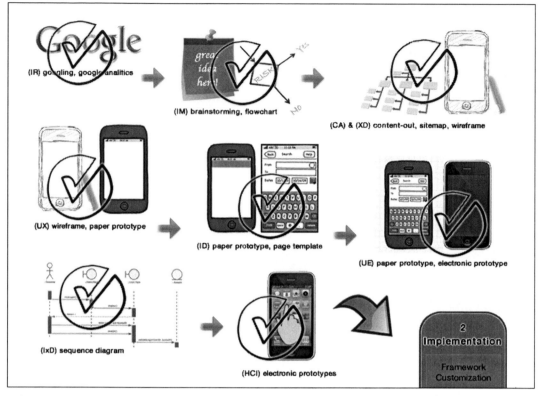

Figure 4–29. *The mobile information process applied to the interface design process.*

As you might notice, we applied the same process that we used in our mobile information architecture process. In fact, the interface design process is a micro-cycle inside the mobile information architecture process and is based on the same pattern.

In the next section, we implement the interface design process, and we design an iPhone and iPad compatible layout for a WebApp.

iPhone and iPad Compatible User Interface Design

For a WebApp to be iPhone and iPad compatible, it must satisfy the first level of Apple device compatibility. As you saw in the Chapter 3, to be iPhone and iPad ready doesn't mean having an HTML5 and CSS3 compliant layout; it means that it is designed in a touch-screen oriented way.

From the standpoint of iPhone development, this problem is less important because, although Safari Mobile has revolutionized the mobile browsing experience in the past three years, a real native-like layout is needed in order to let the user experience an optimized level of interaction with the WebApp. For this reason, if a WebApp is not touch-screen optimized for the iPhone, it's not such a bad thing. The compatible version is not the primary source of information for an iPhone, because a native version of the same layout is also released in most cases.

Things change when we get to the iPad because the 9.7-inch display offers a 1024Í768 pixel resolution. This means that a compatible layout might be a reasonable option in a WebApp mobile strategy. An iPad native-like layout will always offer the best user experience for the user, but for the iPad, a compatible version is still able to offer the next best thing.

Now, let's (re)design a touch-screen oriented version of the official Apple website while making sure to apply all the principles previously presented. The Apple website is well-designed. From an aesthetic point of view, it's impeccable, and we have used it in almost all of our design examples so far, despite the fact that it is not very touch-screen oriented or as cognitively optimized as it could be.

Research

The research phase is based on many techniques, from the simple use of a search engine looking for competitors to advanced market research techniques. In this phase, you use flowcharts and a site map so that you have a visual representation of the content and its deployment.

The research phase aims to understand three points:

- **Competitor Comparison**

  Ascertain how different the actual design is compared with that of your competitors. This is a wide-ranging research task and covers many areas from branding to market projection, comparing everything from offered services to user experience.

- **Weak Points Research**

  Identify the weak points in the design structure.

- **Design's Improvement**

  Identify ways to improve the actual design.

Working on the Apple website use-case, we left out the competitor comparison because the Apple brand is one of the most beautiful and functional on the market and doesn't need to be improved. In this use-case, we go straight to point 2: Weak Point Research.

It's a different story when we look at things in terms of usability, especially touch-screen usability. The first thing that the Weak Point Research tells us about the Apple website is that its three-column layout structure leaves something to be desired.

This structure consists of a main content area bordered on either side by a narrow sidebar column. The three-column structure was and remains a popular choice for blogs and online stores. Two of the most famous stores in the world are based on this kind of layout: the Apple Store and Amazon.

Figure 4–30. *The three-columns layout structure used by Amazon.com.*

From a logical point of view, the three-column layout might seem like a good choice because it enables us to isolate three different kinds of content. In a blog, there is usually a menu or assorted links related to the website in the left column, and various kinds of advertisements in the one on the right.

In recent years, many blogs have converted their structure to a more functional and usable two-column layout, but the same thing hasn't happened to the majority of online store sites. With the two-column layout, we usually have the main menu and other links related to the website in the left column, and the shopping cart with some promotional banners in the right column.

We can summarize the pros of three-column layout as the following:

- Symmetry Can Be Pleasing
- Three Columns Offer Three Different Content Areas
- Centered Main Content Helps the User to Focus on It

The following are cons of the three-column layout:

- Symmetry Works Against Visual Content Hierarchy
- Symmetry Consumes More Cognitive Resources from the User

- Two Sidebars Introduce Visual Noise, Distracting from Content
- Three-Column Layout Makes the Reading Pattern Unpredictable

In addition to these layout problems, there is also a lack of usability when users need to interact with the active interfaces using a small screen-based device like an iPhone. In this context, the user is often obliged to use the zoom function in order to increase content readability.

Browsing with an iPad is a different story because the iPad user, with his 9.7-inch display, can browse compatible and native-like WebApps equally well. In this case, the user has a high expectation about the usability of both compatible and native-like contents.

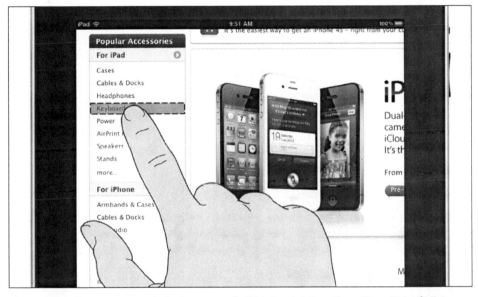

Figure 4–31. *User must zoom in for have a comfortable touch-interaction with a sidebar's link.*

As we suggest in the previous chapter, links must be finger-friendly and touchable without forcing the user to use the zoom function, because the lack of negative space increases the risk of touching the wrong spot. In the Structure phase, we see how to overcome this problem in our current use-case.

Often a report is produced at the end of the Research phase. Usually this report is used to show the client, but it is for our reference in this case. We can summarize the results of our research phase as follows:

- **Web Site Information**

    Apple Store (www.apple.com)

- **Strong Point**

    Use of block model page

Use of visual hierarchy

Brand and identity

▧ **Weak Points**

Three-column layout structure

Most active interfaces are not touch-friendly

▧ **Improvement Points**

Use of two-column layout structure

Use of passive negative space on active interfaces

Now that we collected all the information, we have a better idea of what works and what doesn't work in our project, and we are ready to move to the next step: the (re)design.

Structure

The research phase tells you everything ou need to know about the design, in that you come to know its weak points and how to improve them. The first step is to sketch the structure using a wireframe technique using two-column layout, but it is important to keep in mind the goal you want to achieve.

The structure phase needs to achieve the following goals:

▧ **Offer a Better Layout Structure**

The two-column layout offers a better structure for presenting and finding the content, enabling the user to save his limited cognitive resources for understanding the content instead of looking for it.

▧ **Offer a Touch-Friendly Interface**

Enable the average user to browse the content without using the zoom function, improving the level of user experience.

In the next section, we see how to approach these goals designing a touch-friendly layout and then working on touch-friendly typography.

Touch-Screen Layout

At this point, you need to keep in mind the strong point of the existing design and keep everything working well in the structure. You should keep the original block structure because it's perfect for any kind of touch-screen device with a zoom function, and working in this way you won't have to alter the passive negative space between each single block of content.

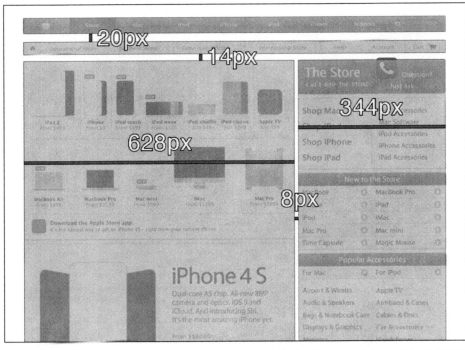

Figure 4–32. *The new iPad two-column layout structure based on the old web three-column layout.*

In Figure 4–34, we can see how, from top to bottom, we have left untouched the Primary Navigation Bar of 980x38 pixels (Figure 4–34, Number 1) and likewise the space between this bar and the Breadcrumb Bar.

We took the Breadcrumb Bar and, without changing its height of 30 pixels, we transformed it into a Secondary Navigation Bar of 980 pixels (Figure 4–34, Number 2), adding several links to the various Apple Store instances.

Figure 4–33. *The new two-column layout structure based on the old three-column layout.*

We moved the main content (Figure 4–34, number 3) to the left and kept the 8-pixel gutter we merged the two sidebars in a semantic way. Instead of placing them side by side, we grouped each single sidebar and its content into a single sidebar composed of a two-column box. Using this box, the user can easily find information about the subject at a glance without scrolling down as far as he would have needed to in the old design.

Inside the sidebar, we increased the box header (Figure 4–34, number 7) height from 24 to 32 pixels and the sub-title row (Figure 4–34, number 8) height from 24 to 30 pixels. We also changed the typography inside the sidebar box, which we will discuss next.

Touch-Screen Typography

So far you have tried to create a more conformable space for user's fingers by increasing various heights in the structure until you reach a minimum height of 30 pixels. As is shown in Chapter 3, we can be pretty safe with a target of 30 pixels, considering the average finger dimensions of our users. If you have the opportunity, you can set a lower-bound of 40 pixels for each single space in our layout, but in this case, it's not possible without introducing the risk of breaking the light visual equilibrium of the design.

From top to bottom, we change the font size in the Primary Navigation Bar (Figure 4–35, number 1), increasing the value from 12 to 14 pixels, and, in the Secondary Navigation Bar (Figure 4–35, number 2), we increase the value from 10 to 12 pixels.

Figure 4–34. *The (re)design order of the new two-column layout structure.*

In the Sidebar main menu, we change the font side from 14 to 16 pixels and set a line height of 20 pixels for the left column (Figure 4–35, number 5) and a font size of 14 pixels with a line height of 18 pixels for the right column (Figure 4–35, number 6).

In the Sidebar Box Header (Figure 4–35, number 7), we increased the font size from 12 to 14 pixels and the size of the call-to-action circle from 13 to 16 pixels. In the content list part of the sidebar box (Figure 4–35, number 9), we increased the font size value from 10 to 12 pixels and we set the line height to 20 pixels.

Aesthetic

The aesthetic part of the design is almost the same; we want to change a few things so they work better with the new structure.

We integrate the call center icon into the Sidebar Main Header (Figure 4–35, number 4) and we remove the search engine box in order to avoid redundancy in the design after we move the Sidebar Main Header from the left to the right side of the page. In the right part of the (re)design, the sidebar main header is under the Primary Navigation Bar, which already includes its own search engine box.

Figure 4–35. *The before (left) and after (right) the (re)design. Interfaces are more accessible and finger friendly.*

The call center icon in the Sidebar Main Header (Figure 4–35, number 4) uses the same technique we saw in Figure 4–10 for creating dominance in the visual hierarchy and attracting the user's attention. The icon eats some of the negative space between the Sidebar Main Header and the Secondary Navigation Bar.

Interaction

What we have done so far serves to guarantee a touch-friendly interaction that, in most cases, doesn't require any use of the zoom function. Increasing the font size value, resetting the line height values, and increasing the row space in the sidebar enables the user to touch every link without the risk of tapping on the wrong spot. These simple changes have had an enormous impact on the quality of user experience.

Figure 4-36. *The (re)designed iPad interface now offers the user a conformable touch-interaction.*

Once all the interfaces are ready to be tested, you need to develop some use-cases and then implement it using the Sequence diagrams or the Use-Case diagrams if we work with low complexity cases. Figure 4-35 represents an example of a Use-Case diagram for the two use-cases: Buy the New iPhone and Search the New iPhone.

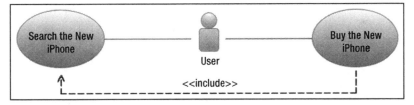

Figure 4-37. *An example of UML Use-Case diagram for representing a user interface interaction.*

Please note that the user icon is not the standard one. We use this icon for two reasons. The first is because, when possible, we always try not to offend our eyes when we work, and so we avoid the sort of generic "We are a PC" styles that are too often adopted as standard. The second is because these diagrams are exclusively for our own reference, or at least for our small team. If we need to share our diagrams with our teams or when we work for a big company, we must use standard notation.

The next step is to test the use-case/s using an electronic prototype. In order to do that, we need to use an HTML5, CSS3, and Javascript framework. By using electronic prototypes, we can have a realistic idea of the real finger-friendly capabilities of our interfaces. If, for some reason, we must move on in the process without having the time or the budget to do any electronic prototypes tests, we have to be sure to do at least few quick tests with paper prototypes.

Deliverables

When the interaction phase is complete, we need to prepare deliverables for the next phase in the process: the implementation. If you are working by yourselves, deliverables are useful only if you need to get back on the project months after it is released, so that you can remember at a glance important points about your design. When you work in a team, you must be sure that your deliverables "talk for us" and show your design clearly, avoiding any possible doubt in the developer's mind.

As previously explained, you produce three kinds of deliverables: a design composition, a design style guide, and an electronic prototype. The design composition, as the name implies, shows the composition of your design, and the design style guide shows, using templates, how to apply our design to various types of pages. If you have an important message to pass on, you can also analyze, explain, or highlight a specific part of your design, adding notes and description. The electronic prototype shows how the design works in an interactive way. The same prototype is used by us and the developer for the startup phase of implementation.

iPad Native-Like User Interface Design

Designing an iPad version of your website and web application is not as important because you are creating the iPhone version. If the compatible version has a touch-screen optimized structure and offers a high quality user experience, it's most important to first focus your energy on designing an iPhone version of your content.

The iPad's browsing capabilities enables the user to do so with a high level of user experience through any desktop content. Nevertheless, developing a native-like experience for an iPad user should always be your first priority. A native-like structure always offers a higher level of user experience.

You will be seeing many iPad native-like WebApps in the near future, so we suggest that you don't omit this option, but make sure to include it in your project roadmap.

Research

When you perform the research phase for the compatible version, you are working on all our planned versions simultaneously. This is because we reuse our research results for our other iPad versions and later for the iPhone research step. In this way, we optimize the budget, saving money and time, and amortize a fixed cost in our process.

Market research tells us which portion of our content to insert in our iPad version and which is better left exclusively for the compatible version.

Structure

When you work on the native-like version of your site or application, you can't redesign the structure as you previously did in the compatible version. The compatible version was focused on improving the structure in order to offer a finger-friendly user experience. Here, the emphasis is on how to prioritize the content with respect to the native-like structure.

How to prioritize your content is a choice that relies on market research and is not up to the designer. When the research phase has determined which part of the content to include and which parts to leave for the desktop version, only then can you start to organize the native-like layout.

Compared with an iPhone native-like version, the iPad native-like version can offer a large portion of the desktop content, and it can include all of it in some cases. When that happens, our job is simply to give it a native-like and optimized structure, without having to cut anything.

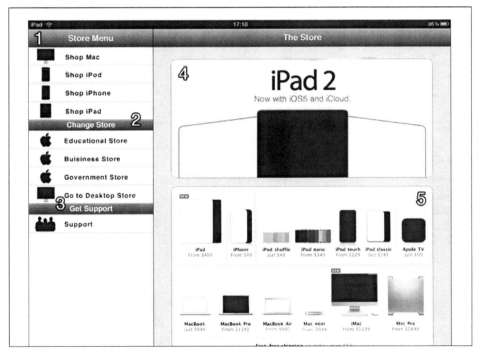

Figure 4–38. *The iPad native two-column layout structure and its (re)design order.*

As seen in Figure 4–39, from top to bottom and left to right, you insert the Store menu (Figure 4–39, number 1) in the top position in order to enable the user to choose a contextualized path from his/her first touch.

Just below that, we insert the option to change the store and its configuration (Figure 4–39, number 2), and then we insert the option to directly access service support (Figure 4–39, number 3).

The main content, which is not related to the links in the sidebar, shows the hero image (Figure 4–39, number 4) and, below that, all of the entry level products (Figure 4–39, number 5) with a link to their specific pages. This zone is exactly the same as the compatible and original designs, because it is the most finger-friendly part of the entire site.

Aesthetic

The iPad native-like structure offers a lot of space in the content column. The main goal is to be consistent with a strong brand aesthetic and to be able to offer it with an optimized structure. In the iPad version, it's easy because we just need to scale it to the content column size and the work will be done. This time the room offered by the 9.7-inch iPad display made our job easy.

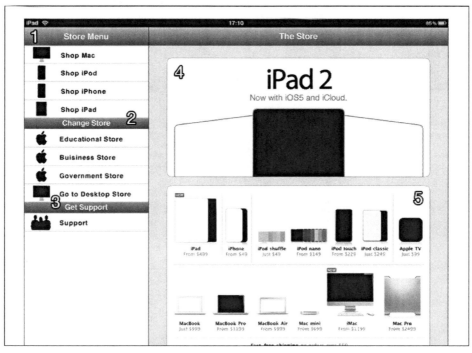

Figure 4–39. *The iPad native-like (re)design of our Apple Store use-case.*

From top to bottom in the content column (Figure 4–40, number 4), you insert the hero image, which in the compatible version played the role of an intro page. As we said, the style is exactly the same as what you saw in the original and compatible versions.

Below the hero image, you insert the entry level product box. Every product has its entire visible area touchable, and it is just like inserting another menu in the content column. In this way, we can insert just the essential entries in the Store menu (Figure 4–40, number 1), reducing the cognitive noise in the user experience.

Interaction

What you need to do in this phase is test the consistency of your interfaces and see whether the user using these interfaces is able to access the specific content that he/she is looking for. We can set up some preliminary tests based on the most important use-cases for checking the user interface consistency and the quality of the user experience.

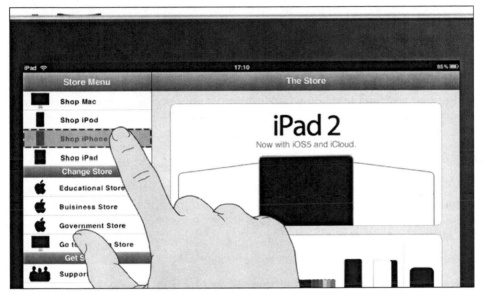

Figure 4–40. *The (re)designed iPad native-like interface offer is now the highest level of user experience.*

The big advantage to using a native-like structure is that you have a solid foundation for your content. Nevertheless, that doesn't prevent us from inserting the wrong content, the wrong links, or using the wrong typography. We must pay attention to these details, because they are exactly what we test for in this phase.

Deliverables

At the end of the process, you need to produce the same deliverables as you did for the compatible version based on design composition, style guide, and electronic prototype.

iPhone Native-Like User Interface Design

An iPhone native-like interface is the only way to offer a quality user experience, because a native-like interface is the only solution that optimizes the use of the 3.5-inch built-in iPhone display. Unfortunately, the Apple Store offers an incredible amount of content and so prioritizing forces us to make some tough decisions in this example.

When you prioritize the content, as you must do in every mobile WebApp, you are forced to cut some important parts. This is the main reason why an iPhone version of the Apple website has not yet been developed as of this writing. What you can do is prioritize its content and offer a link to the desktop version of the site if the user is looking for something that is not offered by the iPhone version.

Research

What was said about the research phase in the iPad process still applies for the compatible version. In the iPhone interface design process, the research phase even more pressingly needs to address the problem of prioritizing content. We use only the most important content, like we did with the iPad version, and we might even change the presentation order.

Once the market research has told you which portion of your content will be included in your iPhone version, it's time to move on to the next step of the process.

Structure

Working on the iPhone native-like version, exactly as was done with the iPad native-like version, we can't change the structure because that structure is the strength of the native-like solution. As you saw in Chapter 2, the iPhone adopts a structure called "iPhone Page Model."

The structure phase aims to achieve the following goals:

- **Apply the Original Brand to the iPhone Page Model**

    It is important to develop a connection between the compatible and the iPhone versions, ensuring that the brand is carried across the design.

- **Offer the Prioritized Part of Contents**

    If we want to retain a high quality user experience, you can't insert all your content in the iPhone page model. You need to prioritize the content and choose the most important parts to include and leave the rest exclusively for the compatible version.

- **Use an Appropriate Link Structure**

    The right link structure enables the user to access your content in a comfortable way, even if there is a large quantity of information.

- **Provide Orientation to the User**

    In a mobile context, it's easy for the user to lose his orientation inside our site map, and this probability is even greater when there is a lot of content.

What you do, to an even greater extent than you did in the iPad native-like version, is to prioritize your content for the native-like structure. This time, only the most crucial elements of the content will be available to the user. A link to the desktop version guides him/her to the other parts if needed.

> **NOTE:** We always try to avoid deep mobile site maps because the (mobile) user can easily lose his orientation. When for some reason, you have no choice, it is important to use an appropriate navigation structure and to show clearly the navigation path using a breadcrumb or other technique as described in the Chapter 2.

Starting from top to bottom, we find the Branding area (Figure 4–43, number 1) and inside this area, we design the breadcrumb in order to provide orientation to the user. Semantically speaking, the Branding area also contains the part below, called the "hero image" (Figure 4–41, number 2). The hero image visually represents the main message of the page and changes to one of the other images each time the user loads the page. In this case, you have three hero images available.

Figure 4–41. *The iPhone native-like one-column layout structure and its (re)design order.*

Below the Branding area, you design the Content area, adopting edge-to-edge navigation (Figure 4–41, number 3) with only three basic options. Because the iPhone version is loaded automatically, you need to give the user the ability to switch back to the compatible version, or if he/she needs it, direct access to the support page. In case the user needs to enter the store, he can touch the first link and the store homepage will load.

> **NOTE:** In modern web design, you always try to avoid intro pages but in this case we keep the structure of the original design that offers a big visual message using an introductory page.

At the end of the page, you have the Site Information part. You use the same approach used by Apple in mobile pages, like MobileMe with a minimalist approach, inserting only the Apple logo without any kind of supplementary information.

Aesthetic

When we work on a mobile version of a site like the Apple Store with a strong brand and a lot of sexy visual appeal and great design, the aesthetic phase becomes the easiest part of the job. In these cases, what we need to do is just keep the look-and-feel of the desktop site and adapt it for the smaller screen without ruining it.

The (layout) rules in a native-like version are even more strict than those in the iPad version. Here there is little room for fancy design but the laws of perception still help us to offer your user a better visual hierarchy and a pleasant look.

Figure 4–42. *The iPhone native-like (re)design of our Apple Store use-case.*

The Branding area keeps the style of the Sidebar Main Header (Figure 4–35, number 4) designed for the iPad compatible version with the breadcrumb sitting below that. We always insert the hero image in the Branding area. Below that, we apply the same style to the Content area.

Usually, designers don't use too much space to display an image in an iPhone version because the limited available room in a 3.5-inch display is often perceived as a problem to solve instead of an opportunity. With this (re)design, we want to break this rule and we are happy to report that the latest (native) application called Apple Store and developed by Apple uses the same approach.

Interaction

If the Aesthetic phase is limited by the strict layout rules of the native-like structure, the same rules make it much easier to work on the Interaction phase because they offer some standard structures that have been specially developed to enable the user to have a comfortable interaction with the mobile device.

Figure 4–43. *The (re)designed iPhone native-like interface offer now the highest level of user experience.*

Exactly as we did for the iPad version, we just need to test the right use of the interfaces offered by the native-like environment. If the user touches a link intending to access a specific piece of information and is successful, this means that your interface works correctly and you did a good job. If this doesn't work, you can try inserting different interface parts, as you might with pieces in a jigsaw puzzle, until everything works correctly (at least inside the test context) and you have created a semantically correct structure.

Deliverable

At the end of the process, if you created compatible iPad and iPhone versions in your project, you might have the option of sending all the deliverables together to the developer team but this is possible only when working on small projects. For a larger project, and where possible, it is always preferable to create some sort of parallel workflow between the different parts of the team.

Tools for User Interface Design

Tools used in this chapter are both application and web application types. Table 4-3 lists some of the useful tools that you can use for designing your next user interfaces.

Table 4–3. *Tools Used for Design iPhone and iPad User Interfaces.*

Name	Type	URL	Operative System
Feng-Gui	Web App	http://www.feng-gui.com/	OSX – Win - Linux
ColoRotate	Web App	http://www.colorotate.org/	OSX – Win - Linux
ColorGrab	Web App	http://colourgrab.com/	OSX – Win - Linux
Pictaculos	Web App	http://pictaculous.com/	OSX – Win - Linux
Contrast-A	Web App	http://www.dasplankton.de/ContrastA/	OSX – Win - Linux
WhatFontls	Web App	http://www.whatfontis.com/	OSX – Win - Linux
Little Snapper	Application	http://www.realmacsoftware.com/littlesnapper/	OSX

Summary

In this chapter, we introduced the interface design process. You saw that designing for a touch device means having a different approach to the interface design concept because of the zoom function that every device offers to the user, so that everything becomes touchable and everything becomes an interface.

We introduced a new concept, defining what active and passive interfaces are in a touch-screen design process, and learning how we can use them for optimizing the structure inside our WebApp.

Following this new approach, we also explored the use of active and passive negative space, the foundation of color psychology, and how colors affect users' moods.

We introduced the visual hierarchy concept, the most common user reading patterns, and discussed how to use a strong visual hierarchy to influence those patterns and achieve specific goals in your design.

In the second part, we worked on a compatible design using the Apple Store use-case. We presented the use of negative space and touch-oriented typography to optimize the user experience of a desktop-based website for Apple's tablet and its 9.7-inch display. In the third part, we used the same approach but oriented to an iPad native version of our Apple Store use-case. Always following the same interface design process, we designed an iPhone version of the Apple Store website in the fourth part.

## Chapter 5

iPhone UI Design: Think Simple

"Less is more..."

—Ludwing Mies van der Rohe

This chapter is all about user interface design for the iPhone. We will first introduce the basic concept for designing that interface, which is "think simple" and will then look at iPhone users' experiences and the nature of users' cognitive resource limitations.

After this brief introduction, we will explore the anatomy of sketching using freehand sketching techniques and will explain how to mock up a user interface with some useful tools, such as Balsamiq. We will explore Balsamiq's interface and show how to optimize it.

Next, we will jump directly into Adobe Fireworks and explain how to design a user interface pixel by pixel. When designing a user interface, you need to control every pixel of all the elements. Adobe Fireworks provides better tools and interfaces for working with pixels because it enables you to keep the user interface elements under more constant control and move and modify them more easily than with Adobe Photoshop. Adobe Fireworks also offers a better export tool compared to Photoshop, allowing you to better optimize the weight of each graphic element. Everything you design in this book can also be achieved using Adobe Photoshop, so feel free to use it if you prefer.

In the last part, we will show you how to reuse your design to create a use case and provide a visual representation of the user experience.

User Interface Sketching

In Chapter 4, you learned about the interface design process and saw an iPhone version of "The Store" use case. Chapter 4 focused on the interface design principles used to design an amazing touch interface.

In this chapter and the next, we will explain in detail how we designed our touch-optimized interface. We will also go through the whole creativity process from the sketch to the final product.

Think Simple

Less is often more. Therefore, "think simple" is the *leitmotif* of our iPhone design and development activities. In previous chapters, we built the foundation to better understand why the "think simple" concept is the right approach to optimize the mobile experience on a small device like the iPhone.

> **NOTE:** A leitmotif is a musical term referring to a recurring theme associated with a particular idea. By extension, the word has also been used in other life contexts to mean any sort of recurring theme, practice, or idea.

In the next paragraphs, we discuss the main points behind the "think simple" concept, thus tying together what you learned in the previous chapters.

The iPhone is an On-the-Go Device

For the majority of users, the iPhone is used on the go. If you are at home or work and have a desktop, notebook, or tablet, you will probably not use the iPhone.

This probability is even greater since the iPad was released. Before the iPad, it was likely someone who needed to use a mobile service would use the iPhone. However, this has changed now that millions of iPads have been sold.

To use an iPhone on the go, users require resources with a simple structure that allow the device to function in various contexts.

The Essence of the iPhone Page Model

The iPhone page model is the basic structure of all our works. It is a linear and simple structure and works perfectly with the iPhone. However, it doesn't allow designers and developers to present content in a more detailed way.

The linear flow of the content browsed with the iPhone is perfect for a mobile context and it is important to stick with this concept without trying to add any techniques used with desktops or tablets. Even the multitasking feature introduced in iOS4 used the page model, which enabled users to use multiple applications, although just one page at a time.

iPhone Limitations

The iPhone is based on a 3.5–inch display and no matter how brilliantly designed or developed a WebApp is, the amount of screen estate remains the same. Even the retina display has the same dimensions and user interface proportions inside the visible area are the same. This means that, despite better readability of the user-interface elements, the level of user experience remains the same.

We also need to remember that, despite the fact the iPhone revolutionized the user experience and the paradigm behind browsing the mobile web, it still remains a small phone optimized for mobile content that has limited hardware features. For example, the new touch keyboard was a huge improvement over the qwerty used in the old smartphones because it can change following the application needs and can be used in portrait and landscape modes. However, with a 3.5–inch display, it will always be limited to a subset of possible use cases.

The Nature of Users' Cognitive Resources

Everything in this world is finite and most things are accessible in a limited way. This is just the way things are. In our mobile context, the screen dimension is limited, as is the available bandwidth, the services offered, and the RAM. Thus, users' cognitive resources are limited.

Because user experience is born and develops in the brain, users' cognitive resources affect their iPhone experiences. It is important to be aware of this. Limited cognitive resources imply the user interface must be optimized in a simple way and we must realize that some contexts require more cognitive resources than others.

In the end, the best we can do is never forget the words of Leonardo da Vinci: "Simplicity is the last sophistication."

Anatomy of Sketching

Sketching might appear to be an easy part of the whole design process. You take a pen and a piece of paper and you're done. After all, you don't have to paint the Sistine Chapel! However, nothing could be further from the truth. Sketching a view, as it is called in native development, means syncing your hand with the creative part of your mind. For this reason, a simple thing like sketching requires years of practice.

> **HISTORICAL NOTE:** The first example of modern sketching dated back to the first half of the fifteenth century in Siena when Mariano di Jacobi detto Taccola produced a set of four volumes on civil and military technology called *De Ingenisis*.

Fortunately for us, sketching a view is simpler than other kinds of engineering or architectural sketching; however, the foundations are the same. Before sketching a use case, you must keep the following points in mind.

- **Quick**

  A sketch must aim to give only an impression.

- **Direct**

  A sketch uses simple and clear wording.

- **Minimal**

  A sketch includes only what is required to communicate the message.

- **Freedom**

  A sketch gives a sense of openness because it is composed of instinctual lines instead of tight, precise lines.

- **Grouped**

  A sketch makes sense in contexts created by other sketches.

- **Suggest**

  A sketch doesn't explicitly state something, but explores a concept that suggests a design and development path.

Now that you have a better idea of what a sketch means, the first step is to sketch your ideas using pen and paper. This is an important step because your mind is better connected to your hand than your mouse.

In the sketching phase, you will:

1. do some freehand sketching on white paper,

2. create logical connections between sketches, and

3. redesign your freehand sketches using a stencil.

Figure 5–1 shows three iPhone views sketched on paper. For these sketches, we used a handmade wood stencil with 1:1 dimensions. As you might notice, a standard X box was used to represent all the images. This is a standard practice for wireframe design but is also recommended for sketching in order to focus solely on representing the page structure. More information regarding the best practices for sketching a user interface will follow in chapter 6 when we detail the iPad use case.

When starting a project from scratch, creating logical connections between views will help you clarify your ideas and contextualize your design. It is a good idea to print all the views, post them on a wall, and discuss your ideas with others.

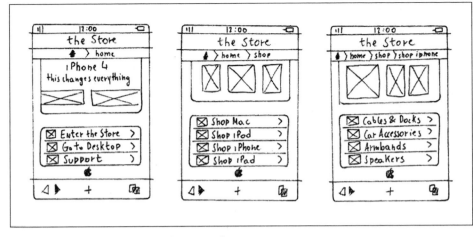

Figure 5–1. *A freehand sketch of "The Store" use case.*

For this use case, you don't need to work on logical (content) connections because you are working on a (re)design. Working on a (re)design means you already prioritized the content from the desktop version and produced an optimized iPhone site map showing the content structure and relationships.

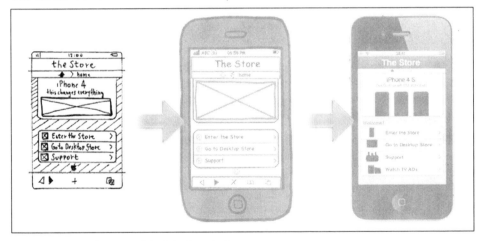

Figure 5–2. *The first step of the interface design process.*

If you work with a development team and need to present your work, you might need to redesign your sketch using a stencil. Figure 5–3 shows how a freehand sketch can be redesigned using a stencil.

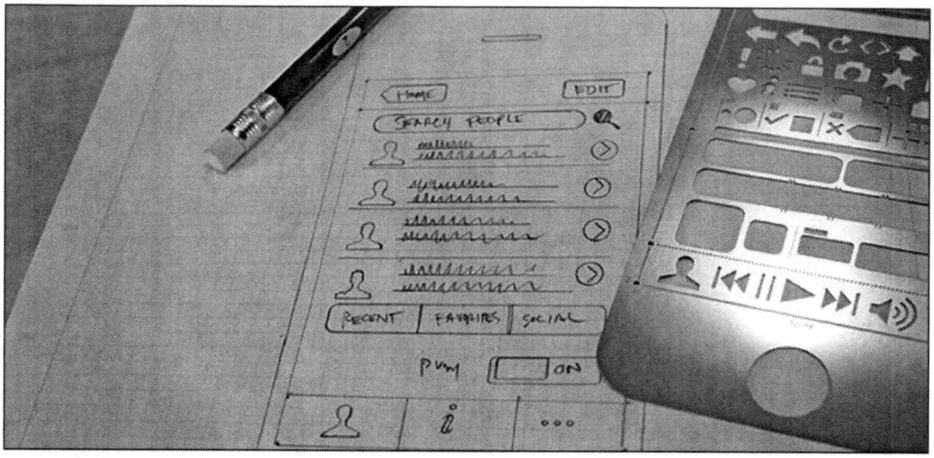

Figure 5–3. *Redesigning a sketch using the UI stencil for the iPhone.*

Once you have sketched your idea using pen and paper and redesigned it using a stencil, you are ready to compose your view using a tool. In the next section, you will see how to use a tool to transform your original sketch into the final design using Adobe Fireworks.

Design Using Tools

When the idea is clear in your mind, move to the second step of the process, which is designing a version of your views using tools. For our project, we chose Balsamiq Mockups (we inserted links to the appropriate web pages at the end of the chapter for all the other tools used in this book).

Balsamiq is a *zenware* program, meaning it helps you get "in the zone" and stay there. Balsamiq is the perfect program for the second step of the interface design process (see Figure 5–4).

> **NOTE:** Zenware means zen software, software that helps you get focused, achieve the ultra-productive cognitive state known as flow, and stay there. The goal of zenware is to disappear, supporting you when you need it but staying out of your way as much as possible. You should forget the software is there at all.

This program offers almost the same speed and rough feel as sketching with a pencil, but with the advantage of the digital medium. For example, enlarging containers is just a drag operation, rearranging elements doesn't require starting over, and your wireframes will be clear enough that you'll be able to make sense of them tomorrow.

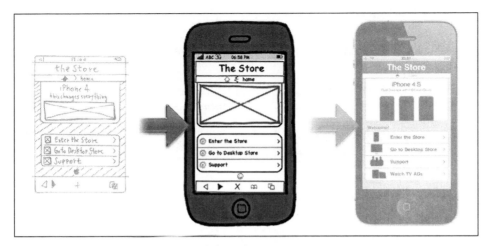

Figure 5–4. *The second step of the interface design process.*

Explore the Balsamiq Mockups Interface

Balsamiq Mockups have a tool bar from which you can select an element category, as follows.

- **All**
  You can see all the available elements.

- **Big**
  You can see all the big elements in all the categories, including the iPhone and many other images, such as the cover flow.

- **Buttons**
  You can see all the buttons, including the iPhone ON/OFF switch toggle.

- **Common Elements**
  You can see all the common elements in all the categories.

- **Containers**
  You can see all the container elements. Despite having a general rectangle container, this category is more useful for desktop projects.

- **Layout**
  You can see all the elements in order to compose a layout.

- **Markup**
  You can see useful elements to mark up your work.

- **Media**
  You can see all the media elements, including icons, cover flow, images, and video player elements.

■ **Text**

You can see all the text elements, such as titles, navigation bars, breadcrumbs, tree panes, and other desktop-like objects.

■ **iPhone**

You can see all the iPhone elements, including the keyboard, value picker, iOS menu, and the alert box. This category is shown in Figure 5–5.

Figure 5–5. *The Balsamiq Mockups application: the iPhone section.*

The Balsamiq paradigm is pretty simple. Drag and drop your element, modify it, and compose your mockup. Figure 5–6 shows some of the elements used to compose "The Store" use case mockup.

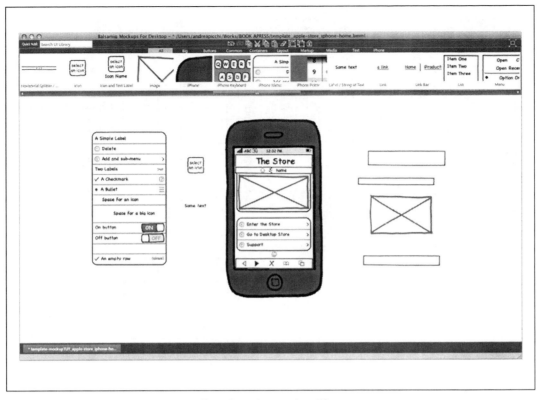

Figure 5–6. *The Balsamiq Mockups paradigm: drag, drop, and modify.*

Represent Connections

When the first view is ready, copy and paste it in order to create another instance to modify. The goal now is to create a few views side by side to represent a relationship and give a visual feeling about the context.

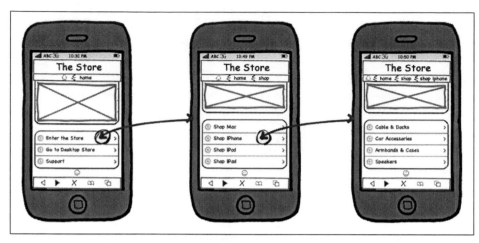

Figure 5–7. *The sketching phase with Balsamiq Mockups.*

Figure 5–7 shows the link between three views. This image shows the action "Go to the iPhone Accessories Page" in "The Store" use case.

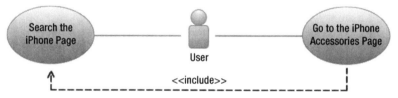

Figure 5–8. *The Unified Modeling Language (UML) use case diagram for "Go to the iPhone Accessories Page".*

Once all your views and relationships are worked out, the work with Balsamiq Mockups is finished and you are ready to refine the aesthetic part of your views using a graphic program.

Designing with Adobe Fireworks

After using a tool such as Balsamiq to compose a mockup from your sketch, it's time to enter the third phase of the process and switch to a graphic program such as Adobe Photoshop or Fireworks to work on the aesthetic aspect. Adobe Photoshop is probably the best graphic program for manipulating bitmaps, but if you work on a WebApp design using many vector shapes and need to control, move, transform, or modify pixels, Fireworks is the best option.

Adobe Fireworks is much more web-oriented than Photoshop. A good example of this is the property tool, located in the lower left corner of the interface. The property tool provides constant feedback to the designer about the X and Y coordinates of an element and its dimensions in pixels. The Property box is useful during the user interface design process. Another example is the export tool; the Fireworks optimization algorithm works much better and gives better results compared with the one in Photoshop. From this point of view, Fireworks is even better than Photoshop.

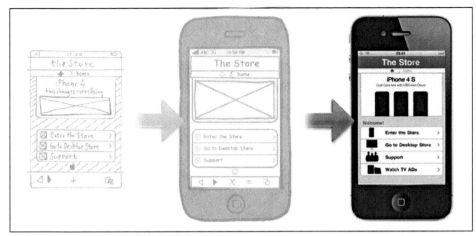

Figure 5–9. *The third step of the interface design process.*

> **NOTE:** In the next section, we introduce the functions used to design "The Store" use case. We show all the *commands*, where they can be found, and the *keyboard shortcuts* inside parentheses.

We learn this lesson from Andy Clarke, the author of *Transcending CSS: The Fine Art of Web Design*.

Creating a Canvas

With Adobe Fireworks open, you need to create a new document. Choose File➤New (⌘N).

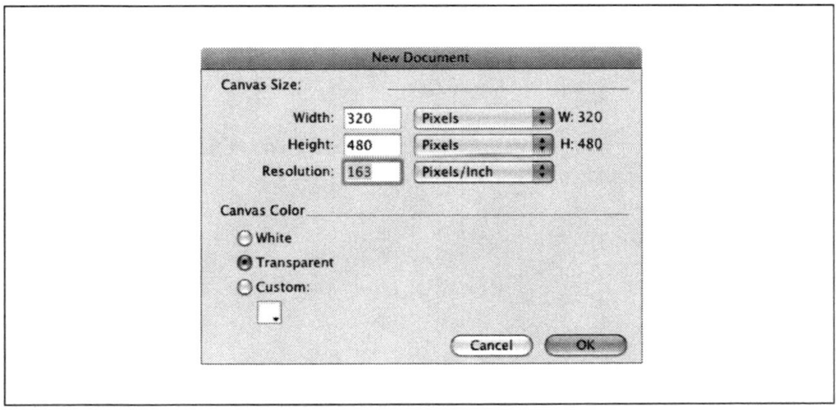

Figure 5–10. *Adobe Fireworks: create a new document.*

Now create a new document with the following canvas size.

- ▪ **Width:** 320 (px)

- ▪ **Height:** 480 (px)

- ▪ **Resolution**: 163 (ppi)

This canvas size follows the iPhone 2G, 3G, and 3GS display capability, but if you want to work with the new Retina Display, you need to set the following canvas size.

- ▪ **Width:** 640 (px)

- ▪ **Height:** 960 (px)

- ▪ **Resolution**: 326 (ppi)

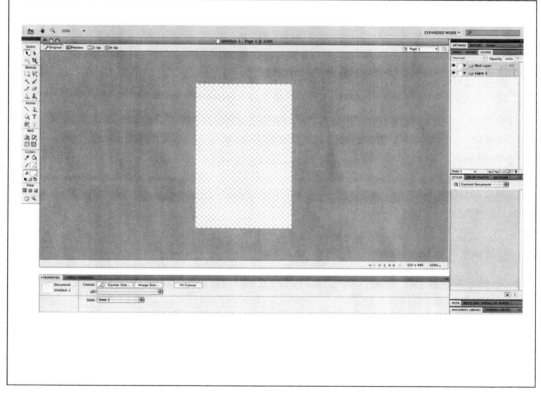

Figure 5–11. *Adobe Fireworks: a new blank document.*

Both resolutions have the same proportion inside the 3.5–inch iPhone screen.

Organize Levels

Your design will be deployed on a few levels. For this reason, the first thing to do is create some folders to organize your assets and keep your environment clean. Using a semantic approach, create the following folders.

- **iOS ui**
- **Branding Area**
- **Content Area**
- **Info Area**
- **Background**
- **Templates**

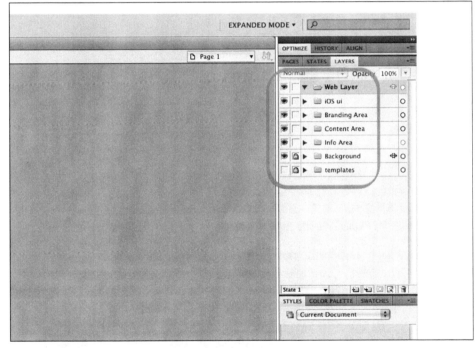

Figure 5–12. *Adobe Fireworks: a semantic structure for the asset's folders.*

The first folder, called "iOS ui", will contain the Status Bar and the Bottom Bar. The next folders—Branding, Content, and Info Area—will contain the WebApp. Below these folders, create two levels called "Background" and "Templates." Inside the Branding, Content, and Info Area, add two more folders, one called "Text" and another called "Icon."

Layout Design

The first thing to do is add another folder called "Rulers." This folder will contain four lines, two lines for fixing the Visible Screen boundaries and two lines to fix 10 px padding on the side. After adding the rulers, insert a background layer by choosing Select▶Rectangle Tool (U).

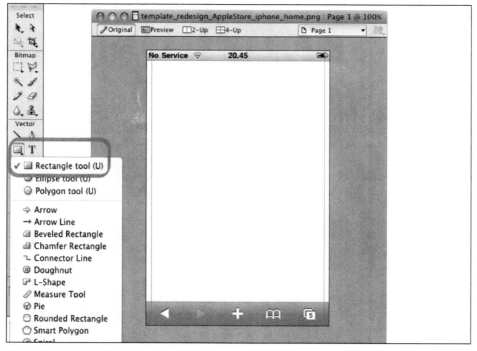

Figure 5–13. *Adobe Fireworks: the Visible Area and Padding Rulers.*

Now draw a rectangle measuring 320 × 480 px. This rectangle will be the basic background color for your canvas, but more importantly, it will be used to align the canvas object with the Align function. The new rectangle is drawn inside the Background folder in order to be under the iOS interface assets of the iOS folder.

> **NOTE:** The Align function is a relative function. We can't just select an object and look for the Align function because it will be unavailable. Being a relative function in this environment means you need to pass two or more objects to the function to align. This is necessary because the function will align "something" to "something else."

Now that you have prepared your canvas, you are ready to add the design elements.

Interface Design

Using the Rectangle tool, add the following elements.

- **Header Bar**

     Rectangle: 45 × 480 px

     Gradient: Linear

     Color: #566E93, #314F7B

- **Breadcrumb Bar**

     Rectangle: 20 × 480px

     Color: #FFFFFF

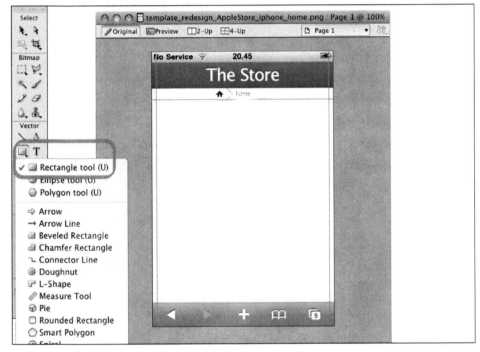

Figure 5–14. *Adobe Fireworks: the Branding Area.*

After adding the two bars, add the text by choosing **Select▶Text tool** (T). The text is defined as follows.

- **Header Text**

     Font: Myriad Pro, Regular, 30 pt

     Drop Shadow: 1 px solid, #3B4C66, 270 deg

■ **Breadcrumb Text**

Font: Myriad Pro, Light Semi-Condensed, 12 pt

To align the Page Title in the middle of the Header Text, select the Header Text and the White Background by choosing **Modify▶Align▶Center Horizontal** (⌥⌘5).

The last element to add is the House Icon. Draw this manually, defining it as follows:

■ **House Icon**

Size: 14 × 11 px

Color: #2B2B2B

Now that the Branding Area is complete, move to the Content Area. Select the Background Level and use the Rectangle tool to draw a rectangle as content background, defined as follows.

Content Background

Rectangle: 350 × 480 px

Color: #D8D8D8

Now that the gray background is defined, add some light to the top part of the Content Area by choosing **Select▶Line tool** (N). The line is defined as follows.

■ **Content Area Light**

Line: 1× 480 px

Color: #FFFFFF

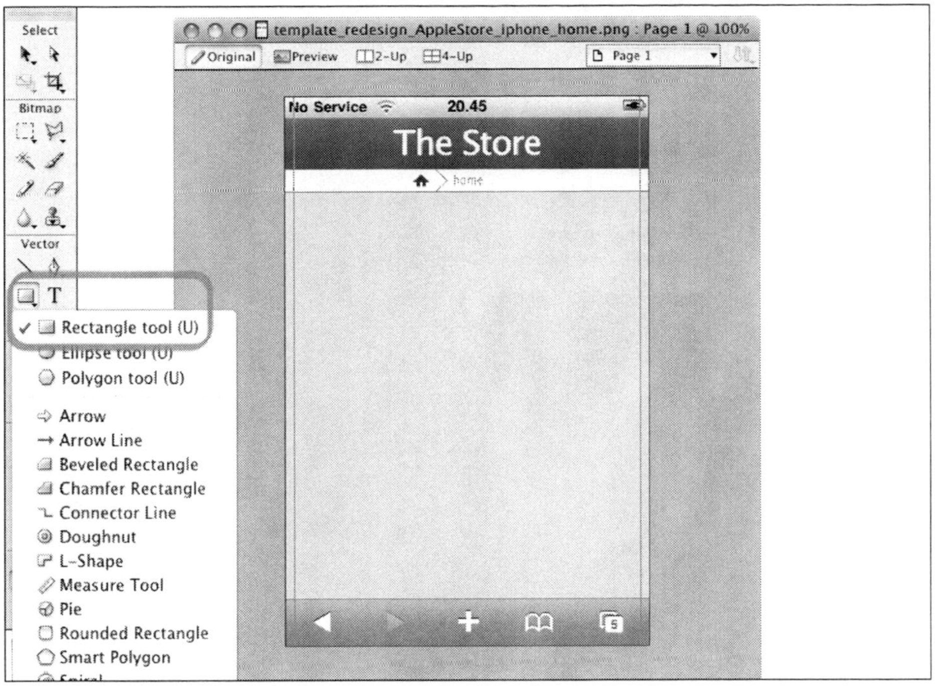

Figure 5–15. *Adobe Fireworks: the Content Area.*

The next step is to insert the Hero Content by choosing **Select▶Rounded Rectangle**. Create two Rounded Rectangles, as follows.

- **Hero Content 1**

    Rectangle: 190 × 300 px

    > Color: #FFFFFF

- **Hero Content 2**

    Rectangle: 190 × 302 px

    > Color: #FFFFFF

    > Border: 1 px solid #000000

When the rounded rectangle is drawn, select both rectangles, resize the corners, and flatten the images by choosing **Modify▶Flatten Selection** (⌥⌘Z).

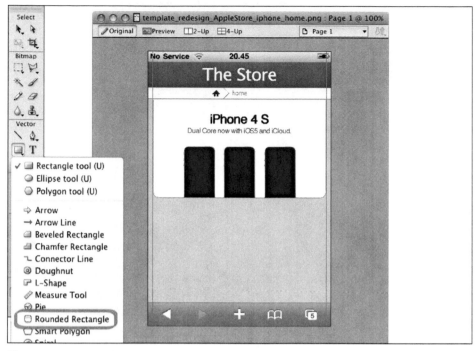

Figure 5–16. *Adobe Fireworks: the Hero Content Area.*

NOTE: When using a Soft Line border, it's hard to have a sharp 1 px angle border because of the anti-aliasing. It is therefore necessary to use a little trick in order to have the same sharp border effect as in the implementation phase when working with the CSS. Put the Hero Content 1 on top of the Hero Content 2. Because the Hero Content 2 is 302 px wide and the Hero Content 1 is only 300 px, only a 1 px border will remain visible.

When the Hero Content Area is ready, insert the text, as follows.

- **Hero Heading**

  Font: Helvetica, Bold, 22 pt

  Color: #000000

- **Hero Sub-Heading**

  Font: Helvetica, Regular, 12 pt

  Color: #666666

Below the two headings, insert the iPhones 4 image and three 6 px circles representing the Hero Carousel.

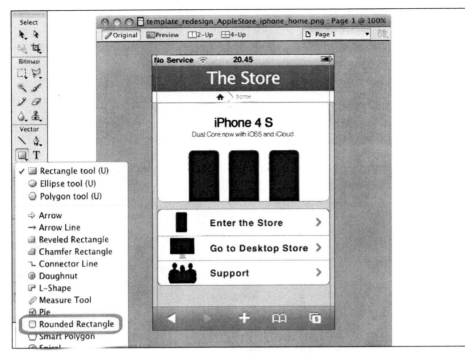

Figure 5–17. *Adobe Fireworks: the Edge-to-Edge menu in the Content Area.*

After the Hero Content, design the Menu Area based on an edge-to-edge structure. Use the Rounded Rectangle tool to design a rectangle, as follows.

- ■ **Menu Area**

    Rectangle: 300 × 132 px

    Color: #FFFFFF

    Border: 1 px solid #000000

The height of the menu is the standard 44 px of each menu entry. The text entries are defined as follows.

- ■ **Main Menu Text Entry**

    Font: Helvetica, Bold, 16 pt

    Color: #111111

On the left side of each Menu Entry, we have a 34 px height icon and on the far left, a 6 × 12 px right arrow.

NOTE: As with the Hero Content Area, use a Soft Line border. This means that if you want to achieve a sharp 1 px border, you need to apply the same technique that uses two overlapped boxes.

Now that the designs for the Menu Area and Content Area are completed, add the Info Area. Like the Apple brand logo, the design for this area should be minimalist, containing only the logo and nothing else. Figure 5–18 shows the whole design with the Info Area in the bottom part.

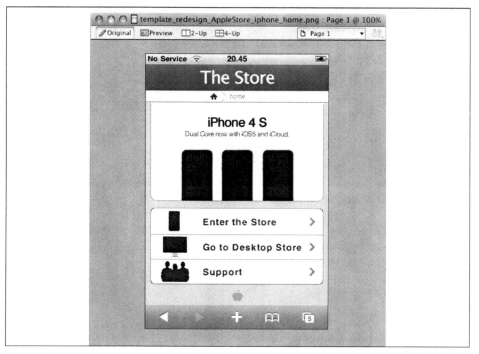

Figure 5–18. *Adobe Fireworks: the entire design with the Info Area in the bottom part.*

At this point, the process is complete. The assets produced in this process are reused to create the electronic prototype useful for a humble first test of the usability and to prepare the next implementation step in the mobile information architecture process.

Reuse Design

Reuse is an important word in the design and development world. Reusing generally saves both time and effort, providing a solid and tested base for projects. This practice is more useful in native development, where reusable code is a fundamental part of the process; even a small piece of tested code can save developers a lot of effort. Design patterns share the same paradigm with code or design reuse practices, where we identify problems or requirements and provide a solution or code/design/pattern.

In our design project flow, we used the view we created for "The Store" home page in designing two other views, "The Store" shop page and "The Store" shop iPhone page. We encourage you to implement this reuse approach in all your future projects.

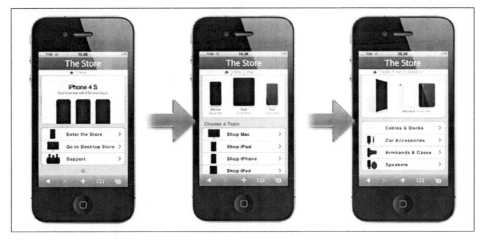

Figure 5–19. *"The Store" use case: the three iPhone views.*

In our process, we reused the view we designed for "The Store" home page to design two more views. This helped give a more tangible feeling about the final WebApp design would look like. The other views we designed are "The Store" shop, the "Shop" page, and "The Store" shop iPhone page.

Looking at Figure 5–19, you can see a few small differences between the home page and the other two pages. This is because we wanted to create dominance in the home page using a bigger Hero Content page based on an image carousel. Achieving this result was possible thanks to the only three text entries in the Main Menu. In this way, both the Hero Content Area and the Main Menu are in the Visible Area and do not require users to scroll.

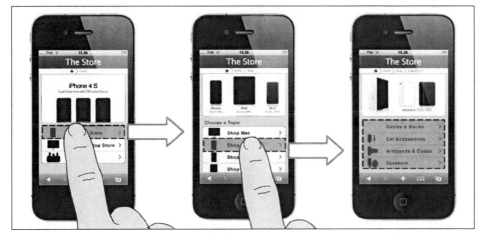

Figure 5–20. *User interface interaction in the "Go to the iPhone Accessories Page" use case.*

On the home page, the main message relies on the Hero Content Area; the Main Menu offers only obvious options, such as "Enter the Store". In the other views, the main message is contained in the Main Menu and the (reduced) Hero Content Area merely lets users know at a glance whether their page is desired. The Hero Content Area also offers information about some products and tempts users to buy them. However, this is not related to the user experience and is only a secondary goal from a marketing point of view.

Once all the views or pages for your WebApp are designed, you can give users a visual representation by creating a few use cases, as shown in Figure 5–20, or by giving an overview of the interface-content relationship, as shown in Figure 5–21. Both are useful for the other members of the team and for yourself in case you need to check the interface consistency before moving to the implementation phase.

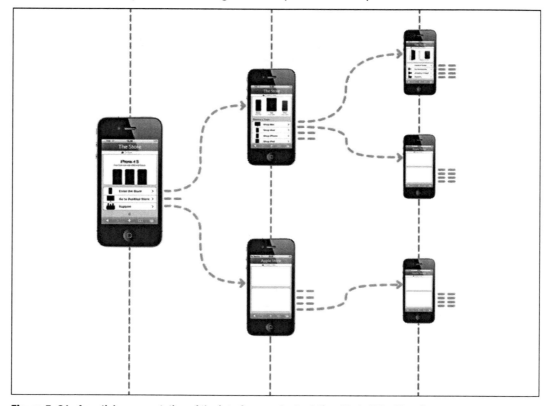

Figure 5–21. *A partial representation of the interface-content relationship in "The Store" use case.*

Tools for User Interface Design

The tools used in this chapter are both physical tools and software applications. Table 5–1 lists some useful tools you can use to design your next user interface.

Table 5–1. *Tools used to design iPhone and iPad user interfaces.*

Name	Type	URL	Operating System
UI Stencil	Tool	www.uistencils.com/	--- --- ---
Balsamiq Mockups	Application	http://www.balsamiq.com/	OSX/Win/Linux
Adobe Fireworks	Application	www.adobe.com/products/fireworks.html	OSX/Win
Adobe Photoshop	Application	www.adobe.com/products/photoshop.html	OSX/Win
Gimp OSX	Application	http://gimp.lisanet.de/	OSX
Gimp	Application	www.gimp.org/	Linux

Summary

In the first part of this chapter, we analyzed the interface design process and discussed the anatomy of sketching and the "think simple" paradigm. We discussed how the iPhone limitations, the iPhone page model, and users' cognitive resources influence design style and explained how all these elements are the source of the "think simple" design paradigm.

In the second part, we explained how to improve a basic sketch made with pen and paper using a tool like Balsamiq Mockups. We explained that you can start to create some content and interface connections to create an initial visual representation of the concept design.

In the third part of this chapter, we told you how to design a user interface using Adobe Fireworks. We approached the process step-by-step, from the creation of a new canvas to the interface design. At the end of the process, we introduced the idea of reusing your design to create two more views or pages and we suggested making a visual representation of the interface-content relationship as a deliverable for the implementation phase.

## Chapter 6

iPad UI Design: Think Inverted

*" . . if you would create something,
you must be something . . ."*

—Johann Wolfgang von Goethe

After working on the iPhone user interface in the previous chapter, you will now be able to start working on the iPad version of your project. When you work on a project for Apple's tablet, you need to choose if you want a compatible user interface or a native-like user interface. There is no right or wrong approach, because everything is dictated by the project requirements.

In this chapter, you will see how to apply both approaches. In the past chapter, you saw how "think simple" was the basic concept for designing an iPhone user interface. Now, you will see how the iPad design requires a switch of perspective for optimizing the device capabilities.

First, a new approach to simplicity called "think inverted," will be introduced, and then you will learn how to design an iPad-compatible user interface from a desktop interface, showing the principles behind this important step of the project flow.

Then, like in the iPhone chapter, you will learn how to sketch the user interface, and after that, you will learn how to design it with Adobe Fireworks. The whole design process will be presented separately for both the iPad-compatible and iPad native-like versions.

User Interface Sketching

In Chapter 5, you designed the iPhone version of your Apple Store use case. In Chapter 6, you will work with the same procedure, but you will be presented with both the compatible and the iPad native-like versions. Since both versions share most of the iPad principles but not exactly the same ones, it will be identified when something is specifically needed for one of the versions.

Instead of using the iPhone for presenting the compatible version, you will use the iPad, because, for the iPhone, it is better to switch to a native-like version every time it is possible, while with an iPad this is not always true.

Think Inverted

This section's heading doesn't say everything, and it probably doesn't show any direct relationship with the iPad. The meaning behind this title could sound like: continue to think simple, but in an inverted way. This defines an inverted (simple) approach. The inverted approach arises from the intermediate position of this new device, just between a pure mobile device like the iPhone and a pure fixed desktop like an iMac or a Mac Pro. The term "inverted" stands for a different approach that requires an opposite approach to achieve the same goals achieved with the iPhone version.

In the iPad native-like version, it is necessary to re-factor your thinking because of the new concepts behind the portrait and landscape orientations. In the portrait mode, the device presents a one-column layout, and in landscape mode, it presents a two-column layout.

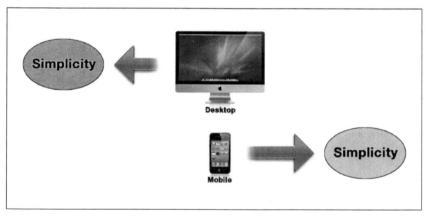

Figure 6–1. *The achieving process of simplicity from a desktop and mobile point of view*

This means that you will often need to use two opposite approaches for the same content in order to optimize both orientations. In the two-column design offered by the landscape orientation, you should use the left (small) column as support for the main content. The left column provides orientation to the user and makes it easier to browse complex sites or application contents.

In the portrait orientation, the single-column design doesn't have this navigation support, and for this reason, the user must access the left column as a pop-up menu, using the button placed in the header. This fact suggests using a second CSS file for modifying the main content structure, including some design elements that will compensate for the missing left column. Providing some navigation information inside the main content, you will be able to reduce the access to the left column through the pop-up menu, and increase the quality of the user experience.

In the iPad-compatible version, re-factoring is necessary because you will work on a desktop version, but you will need to apply some rules from the mobile (touch) environment in order to optimize the user touch experience. Desktop and mobile rules, before the iPad, lived and were applied in two separate worlds. In this new kind of design style, you will merge two types of approaches, like the desktop and the mobile one, using a common background that is based on the simplicity concept. Before the iPad came out, these two types of approaches pointed in opposite directions.

As can be learned from the chaos theory, sometimes making things simpler requires more complex procedures in the design phase. As you will see in the next section, sometimes you will need to add features to reduce complexity and make a pattern simpler.

Inverted Simplicity

How can you use simplicity to point in a direction, in order to achieve your design goals, which point in the opposite direction? Examples of this concept are prioritizing the content (mobile approach), keeping a desktop-like structure (desktop approach), or presenting the content with a desktop structure (desktop approach) and a mobile-oriented structure (mobile approach). Each case is an example of two forces that point in opposite directions.

Now you will see, one more time, how the simplicity concept will be a fundamentally common factor between apparently different things, and you will see that your design goals influence these opposite forces to point in the same direction.

> **NOTE:** The simplicity theory is a cognitive theory that seeks to explain the attractiveness of some kind of human-environment interaction with human minds. This theory claims that interesting situations appear simpler than expected to the observer. A well-known implementation of this theory is Ockham's razor (from the name of the English logician and theologian, and Franciscan friar, William of Ockham).
>
> From a cognitive perspective, simplicity is the property of a domain that requires very little information to be exhaustively described. The opposite of simplicity is complexity.

The Google home page is the perfect example of inverted simplicity—how to present a very complex thing in a very easy way. As Marissa Mayer, vice president of Search Products and User Experience at Google said, "Google has the functionality of a really complicated Swiss army knife, but the home page is simple, elegant, and can slip in your pocket."

NOTE: Marissa Mayer graduated with honors in computer science at Stanford University, has notable public involvement with Google Search and Gmail, and can be considered highly responsible for the success of these UIs. *Fortune* magazine lists her as one of the 50 most powerful women in the world, and the youngest woman ever to make the list. She is credited with shaping the design of Google Maps, Google Earth, iGoogle, and more.

Google makes good use of this concept, and so does Apple. Its all-in-one iMac is the perfect example of how to reduce complexity by making things simpler.

Before starting to sketch out an iPad use case, in the next section, you will see how to apply simplicity to your design, and apply some of the rules behind this concept.

Remove and Prioritize

"Remove" sounds easy, but think about it—how will you know what to take away from your design? This is the main question that every designer will face when trying to achieve simplicity. This question triggers three main fears

- *Fear of missing something*: Designers fear that removing elements from the design will decrease the probability of the user finding what he needs. Designers struggling with this fear add endless content without applying any sort of content prioritizing.

- *Fear of being misunderstood*: Designers fear that removing elements from the design will decrease the probability of the user understanding the content's message. Designers struggling with this fear add technical information or many instructions where they are not strictly necessary.

- *Fear of failure*: Designers fear that removing elements from the design will increase the probability of failure. Designers struggling with this fear rely on the quantity of information instead of the quality.

Overcoming these fears is important for a designer. Through the simplicity concept, you can reduce the noise level in your web site or web application, and this fact will make useful content or features more prominent. This is a fundamental concept behind every great (simple) design.

The next question is how will you know when you have made something as simple as possible? Unfortunately, there isn't an answer for that; your experience will help you the most, besides a good phase of testing. In your interface design process, good guidelines should be as follows

- *Understand the core of a design element*: See the element globally in the web site or web application context.

- *Decide if removing the element could increase the global design value*:
  You need to be sure that removing the element will not disrupt the
  design.

When you remove an element, it is always because you saw it as a part of a puzzle, and
you decided to remove it. If you do not see its global meaning in the design, you'll never
have a chance to increase the global value of your design.

Hide and Shape

Sometimes it is not possible to remove elements or sub-elements from your design.
What you can do in this case is hide these elements, in order to focus the (limited) user-
cognitive resources only on the most important parts and keep these elements available
for a secondary type of user.

It's important to remember your secondary users, but you don't want to confuse or
distract your main target user from the main design message. A good example of this
concept is the structure of the product pages of the Apple Store web site. The message
is nice and clean in the main product page, but there is a toolbar on the top of each
product for letting the advanced user have access to the hardware specifics.

Figure 6–2. *The iPhone 4 page: Hiding and shaping in content design*

In Figure 6–2, you can see how the main target user isn't distracted from the message
behind the design, but the advanced user is also satisfied with all of the specifics; note
that this type of strategy works well because the advanced user is not frustrated when
looking for content, due to the fact that they don't have to scan a web site or web

application's content structure. This kind of user interaction doesn't happen with a beginner user.

This step will dramatically impact the global level of user experience, because if you forget about one kind of audience, you will lose a great number of potential users. Picture the following two situations

■ The Apple Store shows, in the iPhone main page, all the hardware features without hiding any type of element or content—CPU, RAM, Wi-Fi, features, applications; everything. A beginner user will get lost in the endless list of incomprehensible words, and he will probably not establish any kind of relationship with the new phone. This will mean only one thing: in 90% of cases, he will never buy an iPhone 4.

■ The iPhone main page shows only basic information about the phone, and no links to specific hardware information are provided. The advanced user will probably see the new phone as a phone for the inexperienced user, will not be satisfied by the type of relationship established with the brand through the web page, and he will never buy the new iPhone.

Figure 6–3. *The Apple Support page: Hiding and shaping in content design*

Figure 6–3 shows another example of shrinking a portion of content, and at the same time, hiding entries in a classic drop-down menu. The drop-down menu can replace a horizontal menu in a design. The Apple Store uses this approach in the Support page when this type of menu hides a portion of content, and at the same time an entry from an alternative horizontal menu.

These are only two kinds of examples of how using the hide and shape concept in a strategic manner can really increase the level of user experience.

Shrink and Group

Sometimes there is also a situation where an element or a portion of content can't be removed or hidden. The typical situation is when this element or portion of content is very important to the secondary type of user and must be accessed quickly. In this case, you will use the shrink and group approach. To achieve a perfect level of organization in your groups, a scheme has to be developed. Shrinking an element or a portion of content could mean visually reducing its size, and in doing so, reducing the impact of the user's attention. The element or portion of content is still available but it doesn't have a primary role in the message for the user anymore.

Figure 6–4. *The iTunes page: Shrinking and grouping in content design*

Figure 6–4 shows how the three portions of content are too important for the general understanding of the page to hide or take away from the design. The solution is to shrink it and group it below the main image, giving the user the opportunity to read it easily, if necessary. In the element highlighted in Figure 6–4, designers from Apple applied the laws of similarity, proximity, and symmetry.

As a last point, it is important to remember that for shrinking and grouping, sometimes you need to add, instead of take away an element or a portion of content in your design.

Key Points of the Simplicity-Complexity Paradox

So far, you have seen that by applying these three fundamental concepts you can reduce complexity and increase simplicity in your design. You can also see that, in a mobile context, simplicity is deeply related to a high quality of user experience.

The important fact is that simplicity is naturally related to complexity, and both are just two different expressions of the same event that happens in our minds. For this reason, it is totally futile trying to eliminate complexity using simplicity because, as the chaos theory suggests about the simplicity-complexity paradox, complex patterns contain simpler patterns within them that are reflections of more complex patterns.

A few important key points:

- *Simplicity can't eliminate complexity*: Using the simplicity concept, you can't eliminate complexity from your design; simplicity needs complexity in order to stand out in our minds.

- *Simplicity can drive you to complexity*: Removing, hiding, or shrinking the wrong element in your design increases the global-level complexity.

- *Simplicity is subjective*: Simplicity is a perception and has its origin in the user's mind. You can't assume that every user will perceive the same level of simplicity in your design.

Now, it's time to go to the practical part and start to analyze the compatible and native-like iPad versions of your Apple Store use case.

Sketching the UI

In this section, you will learn how to apply the three simplicity principles to your compatible and native-like versions. Starting from the iPad-compatible version, you can see the relationship between the sketch and the final design composition in Figure 6–5. When working on this version, besides the fact of being finger-friendly and optimizing the structure for an effort-free touch user experience, the design approach is not so far from the one you use for a desktop version.

Apply the Remove and Prioritize principle, by removing the Special Deals box and the Financing Option box. Despite that, the most important step is removing the layout dominance over the content.

The user needs more cognitive resources in his browsing experience if he needs to look for important information in two opposite places. As you well know, since the cognitive resources are limited, if the navigation structure takes away too many resources from the user, a small quantity will remain available to the user for understanding the content. This will decrease the level of user experience.

As a result of this step, you will prioritize the main content over the content structure and some navigation elements over others.

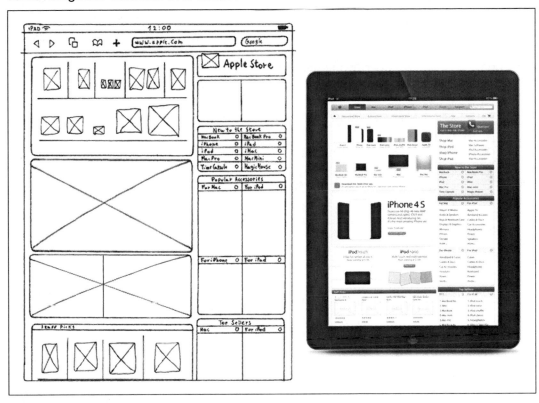

Figure 6–5. *The iTunes page: Shrinking and grouping in content design*

You should apply the Hide and Shape principle, hiding the Software box and the Gift Cards box from the Popular Accessories box. These boxes will be hidden but still accessible with one touch from the new Popular Accessories box, using one of the "more.." links. You should also hid some of the iPhone and iPad top sellers items; the box will show random items from the top ten, and the complete top ten is available using the "more.." link at the bottom of the list.

You should apply the Hide and Group principle, merging and hiding the two side bars into one bigger side bar. Merging the two columns will group the navigation elements, and as result, you will group the user focus into (only) one zone of your layout. More than any other design improvements, it is the level of use experience that really changes.

Analyzing the native-like iPad version of your use case in Figure 6–6, you can see how the design approach is much more mobile-oriented compared to the previous compatible version.

This time, because of the limited screen real estate available, compared to a desktop monitor, you will apply the Remove and Prioritize principle in a more aggressive way.

You will need to integrate the Hero Image from the store index page in the home page, and insert only the Main Content box as a support for the main Hero Image message.

In the side bar, you need to prioritize the four shop options for contextualizing your shopping according with one device and the possibility of a non-standard user changing the profile of the shop. Because you have aggressively prioritized the navigation and main content, you have opened the possibility of switching to the compatible version of the store, and, as a last option, you should insert a shortcut to customer support.

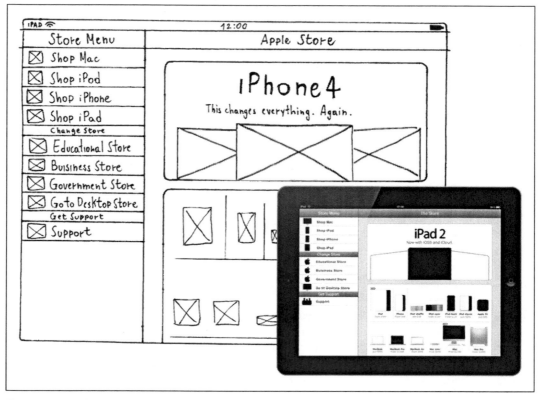

Figure 6–6. *The iTunes page: Shrinking and grouping in content design*

The first principle, Remove and Prioritize, is the dominant in this mobile approach, and the Hide and Shape principles and the Shrink and Group principles have less application. Once you understand this fact, you will be able to hide almost all of the content behind the following four options, Shop Mac, iPod, iPhone, and iPad, and you won't need to shrink any part of the design because you applied the remove principle to some sensible design elements.

Design Using Tools

The sketches are ready, and this means that you are ready to use the Balsamiq Mockups tool, the same one you used for your iPhone mockup. The Balsamiq Mockups tool offers some great design elements for your compatible version that, even while touch-oriented, still has a desktop-like structure. The native-like version will be designed using Adobe Fireworks because, so far, you don't have any optimized tools for representing an iPad sketch.

Select the Big Menu, and use the Browser Window element to represent your iPad Safari application, as in Figure 6–7. It doesn't look exactly like the iPad Safari window, but it will work for your purposes:

- **Browser Windows**

    Width: 1024px

    Height: 2000px

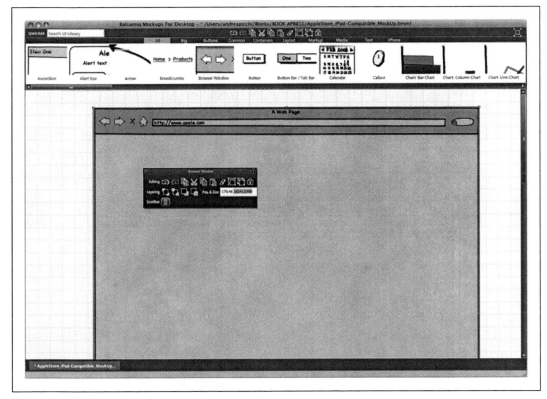

Figure 6–7. *Balsamiq Mockups: The browser window.*

Once your browser window is open, select the Common Menu, and drag a Menu Bar element for the primary navigation bar, and another Menu Bar element for the secondary navigation bar, as follows:

- **Primary Navigation Bar**

    Width: 980px

    Height: 36px

- **Secondary Navigation Bar**

    Width: 980px

    Height: 30px

Figure 6–8 illustrates how you can complete the primary navigation bar by using the Button element for representing the search engine bar.

Now that the navigation area is done, you can drag the Rectangle/Canvaz/Panel element from the Common Menu, and design it as follows:

- **Content Main Area**

    Width: 626px

    Height: 385px

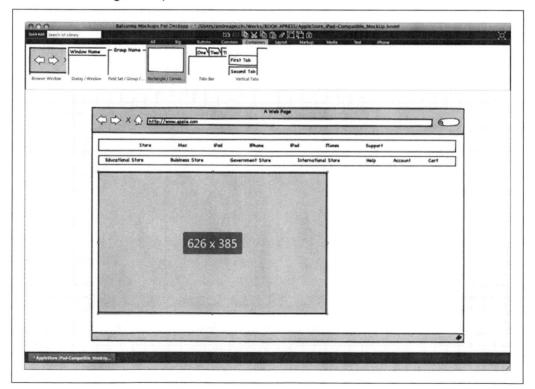

Figure 6–8. *Balsamiq Mockups: The primary and second navigation bar and the content main area*

Below the content main area, there is the spotlight area, which can be drawn by
dragging an Image element from the Common Menu with the following dimensions:

- **Spotlight Area**

    Width: 628px

    Height: 250px

Next is the Staff Picks box. It is drawn by using a Dialog/Window element from the
Common Menu, as seen as follows:

- **Staff Picks Box**

    Width: 628px

    Height: 425px

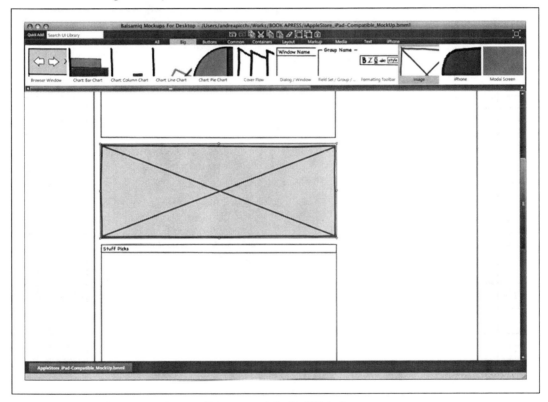

Figure 6–9. *Balsamiq Mockups: The spotlight area and the Staff Picks box*

Below the Staff Picks box, draw the Accessories box using the Rectangle/Canvas/Panel
element, and after that, draw the Informational box using the Dialog/Window element.
Both of these elements should be selected from the Common Menu. The two elements
have the following dimensions:

- **Accessories Box**

    Width: 628px

    Height: 215px

- **Informational Box**

    Width: 628px

    Height: 395px

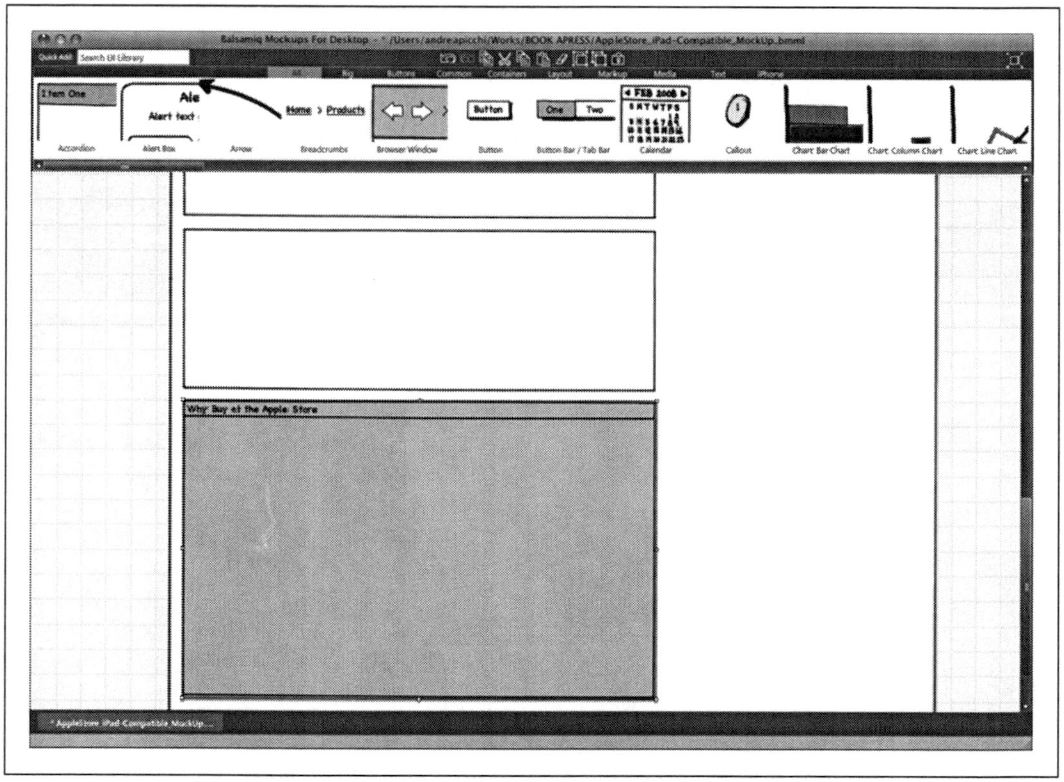

Figure 6–10. *Balsamiq Mockups: The Accessories box and the Informational box*

You are now finished with the content-related part of your design. Now, you need to insert the navigation-related area, and draw the side bar. Using the Rectangle/Canvas/Panel, draw the side bar main header, and add another Rectangle/Canvas/Panel element for the side bar main menu. The two elements have the following dimensions:

- **Side Bar Main Header**

    Width: 340px

    Height: 80px

■ **Side Bar Main Menu**

Width: 340px

Height: 165px

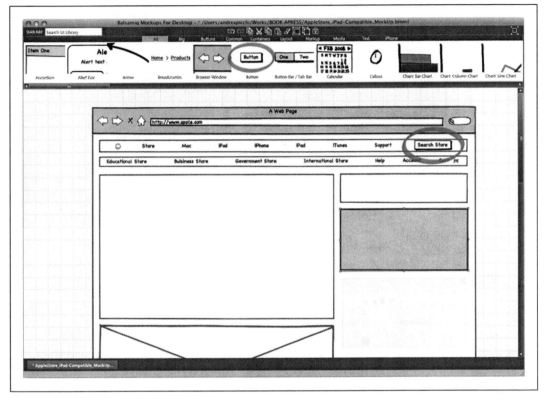

Figure 6–11. *Balsamiq Mockups: The side bar main header, the side bar main menu, and the search engine bar*

Next, the New to the Store box is drawn by using a Dialog/Window element. Below the New to the Store box, in order to design the Popular Accessories box, the two Balsamiq elements are combined. Drag a Rectangle/Canvas/Panel element for the Popular Accessories box header and a Dialog/Window element for the rest of the box, including the side bar subtitle row, plus the side bar content list.

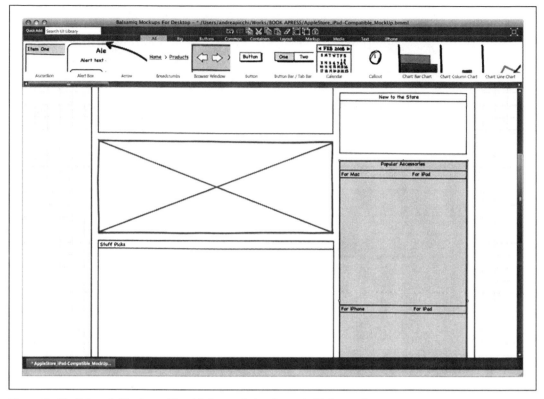

Figure 6–12. *Balsamiq Mockups: The side bar main header and side bar main menu*

In the end, the site information area will have many links. In order to draw these links, select the Text Menu and drag two Label/String of Text elements. Use a Horizontal Rule/Separator element to select the Layout Menu.

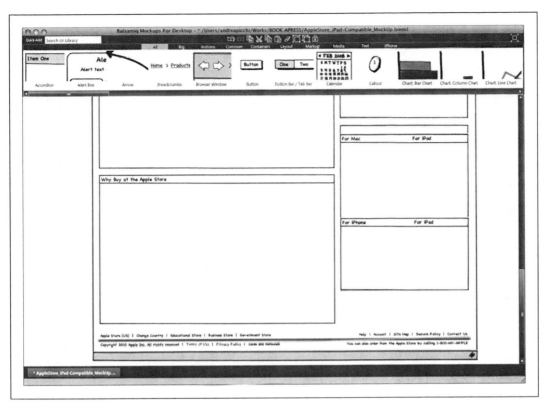

Figure 6–13. *Balsamiq Mockups: The site information area*

The mock up is now ready and can be exported by using Mockup Export Snapshot, and then transferred to a PNG File. For the native-like iPad version, you will need to change your approach, because, so far, there isn't an optimized mockup tool on the market. If you need to mock up a design composition, you can use OmniGraffle. But you need to design a sketch, and it's much better to jump directly inside Adobe Fireworks and merge the sketch and design phase in one single step. This is what you will do for the native-like iPad version in the next section.

Design with Adobe Fireworks

So far, you have sketched both the compatible and native-like iPad versions, but you have mocked up only the compatible one using the Balsamiq Mockups tool. In the next section, you will learn the standard design composition approach for the compatible version, and then, learn how to merge the sketch and design phase using a gray box design for the native-like version.

iPad-Compatible Version

In this section, you will start to work on the compatible version, and then you will present the native-like one, with both versions following the same process used for the iPhone process.

Create a Canvas

Once you've opened Adobe Fireworks, you'll need to create a new document, using File ➤New (⌘N).

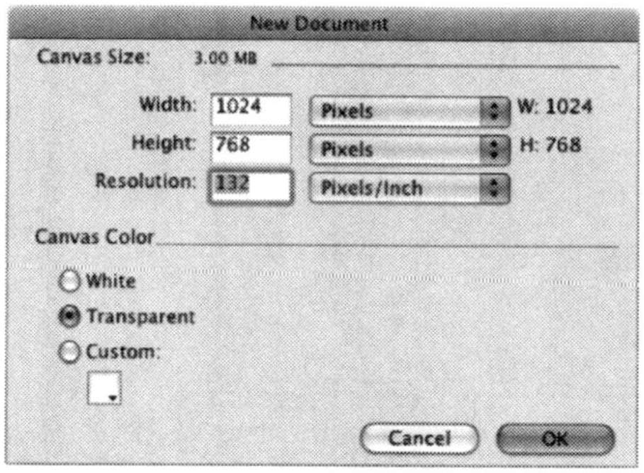

Figure 6–14. *Adobe Fireworks: Create a new document*

Your document should have the following canvas sizes:

- ▧ Width: 768 (px)

- ▧ Height: 1024 (px)

- ▧ Resolution: 132 (ppi)

This canvas, in accordance with the iPad 9.7-inch IPS display, uses a 132-ppi resolution. Remember that the iPhone, with its traditional LCD 3.5 display, uses 163 ppi on the standard display, and a 326–ppi resolution on the Retina display.

> **NOTE:** The IPS (in-plane switching) is an LCD technology that aligns the liquid crystal cells in a horizontal direction. In this method, the electrical field is applied through each end of the crystal, but this requires two transistors for each pixel instead of the single transistor needed for a standard thin-film transistor (TFT) display.
>
> While most older LCD technologies on smartphones have a 35-degree viewing angle, the new IPS display offers the Apple users a viewing angle of up to 180 degrees. This technology can be found in the Apple iMac, iPad, and in the latest iPhone 4 with its Retina display.

The good news about working with the iPad is that you don't have to deal with different display resolutions like with the iPhone—at least not until the next iPad version comes out.

Organize Levels

Your design will be deployed on several levels, so the first thing you'll want to do is create some folders for organizing assets and keeping the working environment clean.

As you know, the iPad and the iPhone run off of the same operating system; the iOS. This means that the user interface elements have different widths and heights but have the same semantic meanings, so the levels of organization of your workspace will look exactly the same, except for an extra folder called Safari, where you will insert the Safari user interface asset.

Based on the semantic approach, you will create the following folders:

- iOS
- Safari
- Branding Area
- Content Area
- Info Area
- Background
- Templates

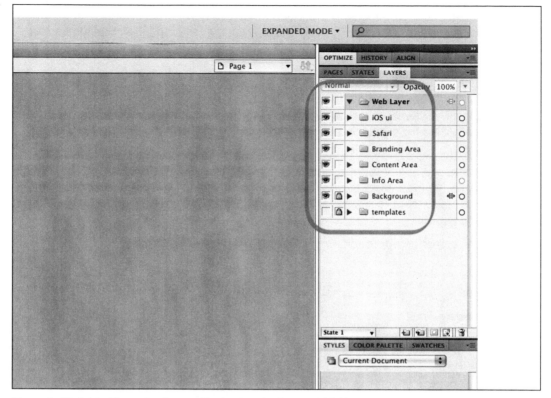

Figure 6–15. *Adobe Fireworks: A semantic structure for the assets' folders*

The last folder is the Template folder, which is used to collect a copy of certain important assets that you can use for the critical part of your design composition.

Layout Design

Now, you will add the Rulers folder for your design composition boundaries. You will draw four lines, but this time, working inside the Safari environment, you will not have a bottom bar, instead, you will have the Safari URL bar.

On the sides, the boundary lines limit a 15px margin, on the top they limit a 20px for the iOS status bar, and on the bottom the limit is 58px for the Safari URL bar. Once you've added the rulers, you can add a background layer, using the Select Rectangle Tool (U).

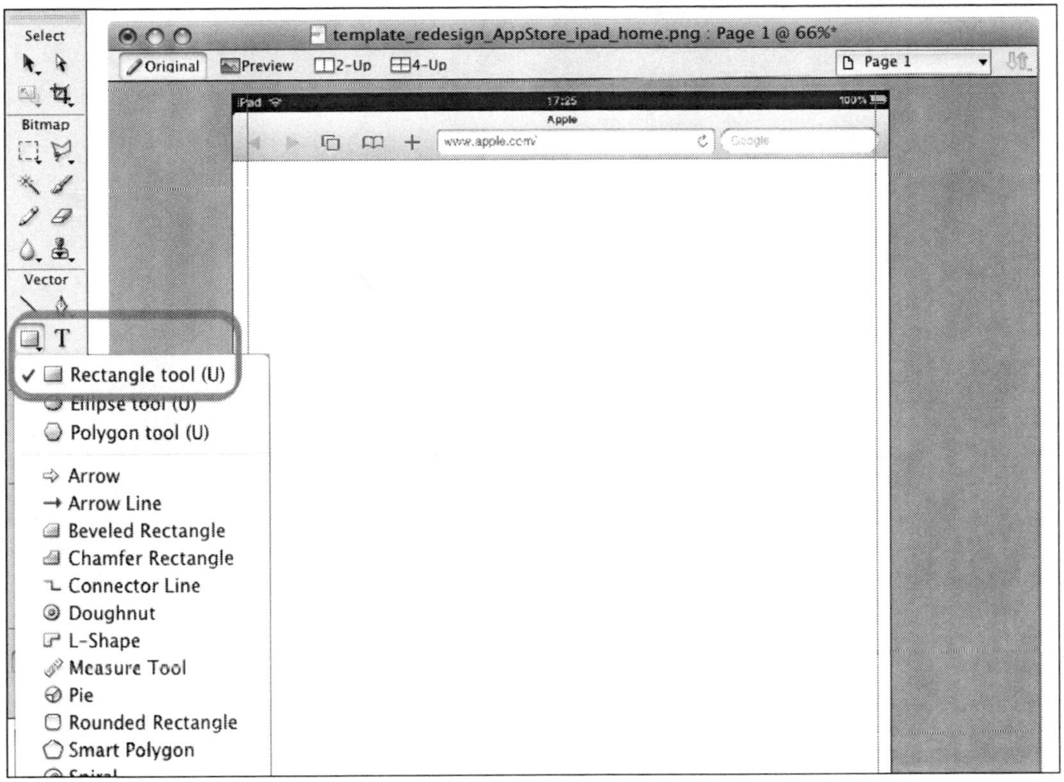

Figure 6–16. *Adobe Fireworks: The visible area and padding rulers*

Now, you'll draw a white rectangle, with the dimensions of 768 x 1024px, in the Background folder. This rectangle will be the basic background color for your canvas, and as you saw with the iPhone version, it will also activate the Align function for the canvas objects.

Now that you've prepared your canvas, everything is ready to start adding the design elements.

Interface Design

Starting at the top, you will design the primary navigation bar (PNB) and the secondary navigation bar (SNB). You will leave 22px of margin on each canvas side, and 20px on the top and bottom. The following elements will be added by using Select Rounded Rectangle:

- **Primary Navigation Bar**

    Width: 980px

    Height: 36px

    Gradient: Linear

Color: #848484, #CACACA

- **Secondary Navigation Bar**

    Width: 980px

    Height: 30px

    Gradient: Linear

    Color: #ECECEC, #F7F7F7

    Border: 1px solid #CBCBCB

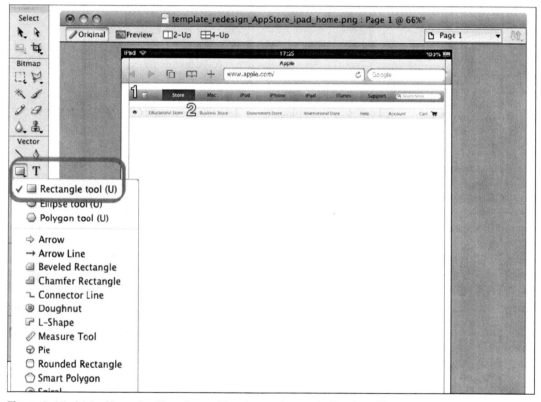

Figure 6–17. *Adobe Fireworks: The primary (1) and secondary navigation bars (2)*

Every single primary navigation bar button has a fixed dimension. It is as follows:

- **Primary Navigation Bar Button**

    Width: 100px

    Height: 36px

    Right Border: 3px (1px + 1px + 1px)

    Height: 36px

The right border of the primary navigation bar button is composed of 3px, and each single pixel is defined as follows:

■ **PNB Right Border Left Vertical Line**

  Gradient: Linear

  Color: #8C8C8C, #CECECE

■ **PNB Right Border Center Vertical Line**

  Gradient: Linear

  Color: #727272, #B6B6B6

■ **PNB Right Border Right Vertical Line**

  Gradient: Linear

  Color: #8C8C8C, #CECECE

Next, add your text by using the Select Text tool (T). The text will be defined as follows:

■ **Navigation Bar Text**

  Font: Myriad Pro, Regular, 16pt

  Color: #262626

  Drop Shadow: 1px solid, #FFFFFF, 270deg

■ **Breadcrumb Bar Text**

  Font: Lucida Grande, Regular, 12pt

  Color: #666666

Moving down in your design, the next area to work on is the content main area. Select the Background Level, and use the rounded rectangle tool (Select Rounded Rectangle) to draw a rectangle in the content background. This is defined as follows:

■ **Content Main Area**

  Width: 628px

  Height: 385px

  Color: #FFFFFF

  Border: 1px solid #CBCBCB

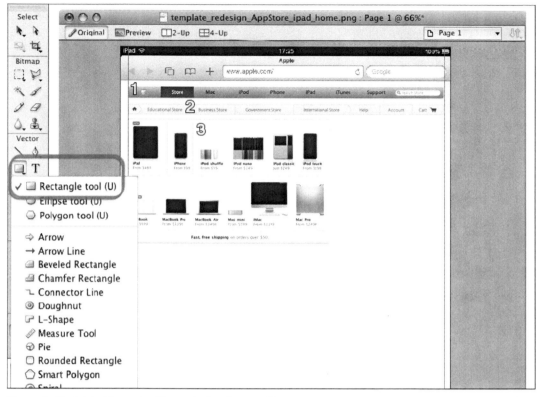

Figure 6–18. *Adobe Fireworks: The content main area (3)*

Below the content main area, draw another rounded rectangle (Select Rounded Rectangle) for the spotlight area. This should be drawn as follows:

- **Spotlight Area**

    Width: 628px

    Height: 250px

    Color: #FFFFFF

    Border: 1px solid #CBCBCB

Below the spotlight area, draw three more rounded rectangles (Select Rounded Rectangle) for the Staff Picks, Accessories, and Information boxes. This should be drawn as follows:

- **Staff Picks Box**

    Width: 628px

    Height: 425px

    Color: #FFFFFF

Border: 1px solid #CBCBCB

- **Accessories Box**

  Width: 628px

  Height: 215px

  Color: #FFFFFF

  Border: 1px solid #CBCBCB

- **Information Box**

  Width: 628px

  Height: 395px

  Color: #FFFFFF

  Border: 1px solid #CBCBCB

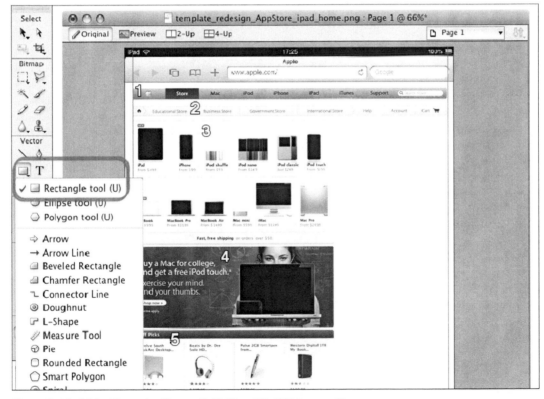

Figure 6–19. *Adobe Fireworks: The spotlight (4) and Staff Picks area (5)*

The height of each box is not very important here because it changes according to the type of content. What is important, in order to keep the same look-and-feel of the desktop version, is to be consistent with the (general) content box header. This is done by using the following values:

- **(General) Content Box Header**

     Width: 628px

     Height: 24px

     Gradient: Linear

     Color: #224272, #5C6F8D

- **Informational Content Box Header**

     Width: 628px

     Height: 24px

     Gradient: Linear

     Color: #999999, #C2C2C2

The text used in the (general) content box header is as follows:

- **(General) Content Box Header Text**

     Font: Lucida Grande, Regular, 12pt

     Color: #FFFFFF

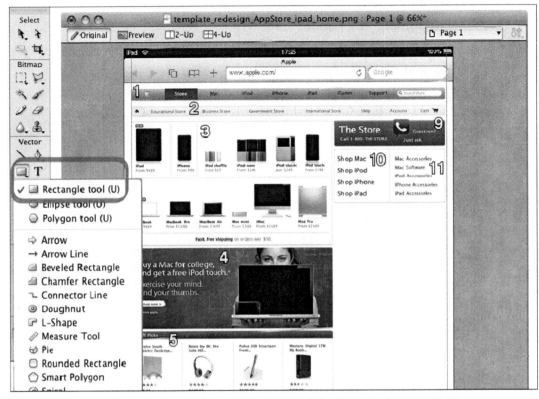

Figure 6-20. *Adobe Fireworks: The side bar main header (9) and the side bar main menu (10-11)*

The next step is to insert the side bar main header by using the Select Rounded Rectangle tool. You'll need to create a rounded rectangle with the following qualifications:

- **Side Bar Main Header**

    Width: 340px

    Height: 80px

- **Gradient: Linear**

    Color: #294876, #5B7396, #A9B5C8

    Border: 1px solid #5E7598

> **NOTE:** For designing a linear gradient with three colors, you will need to add one color to the two offered by the default for Adobe Fireworks. For adding a color, just double-click on the color stripe.

The text used in the side bar main header is as follows:

- **(General) Content Box Header Text**

    Font: Myriad Pro, Regular, 30pt

    Color: #FFFFFF

    Drop Shadow: 1px solid, #3B4C66, 90deg

The side bar main menu is located below the side bar main header. Draw the rounded rectangle, using the rectangle tool (Select Rounded Rectangle) as follows:

- **Side Bar Main Menu**

    Width: 340px

    Height: 165px

    Color: #FFFFFF

    Border: 1px solid #CBCBCB

The text used in the side bar main menu is as follows:

- **Side Bar Main Menu Text Right Column**

    Font: Myriad Pro, Regular, 20pt

    Color: #333333

- **Side Bar Main Menu Text Right Column**

    Font: Myriad Pro, Regular, 16pt

    Color: #333333

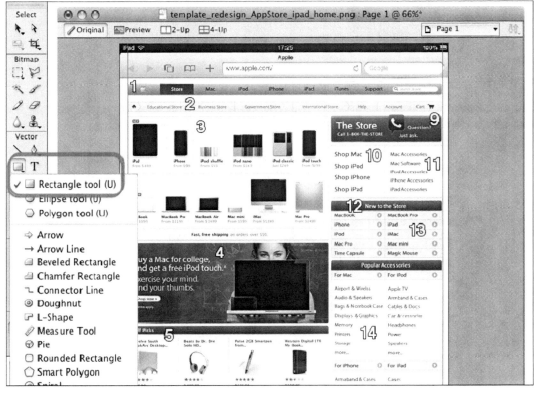

Figure 6-21. *Adobe Fireworks: The side bar content list (14)*

The bottom part of the side bar is composed of three more boxes: the New to the Store, the Popular Accessories, and the Top Sellers boxes. Every box is composed of three parts (except for the New to the Store box, which is composed of two parts), identified as follows:

- **Side Bar Box Header**

    Gradient: Linear

    Color: #224272, #5C6F8D

    Font: Myriad Pro, Regular, 18pt, #FFFFFF

- **Side Bar Sub Title Row**

    Color: #EFEFEF

    Border: 1px solid #CBCBCB

    Font: Myriad Pro, Regular, 16pt

    Icon: Circle, 16px

- **Side Bar Content List**

    Color: #FFFFFF

    Border: 1px solid #CBCBCB

    Font: Myriad Light, Regular, 16pt

The last element of your design is the information area. This area is not wrapped inside a box and shows some general information concerning the following text:

- **Site Information Area Text**

    Font: Myriad Pro, Regular, 12pt

    Color: #999999

- **Site Information Area Link**

    Font: Myriad Pro, Regular, 12pt

    Color: #0085CF

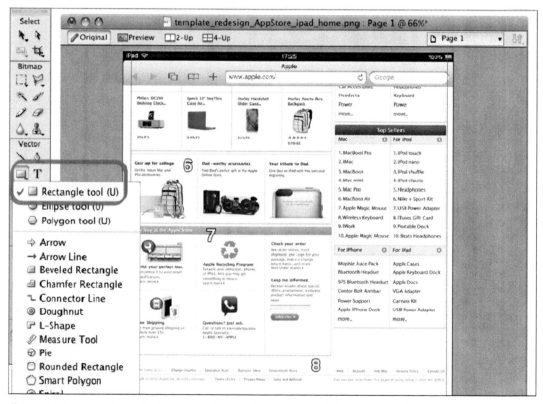

Figure 6–22. *Adobe Fireworks: The Information box (7) and the site information area (8)*

The design composition is complete when your compatible version is complete. Once everything is complete, you are ready to start to work on your native-like version.

iPad Native-Like Version

The canvas values and the workspace organization are the same as the ones you saw for the compatible version. Nothing will change in your design composition setup. What will change is the canvas dimension, because you will have to switch from a portrait orientation to a landscape orientation.

Create a Canvas

Once you've opened Adobe Fireworks, you'll need to create a new document, using **File ➤ New (⌘N)**.

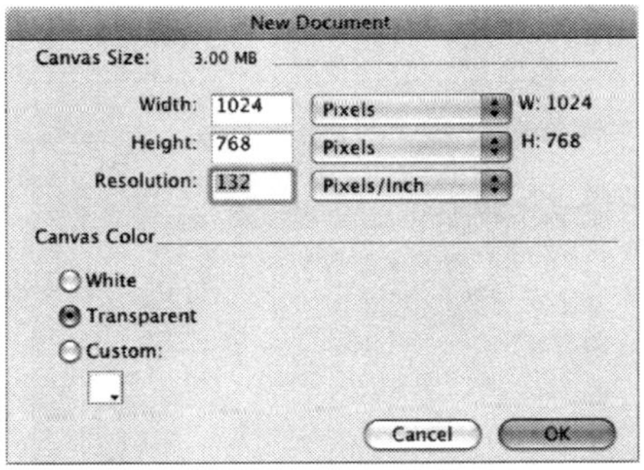

Figure 6–23. *Adobe Fireworks: Create a new document*

Your document should have the following canvas sizes:

■ Width: 1024px

■ Height: 960px

■ Resolution: 132ppi

Gray Box Design

The gray box design will represent your paper sketch-up, and will be the foundation for your design composition. This is another approach to the design phase. The final goal is a design composition for both approaches; every approach is subjective, and it's up to you (or your team) to choose the one to use.

Figure 6–24 shows you that you are reserving 78px in your composition of the browser window, and also shows you how to use the rectangle tool (Select Rectangle Tool (U)) to design the side bar header and content header. The side bar header and the content header should meet the following qualifications:

■ **Side Bar Header**

   Width: 300px

   Height: 44px

Color: #999999

Text: Helvetica, Bold, 20pt

Text Shadow: 1px solid, #333333, 270deg

- **Content Main Header**

    Width: 724px (723px Content + 1px Left Border)

    Height: 44px

    Color: #999999

    Text: Helvetica, Bold, 20pt

    Text Shadow: 1px solid, #333333, 270deg

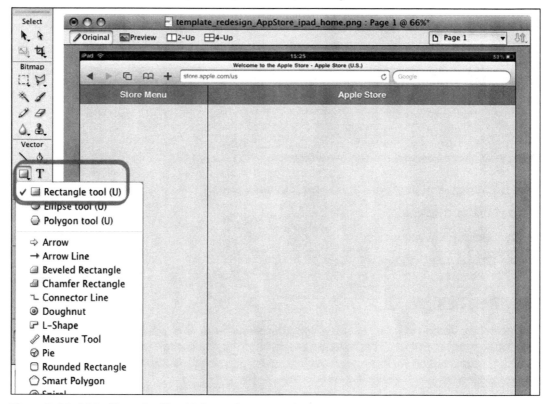

Figure 6–24. *Adobe Fireworks: The side bar and content main header*

Two areas of your design have now been allocated, so you can start to use the side bar to add elements. Using the rectangle tool (Select Rectangle Tool (U)), add nine entries from Menu elements and two menu titles that adhere to the following requirements:

- **Menu Entry**

    Width: 300px

    Height: 44px

    Color: #999999

    Bottom Border: 1px solid, #ADADAD (Last Element #666666)

- **Menu Title**

    Width: 300px

    Height: 26px

    Color: #999999

    Top Border: 1px solid, #CCCCCC

    Bottom Border: 1px solid, #666666

    Text: Helvetica, Bold, 18pt

    Text Shadow: 1px solid, #333333, 270deg

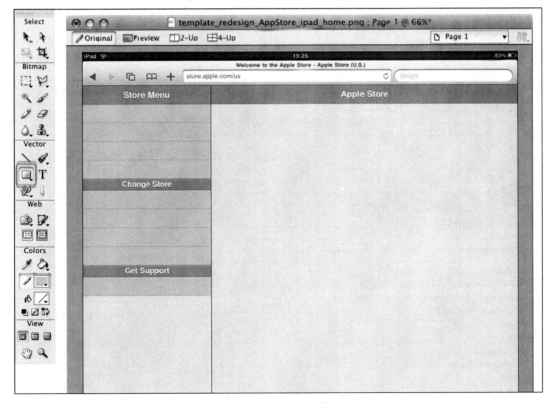

Figure 6–25. *Adobe Fireworks: The side bar menu elements and titles*

The side bar is now finished, and you can now jump to the content main area in the other column. Using the rounded rectangle tool (Select Rounded Rectangle), design the Hero box, the Products box, and the Site Information box, so that they look like the following:

- **Hero Box**

    Width: 644px

    Height: 237px

    Border: 1px solid, #666666

- **Products Box**

    Width: 644px

    Height: 402px

    Border: 1px solid, #666666

- **Site Information Box**

    Width: 644px

    Height: 62px

    Border: 1px solid, #666666

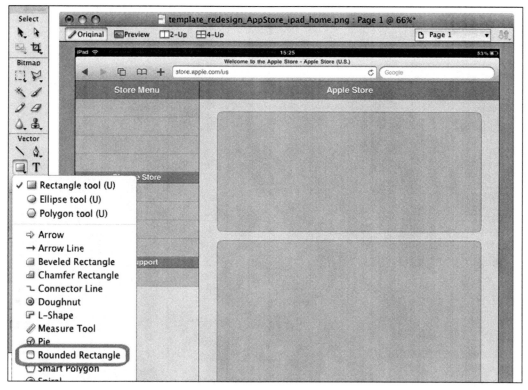

Figure 6–26. *Adobe Fireworks: The Hero box and the Products box*

Figure 6–27 illustrates the final gray box that you will use as a foundation for your design composition. Since the structure was already made in the design phase, you will just need to change the element colors, and add texts, icons, and images.

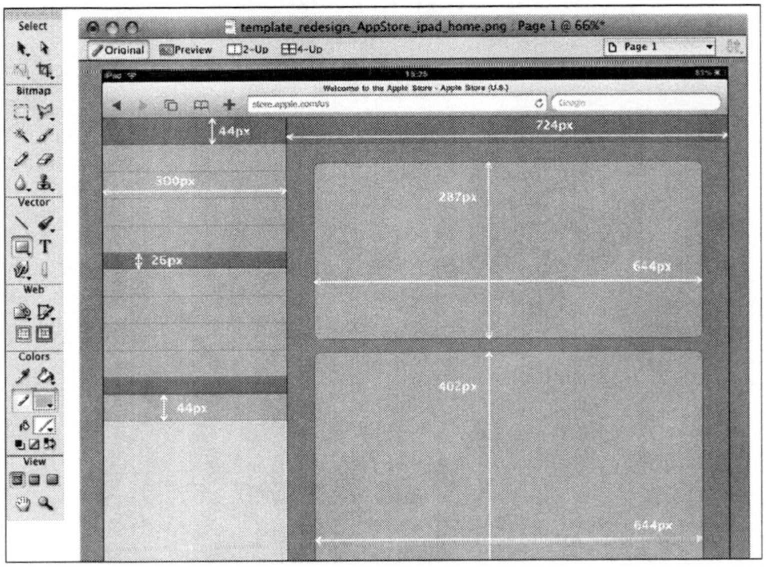

Figure 6–27. *Adobe Fireworks: The gray box design dimensions*

The next step is starting the design composition by organizing the workspace and creating the folders for your assets.

Organize Levels

The workspace will use the same folders, levels, and hierarchy. Based on a semantic approach, you will create the following folders:

- iOS
- Safari
- Branding Area
- Content Area
- Info Area
- Background
- Templates

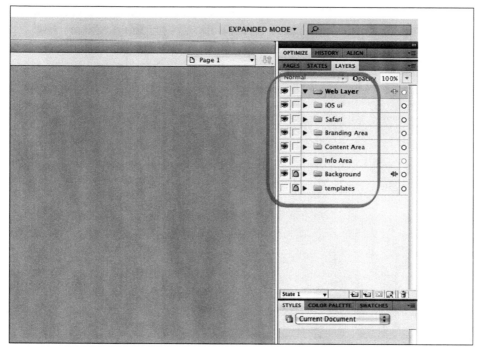

Figure 6–28. *Adobe Fireworks: A semantic structure for the assets' folders*

Layout Design

Now that the gray box is ready, you can add another folder, called Rulers, to your design composition boundaries. Select this folder (layer), and draw four red lines using the line tool (Select Line Tool (N)). The three lines will set the browser window boundary and the 20px padding boundary for the content main area.

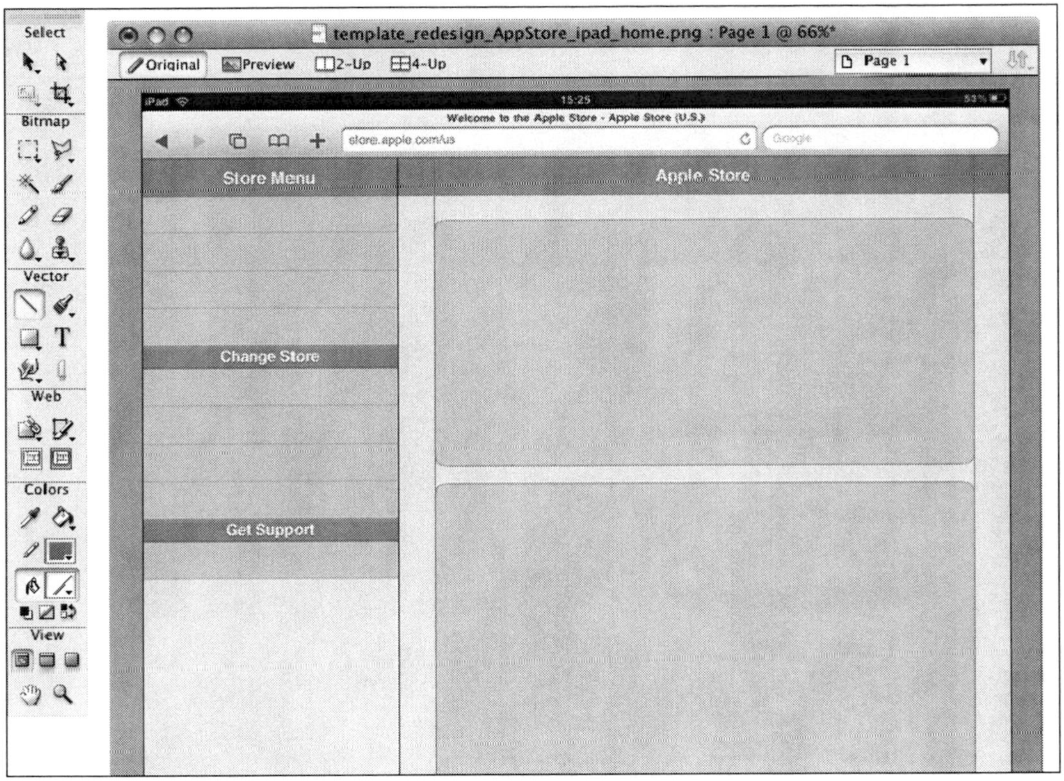

Figure 6–29. *Adobe Fireworks: The gray box design with the rulers*

Due to the gray box design, your work will now be easier. You will no longer need to design any other elements but just change its color. Starting from the side bar, you will change the element colors to the following:

- **Side Bar Area**

  - Background: #FFFFFF

- **Side Bar Header (Store Menu)**

  - Gradient: Linear

  - Color: #294876, #F4F5F7

- **Menu Title (Change Store, Get Support)**

  - Border Top: 1px solid, #CCCCCC

  - Border Bottom: 1px solid, #666666

- **Menu Entry (Generic Menu Element)**

  - Color: #FFFFFF

  - Border Top: 1px solid, #F0F0F0

    ■   Border Bottom: 1px solid, #D1D1D1 (last entry #666666)

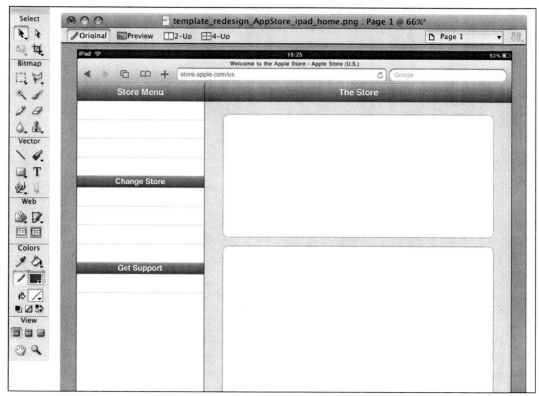

Figure 6–30. *Adobe Fireworks: The colored design without the contents*

Continuing with the content side, you will change the element colors to the following:

    ■ **Content Area**

        Background: #E1E6EB

    ■ **Content Box (Hero Box, Products Box, Site Information Box)**

        Color: #F7F7F7

        Border: 1px solid, #828282

Everything is now ready for the content. In the side bar, start to add the text entry and an icon to its left side, as follows:

    ■ **Menu Entry Icon & Text**

        Width: "variable following the icon design"

        Height: 34px

        Text: Helvetica, Bold, 16pt

The side bar is complete, so now you can jump to the content main area, and add the following text in the three boxes

- **Hero Box**

    Title Text: Helvetica, Bold, 50pt, #000000

    SubTitle Text: Helvetica, Bold, 20pt, #000000

- **Products Box**

    Description Text: Lucida Grande, Bold, 11pt, #000000

    Price Text: Lucida Grande, Bold, 11pt, #666666

- **Site Information Box**

    Text: Lucida Grande, Bold, 10pt, #999999

    Link: Lucida Grande, Bold, 10pt, #0085CF

- **Footer Apple Logo**

    Width: "variable following the icon design"

    Height: 20px

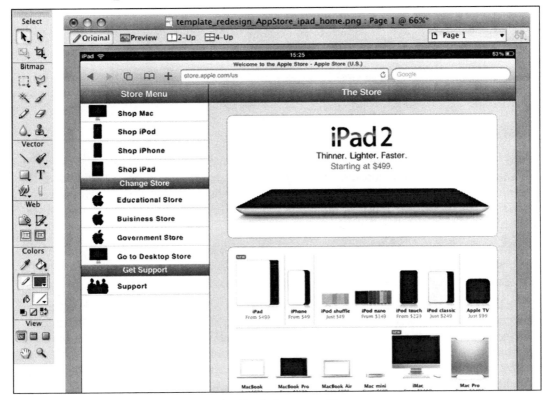

Figure 6–31. *Adobe Fireworks: The final native-like design composition*

Apart from the dimensions of the menu icons that are a part of the layout structure, the image dimensions are related to the content's meaning and can be changed without affecting the global structure. This is the main reason why these design element dimensions weren't reported.

The design compositions are complete. You have everything necessary to advance to the next big step of your project flow; the implementation phase. In Chapter 7, you will start introducing the three languages that are used in this book: HTML, CSS3, and JavaScript.

Tools for User Interface Design

The tools used (and not used but suggested) in this chapter are both physical tools and applications. Table 6–1 lists some of the useful tools for designing your next user interface.

Table 6–1. *Tools Used for Designing iPhone and iPad User Interfaces*

Name	Type	URL	Operative system
UI Stencil	Tool	www.uistencils.com/	- - -
OmniGraffle Pro	Application	www.balsamiq.com/	OSX - iOS
Adobe Design Suite	Application	www.adobe.com/products/creativesuite/design/	OSX – WIN - LINUX
Gimp	Application	www.gimp.org/	OSX – WIN - LINUX

Summary

In the first part of this chapter, you analyzed the interface design process, and presented the anatomy of sketching and the "think simple" paradigm. The iPhone's limitations, the iPhone's page model, and how cognitive resources influence your design style were all discussed. How all three of these elements are the foundation of the "think simple" design paradigm was also discussed.

In the second part of this chapter, the Balsamiq Mockups tool was used to improve the basic sketch made with pen and paper. The content, an interface connection, and the first visual representation of the concept design were all created.

In the third part of this chapter, Adobe Fireworks was used to design a user interface. This process was approached step-by-step, from the creation of a new canvas to the interface design. At the end of the process, design reuse for creating two more views or pages from the presented home page was introduced, and a visual representation of the interface-content relationship as a deliverable for the implementation phase was also introduced.

## Chapter 7

Web Standards for WebKit: Maximizing Mobile Safari

"It's not just what it looks like and feels like..
Design is how it works."

—Steve Jobs

In this rather long chapter, we talk about web standards from a mobile Safari point of view. In the first part, we introduce HTML5, its markup syntax, its new tags, and how it has redefined some tags from HTML4. We discuss the semantics of HTML5 and the `<video>` and `<audio>` tags. We also introduce the `<canvas>` tag, and at the end of this section, we show a live example of a slideshow implemented in the "Store" use case.

In the second part, we look at CSS Level3, its new properties, and its syntax. We enumerate all of the values that can be used with these new properties.

In the last part of the chapter, we discuss Javascript's fundamentals: its syntax, statements, functions, and methods. We also look at the Browser Object Model (BOM) and the Document Object Model (DOM), and we show how you can use these to change a webpage dynamically.

> **NOTE:** This chapter covers the basics of each technology area, so if you are confident in HTML5, CSS3, and Javascript, feel free to skip to the next chapter, or to the relevant section in this chapter, for a refresher on those areas in which you are rusty.

Comparing iPhone and iPad for Web Presentation

As discussed previously, the iPhone and iPad are two different devices. One common denominator between these two devices is their HTML5 semantic structure.

What is different in these two devices is how they present the content represented in our projects by two different CSS3 style sheets and Javascript behavior. The iPhone is based on a **Page Model Paradigm,** whereas the iPad is based on a **Block Model Paradigm**, or a Multiple Page Model Paradigm.

In this chapter, we look at how the web standards play a common role behind these differences and how to use them to develop better web sites and web applications.

HTML5

The physicist Tim Berners-Lee developed the Hypertext Markup Language (HTML) in 1989 while he was working at Organisation Européenne pour la Recherche Nucléaire (CERN).

In 1991, HTML was mentioned publicly for the first time and in 1995, it reached the 2.0 version. HTML passed through the 3.2 and 4.0 versions in 1997 and reached the well known 4.0.1 version in 1999. Work on HTML5 started in 2004 and will reach the status of "proposed recommendation" version, which is scheduled for 2022.

The 2022 date might sound too far away for designers and developers, but we can focus ourselves on what we can do with this language today. In 2012, HTML5 will reach the status of candidate recommendation, which means that some of the most interesting features such as audio, video, and canvas tags, web workers, geolocation, application caches, and the HTML5 semantic tags are currently available and can be used.

We introduce application caches in Chapter 10, but the following sections introduce the foundation of this new web standard.

HTML5 Markup Syntax

A markup language is designed for the processing, definition, and presentation of text; the codes used to specify the formatting are called *tags*. HTML5 defines an HTML markup syntax that is compatible with HTML4 and XHTML1; most of HTML4.0.1 has survived in HTML5.

HTML5 is designed to be the successor to HTML4 and aims to improve interoperability and reduce development costs by making precise rules on how to handle all HTML elements, and for the first time for a markup language, on how to recover from errors. Error handling is not as important for web designers and web developers as it is for browser makers and testers.

Those who have used XHTML know that XHTML forced us to use XML syntax, with quotes on all the attributes, closed tags, and lowercase code. Everything is valid code in HTML5: uppercase, lowercase, quotes, no quotes, self-closing tags or not, and so on. This attitude brings us back to the late '90s where, before XHTML 1.0, this non-rule produced the worst HTML code ever seen since Berners-Lee turned on his first server in 1989.

As you might understand, we don't like the looseness of the HTML5 syntax and encourage bringing an XHTML-like clean style to HTML5—even more if you work in a team where consistency is important at every level.

A new approach in HTML5 embraces the *deprecated element*. In past HTML versions, the designer or developer was advised to not use deprecated elements in code and browsers didn't include deprecated elements in their specifications. Because HTML5 aims to be backwards compatible, instead of declaring an element as deprecated and deleting it from its specification, it declares it as obsolete, maintaining the rendering element rules in its specification. We can define this type of approach as user-friendly or user experience oriented because, from HTML5 on, if an HTML5 compatible browser encounters an *obsolete element*, it will still be able to render it and offer a higher level of user experience.

We can also notice how, in many areas, the new HTML5 syntax is simplicity driven. The doctype declaration is a good example of this attitude. We compare the iWebKit Framework 5.0.4 XHTML and the new HTML5 doctype declaration in the following code:

```
<!-- XHTML DocType -->
<!DOCTYPE html PUBLIC "-//W3C//DTD XHTML 1.0 Strict//EN"
"http://www.w3.org/TR/xhtml1/DTD/xhtml1-strict.dtd">

<!-- HTML5 DocType -->
<!DOCTYPE html>
```

We can see how the new doctype declaration is simpler. This approach also simplifies the character encoding declaration, where the `charset` attribute is the only attribute necessary to specify UTF-8 encoding. The next example shows the new HTML5 character encoding declaration syntax compared with the old (and still allowed) HTML4.0.1 used for the iWebKit Framework 5.0.4.

```
<!-- XHTML DocType -->
<meta content="text/html; charset=utf-8" http-equiv="Content-Type" />

<!-- HTML5 DocType -->
<meta charset="UTF-8">
```

This evolution also brings about a change in the syntax of the most representative tag in the whole HTML history—the one that turned our text into hypertext: the <a> tag. The (X)HTML specifics implement the <a> tag as an inline element, forcing us to use multiple tags every time we need to create a headline. In HTML5, the <a> tag is still an inline tag with the difference that, in HTML5, nesting block level elements are no longer invalid.

The following code is an example of the <a> tag in (X)HTML and in HTML5.

```
<!-- (X)HTML <a> Tag -->
<h2><a href="/portfolio.html">Portfolio</a></h2>
<p><a href="/portfolio.html">Find out more about my last Book.</a></p>

<!-- HTML5 <a> Tag -->
<a href="/portfolio.html">
<h2>Portfolio</h2>
<p>Find out more about my last Book.</p>
</a>
```

As you might have noticed, HTML5 is more evolutionary rather than revolutionary, and it does not dramatically change the story of markup.

HTML5 Re-Definitions

Although many HTML4 elements have been brought into HTML5 essentially unchanged, several historically presentational ones have been given semantic meanings (Figure 7–1). The WC3's HTML5 recommendation redefines the elements shown in Table 7–1.

Table 7–1. *Video Tags Attributes in HTML5 (Ordered Alphabetically)*

Tag	HTML4 Definition	HTML5 Definition
`<i>`	Italic	Span of text offset from its surrounding content without conveying any extra emphasis or importance, and for which the conventional typographic presentation is italic text
`<b>`	Bold	Span of text offset from its surrounding content without conveying any extra emphasis or importance, and for which the conventional typographic presentation is bold text
`<em>`	Emphasis	Span of text with emphatic stress
`<strong>`	Strong emphasis	Span of text with strong importance

HTML5 Semantics

Besides the few new syntax rules introduced so far, the most notable feature embraces the tag's semantic. HTML5 has a natural semantic-oriented attitude and enables developers to create cross-platform design through expressing the content more semantically. To achieve this, HTML5 introduces some new tags, such as `<header>`, `<nav>`, `<section>`, `<aside>`, and `<footer>`, to structure our web site or web application and render the content more machine-readable and therefore make it easier for the mobile browser and search engine to treat content properly.

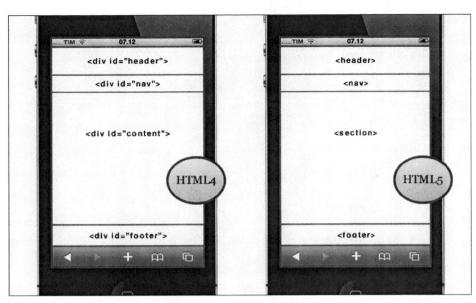

Figure 7–1. *HTML4 and HTML5 comparison in two simple iPhone page structures*

HTML5 also introduces a few new inline elements such as <mark>, <time>, <meter>, and <progress> that, with the previous elements (such as <strong>, <em>, <span>, and so on), are renamed from "inline" to "text-level semantics." In Table 7–2, we alphabetically list all the new tags in HTML5. These tags are added to the previous, supported, and non-deprecated tags from (X)HTML specifics. Some of the new media tags are introduced in the next section.

Table 7–2. *New Tags in HTML5 (Ordered Alphabetically)*

HTML5 STRUCTURE TAGS

Name	Description
<article>	Defines an article
<aside>	Defines content aside from the page content
<command>	Defines a command button
<datalist>	Defines a drop-down list
<details>	Defines details of an element
<figcaption>	Defines the caption of a figure element
<figure>	Defines a group of media content, and its captions
<footer>	Defines a footer for a section or page

Name	Description
<header>	Defines a header for a section or page
<hgroup>	Defines information about a section in a document
<keygen>	Defines a generated key in a form
<mark>	Defines marked text
<meter>	Defines measurement within a predefined range
<nav>	Defines navigation links
<output>	Defines some types of output
<progress>	Defines progress of a task of any kind
<rp>	Used in Ruby annotation for the benefit of browsers that don't support Ruby annotation
<rt>	Defines explanation to ruby annotation
<ruby>	Defines ruby annotation
<section>	Defines a section
<summary>	Defines the header of a "detail" element
<time>	Defines a date/time

HTML5 MEDIA TAGS

Name	Description
<audio>	Defines audio content
<canvas>	Defines graphics
<embed>	Defines external interactive content or plug-in
<source>	Defines a media resource
<video>	Defines a video

HTML5 Media

Web standards such as XHTML, CSS, and Javascript provide us everything we need to publish text and images and they add interaction to our projects. The problem comes when we are working with audio and video. In order to insert audio and video contents, we used to rely on external plug-ins like Adobe Flash. HTML5 fills this gap by introducing new tags to embed audio and video without requiring external plug-ins.

The Video Tag

The new `<video>` tag is by far the most famous tag in the HTML5 list, because of the well-known controversy between Apple and Adobe about Flash technology support. It enables us to play a video in our web site or web application directly in the browser. This feature is valid only for the desktop browser. In an iPhone or iPad environment, the video is not a real embedded video because it doesn't play directly in the browser.

iOS always launches the built-in media player, which occupies the full screen, where the user can use the Done button to return to the web site or web application. The `<video>` tag structure used for the TV Ads page of our "The Store" use-case is the following:

```
... ... ...

<div id="heroTvads">

        <video width="100%" height="148" src="videos/iphone_facetime.mp4" controls
poster="pics/poster-facetime.jpg"></video>
</div>

... ... ...
```

The `controls` attribute tells the browser whether it has to show the video controls, and the `poster` attribute is an image used as a placeholder for the video. Not only is it a good practice to always add the control attribute to the <video> tag, it must be remembered that Safari Mobile ignores the control attribute. Controls are always visible, and the true/false attribute is not required (even on Safari Desktop). Another important behavior to remember about the <video> tag is that the autoplay attribute is ignored by Safari on iOS.

The `<video>` tag can be styled through CSS like every other HTML5 element. In the example we use only four attributes, but this new tag has many other attributes that help us to offer a more rich experience to our user. In Table 7–3 we show each `<video>` attribute with its related description.

Table 7–3. *Video Tag Attributes in HTML5 (Ordered Alphabetically)*

Attribute	Value	Description
audio	muted	Defines the default state of the audio
autoplay (*)	true | false	Boolean value for automatically play the file
controls (*)	true | false	Boolean value for display the audio controls
end	numeric value	Defines the endpoint of a video (if it's not defined, the video plays to the end)
height	pixels	Defines the height of the video player
loop	true | false	Boolean value for repeatedly play the file
loopend	numeric value	Defines the ending point of a loop
loopstart	numeric value	Defines the starting point of a loop
playcount	numeric value	Defines the number of times a video clip is played (default value is set to 1)
poster	src	Defines the URL of a "poster image" to show before the video begins to play
preload	true | false	Boolean value for load the video when the page loads
src	url	Defines the URL of the video file
start	numeric value	Defines the startpoint of a video (if it's not defined, the video starts from the beginning)
width	pixels	Defines the width of the video player

(*) ignored by Safari Mobile on iOS

Table 7–4 shows the video formats supported by iOS.

Table 7–4. *Video Formats Supported by iOS*

Video Format	Profile
H.264	Up to 720p, 30 fps
MPEG-4	Up to 2.5 Mbps, 640x480 px
M-JPG	Up to 35 Mbps, 1280x720 px

The Audio Tag

The <audio> tag is the other important media tag introduced in HTML5. It enables us to play audio files with a native audio playback within the browser. The <audio> tag works in the same way as the <video> tag, although its attributes are a subset of the <video> tag. The <audio> tag has the following structure:

```
<audio src="audioName.mp3" controls autobuffer></audio>
```

In this example, we use one attribute to show the audio control to the user and one attribute to buffer the audio file in advance. Like some of the <video> attributes, these are Boolean attributes that don't have a value to specify, as shown in the following example:

```
// (X)HTML5 syntax
<audio src="audioName.mp3" controls="true" autobuffer="true"></audio>
// HTML5 syntax
<audio src="audioName.mp3" controls autobuffer></audio>
```

If you prefer an XML-like syntax, you can specify the attribute value, but it isn't necessary. All of the attributes defined for the <audio> tag are reported in Table 7–5.

Table 7–5. *Audio Tag Attributes in HTML5 (Ordered Alphabetically)*

Attribute	Description
autobuffer	Boolean value to buffer the file in advance
autoplay	Boolean value to automatically play the file
controls	Boolean value to display the audio controls
loop	Boolean value to repeatedly play the file
loopend	Defines the ending point of a loop
loopstart	Defines the starting point of a loop
playcount	Boolean value to load the video when the page loads
src	Defines the URL of the audio file
start	Defines the startpoint of a video (if it's not defined, the video starts from the beginning)

Table 7.6 shows the audio formats supported by iOS.

Table 7–6. *Audio Format Supported by iOS*

Audio Format	Profile
AAC	8-320 Kbps
HE-ACC	8-320 Kbps
MP3	8-320 Kbps
MP3 VBR	- - -
Audible	- - -
Audible Enhanced Audio	- - -
AAX, AAX+	- - -
Apple Lossless	- - -
AIFF	- - -
WAV	- - -

The Canvas Tag

The <audio> and <video> tags are two of the most important tags in the evolution of HTML5, and we use these tags often in our Web Site or Web application. The <canvas> tag represents a huge step forward in graphic capabilities for the web, as it enables Web developers to build many of the same events and effects that native applications have had for years. In spite of the downside of a GPU overhead, we can use dynamic images to save bandwidth and reduce image loading latency.

HTML Canvas vs. SVG; Pixels vs. Vectors

HTML5 Canvas and Scalable Vector Graphics (SVG) are both web technologies that enable us to create rich graphics in the browser, but they are fundamentally different from each other.

The HTML5 Canvas specification is a Javascript API that enables us to code programmatic drawing operations. Canvas, by itself, enables a web developer to define a canvas context object, which can then be drawn. We can also insert images (for example, .png or .jpg) and anything else the browser is capable of loading.

To do the actual drawing, you have two options:

- 2D drawing context
- 3D drawing context

On the other hand, SVG is an XML-based vector graphics format. SVG content can be static or it can be dynamic, interactive, and animated. With SVG, we can do more than simple vector graphics and animations; we can develop highly interactive WebApps with scripting, advanced animation events, and filters.

SVG is still in the process of being optimized for even closer integration with HTML and CSS in the browser. SVG 1.1 is a W3C Recommendation and is, at the time of this writing, the most recent version of the full specification. Besides SVG 1.1, we have SVG Tiny 1.2 (www.w3.org/TR/SVGTiny12/), which is also a W3C Recommendation that targets mobile devices. We can follow the SVG roadmap at www.w3.org/Graphics/SVG/WG/wiki/Roadmap.

The HTML Canvas and SVG also represent a good alternative to Adobe Flash on iOS devices. For this reason, we hope that the future web, based on open HTML5 standards, will fully accommodate SVG.

HTML Canvas and SVG Comparison

At first glance, Canvas and SVG appear to be different techniques that achieve the same thing; however, several important differences exist between the two. Table 7–7 shows some of these.

Table 7–7. *Differences between HTML Canvas and SVG*

HTML Canvas	SVG
Drawing is done with pixels	Drawing is done with vectors
Elements are drawn programmatically	Elements are part of page's DOM
High performance for pixel-based operations	High accessibility because of XML syntax foundation
Animation is not built in	Animation and effects are built-in

HTML Canvas and SVG are not mutually exclusive, and we can find good ways to use them together in the same web page (for example, canvas as background with SVG on top); we can draw SVG on a canvas or vice versa. Here's a list of some of the advantages and disadvantages of HTML Canvas and SVG.

HTML Canvas

Advantages

- High 2D drawing performance
- Constant performance level on fixed canvas dimensions
- Option of saving the resulting images as png or jpg

Disadvantages

- No DOM nodes for drawn elements
- No animation API
- Poor text-rendering capabilities

SVG (Scalable Vector Graphics)

Advantages

- Resolution independent
- Built-in animation support
- Full control of each element using SVG DOM API

Disadvantages

- Introduce (DOM) rendering latency

In terms of practice implementations, the bottom line is that, other than in an HTML Canvas+SVG approach (as in game applications where we can render raster graphics dynamically using canvas and animate them with SVG), HTML Canvas should be used to generate raster graphics. SVG, on the other hand, should be used for resolution-independent user interfaces and highly interactive animations.

The Canvas Element

The HTML Canvas element provides web pages with a place (a canvas) where, using Javascript code, a Web developer can draw free-form graphics of all kinds, such as lines, shapes, images, and even texts on-the-fly. The downside is that once we draw something in the <canvas>, they become part of the page's DOM and the Javascript engine forgets them.

A web page can have more than one <canvas>, and these can overlap and be used beside other standards like SVG. When we draw an object in the <canvas>, the coordinate system starts at the upper left, with increasing value of x going from left to right and increasing value of y from top to bottom, as shown in Figure 7–2.

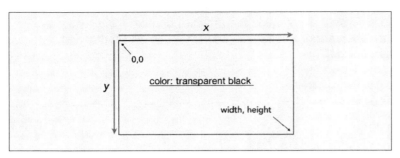

Figure 7–2. *The starting Canvas coordinate system and background color*

The following code shows the basic canvas syntax and attributes:

```
<canvas id="heroCanvas width="460" height="300">
        Fallback Content
</audio>
```

The <canvas> tag typically has an ID attribute because Javascript uses it to access the drawing area. The default <canvas> dimensions are 300x150, but we can set them using width and height attributes in the tag.

If the user has disabled the Javascript engine and the browser doesn't understand what the <canvas> tag is, the Fallback Content will be displayed. In this particular case, even the width and height attributes are ignored; to avoid this problem, we can set width and height using CSS in order to keep the design behavior unchanged.

```
#canvasHero
{
        display: inline-block;   // only on non-floated element
        height: 300px;
        width: 460px;
}
```

Table 7–8. *The HTML Canvas Basic Attributes and Methods*

Attribute	Description
width	Width in pixels of the canvas
height	Height in pixels of the canvas
Methods	**Description**
toDataURL(type)	Convert the content into static image
getContext(ctxID)	Get the drawing context

The toDataURL() method in Table 7–8 converts the content of the image into a static image, typically .png. In the HTML Canvas specifications, only image/.png support is mandatory but other formats can be supported.

The getContext() method in Table 7–8 retrieves the drawing context for the canvas. This context contains information about the canvas and provides all the drawing methods for that particular context.

```
<html>
<head>
        <title>Canvas Test</title>
        <style type="text/css">
                #canvasTest01 {
                        border: solid 2px black;
                        background-color: #CCC;
                }
        </style>
</head>
<body>

        <h1>Canvas Example 01</h1>
<canvas id="canvasTest01" width="300" height="200">
        Please Enable Javascript Engine
</canvas>
</body>
</html>
```

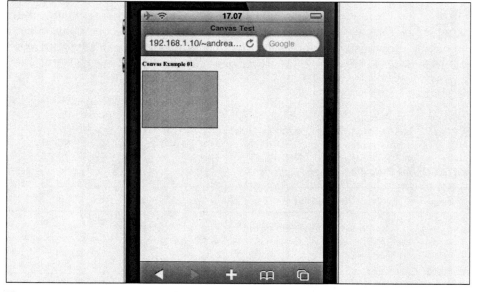

Figure 7–3. *The HTML 2D API in action: drawing a basic shape using Canvas and CSS*

Basic Shapes and Lines

In the first example shown in Figure 7–3, we see how to draw the canvas using CSS. Now, let's move to the next level and see how we can use Javascript to affect the way the canvas looks in the browser. Drawing on a <canvas> requires the following steps:

1. Retrieve a reference to Canvas element.

2. Get the drawing context from the element using getContext().

3. If the getContext returned result is not null we can use the drawing API.

An example of this approach is the following example:

```
<canvas id="canvasTest" width="300" height="200">
        Please Enable Javascript Engine
</canvas>
        function drawOnCanvas() {
                var ctxElement = document.getElementById("canvasTest");
                var ctx = ctxElement.getContext("2d");
                if (ctx != null) {
                        // we can draw using Canvas 2D API
                }
}
```

We define a function and in the body function we retrieve the reference to the canvas that we stored in the variable ctxElement, and then we make a request for the 2D API. If the result of the test is not null, we can draw using the 2D API.

The 2D Canvas API provides several methods and is broken up into three groups, as shown in Figure 7–4.

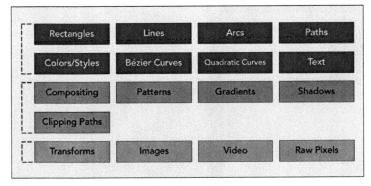

Figure 7–4. *The HTML 2D API divided into three groups*

In the next example, we see how to fill the rectangle using a method from the 2D API. First, we get a reference for the canvas element using the getElementById method, and we make a request for the 2D API exactly as in the previous example. Then, we fill the rectangle using the fillStyle and fillRect methods. Rectangles are the only primitive shape supported by canvas. This differs from SVG, which also supports the ellipse as a primitive shape. In Table 7–9, we can see the three basic methods that operate on rectangles.

Table 7–9. *The HTML Canvas Rectangle Methods*

Method	Description
fillRect(x,y,w,h)	Fills the rectangle with the current fillStyle
strokeRect(x,y,w,h)	Outlines the rectangle with the current strokeStyle
clearRect(x,y,w,h)	Erases the rectangle, making the area transparent

(x,y) are the starting points from the upper-left corner of the rectangle

(w,h) are the width and height of the rectangle

The fillStyle method sets the color of the style to be applied to the rectangle and the fillRect sets the starting and the ending coordinates for the operation. The ending coordinates are retrieved from the width and height <canvas> attributes value. In Figure 7–5, we can see the final result.

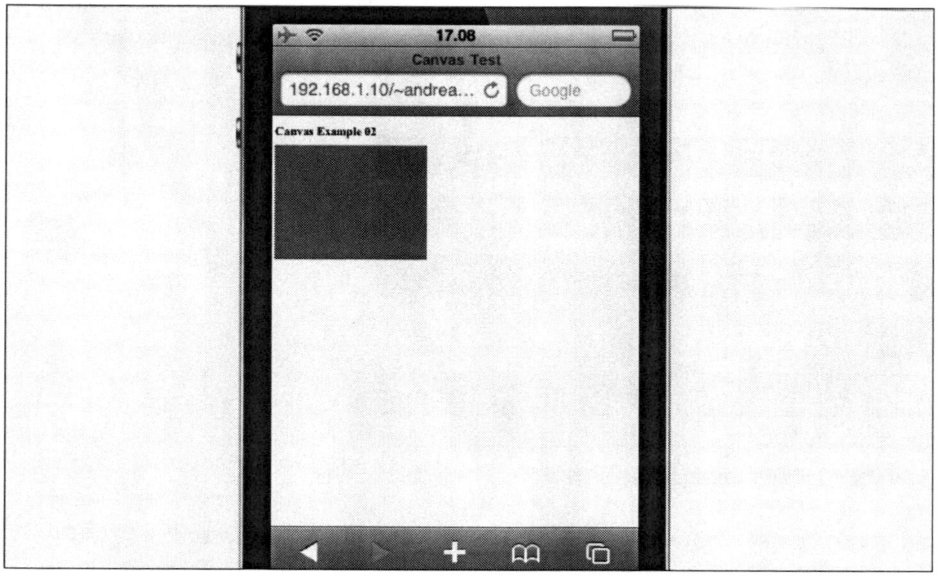

Figure 7–5. *The HTML 2D API in action: drawing a basic shape using Canvas and Methods*

The following full code is from our current example.

```
<html>
<head>
        <title>Canvas Test</title>
        <script>
                window.onload = function() {
                        var ctxElement = document.getElementById('canvasTest02');
                                var ctx = ctxElement.getContext("2d");
                                if (ctx) {
```

```
                                        ctx.fillStyle = "#F00";
                                        ctx.fillRect(0,0, ctx.canvas.width,
ctx.canvas.height);
                        }
                }
        </script>
</head>
<body>

        <h1>Canvas Example 02</h1>
        <canvas id="canvasTest02" width="400" height="300">Please Enable Javascript
Engine</canvas>
</body>
</html>
```

In the next example, we can see how to draw two shapes—one filled with a color as we did previously and one with a stroke. We also see how to use the clearRect(x,y,w,h) method over the two drawn shapes. In Figure 7–6 we can see the final result.

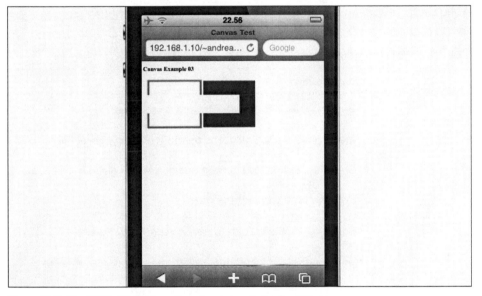

Figure 7–6. *The HTML 2D API in action: drawing and clearing shapes*

Let's look at the following code from our drawing and clearing shapes example shown in Figure 7–6.

```
<html>
<head>
        <title>Canvas Test</title>
        <script>
                window.onload = function() {
                    var ctxElement = document.getElementById('canvasTest03');
                              var ctx = ctxElement.getContext("2d");
                              if (ctx) {

                                        ctx.strokeStyle = "#F00";
                                        ctx.lineWidth = 10;
```

```
                                        ctx.strokeRect(25,25,280,250);

                                        ctx.fillStyle = "#333";
                                        ctx.fillRect(320, 25, 280, 250);

                                        ctx.clearRect(15, 100, 500, 100);
                            }
                    }
            </script>
    </head>
    <body>

            <h1>Canvas Example 03</h1>
            <canvas id="canvasTest03" width="600" height="300">Please Enable Javascript
    Engine</canvas>
    </body>
    </html>
```

Lines are somewhat different from shapes. Lines can be created using a variety of settings that determine how they join together and how they end. In Table 7–10, we can see the methods that operate on lines.

Table 7–10. *The HTML Canvas Line Methods*

Method	Description
beginPath()	Begins a new set of path-drawing operations
moveTo(x,y)	Moves (without drawing) the pen to the given coordinates
lineTo(x,y)	Draws a line from the current position to the given coordinates
lineWidth	Sets the pixel width of the line
lineCap	Sets how lines end: butt (default), round, and square
lineJoin	Sets how lines join together: miter (default), round, and bevel
miterLimit	Sets the limit at which line joins are cut off
Stroke()	Collects all of the current path commands and draws them

In the following example, we see how to draw a line and how the threelineCap method's attributes work. As shown in Figure 7–7, by using the three attributes we can achieve three different effects.

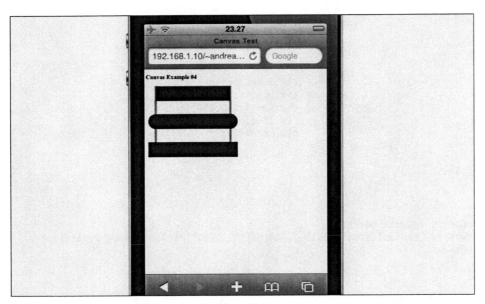

Figure 7–7. *The HTML 2D API in action: lineCap method*

The following code is from the lineCap method example shown in Figure 7–7.

```
<html>
<head>
        <title>Canvas Test</title>
        <script>
                window.onload = function() {
                        var ctxElement = document.getElementById('canvasTest04');
                                var ctx = ctxElement.getContext("2d");
                                if (ctx) {

                                        ctx.strokeStyle="#F00";
                                        ctx.lineWidth=10;

                                        ctx.beginPath();
                                        ctx.moveTo(50,10);
                                        ctx.lineTo(50,390);
                                        ctx.moveTo(450,10);
                                        ctx.lineTo(450,390);
                                        ctx.stroke();

                                        ctx.lineWidth = 80;
                                        ctx.strokeStyle="#000";

                                        ctx.lineCap="butt";
                                        ctx.beginPath();
                                        ctx.moveTo(50,50);
                                        ctx.lineTo(450,50);
                                        ctx.stroke();

                                        ctx.lineCap="round";
                                        ctx.beginPath();
```

```
                                  ctx.moveTo(50,200);
                                  ctx.lineTo(450,200);
                                  ctx.stroke();

                                  ctx.lineCap="square";
                                  ctx.beginPath();
                                  ctx.moveTo(50,350);
                                  ctx.lineTo(450,350);
                                  ctx.stroke();
                          }
                  }
          </script>
  </head>
  <body>

          <h1>Canvas Example 04</h1>
          <canvas id="canvasTest04" width="600" height="600">Please Enable Javascript
  Engine</canvas>
  </body>
  </html>
```

We use a red line to show how the lineCap method works; in this way we can see from which point the end of the line is modified. In the next section, we see how to draw complex shapes.

Complex Shapes

We have seen how to draw simple shapes and now we draw some shapes with more complexity, such as paths. A path is a set of points, like a straight line is a set of points in mathematics.

A path can be either open or closed; a closed path always has an end point that is the same as the start point. A context can have one and only one current path. In Table 7–11, we can see the methods that operate on a type of path called an *arc*. Arcs are curves that are a portion of a circle; a circle is considered a 360-degree arc.

Table 7–11. *The HTML Canvas Arc Methods*

Method	Description
beginPath()	Begins a new set of path-drawing operations.
arc(x,y,r,sA,eA,aC)	Adds an arc to the current path. The arc starts at x,y with a radious of r, a starting angle of sA and an ending angle of eA. The aC argument is false if the arc is clockwise.
arcTo(x1,y1,x2,y2,r)	Adds an arc to the current path that starts at the current pen position. The arc has a radious of r.
closePath()	Closes the current drawing path.

Note: Angles are in radians.

In Figure 7–8 we can see a simple path drawn using arcs.

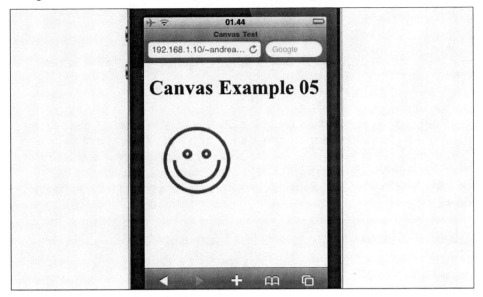

Figure 7–8. *The HTML 2D API in action: drawing using arcs*

The following code is an example shown in Figure 7–8.

```html
<html>
<head>
      <title>Canvas Test</title>
      <script>
            window.onload = function() {
                  var ctxElement = document.getElementById('canvasTest06');
                        var ctx = ctxElement.getContext("2d");
                        if (ctx) {

                              ctx.strokeStyle = "#C00";
                              ctx.fillStyle = "#CCC";
                              ctx.lineWidth = 5;

                        ctx.beginPath();
                        ctx.arc(75,75,50,0, Math.PI*2, true);

                        ctx.moveTo(110,75);
                        ctx.arc(75,75,35,0, Math.PI, false);

                        ctx.moveTo(65,65);
                        ctx.arc(60,65,5,0, Math.PI*2, true);

                        ctx.moveTo(95,65);
                        ctx.arc(90,65,5,0, Math.PI*2, true);

                        ctx.stroke();

}
```

```
            }
        </script>
    </head>
    <body>

        <h1>Canvas Example 06</h1>
        <canvas id="canvasTest06" width="800" height="600">Please Enable Javascript
Engine</canvas>
    </body>
</html>
```

Arcs are not the only paths we can draw using the Canvas 2D API. Canvas also lets us draw Bezier and quadratic curves. Bezier curves are drawn from a start point to an end point using two control points to determinate the curve. Quadratic curves are like Bezier curves but they use only one control point to determine the curve. This means that Bezier curves using two control points can draw curves of more complexity compared to quadratic curves.

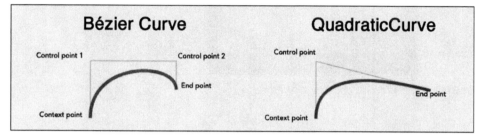

Figure 7–9. *The HTML 2D API in action: Canvas curves implementation*

In Figure 7–9, we can see the difference between a Bezier curve with two control points and a quadratic curve with only one control point. In Table 7–12 we can see the methods that operate on Bezier and quadratic curves.

Table 7–12. *The HTML Canvas Curve Methods*

Method	Description
beginPath()	Begins a new set of path-drawing operations
bezierCurveTo(cx1,cy1,cx2,cy2,end1,end2)	Draws a Bezier curve from the current pen position using the two control points cx1,cy1 and cx2,cy2 and ending at the point end1,end2
quadraticCurveTo(cx,cy,x,y)	Draws a quadratic curve from the current pen position using the control point cx,cy and ending at the point x,y
closePath()	Closes the current drawing path

Note: Angles are in radians.

In Figure 7–10, we can see how to draw a simple golf club using quadratic curves.

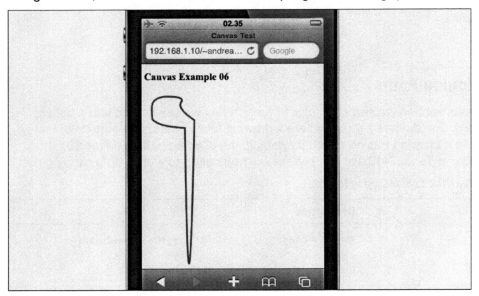

Figure 7–10. *The HTML 2D API in action: drawing using quadratic curves*

The following code is the example shown in Figure 7–10.

```
<head>
      <title>Canvas Test</title>
      <script>
            window.onload = function() {
                  var ctxElement = document.getElementById('canvasTest06');
                        var ctx = ctxElement.getContext("2d");
                        if (ctx) {

                                    ctx.strokeStyle = "#C00";
                                    ctx.fillStyle = "#CCC";
                                    ctx.lineWidth = 5;

                                    ctx.beginPath();
                                    ctx.moveTo(75,25);
                                    ctx.quadraticCurveTo(25,25,25,62.5);
                                    ctx.quadraticCurveTo(25,100,30,100);
                                    ctx.quadraticCurveTo(50,120,130,125);
                                    ctx.quadraticCurveTo(140,1000,160,100);
                                    ctx.quadraticCurveTo(100,60,120,40);
                                    ctx.quadraticCurveTo(125,25,75,25);

                                    ctx.stroke();

}
                  }
      </script>
</head>
<body>
```

```
    <h1>Canvas Example 06</h1>
    <canvas id="canvasTest06" width="800" height="600">Please Enable Javascript
Engine</canvas>
</body>
</html>
```

Using Clipping Paths

In the previous section we saw examples of paths. Now we see how to use a path to define a mask that defines a region where a drawing takes place, and outside of that space, where a drawing has no effect. By default, the clipping path is defined by the entire canvas. In Table 7–13, we can see the methods used to work with a clipping path.

Table 7–13. *The HTML Canvas Clipping Methods*

Method	Description
clip()	Create a clipping region defined on the current path
drawImage	Insert the clipped image in the canvas

In the following example, we use an arc to define a 360-degree circle mask. The code for this example is shown in the following:

```
<html>
<head>
    <title>Canvas Test</title>
    <script>
        window.onload = function() {
            var ctxElement = document.getElementById('canvasTest07');
                var ctx = ctxElement.getContext("2d");
                if (ctx) {

                    var img = document.getElementById("spartan");

                    ctx.arc(ctx.canvas.width/2, ctx.canvas.height/2,
150,0,2*Math.PI);

                    ctx.clip();

                    ctx.drawImage(img,0,0);

}
            }
    </script>
</head>
<body>

    <h1>Canvas Example 07</h1>
    <canvas id="canvasTest07" width="800" height="200">Please Enable Javascript
Engine</canvas>
    <img id="spartan" src="pics/canvas_spartan.jpg" />
</body>
</html>
```

Next, we see how to manipulate canvas objects.

Manipulate Canvas Objects

Besides the possibility to draw some complex shapes, canvas also provides some advanced operations to transform, scale, or rotate canvas objects. In Tables 7–14 and 7–15, we can see the methods used for these advanced operations.

Table 7–14. *The HTML Canvas: Advanced Methods and Operations*

Method	Description
translate(x,y)	Moves the origin by the amounts of x,y
scale(x,y)	Scales drawing operation by multiplies x,y
rotate(angle)	Rotates subsequent drawing operations by angle

In addition to the built-in transforms in Table 7–14, we can also define our own transformation using the two methods in Table 7–15.

Table 7–15. *The HTML Canvas Custom Transformation Methods*

Method	Description
transform(a,b,c,d,e,f)	Adds the given transform to the current one
setTransform(a,b,c,d,e,f)	Sets the current transform to the given arguments

Canvas also has a setting for the default compositing method that determines how new content is drawn onto the canvas surface. We have 12 different compositing methods listed in Table 7–16.

Table 7–16. *The HTML Canvas Compositing Methods*

Method	Description
source-over	Adds the shape on top of the existing content.
source-in	Shape is drawn only where both shapes overlap.
source-out	Shape is drawn only where two shapes don't overlap.
source-atop	Shape is drawn only where there is overlap in the existing content.
lighter	Color values determine color of overlapping shapes.
xor	Shapes are transparent where both overlap.

Method	Description
destination-over	Shape is drawn behind the existing one.
destination-in	Existing content is kept where shape and existing content overlap.
destination-out	Existing content is kept where it doesn't overlap.
destination-atop	Existing canvas is kept where it overlaps. Shape is drawn behind the existing content.
darker	Color values are subtracted where shapes overlap.

In Figure 7–11, we can see how the method in Table 7–16 operates.

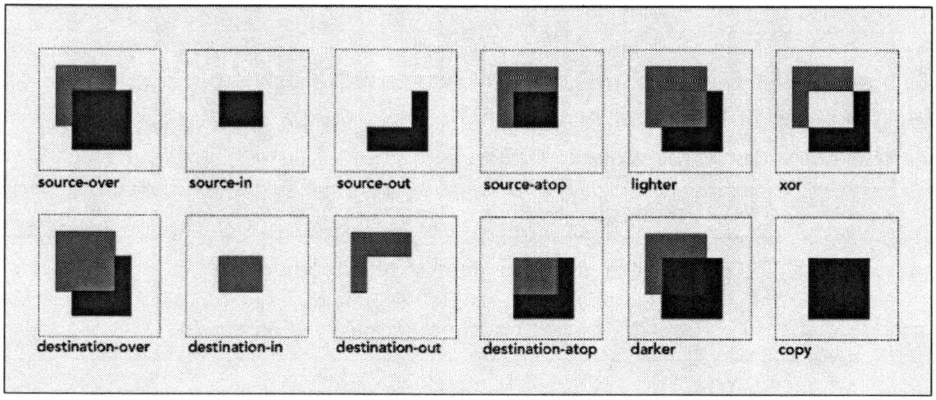

Figure 7–11. *The HTML 2D API in action: composition methods*

The previous canvas advanced operations are used when we need to develop a web game using HTML; however, it's important that a developer know all the possibilities provided by a "standard" like the fifth version of HTML.

The Canvas State

Each context we draw in our canvas maintains a *drawing state*. The drawing state is accessible and manageable using some specific methods.

This state is saved on a stack of saved states. This means that we can save a state by inserting it on top of the stack and restore a state by popping off the last state on top of the stack and restoring it.

The drawing state, also called the *canvas state*, keeps track of several values from different properties and attributes such as the following:

1. Current method values (for example, fillStyle, strokeStyle, and so on)

2. Current transformation matrix

3. Current clipping region

The canvas state is used to restore a set of values for a shape without having to manually keep track of them. Table 7–17 shows the state methods for HTML Canvas.

Table 7–17. *The HTML Canvas State Methods*

Method	Description
save()	Saves the current state on top of the stack
restore()	Restores the first state on top of the stack

In the following example, we first draw a rectangle with some color and stroke values, and then we save the canvas state. Next, we draw another rectangle with different color and stroke values, and then, before drawing a third rectangle, we restore the canvas state. The restore method applies the previously saved state to the third rectangle, as shown in Figure 7–12.

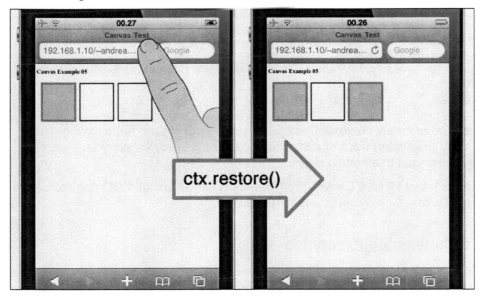

Figure 7–12. *The HTML 2D API: save() and restore() methods in action*

The code of the preceding example shown in Figure 7–12 is the following:

```
<html>
<head>
        <title>Canvas Test</title>
        <script>
                window.onload = function() {
```

```
                        var ctxElement = document.getElementById('canvasTest05');
                             var ctx = ctxElement.getContext("2d");
                             if (ctx) {

                                   ctx.strokeStyle = "#F00";
                                   ctx.fillStyle = "#CCC";
                                   ctx.lineWidth = 10;

                                   ctx.fillRect(25,25,180,200);
                                   ctx.strokeRect(25,25,180,200);

                                   ctx.save();

                                   ctx.strokeStyle = "#000";
                                   ctx.fillStyle = "#FFF";
                                   ctx.lineWidth = 5;
                                   ctx.fillRect(230,25,180,200);
                                   ctx.strokeRect(230,25,180,200);

                                   ctx.restore();

                                   ctx.fillRect(435, 25, 180, 200);
                                   ctx.strokeRect(435,25,180,200);
}
                        }
            </script>
</head>
<body>

        <h1>Canvas Example 05</h1>
        <canvas id="canvasTest05" width="800" height="600">Please Enable Javascript
Engine</canvas>
</body>
</html>
```

When we work on complex contexts, the save() and restore() methods save us from
the manual work of keeping track of current and past canvas states every time we need
to apply minor changes to a certain shape.

For a look at the latest HTML5 Canvas draft version, visit the official W3C page available
at www.w3.org/TR/html5/the-canvas-element.html.

Creating a Canvas Slideshow

Now we build a slideshow for our "The Store" use-case. We use three different images
that are drawn by the canvas, as well as a Javascript function that takes care of sliding
the three images over time. For a review of Javascript, see the section, "Javascript,"
later in this chapter.

The first step is to open our index.html and insert the <canvas> in our hero area, as
follows:

```
... ... ...
<div id="hero">
        <canvas id='heroCanvas' width='298' height='150'></canvas>
```

```
</div>
… … …
```

Now we need to create a new file called *heroCanvas.js* and save it in the Javascript folder of our framework.

```
var imagePaths = [
        "pics/hero-slide_01.png", "pics/hero-slide_02.png", "pics/hero-slide_03.png"
];
var showCanvas = null;
var showCanvasCtx = null;
var img = document.createElement("img");
var currentImage = 0;
```

The first part of the code shown previously initializes the variables we need for the slideshow. The variable `imagePaths` is an array with all the images that are displayed in the slideshow, a couple of variables that refer to the canvas context, a variable img that stores a new image element created using the `createElement()` DOM method, and then an index variable that keeps track of the current image displayed in the slideshow.

```
window.onload = function () {
        showCanvas = document.getElementById('heroCanvas');
        showCanvasCtx = showCanvas.getContext('2d');

        img.setAttribute('width','298');
        img.setAttribute('height','150');
        switchImage();

        setInterval(switchImage,2500);
}
```

Now we can write and set of functions that start when the window's object is loaded. In the first block of the function's code, we get a reference to the canvas, and then we make a request for the Canvas 2D API. In the second block, we set the width and height of the images to be displayed and then we call the `switchImage()` function, which we see later in the chapter. In the last block, we set the slideshow interval between each image at 2.5 seconds.

```
function switchImage() {
        img.setAttribute('src',imagePaths[currentImage++]);
        img.onload = function() {
                if (currentImage >= imagePaths.length)
                        currentImage = 0;

                showCanvasCtx.drawImage(img,0,0,298,150);
        }
}
```

Now we come to the `switchImage()` function, which does all the hard work in this example. First, this function sets the source of the image function to the current image index value in the array. When the image loads we run a function that checks to see whether the current image is greater than the image path array. If it's greater, the function resets the index to zero restarting the counter to the beginning. Lastly, we call the `drawImage()` function on the canvas context to draw the image using the given coordinates. The `switchImage()` function is called each time the interval time goes off, or in other words every 2.5 seconds. In the following, we have the entire Javascript code with the function definition on top of the Javascript file, which is the recommendation.

```
<head>
        ... ... ...
        ... ... ...
        ... ... ...
        <script type="text/Javascript" src="Javascript/heroCanvas.js"></script>
</head>
```

As the last step, we need to import the Javascript file as an external file inserting a <script> in the <head> section as shown previously. In Figure 7–13, we can see the canvas slideshow in action.

Figure 7–13. *The HTML 2D API: the Canvas slideshow in action*

As we have now seen, canvas brings to the table a new set of opportunities for those who are interested in developing a WebApp. Next, we see how the new CSS level 3 gives us more help in developing WebApp for iOS devices.

CSS3

The old CSS2 specification was too large and complex to be updated in one large document specification, so it is divided into smaller document specifics from the World Wide Web Consortium (W3C). Some modules include the following:

- The Box Model
- Multi-Column Layout
- Background and Borders
- Lists Module

- ▓ Text Effects

- ▓ Hyperlink Presentation

- ▓ Speech Module

> **NOTE:** CSS3 is still a "work in progress" project, and you can have a look at the complete list of modules here: www.w3.org/Style/CSS/current-work.

The main impact of CSS3 is the capability to achieve the current design features in a much easier way and to use new selectors and properties to introduce new design features, such as animation or gradients effects.

Now we see some of the most common properties that are found in every iPhone and iPad framework available to design and develop for iPhone and iPad. We master these properties in Chapter 8 when we expand on our frameworks.

Prefixes

Until all of the CSS3 modules reach recommended status, every browser vendor has the faculty to decide how to implement these properties. For this reason, a proprietary prefix is placed in front of every property.

The point of vendor-specific prefixes is to let other rendering engines know that the property can be safely ignored without creating an error. At the same time, it lets the developer know that those properties are experimental and not fully supported, even if planned by the W3C.

Once CSS3 has been completely defined, supported, and officially becomes a Web Standard, all of these prefixes will be removed.

An example is the following:

```
border-radius: 3px;
-webkit-border-radius: 3px; (WebKit-based Browser implementation)
-moz-border-radius: 3px; (Gecko-based Browser implementation)
```

At present, when working with desktop websites and web applications, we need to specify the same property several times, at least once for each of the most common browsers, in order to achieve a minimum level of CSS3 properties accessibility.

In our Apple devices context, we need to take care of WebKit CSS3 implementation, because we use only WebKit-based browsers like Safari.

Rounded Borders

Achieving rounded borders using CSS2 coding is not a simple task. As we well know, iOS has rounded borders everywhere. Numerous methods are available to create CSS2 rounded borders, but these require additional markup and individual images for each border.

Using CSS3, creating a rounded border is incredibly fast and easy. We can apply this property to one or to all corners, or to individual corners. Table 7–18 shows the CSS Level 3 rounded border property.

The CSS syntax is the following:

```
-webkit-border-radius: <length>;
```

Table 7–18. *The CSS Level 3 Rounded Border Property*

Name	border-radius
Value:	[length	percentage]
Initial:	[0]
Applies to:	all elements
inherited:	no

Border Images

Border images are one of the most useful additions; note that all of the big buttons that slide from the bottom on the iPhone can also be designed with this property. CSS3 has the capability to repeat or stretch a border image as you choose. Table 7–19 shows the CSS Level 3 border image property.

The CSS syntax is the following:

```
-webkit-border-image: <source> <slice> <width> <outset> <repeat>;
```

Table 7-19. *The CSS Level 3 Border Image Property*

Name	border-image
Value:	[none | length]
	[number | percentage]
	[length | percentage | number | auto]
	[length | percentage]
	[stretch | repeat | round]
Initial:	[none]
	[100%]
	[1]
	[0]
	[stretch]
Applies to:	all elements

Gradients

A *gradient* is a browser-generated image specified entirely in CSS, which consists of smooth fades between several colors. Gradients are specified using the -webkit-gradient function and can be passed in place of an image URL. Two types of gradients are recognized: linear and radial. You can specify multiple in-between color values, called *color stops*, and the gradient function interpolates the color values between them.

The function you use to create a color stop is called color-stop. You pass this function as a parameter to the -webkit-gradient() function to specify the start, intermediate, and end colors in both a linear and a radial gradient. The colors between the specified color stops are interpolated. Table 7–20 shows the CSS Level 3 gradient property.

The CSS syntax is the following:

```
-webkit-gradient ( <gradient-line> <color-stop1> <color-stop2> <color-stopN> );
-webkit-gradient ( <gradient-line> <color-stop1> <color-stop2> <color-stopN> );
```

Table 7–20. *The CSS Level 3 Gradient Property*

Name	gradient()
Value:	[gradient-line]
	[color-stop]
	[color-stop]
	[color-stop]
Initial:	[top]
	[transparent]
	[transparent]
	[transparent]
Applies to:	all elements
Name	**color-stop()**
Value:	[color]
	[length | percentage]
Initial:	[transparent]
	[0%]
Applies to:	all elements
Percentages:	N/A

Box Sizing

The new Box model is one of the most extensive areas of the CSS3 draft. This box-sizing aspect enables you to define certain elements to fit an area in a certain way. If we want to design a two-column bordered box in our user interface and place the two boxes side by side, it can be achieved using this property. This forces the browser to render the box with the specified width and height, and place the border and padding in the box. Table 7–21 shows the CSS Level 3 box sizing property.

The CSS syntax is the following:

```
-webkit-box-sizing: <box-sizing value>;
```

Table 7–21. *The CSS Level 3 Box Sizing property*

Name	box-sizing
Value:	[content-box | border-box | inherit]
Initial:	[content-box]
Applies to:	all elements

Box Shadow

Adding a box shadow is another effect that is difficult to achieve using CSS2 specification because usually we need to use additional image and markup. Although we wait to switch to a full CSS3 website in the near future, for the time being we add an additional <div> to our desktop website in order to add a paper-shadow effect to the main content. The CSS3 alternative is more elegant and clean. Table 7–22 shows the CSS Level 3 box shadow property.

The CSS syntax is the following:

```
-webkit-box-shadow: <offset-x> <offeset y> <blur radius> <color>;
```

Table 7–22. *The CSS Level 3 Box Shadow Property*

Name	box-shadow
Value:	[offset]
	[offset]
	[offset }
	[color]
Initial:	[0]
	[0]
	[0]
	[transparent]
Applies to:	all elements

Outline

Setting an element outline is already available in CSS2, but in CSS3 includes the capability to offset the outline away from its element, by a value we define. It differs from a border in two ways:

- Outlines do not take up space.
- Outlines can be non-rectangular.

Table 7–23 shows the CSS Level 3 outline property. The CSS code is the following:

```
outline: <width> <style> <color>;
outline-offset: <offset>;
```

Table 7–23. *The CSS Level 3 Outline Property*

Name	Outline
Value:	[width | inherit]
	[auto | style | inherit]
	[color | invert | inherit]
Initial:	[medium]
	[none]
	[invert]
Applies to:	all elements

Background Size

Before CSS3, background size was determined by the actual size of the image used. With this new CSS3 property, it is possible to specify, in terms of percentage or pixels, how large a background image should be. Emulating the iOS user interface, we always try to use CSS properties, instead of images everywhere possible.

In any case, the background size property, where it is needed, enables us to reuse images in several different contexts and it also expands a background to fill an area more accurately.

Table 7–24 shows the CSS level 3 background size property. The CSS syntax is the following:

```
-webkit-background-size: <length-x> <length-y>;
```

Table 7–24. *The CSS Level 3 Background Size Property*

Name	background-size
Value:	[auto	length	percentage]
Initial:	[auto]
Applies to:	all elements

Background Origin

CSS3 also enables us to specify how the position of a background is calculated. This enables great flexibility in terms of placing a background image.

Table 7–25 shows the CSS background origin property. The CSS syntax is the following:

```
background-origin: <origin-value>;
```

Table 7–25. *The CSS Level 3 Background Origin Property*

Name	background-origin
Value:	[content-box	border-box	padding-box]
Initial:	[padding-box]
Applies to:	all elements

Multiple Backgrounds

The new CSS3 capability to use multiple backgrounds is a great time saver and it enables us to achieve effects that previously required more than one <div>. This property, combined with the background size, gives us a powerful tool for reducing the gap between a native UI look-and-feel and our emulated (web) user interface.

Table 7–26 shows the CSS Level 3 multiple background property. The CSS code is the following:

```
background: <source-1> <position> <repeat>, <source-n> <position> <repeat>;
```

Table 7–26. *The CSS Level 3 Multiple Background Property*

Name	background
Value:	[image | none]
	[length | percentage]
	[repeat | no-repeat]
Initial:	[none]
	[0% 0%]
	[repeat]
Applies to:	all elements

Text Shadow

Text shadow is a fundamental CSS3 property to emulate the native iOS user interface. Almost all of the text in iOS is embossed and very readable.

Table 7–27 shows the CSS Level 3 text shadow property. The CSS code is the following:

```
-webkit-text-shadow: <offset-x> <offeset-y> <blur radius> <color>;
```

Table 7–27. *The CSS Level 3 Text Shadow Property*

Name	text-shadow
Value:	[image | none]
	[length | percentage]
	[repeat | no-repeat]
Initial:	[none]
	[0% 0%]
	[repeat]
Applies to:	all elements

Text Overflow

Text overflow is another fundamental property involved in iOS native user interface emulation. Often, in the iPhone environment, the title overflows the Header Bar, even more often if we use buttons on the left and right of this bar to help navigate the content.

This property enables us to clip the text with ellipsis ("...") as a visual hint to the user that the text has been clipped. With the iPad, this problem no longer exists because of the larger screen.

Table 7–28 shows the CSS Level 3 text overflow property. The CSS syntax is the following:

```
text-shadow: <overflow-value>;
```

Table 7–28. *The CSS Level 3 Text Overflow Property*

Name	text-overflow
Value:	[clip | ellipsis | ellipsis-word | inherit]
Initial:	[clip]
Applies to:	all block-level elements

Word Wrapping

With CSS2, if a word is too long to fit within one line of an area, it expands outside. This is not a common occurrence but happens from time to time. The new word wrapping capability enables us to force the text to wrap, even if it means splitting it mid-word. Table 7–29 shows the CSS Level 3 word wrapping property.

Table 7–29. *The CSS Level 3 Word Wrapping Property*

Name	word-wrap
Value:	[normal | break-word]
Initial:	[normal]
Applies to:	all elements
Inherited:	yes

The CSS syntax is the following:

```
word-wrap: <wrap-value>;
```

The CSS code is the following:

```
word-wrap: break-word;
```

Web Fonts

Although this new property is a revolutionary change for web design, for those of us who need to work with the native iOS user interface this property is not that useful, because we have Helvetica in the Safari Font Stack. The property can end up being a handy tool if we should ever have some strange logos to represent textually.

Table 7–30 shows the CSS Level 3 web fonts property. The CSS syntax is the following:

```
@font-face { <font-family>; <source>; }
```

Table 7–30. *The CSS Level 3 Web Fonts Property*

Name	@font-face
Value:	[family-name]
Initial:	[N/A]
Applies to:	all font face and font family

Tap Highlight

In the touch-screen device paradigm, the hover status (as we know it in the desktop user experience) doesn't exist, but with this useful WebKit extension we can highlight a link or a Javascript-clickable element. The alpha channel is also supported.

Table 7–31 shows the CSS level 3 tap highlights property. The CSS syntax is the following:

```
-webkit-tap-highlight-color: <color>;
```

Table 7–31. *The CSS Level 3 Tap Highlights Property*

Name	tap-highlight-color
Value:	[color]
Initial:	[rgba(0,0,0,0)]
Applies to:	link, Javascript clickable elements
Inherited:	yes

Multiple Columns

The multi-columns property is much more exciting from a desktop prospective, because the iPhone and iPad user interface doesn't use a multi-columns layout very often. In some cases, this property can still be used to achieve some nice content presentation. This property enables us to specify how many columns our text should be split, and how they should appear.

Four properties relate to the multiple column layout in CSS3, enabling us to set the number of columns, width, amount of gap separating each column, and the border between each. The four properties are

- Column-count (number of columns)
- Column-width (width of columns)
- Column-gap (gap between columns)
- Column-rule (border between the columns)

Table 7–32 shows the CSS Level 3 multiple columns property. The CSS syntax is the following:

```
.twoColumnLayout { <number-of-column> <width> <gap> <rule> }
```

Table 7–32. *The CSS Level 3 Multiple Columns Property*

Name	column-span
Value:	[integer	auto]
	[length	auto]
	[length	normal]
	[color]
Initial:	[auto]
	[auto]
	[normal]
	[same as for 'color' in CSS21]
Applies to:	non-replaced block-level elements (except table elements), table cells, inline block elements

Spanning Columns

This property is used in case we want an element to span more than one column; usually we use it for headings, tables, and images.

Table 7–33 shows the CSS Level 3 spanning columns property. The CSS syntax is the following:

```
column-span: <number-of-column>;
```

Table 7–33. *The CSS Level 3 Spanning Columns Property*

Name	column-span
Value:	[1	all]
Initial:	[1]
Applies to:	static, non-floating elements

Transitions

The transition property can be used to modify a CSS property such as height, width, or color over time. Not all properties can be animated with a transition, but all the important properties for iPhone and iPad development are in the list.

The first value refers to the property that is transitioned, the second value controls the duration, and the third controls the type of transition.

Table 7–34 shows the CSS Level 3 transition property. The CSS syntax is the following:

```
-webkit-transition: <property> <time> <function>;
```

Table 7–34. *The CSS Level 3 Transition Property*

Name	transition
Value:	[none	all	property]
	[time]
	[ease	linear	ease-in	ease-out	ease-in-out	cubic-bezier]
Initial:	[all]
	[0]
	[ease]
Applies to:	all elements, :before and :after pseudo elements

Transforms

Transforms are used to modify the geometry of objects through mathematical operations. This property is fundamental for emulating some of the typical iOS effects between pages, and is used to create interesting visual effects and animations.

In the transform property, a list of transform functions are used as values and are applied in the order provided. Exactly as they are for the other CSS3 values, the individual transform functions are separated by white space.

The transform property works together with the transform-origin property to set the point of origin from where the transition takes place.

Available transform functions are

matrix(number, number, number, number, number, number)
Specifies a 2D transformation in the form of a transformation matrix (3X3) of six values. Matrix (a,b,c,d,e,f) is equivalent to applying the transformation matrix [a b c d e f].

translate(translate-value, translate-value)
Specifies a 2D translation by the vector [tx, ty], where tx is the first translation-value parameter and ty is the optional second translation-value parameter. If <ty> is not provided, ty has a zero value.

translateX(translation-value)
Specifies a translation by the given amount in the X direction.

translateY(translation-value)
Specifies a translation by the given amount in the Y direction.

scale(number, number)
Specifies a 2D scale operation by the [sx,sy] scaling vector described by the two parameters. If the second parameter is not provided, it is takes a value equal to the first.

scaleX(number)
Specifies a scale operation using the [sx,1] scaling vector, where sx is given as the parameter.

scaleY(number)
Specifies a scale operation using the [1,sy] scaling vector, where sy is given as the parameter.

rotate(angle)
Specifies a 2D rotation by the angle specified in the parameter about the origin of the element, as defined by the transform-origin property.

skew(angle, angle)
Specifies a skew transformation along the X and Y axes. The first angle parameter specifies the skew on the X axis. The second angle parameter specifies the skew on the Y axis. If the second parameter is not given, a value of 0 is used for the Y angle (for example, no skew on the Y axis).

skewX(angle)

Specifies a skew transformation along the X axis by the given angle.

skewY(angle)

Specifies a skew transformation along the Y axis by the given angle.

Table 7–35 shows the CSS Level 3 transform property. The CSS syntax is the following:

```
-webkit-transition: <transform function> <type of effect>;
-webkit-transition-origin: <transform origin>;
```

Table 7–35. *The CSS Level 3 Transform Property*

Name	transform
Value:	[none | transform function | transform function]
Initial:	[none]
Applies to:	block-level and inline-level elements
Percentages:	Refer the size of the element's box
Name	**transform-origin**
Value:	[percentage | length | left | center | right]
Initial:	[50% 50%]
Applies to:	block-level and inline-level elements
Percentages:	Refer the size of the element's box

Animation

Animation, similar to transition, modifies properties over time. Using the transition property, we achieve a one-way effect from one value to another; this kind of property is useful for page transition, but has a limited value for building any kind of visual effect.

Using the Animation property, we can provide any number of intermediate values that are not necessarily linear, to achieve complex animations. These intermediate values are called *keyframes* and are the foundation of all animation processes.

> **NOTE:** keyframe in animation and filmmaking is a drawing that defines the starting and ending points of any smooth transition. They are called "frames" because their position in time is measured in frames on a strip of film. A sequence of keyframes defines which images the viewer will see, whereas the position of the keyframes on the film, video, or animation timeline defines the timing of the movement.

Table 7–36 shows the CSS Level 3 animation property. The CSS syntax is the following:

```
animation-name: <name>;
animation-duration: <time>;
animation-iteration-count: <integer>;
animation-timing-function: <function>;
@keyframes <name> {
        from {
                left: <start-x>;
                top: <start-y>;
        }
        to {
                left: <destination-x>;
                top: <destination-y>;
        }
}
```

Table 7–36. *The CSS Level 3 Animation Property*

Name	Transform
Value:	[animation-name]
	[animation-duration]
	[animation-timing-function]
	[animation-delay]
	[animation-iteration-count]
	[animation-direction]
Initial:	see individual properties
Applies to:	block-level and inline-level elements

In our frameworks, the Javascript takes care of the user interface's behavior, but the animation property offers a valid alternative in many situations. This property is also the most complex of all CSS3 modules; for this reason, we analyze all its properties in detail, as shown in Table 7–37.

Table 7–37. *The CSS Level 3 Animation Property*

Name	animation-name
Value:	[none	name]
Initial:	{ none]
Applies to:	block-level and inline-level elements

Name	animation-duration
Value:	[time]
Initial:	[0]
Applies to:	block-level and inline-level elements
Name	**animation-timing-function**
Value:	[ease | linear | ease-in | ease-out | ease-in-out | cubic-bezier]
Initial:	[ease]
Applies to:	block-level and inline-level elements
Name	**animation-iteration-count**
Value:	[infinite | integer |
Initial:	{ 1]
Applies to:	block-level and inline-level elements
Name	**animation-direction**
Value:	[normal | alternate]
Initial:	[normal]
Applies to:	block-level and inline-level elements
Name	**animation-play-state**
Value:	[running | pause]
Initial:	[running]
Applies to:	block-level and inline-level elements
Name	**animation-delay**
Value:	[time]
Initial:	[0]
Applies to:	block-level and inline-level elements

Keyframes

Keyframes are used to specify the values for animating properties at various points during the animation. The keyframes specify the behavior of one cycle of the animation; the animation might iterate one or more times.

Keyframes are specified using a specialized CSS at-rule. A @keyframes rule consists of the keyword "@keyframes", followed by the identifier "animation-name" that gives a name for the animation, followed by a set of style rules.

The CSS grammar for the keyframes rule is the following:

```
keyframes-rule: '@keyframes' IDENT '{'keyframes-blocks'}';
keyframes-blocks: [ keyframe-selectors block ] ;
keyframe-selectors: [ 'from' | 'to' | PERCENTAGE ] [ ',' [ 'from' | 'to' | PERCENTAGE ]
];
```

Reflections

No other CSS3 property is so typically Apple-style as is the reflection property. Reflection is used on every product presentation in the Apple store, and combined with the use of negative space, it is a valuable tool for achieving clean design.

> **NOTE:** As we saw analyzing the Laws of Perceptions, negative space, in art, is the space around and between the subject(s) of an image.
>
> Negative space is most evident when the space around a subject, and not the subject itself, forms an interesting or artistically relevant shape. This space is occasionally used as an artistic effect of the "real" subject of an image. The use of negative space is a key element of artistic composition and visual design.

The reflection property is composed of three arguments or values in order to achieve the final effect. The first argument sets the direction of the reflection. The second argument specifies the offset of the reflection. The third argument is a mask applied to the reflection passed using the gradient property.

Table 7–38 shows the CSS Level 3 reflection property. The CSS syntax is the following:

```
-webkit-box-reflect: <direction> <offset> <mask-box-image>;
```

Table 7–38. *The CSS Level 3 Reflection Property*

Name	box-reflect
Value:	[above	below	left	right]
	[offset]
	[gradient()]
Initial:	None
Applies to:	all images
Name	**Gradient**
Value:	[gradient()]
	[from()]
	[color-stop()]
Initial:	None
Applies to:	all images

Javascript

So far, using the HTML5 markup language, we have built the structure of our web site or Web application. We have then used the CSS3 style sheet to modify its visual presentation. Now it's time to work on its behavior and it's at this point that Javascript comes into the picture. Javascript is a complicated subject that is difficult to cover comprehensively here, so this section is a crash-course.

Javascript was developed in 1995 by the Netscape team and appeared for the first time in Netscape 2. Javascript's original name was LiveScript, but in 1996, since the Sun Java Language was a big deal at the time, Netscape and Sun worked out an agreement to change its name to Javascript. In retrospect, this was a big mistake because Javascript and Java have nothing to do with each other; Javascript is not based on Java and it's not a light version of Java. Calling this scripting language Javascript might have served some marketing purpose, but it also created a lot of confusion around it.

In 1996, Microsoft made its own version for Internet Explorer 3, which was called Jscript. In 1997, Netscape submitted the Javascript language to the European Computer Manufacturers Association (ECMA) in order to create an independent and official standard edition that was called ECMAScript (ECMA-262), although everybody in the IT world continued to call it Javascript. In 1999, ECMAScript 3 was published and in 2009 came ECMAScript 5, retrocompatible with ECMAScript 3 versions of the language. Mobile Safari partially supports ECMAScript 5 from iOS4.3.2 whereas almost all new features are supported with iOS5.

Javascript is a client-side scripting language for interacting with web pages. Unlike other non-scripting program languages, Javascript works only inside specific applications (for example, web browsers such as Safari Mobile). The operating system (such as iOS) runs the web browser, the web browser contains a page, and the page contains the Javascript. We can see this principle in Figure 7–14.

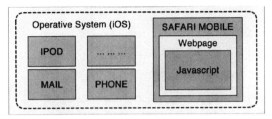

Figure 7–14. *Relationship between web browser, web page, and Javascript code*

Javascript is a scripting language and is intentionally limited, which means, for example, that it can't access the file system, a database, or hardware. The reason for this approach is that Javascript is not meant to be a general-purpose programming language, but is designed to manipulate web pages.

When a user opens the browser and requests a webpage from a webserver, the webserver sends HTML and CSS back to the browser as plain text, letting the browser take care of interpreting, rendering, and finally displaying the final content. As discussed, Javascript is a client-side language, and this means that it works in the same way as HTML and CSS files: the webserver sends the Javascript to the browser, which then interprets and runs it. We can see these steps in Figure 7–15.

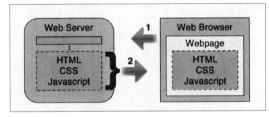

Figure 7–15. *Interaction between a web browser and a web server*

The client-side approach is opposite to the server-side approach that we have with languages such as PHP or Ruby on Rails, which are executed on the webserver and whose results are delivered to the browser.

Adding Javascript to a Webpage

The Javascript code is embedded on a webpage using the <script> element. In the CSS rules, a piece of Javascript code can be inserted using two approaches:

Inline
The code is written directly in the HTML document.

Imported
The code is imported, referring to an external Javascript document.

In this book, we use inline Javascript for demonstration purposes, but for most real projects, importing the Javascript code is considered to be a good practice. In the following two examples, we start with the first program in any programming language, the Hello, World! program.

```
<html>
<head>
      <title>Javascript Test</title>
</head>
<body>
      <h1>Javascript Test Page</h1>
      <script>
            alert("Hello, world!");
      </script>
</body>
</html>
```

The previous Javascript code shows the inline technique in which the code is inserted inline between the two <script> tags.

```
<head>
<link href="css/style.css" rel="stylesheet" media="screen" type="text/css" />
<script src="Javascript/helloWorld.js"></script>
<title> Javascript Test Page </title>
</head>
```

The previous code shows the imported technique, where the code is imported using the src attribute.

At this point, we might ask ourselves, "Where do we insert the Javascript code?" The browser reads and interprets all the code from top to bottom, meaning that Javascript is interpreted and run as soon as the browser has read it. This means that, according to the position of the code in the web page, Javascript can cause page rendering delays, slowing all of our pages down. In addition, it's considered a good practice to insert the Javascript code at the bottom part of the <body> section, just before the closing </body> tag, as shown in the previous Hello World example.

Javascript Structure

Javascript is an *interpreted* language, as opposed to *compiled*, another type of language. Compiled languages need to be run through a special program called a *compiler* that converts the code we wrote into machine code that can be run by the CPU that's controlled by the operating system. As we have seen, we don't need to do that with Javascript; using the browser, we simply make a request to the webserver that sends back to the browser the plain text version of the Javascript code that the browser interprets and runs.

Javascript is also case sensitive, meaning that the following pieces of code are different from each other in Javascript:

```
alert("Hello World!");        // correct Javascript syntax
Alert("Hello Wolrd!");        // incorrect Javascript syntax
```

A Javascript statement is typically written on one line and must finish with a semicolon, as shown in the previous example. The semicolon has the same role as the full stop or period in English. When we have a long statement, we can promote readability by splitting it into multiple lines, using the semicolon only at the end of the statement.

Javascript is case sensitive but space insensitive, meaning that it doesn't care about blank space between different pieces of the language. The following statements are all correct and interpreted in the same way:

```
alert("Hello World!");        // correct Javascript syntax
alert ("Hello World!");       // correct Javascript syntax
```

We can insert single-line comments into Javascript code by using two forward slashes, as in the preceding examples. If we need to insert a multiple-line comment, we can use the combination forward slash asterisk, and close the comment using its flip side, the asterisk forward slash, as shown in the following example.

```
/* this is
a multiple line
comment */
```

Data Categories

In Javascript, we have two types of data: Primitive and Reference. The Primitive data type is irreducible and the primitive value is stored on the *stack*, which means directly in the location of the variable access. The Reference data type is composed and is an object, and the reference value is stored in the *heap*, which means that the value in the variable is a pointer to a location in memory where the object is stored. The following list shows the two categories of data:

Primitive Data
Number
Boolean
String
Null
Undefined

Reference Data
Object
Function
Array
Date
Error
RegExp

Those new to stack and heap will be a little bit disoriented trying to understand their nature. For our purpose, the concept that is important to understand is that a stack is a zone of memory with a Last In First Out (LIFO) policy, where the application keeps track of its memory needs. The heap is another zone in the memory, where objects are stored and reachable by pointers at any moment of time. Figure 7–16 show how primitive and reference type works in practice.

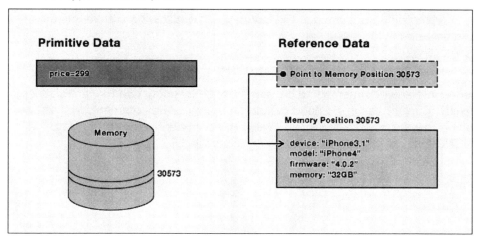

Figure 7–16. *Primitive and reference data in Javascript*

Figure 7–17 shows how stack and heap works with primitive and reference data types.

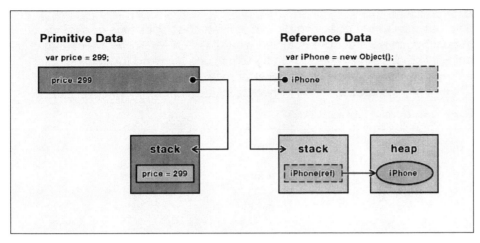

Figure 7–17. *Primitive and reference data in Javascript*

From a developer point of view, this different way to store data in memory doesn't have any visible effect on the program perception.

Reserved Words

Reserved words have a place in every language, Javascript included. Javascript describes a set of *reserved words* that we can't use as identifiers for functions and variables. If we use a reserved word, naming a function or a variable often will not receive an error, and then the word will be considered a keyword and we will get a keyword error.

In Table 7–39, we can see the most common reserved words in Javascript.

Table 7–39. *Reserved Words in Javascript (Alphabetic Order)*

abstract	enum	int	short
Boolean	export	interface	static
byte	extends	long	super
char	final	native	synchronized
class	float	package	throws
const	goto	private	transient
debugger	implements	protected	volatile
double	import	public	

Javascript also describes a set of keywords that indicate the beginnings or endings of Javascript statements. Keywords, like reserved words, are reserved and we can't use them for naming functions or variables. If we try to use one keyword for naming a variable or a function, we will probably get an error message, such as "Identifier expected." Table 7–40 displays all of the keywords in Javascript.

Table 7–40. *Keywords in Javascript (Alphabetic Order)*

break	else	new	var
case	finally	return	void
catch	for	switch	while
continue	function	this	with
default	if	throw	
delete	in	try	
do	instanceof	typeof	

Variables

Working with programming languages means also keeping track of many pieces of different types of data. For this purpose, every program language has variables. A *variable* is a container that abstracts a piece of physical memory that physically stores the data. In Figure 7–18, we can see how we might picture the physical memory in a linear form.

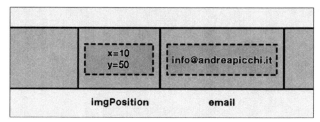

Figure 7–18. *Device memory represented in a linear (vector) form*

When data is stored in memory, we can access it with two basic operations called read and write. Using the read operation we can retrieve the value of a variable stored in the memory, whereas by using write we can update the value of a variable.

In Javascript, we create a variable using the reserved word "var" followed by the name of the variable and then the semicolon. The following examples show some variable declarations. We must remember that Javascript is case sensitive.

```
var varName;           // generic variable declaration
var userEmail;         // variable for an email address
var todayDate;         // variable for a date
```

The name that we use for a variable must be written as one word, with no spaces between letters because spaces aren't allowed in a variable declaration. The name can be made up of letters, numbers, underscore symbols, or dollar signs, but it can't start with a number. The following examples demonstrate this rule.

```
var todayDate;         // correct declaration
var 2012todayDate;     // incorrect declaration
var todayDate2012;     // correct declaration
```

The declaration we saw in previous examples creates an undefined variable, meaning that the variable has no value. In order to assign a value to the variable, we need to use the equal operator followed by an allowed value, as shown in Figure 7–19.

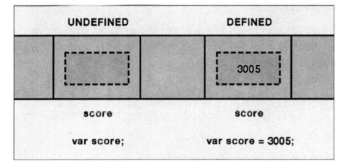

Figure 7–19. *Undefined (left) and defined (right) variables*

The declaration can also be split into two statements, but this approach is rarely used because it increases the number of lines of code and doesn't improve code readability.

```
var score;             // first step of variable declaration
score = 3005;          // second step of variable declaration
var score = 3005;      // compact approach to variable declaration
```

In Javascript, we can also omit the first step and write only the second step, as shown in the preceding example. Javascript first looks for a variable called "score" and if it is not found, it creates it *ex-novo*. It is considered a bad practice to omit the reserved word "var" because that can lead to unexpected behavior by Javascript and decrease code readability.

To declare multiple variables, we can create them using only one line, instead of spreading them across multiple lines.

```
var score;                                 // single approach
var hightScore;                          // single approach
var score, hightScore;                     // compact approach
var score = 3005;                          // single approach
var hightScore = 19733005;                 // single approach
var score = 3005, hightScore = 19733005;   // compact approach
```

In many other programming languages, when we declare a data type (for example, variable) we don't just give the variable a name, but we also need to specify the exact data type that will be stored in the variable itself. In Javascript, we can't do that. Javascript is a "weakly typed language" as opposed to other languages such as Java that are "strongly typed languages." In Javascript, we use the reserved word "var" to create a generic variable that stores any type of data, such as integers, Booleans, strings, and so on. Therefore, Javascript doesn't treat different types of data differently; it uses a generic variable type for storing any type of available data.

Operators

Every statement we write always involves at least one operation: assigning a value, moving data from one place to another, and adding and subtracting are a few examples. In order to perform operations, we need operators.

The most common operators are the arithmetic ones but we also have logic operators, assignment operators, Boolean operators, and many others. We can group these operators into six functional categories, as follows:

Assignment
Assigns a value to its left operand based on the value of its right operand.

Logical
Returns a logical value based on the logical operator.

Comparison
Returns a logical value based on the comparison operator.

Combinational
Returns a result without affecting either operand, including string and mathematical operators.

Bitwise
Returns a number value based on its operands treated as a sequence of 32-bit value.

Other Types

Operators that don't fall into standard groups include the Comma Operator (,), Dot Operator (.), Conditional Operator (?:), Delete Operator (delete), New Operator (new), In Operator (in), Typeof Operator (typeof), Instanceof Operator (instanceof), and the Void Operator (void).

In general, operators require one or more operands as values and an output, following a simple (mathematical) expression structure example:

```
"operand" "operator" "operand" "operator" "output"
90 + 10 = 100
```

Table 7–41 lists some of the most common Javascript operators.

Table 7–41. *Common Javascript Operators*

Operator	Name
=	Assignment
==	Equal (value)
===	Identical (value and type)
+	Addition
-	Subtraction
*	Multiplication
/	Division
%	Modulus
++	Increment
--	Decrement
<<	Shift Left
>>	Shift Right
&	Bitwise AND
|	Bitwise OR
^	Bitwise Exclusive OR
&&	Logical AND
||	Logical OR
!	Logical Exclusive OR
?:	Conditional

In Javascript, as in other programming languages, we have operator precedence, meaning that some operators are treated as having more importance than others. The more important an operator is, the higher its precedence, meaning that it is executed before any other operator with a lower precedence.

```
score = 100 + 100 * 2;        // score value is 210
score = (100 + 100) * 2;           // score value is 400
```

As we can see from our example, if we need to create a specific order, we can use parentheses as we often do in mathematical operations.

As a final example, we see the conditional operator, whose general syntax is the following:

```
Condition ? true : false
```

Essentially, we have a condition, and we specify what happens if the condition is true and what happens if it's false.

```
var gameScore = 500;
var highScore = 350;
highScore = (game > highScore) ? gameScore : hightScore;
```

In our example, we show the assignment with the conditional operator. First, we test whether the game score was higher than the existing high score. In this case, 500 is greater than 350, and the conditional operator returns and assigns 500 to the variable highScore, updating the best record value.

Conditional Statements

Each time we use a programming language, we need to ask and answer two questions{what are they?]. In Javascript, as with other languages, we have some conditional statements that address these needs. The first conditional statement is the if statement, shown in the following code example:

```
if (condition) {
// action code here
}
```

The if statement has a condition in parentheses. If the condition is true, the code in braces will be executed. The part of the code in braces is the body of the statement. Braces are not needed ,to write an if statement, but the approach without using braces is considered a bad practice because the code readability decreases as the code's complexity increases.

The condition can be evaluated only as true or false. To implement this, we usually use operators like those shown in the following example:

```
if (a<10) {
// action code here
}
if (b==10) {
// action code here
}
if (c!=10) {
// action code here
}
```

The if statement enables us to address only one choice: if the condition is true, do something. If we need to have an alternative to our main case, we can use the if-else statement. With the if-else statement, the else-branch is executed if the test on the condition returns false.

```
if (condition) {
// action code here
} else {
        // action code here
}
```

Next, let's look at a simple `if-else` statement. We use the score variable in creating two options:

```
var score = 500;

if (score>100) {
alert("Congrats, New Record!");
} else {
        alert("Sorry, Try Again!");
}
```

In Figure 7–20, we can see what happens when we run the preceding code on Safari Mobile.

Figure 7–20. *The conditional if statement in action*

We can also nest the `if` or `if-else` statement, but it's considered a good practice not to go beyond two levels of nested statements because the code's readability decreases.

```
if (condition) {
// action code here
} else {
        // action code here
        if (condition) {
                // nested code here
        }
}
```

If we have a Javascript code with a complex logic, instead of using a deep nested conditional statement, it's much better to break it apart and implement it in different functions.

Loop Statements

Often we need to execute our code multiple times, such as when we change the background of more than one element, hide multiple elements in some specific context, and so on. The most basic kind of loop is implemented in the while statement.

```
while(condition) {
    // action code here
    increment/decrement operator
}
```

In the while loop, we execute the body of the statement until the condition is true. The increment/decrement operator guarantees that the while exits after a finite number of times; otherwise, the while executes what an infinite loop.

```
var a = 1;

while(a<10) {
    alert(a);
    a++;
}
```

Another loop statement is the do-while. The do-while statement is a variant of the while statement but with one important difference. The do-while statement always executes at least once.

```
var a = 1;

do {
    alert(a);
    a++;
} while(a<10);
```

The do-while executes at least once so that the body of the statement comes before the condition, meaning that the first time the body is executed and only after that the condition is checked for the first time.

The last loop statement we examine is the for statement. The for statement takes all the logical parts we use in the while statement and compacts them into one single line. For this reason we can always convert a for statement into a while statement and vice versa.

```
for(index variable; condition, increment/decrement) {
        // action code here
}
```

The following code shows an implementation of a for cycle using the same logical part used in the while statement:

```
for(var i=1; i<10; i++) {
    alert(a);
}
```

The `for` statement is common in Javascript and, as we have seen, it is also similar to the `while` statement. Only experience tells us when a `for` statement is preferable to a `while` statement and vice versa.

Functions

When our code gets large and complex, it's considered a good practice to break large Javascript elements into smaller reusable modular pieces. We do this by taking different parts of Javascript code, wrapping them up, and giving them a name. This is the logical approach behind creating Javascript functions.

```
function functionName() {
        // action doce here
}
```

`Function` is the reserved word used for creating a function. Next we choose a name followed by parentheses. In the parentheses is the place where the function expects to have data passed into it; in this case, the function doesn't take any data.

After the function is declared, we can call it in our HTML code using its name as shown in the next example.

```
functionName();
```

Writing our function code doesn't officially tells us where we insert our Javascript code because the Javascript engine first scans the entire code checking for functions before running anything. Nevertheless it's considered a good practice to define a function on top of our Javascript file, and then call it later.

```
function functionName() {
        // action here
}
… … …
… … …
… … …
functionName();
```

A function might also have one or more parameters. These are specified in parentheses as shown in the following example:

```
function functionName(parameters) {
        // action here
}
```

In the next example, we write a sum function that takes two parameters and returns the sum using the alert box:

```
<html>
<head>
        <title>Javascript Test</title>
</head>
```

```
<body>
        <h1>Javascript Test Page</h1>
<script>
                function sum(a,b) {
                        var mySum = a+b;
                        alert(mySum);
                }
                sum(10,15);
</script>
</body>
</html>
```

In Figure 7–21, we can see the result tested using Safari Mobile.

Figure 7–21. *The sum() function in action*

In Javascript, we are not required to return any type of value from our functions, but in case we need to send information back from a function, we can use the return reserved word, as follows:

```
function sum(a,b) {
var mySum = a+b;
        alert(mySum);
        return mySum;
}
```

Variable Scope

The concept of *variable scope* refers to the area in which certain variables are accessible. Variable scope is a fundamental concept with every programming language and involves several more concepts. A variable can have a local scope or a global scope.

A local variable has a *local scope* and is a variable declared in a function, meaning that we can't access this variable from outside the function. This kind of variable exists until the function ends. From the other side, we have a *global scope* where the variable is declared at the top-level block of a scripting block, is outside any kind of function declared inside the scripting block, and is accessible from anywhere in the document. This kind of variable exists until the document closes.

When writing the sum function, we use the variable mySum to store the sum result. Every variable declared in a function is a local variable, which means that it is restricted to it and doesn't exist outside the function itself. In this case, mySum is a local variable with a local scope and is not visible outside the function.

```
var mySum;
function sum(a,b) {
mySum = a+b;
        alert(mySum);
        return mySum;
}
```

If we need a variable visible through the entire code, we need to declare the variable outside the function. In this case the variable is a global variable. In the previous example, we declare mySum outside the function, and we assign the add result in the function's body.

In Javascript, variable scope can be only global or local. For those who use other programming languages, this might sound a bit strange, but as we previously mentioned, Javascript is an intentionally limited language that is focused on and oriented to its goals: manipulating web pages.

Arrays

So far, we have learned how to store a value in a variable. Sometimes we need to store multiple values in the same object. This type of object is an *array* and can be declared using one of the following two syntaxes.

```
var myArray = [];              // shorthand declaration
var myArray = new Array();     // longhand declaration
var myArray = Array();   // longhand declaration
var myArray = Array(5); // array with 5 slots
```

In Javascript, we can create an array with a fixed number of elements (as shown in one of our previous examples), but in Javascript, arrays are dynamic and in this language that value is not fixed or specified.

Because arrays are objects, they have properties that we can retrieve. In Table 7–42, we can see these array properties.

Table 7–42. *Javascript Array Properties*

Property	Description
constructor	Returns the function that created the array
length	Sets or returns the number of elements in an array
prototype	Identical (value and type)

Because arrays are objects, they also have methods. In Javascript, we can see a method as a function that belongs to an object. A method can be called using the following syntax.

```
objectName.methodName();
```

In Table 7–43, we can see the methods that operate on the type of object called arrays.

Table 7–43. *Javascript Array Methods*

Method	Description
concat()	Joins two or more arrays and returns a copy of the joined arrays
indexOf()	Returns true if the array is the specified object
join()	Joins the elements of an array into a string
pop()	Removes the last element of an array and returns the element
push()	Adds an element to the end of an array and returns the new length
reverse()	Reverses the order of the elements of an array
shift()	Removes the first element from an array and returns the element
slice()	Selects a part of an array and returns the part
sort()	Sorts the elements of an array
splice()	Adds or removes elements from an array
toString()	Converts an array to a string and returns the string
unshift()	Adds an element to the beginning of an array and returns the new length
valueOf()	Returns the primitive value of an array

Arrays are one of the most used objects in Javascript and in fact are almost everywhere, primarily because most of them are created by the Javascript engine for dealing with many different situations that arise. We see more on this when we work with DOM a little later on.

Strings

To assign a string value to a variable, we need to surround our word or phrase with quotes or double quotes. Both types of quotes are allowed; mixed up quotes, such as those in the next example, are not allowed:

```
var myString = "double quoted string";  // correct syntax
var myString = "single quoted string";  // correct syntax
var myString = 'mixed quoted string";   // incorrect syntax
```

If we use single quotes and we want to insert a quote or a double quote in our string, we need to use the backslash prefix in order to tell the Javascript engine to close the string.

```
var myString = "don't use single quotes";    // correct syntax
var myString = 'don't use single quotes';     // incorrect syntax
var myString = 'don\'t use single quotes';    // correct syntax
```

Strings can be treated as array objects (array of characters) and applied to it one of the methods we previously saw for the arrays. For the same reason, a string object has the same properties previously seen for the array objects, which is shown in the Table 7–44.

Table 7–44. *Javascript String Properties*

Property	Description
constructor	Returns the function that created the array
length	Sets or returns the number of elements in an array
prototype	Identical (value and type)

In the same way, string objects have methods that operate on this type of Javascript object. String object methods are shown in Table 7–45.

Table 7–45. *Javascript String Methods*

Method	Description
charArt()	Returns a character at the specific index
charCodeAt()	Returns the Unicode of the character at the specific index
concat()	Joins two or more strings and returns the joined string
fromCharCode()	Converts Unicode values to characters
indexOf()	Returns the position of the first found occurrence of a specified string
lastIndexOf()	Returns the position of the last found occurrence of a specified string
match()	Searches for a match between a string and a regular expression and returns the match
replace()	Searches for a match between a string and a substring (or a regular expression) and replaces the matches substring with the new substring
search()	Searches for a match between a string and a regular expression and returns the position of the match
slice()	Extracts a part of a string and returns the part
split()	Splits a string into an array of substrings
substr()	Extracts the specified number of characters from a string
substring()	Extracts characters from a string between two specified indices
toLowerCase()	Converts a string to lowercase letters
toUpperCase()	Converts a string to uppercase letters
valueOf()	Returns the primitive value of a string

Remember that Javascript is case sensitive, which is important when we work with strings.

Objects

As previously mentioned, Javascript supports the concept of objects. An object can be pictured as a container for various data and behaviors. Data are stored, for example, in variables or arrays, whereas behaviors are represented by methods and functions.

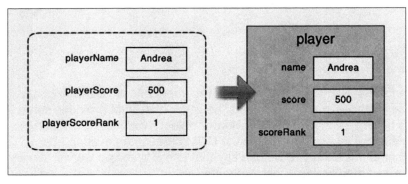

Figure 7–22. *Three variables (left) and three object's properties (right)*

In Figure 7–22, we see how variables can be wrapped into a container (an object). Once we do this, the data are one level deeper in the container object. If we need to access data in an object, we can use the following syntax. When a variable is outside an object, it's called "variable" and when is in an object is called "property."

```
var player = new Object();      // create a new object called "player"
player.name = "Andrea";
player.score = 500;
player.scoreRank = 1;
```

```
objectName.propertyName // generic syntax for property declaration
```

When we declare a Javascript object, we can also use shorthand as shown in the next example. We declare a variable and assign a set of properties surrounded by a pair of braces to it.

```
var player = { name:"Andrea", score: 500, scoreRank:1 }
```

In the braces, we use three name value pairs to create the same object we created previously using four different lines of code.

BOM (Browser Object Model)

The Browser Object Model (BOM) describes methods and interfaces for working with the browser. The browser itself is an object and can be accessed from its top to the bottom status bar by referencing the top-level object window. From the top-level object window, we can access important information contained in other (sub) objects such as the following:

Navigator
Contains information about the browser engine type or version.

Location
Holds the current URL displayed in the browser.

History
Contains the history list of the browser.

Frames

Provides an array of the frames within the current page.

Document

Represents the current page in the browser.

Because no official standards exist for the BOM, each browser defines its own properties and methods for these and other objects; however, the BOM provides some *de facto* standards like having a window and a navigator object. Notice how the BOM also covers the document that is also covered by the DOM creating an overlap effect. Without going any further in this situation, we can say that in our WebApp we will always use the DOM to access and modify document elements.

DOM (Document Object Model)

DOM stands for Document Object Model. The word "document" refers not to the entire WebApp, but just to its single webpage. The word "object" refers to the individual parts of the documents, to all things that can be manipulated as individual pieces. In Figure 7–23, we can see the individual objects of a page from our "The Store" use-case. A single object can be a heading element, an entire ordered list, or a single element in the same unordered list or even the whole document.

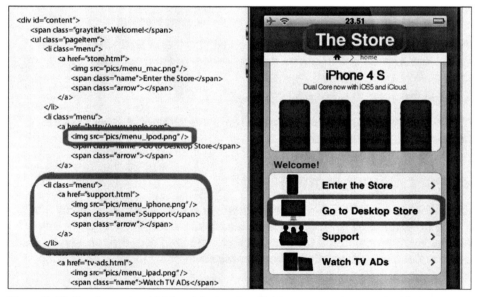

Figure 7–23. *Developer view (right) and design view (right) over some document's objects*

The word "model" refers to the diagram that represents a webpage. This diagram is based on a tree structure that connects the single part of a document; each single part is a node and is represented in the example in Figure 7–24.

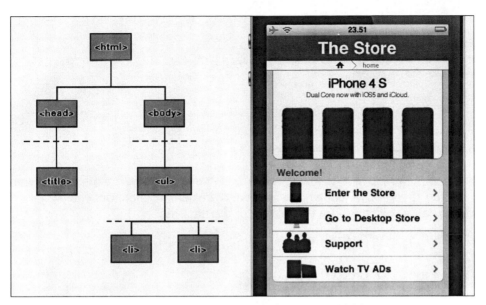

Figure 7–24. *The node structure (left) and the visual design structure (right)*

A node in the diagram can have a parent represented by the node directly above itself and can have children represented by nodes directly below. The model refers to the page diagram structure, but it's actually just a set of terms that we can agree on and a set of standards we can use.

This means that what we have defined so far is an agreed-upon set of terms (Model) that describe how to interact with the single piece (Object) of a webpage (Document). The DOM is not a language; it's a convention and because Javascript agrees on that, it's available in Javascript.

DOM works in terms of nodes, and we don't just have nodes that represent the single document elements, but we also have nodes that represent the various attributes that a node can have. Officially in Javascript there are twelve types of nodes, but in practice we are interested in only three of them: element, attribute, and text nodes. In Figure 7–25, we can see the DOM of an unordered list.

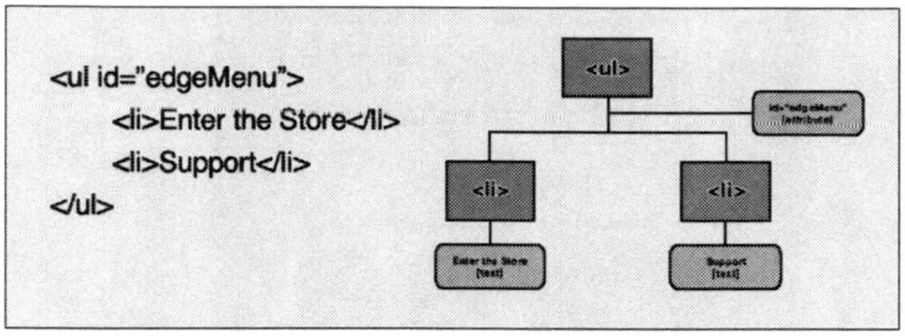

Figure 7–25. *The code (left) and its DOM structure (right)*

The important point to grasp here is that a node doesn't contain (directly) the attribute or the text. According to the DOM, each node relative to an element that contains some text or attributes has a child node for the text or for the attribute.

Now we see how to work with DOM.

Compare DOM and HTML Structure

Just as we saw previously for the DOM map, the HTML document has a hierarchical tree where the single HTML elements are the nodes of the tree. Although this is true, it's important to clarify that the HTML hierarchy structure is not identical to the DOM hierarchy structure. Every HTML element has its own attributes that are not represented in the HTML hierarchy but in order to be accessed must be represented in the DOM node hierarchy. The following example illustrates this point:

```
<html>
        <head>
                <title>DOM Structure Test</title>
        </head>
        <body>
                        <section id="intro">
                        <h1>The DOM Structure</h1>
                        <p id="paragraph1">Lorem ipsum dolor sit amet</p>
                </section>
        </body>
</html>
```

In Figure 7–26, we can see the comparison between the HTML and the DOM structure.

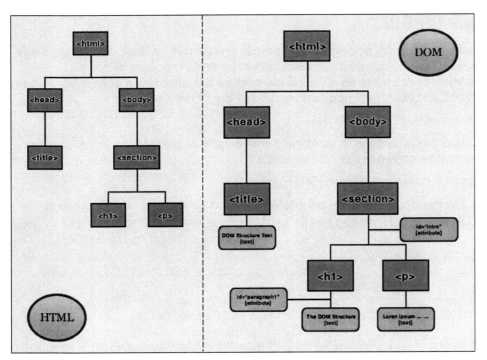

Figure 7–26. *HTML and DOM structure comparison*

Figure 7–26 also shows how HTML attributes that are not represented in the HTML element structure are a type of special node in the DOM structure because they don't participate in the parent-child relationship. Nevertheless, they are still objects and therefore accessible via Javascript call. Table 7–46 shows the most common node types in Javascript.

Table 7–46. *Most Common Node Type in Javascript.*

Node Type	Node Code	Description
Element	1	Represents a single HTML element
Attr	2	Represents a single node attribute
Text	3	Represents the text in an element or attribute node
Comment	8	Represents the contents of an HTML comment
Document	9	Represents the whole HTML document
DocumentType	10	Represents the attributes of a DTD
Document Fragment	11	Represents a (temporary) fragment of HTML document

Working with DOM

The DOM works in terms of nodes, so for us the main question is: how can we grab one of these nodes? The key consideration is whether the node is unique or not and therefore whether or not it has an ID. If the element we are after has a unique ID, we can use what's probably the most important method of the DOM:

```
document.getElementById("elementId");
```

The way we use this method is to combine it with a variable declaration that stores the returned element as shown in the next example.

```
var myElement = document.getElementById("edgeMenu");
```

In this case, the method returns the unordered list used for the previous example in Figure 7–26. In Table 7–47 we can see three of the most useful methods defined by the DOM.

Table 7–47. *Javascript Most Used Methods*

Property	Description
getElementById()	Returns the fist element with the specified id
getElementsByName()	Returns the fist element with the specified name
getElementsByTagName()	Returns the fist element with the specified tagname

If we use the getElementByTagName(), we can grab a set of elements with just one method call. In this situation, Javascript creates an array and inserts all the returned elements. The syntax for the getElementByTagName() is the following, and this code returns all the <li> elements in the documents.

```
var myListElements = document.getElementsByTagName("li");
myListElements[3];       // return the fourth links in position three inside the array
```

In our example, we use the getElementById and getElelmentsByTagName methods on the document object, but we use them on all the document's objects. In the next example we don't want all the links in the document but only the links in a specific menu.

```
var myEdgeMenu = document.getElementsById("edgeMenu");
var edgeMenuLinks = myEdgeMenu.getElementsByTagName("li");
```

First, we grab the edgeMenu element using its ID and then call the getElementsByTagName() on this node. The result is that the method returns only the <li> elements of the edgeMenu.

The next question is: what can we do if we want to not just simply grab a node, but also change it? When we write HTML code, we can change an element modifying its attribute or attributes, sometimes even adding one or more attributes. Examples are changing the src attribute of an image or a link in the heading or some other attributes in a <div> or a list.

Once we grab an element, we can use two different types of elements to achieve our goal: one for getting an attribute and one for setting an attribute. In Table 7–48, we can see these methods.

Table 7–48. *Javascript Setter and Getter Attribute Methods*

Property	Description
getAttribute()	Returns the specified attribute name
setAttribute()	Sets the specified attribute name at the specified attribute value

When we want to get an attribute, we pass the name of the attribute to the method in string format surrounded by double quotes. When we want to set an attribute we pass the name of the attribute and the value of the attribute, always in string format surrounded by double quotes. The syntax is the following:

```
elementName.getAttribute("align");
elementName.setAttribute("align", "left");
```

So far we have changed only the attribute of an element but sometimes we might need to change not only the attribute, but also the content of an element. The best way is by creating it manually and inserting individual DOM nodes in the document, which changes the page on the fly. The process requires two steps:

1. Create the element.

2. Add the element to the document.

In the next example, we add an entry to our edgeMenu or in other words we add a <li> element to the <ul> unordered list that we used for our menu.

```
var newEdgeMenuElement = document.createElement("li");
edgeMenu.appendChild(newEdgeMenuElement);
```

After we create and append a new node to the edgeMenu, we might need to add text to it. We can do this using the following syntax:

```
var newMenuText = document.createTextNode("Watch TV Ads");
newEdgeMenuElement.appendChild(newMenuText);
```

So far, we used two new methods to create nodes, and in Table 7–49, we can see some useful methods for manipulating the DOM tree structure.

Table 7–49. *Javascript Methods to Manipulate the DOM Structure*

Property	Description
appendChild()	Adds a node at the end of the list of childer node
cloneNode()	Clones a node
compareDocumentPosition()	Compares the document position of two nodes
hasAttributes()	Returns true if the node has any attributes
hasChildNodes()	Returns true if the node has any childs nodes
insertBefore()	Inserts a child before an existing child node
isEqualNode()	Checks whether two nodes are equal
isSameNode()	Checks whether two nodes are the same nodes
removeChild()	Removes a child node
replaceChild()	Replaces a child node

Now we insert the same new item into our edgeMenu but this time between the first and the second <li> elements instead of at the end as we did in the previous example.

```
var newEdgeMenuElement = document.createElement("li");
var secondMenuItem = edgeMenu.getElementsByTagName("li") [1];
edgeMenu.insertBefore(newEdgeMenuElement, seconfItem);
```

The first step uses the same code we used in the previous example, so we start by creating the new <li> element. In the second step we grab the second <li> element in the edgeMenu using the getElementByTagName method, because the <li> element doesn't have an ID and we specified the [1] second position in the edgeMenu structure. In the third step we use the insertBefore method that inserts the new <li> before the second <li>element in the edgeMenu.

Some Javascript Best Practices

Generally speaking, a program language has many rules that a developer must to follow to write complain code. These rules specify what you must write to create a valid code. When we approach the best practice, we switch from what we must write to what we should write in order to create high quality code. Essentially, best practice aims to achieve clarity, readability, and meaning.

Name convention

A name for a variable, a function, or an object should be meaningful and should be in camelcase with the first letter in lowercase. The object's name should start with an uppercase letter.

Brace style

The dominant style in Javascript is the most traditional brace style from C-based languages. If we have an if or a while statement, the curly braces opens on the same line as the keyword (if, while, and so on), and the code is indented in the block and closed curly braced in a line by itself.

Function declaration

When we declare a function, we should always define it before any attempt to call it and we always should use curly braces to define a block even if there is only one statement after the keyword (if, while, and so on).

Syntax

Always use semicolons to end of a statement and always use the keyword "var" when declaring a variable.

For more information on this subject, use a search engine and search for Javascript style guidelines. There are guidelines written by individuals from Mozilla, Yahoo, and Google.

Resource on Web Standards

In Table 7–50, we have the official resource about the three web standards presented in this chapter. If you are new to one or more of these technologies, continue to build your web standard foundations using the following official sources.

Table 7–50. *Tools Used to Design iPhone and iPad User Interfaces*

Name	URL
HTML5	http://dev.w3.org/html5/spec/
CSS3	www.w3.org/TR/CSS/
Javascript	https://developer.mozilla.org/en/JavascriptJavascript

Summary

This chapter discussed web standards. In the first part, we introduced HTML5, the web standard that structures all our web site and web applications. We introduced the new markup tags and focused our attention on its new semantic-oriented approach. We also analyzed the new HTML5 media tags such as `<audio>`, `<video>`, and `<canvas>` tags.

In the second part, we presented the new CSS3 properties that enable us to emulate the native iOS environment in a simple and better way compared with the old CSS2 specification.

In the third and final part, we worked on Javascript, viewing its implementation and working on its foundations.

In the next chapters, we use this knowledge to put our hands on and expand the iPhone and iPad HTML5, CSS3, and Javascript frameworks.

## Chapter 8

Native iOS Environment Development

My goal wasn't to die the richest man in the cemetery.
It was to go to bed at night saying, we've done something wonderful.

—Steve Jobs

In this chapter, we will see how to work in an iOS environment, how to emulate it in our WebApp, and how to optimize its use.

First, we will set up an environment for testing our work on a local network. Next, we will introduce a viewport and see how we can optimize it for developing full-screen WebApps. We will explain how to create a springboard icon, as in native applications, and how to customize a startup image.

We will specify the JavaScript code for redirecting a user from a desktop to our iPhone WebApp and from our iPhone WebApp to a desktop, and explain how to emulate native link and design element behavior once a user has approached our WebApp.

We will also see how to interact with iPhone features, such as phone, mail, and GPS, and how to handle user gesture interaction and device orientation change.

Setting up the Environment

Before placing a WebApp on a public, live web server, it is better to work in a private environment, using a server on a desktop computer. This configuration will make the development and testing phases easier.

In order to do this, we need to perform the following steps:

1. Create a folder in: /user/UserName/Sites/MySharedFolder

2. Go to System Preferences Sharing

3. Enable the service Web Sharing

> **NOTE:** The iPhone or the iPad and the desktop computer must be connected to the same Wi-Fi network in order to establish a connection using the local URL address.

From this point on, we will save everything in this local folder and will access it using the local URL: http://desktopIPaddress/~folderName.

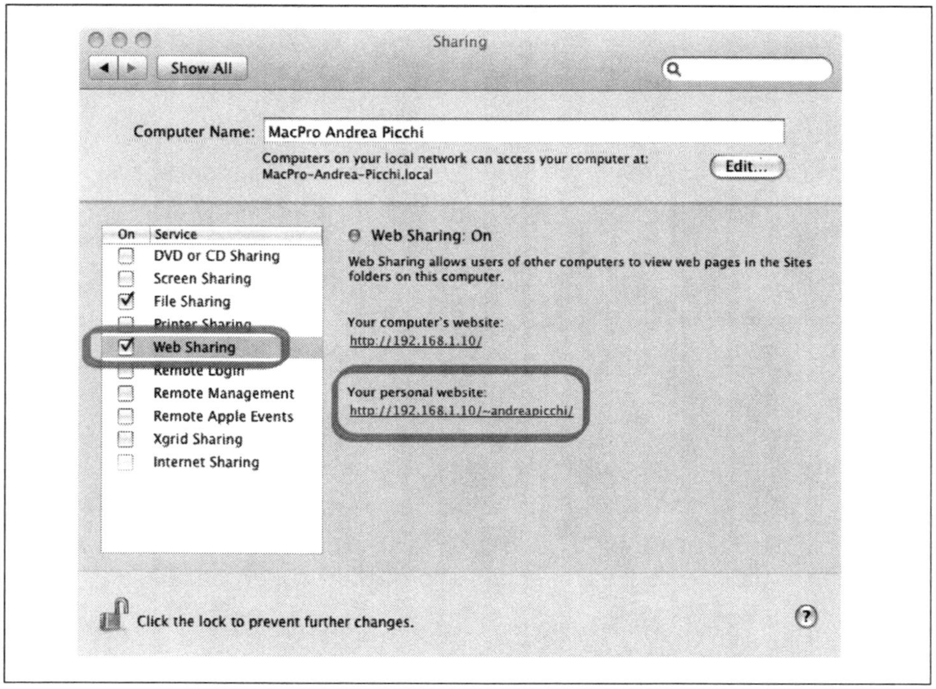

Figure 8–1. *The Sharing box preferences.*

Figure 8–1 shows the Sharing box with the service to enable and the IP address to use. The IP address shown in Figure 8–1 is related to my desktop computer; yours will have the same structure but will be slightly different.

Once the network environment is set, an HTML5-compliant editor is needed. Unfortunately, not every editor currently available is compatible with HTML5 syntax; be sure to check HTML5 compatibility before starting your project.

Defining Viewport

The viewport is the rectangular area that the user sees when looking at the iPhone or iPad display, and represents an important concept in the world of web design. The viewport dimensions are defined by two values: device-width and device-height. As we learned in previous chapters, different models of the iPhone have different display resolutions; nevertheless device-width and device-height values are set by default at the same value for all iPhone models. In both portrait and landscape modes, there will always be a 320 × 480 px viewport area. This approach ensures that, even with double-pixel resolution, the ratio between viewport elements remains unchanged, as shown in Figure 8–2, ensuring that existing iPhone WebApps continue to function as expected.

```
<meta name="viewport" content="width=640"/>
```

Even if it's not indicated by the code just shown, you can still have "full 100% real pixels" on Retina display devices.

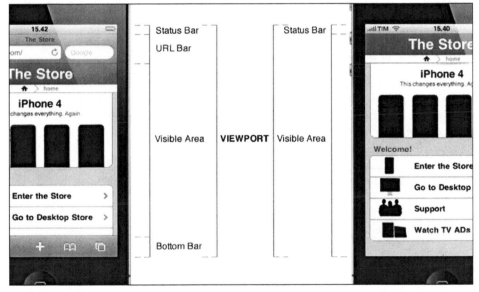

Figure 8–2. *The iPhone viewport and its sections in non-WebApp (left) and WebApp mode (right).*

The default value for the viewport is set to a width of 980 px; this value is the reason a compatible WebApp with a fixed-width structure should be set as 980 px wide. In addition, when the viewport tag is not present, Safari loads the page as a 980 px-wide page and shrinks it to the viewport. This is equal to the following viewport metatag declaration:

```
<meta name="viewport" content="width=980; user-scalable=1;"/>
```

Having a 980 px default value means that the old iPhone models will scale down this value by a factor of approximately 3.06:1 or 2.04:1, while the iPhone4 will scale down by a factor of 2.04:1 or 1.02:1. Furthermore, the best option for iPhone and iPad web designers and developers is using the viewport metatag for letting the web page fit the width of the device; the viewport metatag properties can be seen in Table 8–1.

In order to achieve this, a constant called device-width needs to be used. The following example shows a typical viewport metatag for a WebApp with two meta-keys: name and content.

```
<meta name="viewport" content="width=device-width; initial-scale=1.0;
 maximum-scale=1.0; user-scalable=no;"/>
```

This meta-key content has multiple properties separated by a comma. The constant device-width refers to the width of the device that browses the page. This means that the value will change from device to device, as shown in the following example:

- width=768 (device-width in px for iPad on)

- width=480 (device-width in px for iPhone4 on)

- width=320 (device-width in px for iPhone 2G, 2G, 3GS)

You can also decide to match the device height instead of its width using the constant device-height.

The other property, initial-scale, sets the initial zoom on the web page once it is loaded. The default value of 1 sets the page to the iPhone display resolution.

The last property, user-scalable, sets the capability for the user to zoom in or out using a pinch gesture on the screen. When it is set to *no*, no zooming is allowed. The user scalability property should be set to *no* for every native iPhone and iPad WebApp, while it should be set to *yes* on iPad-compatible projects.

Table 8–1. *Viewport Metatag Properties.*

Name	Default Value	Min Value	Max Value
width	980	200	10000
height	Calculated	223	10000
initial-scale	Fit to Screen	Minimum Scale	Maximum Scale
user-scalable	Yes	- - -	- - -
minimum-scale	0.25	>0	10
maximum-scale	1.6	>0	10

As a final note, remember that the viewport metatag will not in any way affect the rendering of desktop web pages.

Full-Screen Mode Application

The first and major aesthetic difference between a native application and a WebApp is the presence of the Safari URL bar in the latter. Working with Safari and its engine, WebKit, provides a measure of control over this situation.

Figure 8–3. *Comparison between a native application (left) and a WebApp (right) in non-WebApp mode.*

Using the apple-mobile-web-app-capable metatag, you can specify the browser to hide the URL bar, thus providing a native-like look and feel to the user.

```
<meta name="apple-mobile-web-app-capable" content="yes" />
```

The full-screen mode will work only if the web page is launched from a link in the springboard. We will see how to add a web page to the iPhone or iPad springboard in the next section.

The iPhone and iPad status bar is fixed, and we are unable to hide it. Despite that fact, we can change how it looks using the following metatag:

```
<meta name="apple-mobile-web-app-status-bar-style" content="black-translucent" />
```

Table 8–2. *AppleMobileWebAppStatusBarStyle Content Meta-key Properties.*

Name	Description
default (gray)	Set the default (gray) background. Content is displayed below the status bar.
black	Set a black background. Content is displayed below the status bar.
black-translucent	Set a black translucent background. Content is displayed on the entire screen partially obscured.

This metatag works only if the full-screen mode metatag is previously declared; otherwise it will be ignored by the browser. The best approach is always to choose the Status Bar style according to the application color palette, but if you want to increase the visible area, the only option is to use the black-translucent version. The default Status Bar style in the springboard is set to black-translucent from iOS4 onwards.

Adding the Springboard Icon

The second difference between a native application and a WebApp is that a native application is launched from the home screen, also known as a springboard. We can replicate this sort of native pattern by designing a customized icon and adding a web page shortcut to the springboard, and then launch the page directly from there.

The customized springboard icon has some specific characteristics; some are a "must," while others are just a "should," and can be considered best practices.

- Measure: 57 × 57 px (iPhone 2G, 3G, 3GS) (required)
- Measure: 114 × 114 px (iPhone 4 on) (required)
- Measure: 72 × 72 px (iPad, iPad2) (required)
- Corners: 90 Degree
- Style: No Shine or Gloss
- Name: apple-touch-icon.png
- Name: apple-touch-icon-precomposed.png
- Format: Portable Network Graphic (PNG) (required)
- Location: Root Directory (required)

If we want to prevent Safari from adding effects like gloss and shine to our icon, we need to use the name apple-touch-icon-precomposed.png.

When the custom image is ready, we can link it to the web page using the following metatag:

```
<link rel="apple-touch-icon" href="/apple-touch-icon.png"/>
```

Even if, in theory, it's possible to use different springboard icons for different pages, it is strongly recommended that you use only one image for all your web pages—one WebApp, one springboard icon.

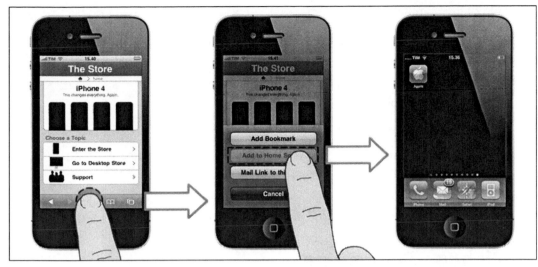

Figure 8–4. *Adding a springboard (home screen) icon.*

Users can add the springboard icon to their iPhone or iPad home screens using the plus button "+" in the Safari bottom bar and then clicking the "Add to Home Screen" button, as shown in Figure 8–4.

Application Startup Image

A web site, and even more often a WebApp, takes several seconds to load completely. We can cover this delay using a startup image, also known as a splash screen, which is displayed while the web page is loading.

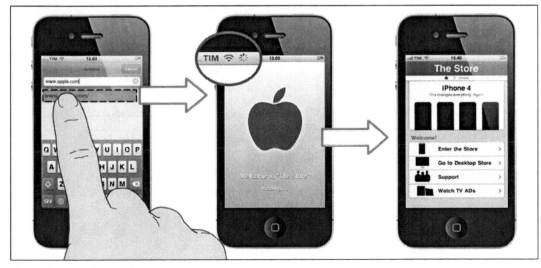

Figure 8–5. *WebApp startup image in action.*

This kind of image must have some specific dimensions based on the principle that we need to cut off from the image the 20 px of space used by the status bar. The startup image is typically a portrait image, is in PNG format, and has exactly the following measurements:

- 320 × 460 px (iPhone 2G, 3G, 3GS)
- 480 × 940 px (iPhone4 on)
- 768 × 1004 px (iPad, iPad2)

Once we have our startup image, we need to link it using the following metatag:

```
<link rel="apple-touch-startup-image" href="/startup-image.png">
```

As for the springboard icon, if we link it using the metatag, the startup image does not need to be placed in the root directory; however, this is considered best practice.

Application Redirecting

When we develop a native-like WebApp for iOS, we need to keep in mind that this optimized mobile version is, most of time, not the first choice in terms of availability for the user.

The first thing that will happen in 99% of cases when a user comes to your index web page is that the web server sends the web client the standard desktop version. In addition, we need to know when a user is browsing from a mobile device in order to redirect him to the specific mobile version of our content.

We can achieve this using one of two techniques: JavaScript or CSS. These are not the only solutions available; we can achieve the same result very efficiently from the server (Apache or PHP, for instance), but in this text we are focusing on web standards in a broader sense. For this reason, we will show only HTML, CSS, and JavaScript solutions.

I recommend that you use JavaScript code for your project, but it's also important to remember that in some other cases, CSS detection via media query can be helpful.

```
<link rel="stylesheet" media="all and (max-device-width: 480px)" href="iphone.css">
<link rel="stylesheet" media="all and (min-device-width: 481px) and (max-device-width:
1024px) and (orientation:portrait)" href="ipad-portrait.css">
<link rel="stylesheet" media="all and (min-device-width: 481px) and (max-device-width:
1024px) and (orientation:landscape)" href="ipad-landscape.css">
<link rel="stylesheet" media="all and (min-device-width: 1025px)" href="ipad-
landscape.css">
```

In this example, we used three CSS files—one for iPhone, and two for iPad. We also used the ipad-landscape.css file for desktop machines, with a minimum width of 1025 px.

Assuming that we developed a compatible version for our project for both desktop and iPad users, the following code will be used in the compatible index web page for redirecting the iPhone user to the iPhone native-like version.

```
<script type="text/javascript">
```

```
        if ((navigator.userAgent.indexOf('iPhone') != -1) ||
(navigator.userAgent.indexOf('iPod') != -1) ||
(navigator.userAgent.indexOf('iPad') != -1))
        {
                document.location = "http://www.iphone.store.com/";
        }
</script>
```

The JavaScript code will do a test on the device "user agent," detecting both iPhone and iPod users. We also need to ensure that an iPad or desktop user will not accidentally browse to the iPhone version, so we need to detect these users employing another small JavaScript code, but this time on the iPhone web page.

```
<script language="javascript" type="text/javascript">
        if((navigator.userAgent.match(/Macintosh/i)) ||
        (navigator.userAgent.match(/Windows/i)) ||
        (navigator.userAgent.match(/Linux/i)))
            {
                location.replace("http://www.store.com/");
            }
</script>
```

This time, the JavaScript code will detect the Macintosh, Linux, and Windows "user agent" and will redirect these desktop users to their specific version.

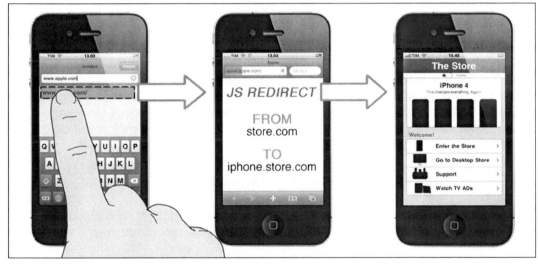

Figure 8–6. *WebApp redirecting in action: From desktop to mobile (iPhone) version.*

Setting up the Head Section

All the code developed so far is to be inserted into the <head> of our web page. Now it's time to take a bird's eye view of the entire <head> section. The following code is the <head> of the Apple Store use case based on iWebKit 5.0.4.

```
<head>
<meta charset="utf-8">
<meta name="apple-mobile-web-app-capable" content="yes" />
<meta name="viewport" content="minimum-scale=1.0, maximum-scale=0.6667,É
 width=device-width, user-scalable=no" />
<meta name="description" content="The Store iPhone Use Case" />
<link rel="apple-touch-startup-image" href="pics/startup-image.png" />
<link rel="apple-touch-icon" href="/apple-touch-icon.png" />
<link rel="stylesheet" type="text/css" media="screen" href="css/style.css" />
<script type="text/javascript" src="javascript/functions.js"></script>
<title>The Store</title>
<script language="javascript" type="text/javascript">
          if((navigator.userAgent.match(/iPhone/i)) ||
          (navigator.userAgent.match(/iPod/i)) ||
          (navigator.userAgent.indexOf('iPad') != -1)))
             {
                    location.replace("http://www.iphone.apple.com/");
             }
</script>
</head>
```

The <head> code intentionally doesn't contain any type of SEO metatags because we will introduce this subject in Chapter 10. Now, we will jump to the <body> section of our web page; in the next section, we'll see how to interact with the native services provided by the Apple mobile device.

Native Link Emulation

The default Safari mobile behavior provides a transparent highlight color as an active state to every link that has been clicked. When designing a web site, this feature could be useful, but when working on a WebApp with, presumably, many well-designed buttons, this feature would not be visually appealing. We can override this default Safari behavior using the following CSS rule:

```
* {
        -webkit-tap-highlight-color: rgba(0,0,0,0);
}
```

The syntax of this CSS rule uses the "*" symbol in order to attach it to all the active design elements. We include the RGBA code for using the alpha channel and specify a total transparent color for the element.

Native Text Emulation

A handy feature on Safari is that it is able to resize text automatically and reformat it for use on a small screen. By default, iOS overwrites the site's font size to allow the text to be read without any problems when the user zooms over a paragraph. When designing a native-like WebApp, we don't need this feature and can disable it with the following rule:

```
* {
        -webkit-text-size-adjust: none;
}
```

A native-like WebApp is designed for use on the iPhone and does not need any help from Safari to make it more readable.

Native Element Emulation

The copy and paste feature is useful while browsing a web site but, as for the active link state, it is less useful with a WebApp. This feature remains active on all the design elements, making even the header bar of your web page selectable. The following CSS rule creates a more comfortable and native-like environment for the user.

```
* {
        -webkit-user-select: none;
}

.copiable {
        -webkit-user-select: text;
}
```

For this purpose, two different CSS rules can be used for disabling the copy and paste feature on all the design elements and texts, using another rule for creating a CSS class that targets only some specific cases where the copy and paste feature can actually be useful. The implementation of this rule depends on the kind of content provided; if we have a lot of "copiable" text, it can sometimes be useful to reverse the rule.

Figure 8–7. *Native design element emulation: Unwanted copy and paste feature in action.*

Another feature that is useful to disable when we work on a WebApp is the default Safari callout behavior. Every time the user touches and holds an element such as a link, the browser displays a callout containing information about the link, such as opening it in another window. We can disable the callout behavior using the following CSS rule:

```
* {
        -webkit-touch-callout: none;
}
```

We want to prevent this behavior because links used in a WebApp are typically dedicated to internal navigation, and we want to prevent the user from using it and going outside it. If this rule is set to *none*, the user can hold any link or image as long as he/she wants without getting the default Safari behavior.

Native Scrolling Emulation

One of the most important features available from iOS5 (beta2) is support for the new CSS rule for overflow-scrolling. Until now, there was a noticeable difference in momentum between scrolling a native app and scrolling a native-like WebApp. This behavior was an obstacle for those who wanted to emulate the native look-and-feel of iOS applications.

This new rule provides a native way to scroll content inside a fixed size (width and height) HTML element—for instance, the main <div>—and to reduce or eliminate the GPU overhead caused by the implementation of custom scrolling. An implementation of this rule follows:

```
.scrollableElement
{
  overflow-y: scroll;
  -webkit-overflow-scrolling: touch;
}
```

The position—fixed and overflow—scroll rules will change the way layouts are designed on iPhone, taking another important step forward in the native look-and-feel emulation process.

Native iOS Service Interaction

Service interaction is one of the drawbacks of developing web applications instead of native applications. Previously, we introduced the pros and cons of this choice; in this section, we will focus only on what we can do and how we can achieve it.

A WebApp is able to interact with the most important, and most used, services provided by iOS: Phone, Mail, SMS, and Maps. This type of user interaction is made using the <a> tag, as with every other ordinary link in our web page, and has the following structure:

```
<a href="protocolServiceScheme:protocolParameter>linkName</a>
```

In the next section, we will see how to implement these special types of links for adding an extra level of interaction to our WebApp.

The Phone Application

We can add a link to the Phone application using the following link syntax:

```
<a href="tel:1-305-555-5555">Call 1-305-555-5555</a>
```

Using this syntax, Safari will automatically create a phone link on your web page. If the Phone application is not installed on the device, as in the iPad and iPod, we will get a warning message when touching this type of link.

Another good practice is to check the iPhone agent in order to prevent this type of error. Checking the iPhone agent filters access to the service, allowing only iPhone users with phone capability. The following code performs this type of check using the JavaScript "onclick" event handler:

```
<a href="tel:1-305-555-5555"  onclick="return (navigator.userAgent.indexOf('iPhone')É
 != -1)">1-305-555-5555</a>
```

iOS provides only partial support to the RFC 2086 protocol. This means that if the number contains special characters like "*" or "#", the device will not attempt to call the number. This happens because iOS, for security reasons, doesn't implement all the special characters in the `tel` scheme.

iOS number detection is on by default; sometimes you don't want some numbers to be interpreted as phone numbers. In this case, switch off the iOS number detection, adding the following metatag in the <head> section, telling the iPhone to ignore it.

```
<meta name ="format-detection" content ="telephone=no">
```

It's important to note that if a phone number is inside an <a> link, it will continue to be displayed as a phone link.

The Mail Application

You can add a link to the Mail application using the following link syntax:

```
<a href="mailto:info@andreapicchi.it">Andrea Picchi</a>
```

Safari will automatically create a link to the Mail application that will be opened in a new window. You can also embed text directly in the e-mail form that will be opened by the link using the following syntax:

```
<a href="mailto:info@andreapicchi.it?subject=Book%20Feedback&body=É
Keep%20Up%20the%20Good%20Work!">Send a Feedback to Andrea Picchi</a>
```

The iOS implements the `mailto` scheme specified in the RFC 236 and allows you to use some optional mailto attributes, as shown in Table 8–3.

Table 8–3. *Optional Mailto Attributes Supported by iOS.*

Name	Syntax
Body Message	body=messageText
Subject Message	subject=subjectText
Multiple Recipients	mailto=emailAddress1,emailAddress2,emailAddressN
CC Recipient	cc=emailAddress
BCC Recipient	bcc=emailAddress

As you can see from the last code example, the HTTP convention says to use the "?" character (?subject=...) for the first attribute and use the "&" for the other follower attributes (&body=...).

The SMS Application

We can add a link to the SMS application using the following link syntax:

```
<a href="sms:1-305-555-5555">1-305-555-5555</a>
```

The sms scheme will tell Safari to open the SMS application. Unlike the Mail application, with the sms scheme, we can't add text.

The target phone number is an optional parameter, and if we just want to open the SMS application with a blank page, we can use the following syntax:

```
<a href="sms:">Launch the SMS Application</a>
```

As for the Phone application, if the SMS application is not installed on the device, as in the case of the iPad and iPod, we will get a warning message when touching this type of link.

```
<a href="sms:1-305-555-5555"  onclick="return (navigator.userAgent.indexOf('iPhone')É
 != -1)">1-305-555-5555</a>
```

The preceding code performs the same agent check used with the tel protocol in order to prevent iPod users from accessing a baseband-based service.

The Maps Application

You can add a link to the Maps application using the following link syntax:

```
<a href="http://maps.google.com/maps?q=cupertino">Cupertino</a>
```

The Maps application doesn't have its own maps scheme, and the map link is specified using a regular HTTP protocol syntax. Safari reroutes the HTTP request to the Google map server at maps.google.com and then opens its HTTP response using the Maps application.

As with the Mail application, we can combine parameters to provide more information to the Maps application using the "?" character. The following example shows my office in Tuscany, Italy:

```
<a  href="http://maps.google.com/maps?q=via+dell+olmo+50,É
+livorno,+italy+(Andrea+Picchi's+Office)&t=h&z=7">Andrea Picchi's Office</a>
```

The "+" character is used for passing the application a phrase composed of multiple words, while the rounded parentheses are used for creating a label. The "t" parameter is used for specifying a hybrid map with the "h" value, and the "z" setting the zoom level at 7.

The Google Maps application has a long list of parameters, but the Maps application doesn't support them all. The Google Maps parameters supported by iOS are shown in Table 8-4.

Figure 8–8. *The Maps application: Cupertino, CA, USA.*

Table 8–4. *Google Maps Application Parameters Supported by iOS (Alphabetical Order)*.*

Name	Description
cid=	Custom ID used by Google for identifying businesses
daddr=	Destination address used with driving directions
latlng=	Custom ID used by Google for identifying businesses
ll=	Latitude and longitude points for the map center point; must be in decimal format and comma-separated
near=	Location part of the query
q=	Query parameter
saddr=	Source address used with driving directions
sll=	Latitude and longitude points for a business search
spn=	Approximate latitude and longitude span
sspn=	Custom longitude and latitude span used by Google
t=	Type of map to display
z=	Zoom level

*Complete list of parameter values at http://mapki.com/wiki/Google_Map_Parameters

Touch Events and Gesture Interactions

Previously, we saw that a mouse pointer is not a finger and how different it is to design for fingers instead of a mouse pointer. Here, we need to do another paradigm switch, exactly as we did for the pointing concept.

Users employ gestures for browsing web pages and emulate behaviors that they formerly used with a mouse. For this reason, finger actions and gestures have to emulate mouse events. Before the touch era, every event on a web page was triggered only by a mouse movement; button rollover, drop-down menus, and simple links are just a few examples of this type of interaction.

However, the flow of events generated by finger actions is not the same as that generated by a mouse pointer, and a finger event flow is generated by one or more finger touches, depending on whether the selected element is touchable, non-touchable, or scrollable.

> **NOTE:** Whenever we use the word "touchable," we refer to a "clickable" design element like a link, a drop-down menu, or whatever element triggers a standard mouse event inside the web page structure.

If a finger touches a non-touchable design element, events are generated or added to the gesture event flow. For this reason, when designing for iOS, we need to switch from a "mouse-oriented design paradigm" to a more appropriate "touchable-oriented design paradigm."

Touch Event Paradigm: Touch Is Not a Click

A touchable element is defined by a design element associated with an event handler. Using the mouse-based web paradigm, we could define it as a clickable element.

Single-finger user actions, two-finger user actions, and more complex gestures are built on top of the WebKit engine used by Safari Mobile. The WebKit engine plays a major role in this game, providing touch support similar to the gesture support built into the native iOS SDK. These types of events are triggered by the user every time his finger or fingers touch the capacitive display of an iOS-based device.

The single- and multi-touch events emulate classic mouse navigation, triggering mouse-related events, while gesture events are captured in addition to the mouse-emulating events, providing an extra level of interaction and possibilities. The WebKit engine and the capacitive display support three types of events:

- *Single-touch events*: Composed of one single touch at a time on the capacitive display, this type of event is comparable to 99% of mouse-based actions. We will see these events in Table 8–5.

- *Multi-touch events*: Composed of two or more simultaneous touches on different parts of the display. We will see these events in Table 8–6.

- *Gesture events*: Composed of one or more touch events plus a specific movement of the finger or fingers on the capacitive display; gesture events are implementable using seven DOM (Document Object Model) event classes, which are shown in Table 8–7.

Single-touch Events

All the basic and browsing-related mouse events are typically triggered by one or two finger touches and are listed in Tables 8–5 and 8–6.

Table 8–5. *Standard DOM Event Classes for Recognizing iOS Single-finger Touch-based Events.*

Description	Finger Gesture	Mouse Event
User touches a non-touchable element	Single touch	(None)
User touches a non-touchable element and an info bubble appears	Single touch	(None)
User touches a scrollable element and pans the display	Single touch	onscroll
User touches a touchable element	Single touch	mouseover mousemove mouseout
User touches a touchable element and the content changes	Single touch	mouseover mousemove mouseout mousedown mouseup click
User touches and holds a touchable element	Single touch	(None)
User zooms in or out on a design element	Double touch	onscroll

Three of the five single-finger touch actions represented in Table 8–5 are visually represented using flow charts in Figure 8–9.

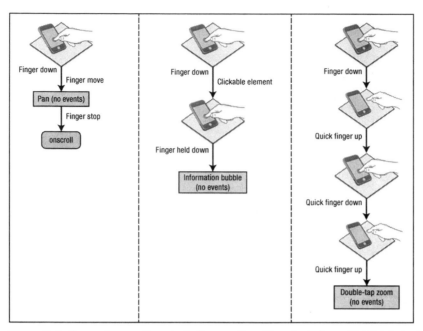

Figure 8–9. *Comparing overtime single-finger actions (flowcharts from official Safari reference).*

Multi-touch Events

In contrast, there are two-finger touch events, not as often used in a browsing session, but equally important in order to provide a solid level of user experience. Table 8–6 shows the two-finger touch events.

Table 8–6. *Standard DOM Event Classes for Recognizing iOS Two-finger Touch-based Events.*

Description	Finger Gesture	Mouse Event
User pinches a design element in or out	Double (separate) touch	(None)
User touches a non-scrollable element and pans the display	Double (separate) touch	mousewheel
User touches a scrollable element and pans the display	Double (separate) touch	onscroll

Two of the three two-finger touch actions represented in Table 8–6 are visually represented using flow charts in Figure 8–10.

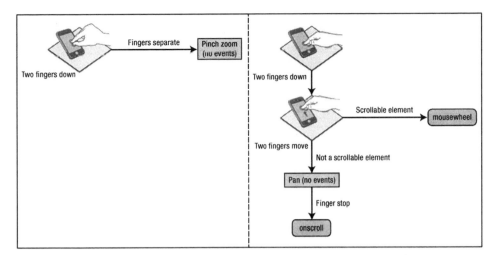

Figure 8–10. *Comparing overtime two-finger actions (flowcharts from official Safari reference).*

Gesture Events

A gesture could be composed of single- or multi-finger movements on the display. The single- and multi-touch actions seen so far are more related to mouse events and emulate the standard mouse-oriented browsing session. Besides the great increase in user experience, this is just one side of the touch era—the retrocompatible one. What really makes the difference is the gesture support provided by Safari and Apple iOS and offered by the iPhone 3.5-inch and the iPad 9.7-inch capacitive display.

Table 8–7. *Standard DOM Event Classes for Recognizing iOS Gesture Touch-based Events.*

Name	Description
touchstart	When a finger touches the display
touchmove	When a finger moves across the display
touchend	When a finger leaves the display
touchcancel	When the system cancels a touch event
gesturestart	When two or more fingers touch the display
gesturechange	When two or more fingers move during a gesture on the display
gestureend	When one or no finger touches the display touches the display

A gesture is composed of one or more finger movements, and a gesture event is a collection of touches triggered by these single or multiple finger movements. Table 8–7 shows the touch and gesture events involved in this context.

In order to use touch or gesture events, we need to convert them into individual touches. This can be achieved using the object properties of every event. Every event is an object and every object has properties. Using the properties of the object shown in Table 8–8, we can reach every single touch inside a gesture event.

Table 8–8. *Event Object Properties: Accessing Single-Touch Objects Inside a Gesture Event Flow.*

Name	Description
touches	Array with all the touches on a web page
changedTouches	Array with the recent changed touches on a web page
targetTouches	Array with all the current touches for a design element
target	The design element that generated the touch event

Because event objects produce standard arrays, we can use JavaScript array functions and syntax to access these properties. This means that if we want the array with all the touch objects on the web page, we can use the following JavaScript syntax:

```
event.touches;
```

If we want to access the first touch object on the web page, we can use the following JavaScript syntax:

```
event.touches[0];
```

We know that we need to access single-touch objects for manipulating gesture events, but what next? Just as every event object has its properties, every touch object has its own properties.

Table 8–9. *Touch Object Properties: Accessing Single-touch Properties Inside a Touch Object.*

Name	Description
identifier	Unique identifying number for the touch event
clientX	X coordinates of the touch object relative to the viewport
clientY	Y coordinates of the touch object relative to the viewport
screenX	X coordinates of the touch object relative to the screen
screenY	Y coordinates of the touch object relative to the screen
pageX	X coordinates of the touch object relative to the web page
pageY	Y coordinates of the touch object relative to the web page
scale	Multiplier of the default (1.0) pinch in or out value
rotate	Finger rotation value of a gesture

In this case, if we want to know the exact coordinates of the first touch object on the web page, we can use the following JavaScript syntax:

```
event.touches[0].pageX;
event.touches[0].pageY;
```

Once we access a single-touch object, we can use its properties, shown in Table 8–9, for creating every type of gesture interaction.

Combining JavaScript code and CSS properties, we can create custom touch handling support. Every time we write custom touch handling support, a good practice is to disable the default Safari behavior. This will be the subject of the next section.

Native and Customized Touch Event Handler

In the previous section, we saw that the most used event inside a typical browsing session is the event related to mouse behavior emulation. Some of these well-known activities are one-finger panning, zoom pinching and unpinching, and touch-and-hold. We also said that most of the DOM events supported by Safari Mobile and related to this type of activity are natively handled by the Apple iOS and are provided for free.

Besides these natively supported events, sometimes a project requires a way to customize multi-touch and gesture events. In this case, we can turn off the default Safari behavior, giving the developer the opportunity to implement his fancy touch and gesture support. For example, to prevent scrolling on an element in iOS 2.0, implement the touchmove and touchstart event handlers as follows:

```
function touchMove(event)
        {
        // prevent scrolling on this element
              event.preventDefault();

        … … …
        }
```

Similarly, we can prevent pinch open and pinch close gestures, implementing gesturestart and gesturechange event handlers as follows:

```
function gestureChange(event)
        {
        // disable browser zoom in and out
              event.preventDefault();

        … … …
        }
```

If we implement the function for the touchmove and touchstart event handlers, we will prevent scrolling in our WebApp, while if we implement it for gesturestart and gesturechange, we will prevent both open and close pinching.

Create Touchable Design Elements

A touch event flow is a collection of single touches, and we know that a design element must be touchable to join this flow during a gesture action. What if we want to interact with a design element that Safari doesn't consider touchable?

```
<span onmousemove="enableTouch(event)" onclick="void(0)">Element Name</span>
```

Paying the price of adding a non-semantic <span> element to the code, we can transform a non-touchable element into a touchable element by adding an empty click handler to the element, as shown in the preceding code. If the element is inside a semantic HTML5 tag, we can use it instead of a semantic-empty <span> element. The following example shows how to register handlers for gesture events inside a generic <div> element:

```
<div
ongesturestart="gestureStart(event);"
ongesturechange="gestureChange(event);"
ongestureend="gestureEnd(event);"
>
</div>
```

After registering the handler in the HTML5 code, we can implement our handler using JavaScript and the following syntax:

```
function gestureStart(event) {
      /* Handler Javascript Code Here */
}

function gestureChange(event) {
      /* Handler Javascript Code Here */
}

function gestureEnd(event) {
      /* Handler Javascript Code Here */
}
```

In the next section, we will see a special type of gesture event; a gesture that doesn't interact with the capacitive display but with the whole device. This gesture is the well-known and widely used device orientation change.

Orientation Change Event

With the iPhone, and even more with the iPad, users change the orientation of their devices constantly according to their needs. Using a framework for a WebApp, we can rely on it for orientation change support. Every time the user changes device orientation, the framework handles it and changes the layout for us. In addition, for a solid developer, it is important to know what's behind the scenes and how to change or add custom behaviors for a specific project requirement.

We can see the device orientation change as a special type of gesture where the user interacts with his/her whole hand on the whole device. The orientationchange event is measured via hardware by the accelerometer. Besides notifying that an orientation change has occurred, iOS also maintains a special "orientation" property in the window object with the four values shown in Table 8–10.

Table 8–10. *The Orientation Values Returned by the "Orientation" Object.*

Value	Description
0	Portrait view
90	Landscape view (turned counterclockwise)
180	Portrait view (flipped over)*
-90	Landscape view (turned clockwise)

* Currently supported only by iPad, not iPhone

The orientation value inside the window object always reflects the current device orientation. The following code adds an orientation handler to the <body> and implements the updateOrientation JavaScript method to display the current orientation.

```
<!DOCTYPE HTML>
<head>
<title>Orientation Change Test</title>
<script type="text/javascript" language="javascript">
function updateOrientation()
{
        var displayString = "Orientation : ";
        switch(window.orientation)
        {
                case 0:
                        displayString += "Portrait";
                break;
                case 90:
                        displayString += "Landscape (left, screen turnedÉ
 counterclockwise)";
                break;
                case 180:
                        displayString += "Portrait (upside-down portrait)";
                break;
                case -90:
                        displayString += "Landscape (right, screen turned clockwise)";
                break;
        }
        document.getElementById("output").innerHTML = displayString;
}
</script>
</head>
        <body onorientationchange="updateOrientation();">
        <div id="output"></div>
</body>
</html>
```

Every time the orientationchange event occurs, the updateOrientation method is invoked and the displayed string inside the <div id="output"> element is updated.

Orientation Change Media Query

Working with the orientationchange event is a solid way to implement any kind of switch based on device orientation, but it is not the only way. The orientationchange event also offers options to a developer, but in some contexts, we can accomplish something similar without using JavaScript. In this case, we will describe how to use a media query.

A media query is a media type composed of one or more expressions that check one or more conditions of certain media features. The concept is the same as the one used with the orientationchange; what will change is the language used and its syntax.

The iWebKit framework used for the Apple Store use case employs the same approach. The following small piece of code shows one example from this framework style.css file.

```css
@media screen and (max-width: 320px)
{
        #topbar {
                height: 44px;
        }
        #title {
                line-height: 44px;
                height: 44px;
                font-size: 16pt;
        }
}
```

As previously mentioned, it is always considered best practice to develop three different versions of the WebApp in order to optimize the iPhone, the iPad, and the desktop PC hardware and software characteristics—or at least one mobile version for the iPhone and one compatible version for both the iPad and the desktop PC. In addition, the next example shows a general case where we need to handle seven CSS style sheets for the same web page.

```css
@media only screen and (device-width: 320px) and (orientation: portrait) {
        /* CSS Rules for iPhone 2G, 3G, 3GS in Portrait Orientation */
}

@media only screen and (device-width: 480px) and (orientation: landscape) {
        /* CSS Rules for iPhone 2G, 3G, 3GS in Landscape Orientation */
}

@media only screen and (device-width: 480px) and (orientation: portrait) {
        /* CSS Rules for iPhone4 in Portrait Orientation */
}

@media only screen and (device-width: 960px) and (orientation: landscape) {
        /* CSS Rules for iPhone4 in Landscape Orientation */
}

@media only screen and (device-width: 768px) and (orientation: portrait) {
        /* CSS Rules for iPad in portrait orientation */
```

```
}

@media only screen and (device-width: 1024px) and (orientation: landscape) {
        /* CSS Rules for iPad in Landscape Orientation */
}

@media only screen and (device-width: 980px) {
        /* CSS Rules for Fixed Width Desktop and iPad Compatible Version */
}
```

The Retina display and its 480 × 960 px display resolution slightly complicated the media query code for the iPhone case, forcing us to add two more cases. Before the Retina display, we always used the min-device-width and max-device-width for targeting the iPhone 320 × 480 px resolution case.

Nowadays, it is no longer possible to use this option because when there is a value of "480" for the device-width property, there is no way of knowing whether it is an old iPhone 2G, 3G, or 3GS in landscape orientation or the new iPhone4 in portrait orientation. Moreover, we added the portrait and landscape test to the media query, creating two new cases for identifying the iPhone model when the "device-width" is set to 480 px.

Expand a Framework for iOS

Frameworks are the Holy Grail for a developer; they reduce development times, offering all the tools required for building a web page. A framework offers the building blocks needed to design and develop our project requirements.

Because perfection isn't possible, sometimes a framework doesn't match all of our needs. In these cases, we are unable to design and develop our specific project requirements with the building blocks offered by our framework. When we face such a situation, the only solution is to expand the framework, adding and developing what we need.

The iWebKit framework contains many files in the root directory; focus on the following:

  ■   css: // style sheet directory

  ■   images: // ui images

  ■   index.html: // index web page

  ■   javascript: // js framework directory

  ■   thumbs: // web page images

When we develop a project, we always need to look for updates, which include both framework core functionality and project specifics. Because newer versions of the framework could be released from its developer at any time, we must maintain, as much as possible, the original framework structure.

If the framework update does not dramatically change its core functions and its folders and files structure, we will easily be able to update our WebApp. Not changing the original framework files and structure will allow us to upload the entire framework, just overriding a few files and directories.

Here is a practical example of what will happen when we start to design the Apple Store use case. The context will be the following:

- *Problem*: Implement the Apple Store use case.

- *Solution*: Emulate the native application behavior using the framework core functions. Use the framework building blocks for designing the web page structure. Expand the framework when we need to add or design something that is not provided or supported by the framework templates.

The iWebKit framework provides some templates, but our "The Store" use case is totally different from all of them. For this reason, we will need to expand our framework. What we will do is use the same folders offered by the framework (keeping the framework directory structure untouched), and, instead of modifying the original framework files, we will add what we need (remaining ready for a future framework update). Despite that fact, the downside of this approach will be that overwriting many rules instead of replacing them will add more code to the framework and more HTTP requests from our WebApp. The right approach will be dictated by the WebApp context.

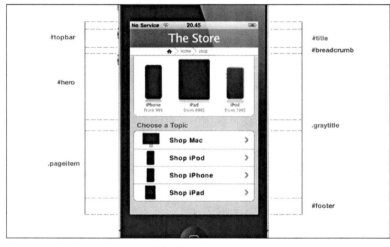

Figure 8–11. *Apple Store use case: The Store home page structure.*

We will work on the HTML5 structure, and save the new document in the root with all the other web pages. Subsequently, we will start to design the layout, working on a CSS style sheet that we'll save in the "css" folder. In addition, we will save all the additional images for the layout design in the "pics" folder.

- #topbar (pre-defined customized)

- #title (pre-defined customized)

- #breadcrumb (designed from sketch)

- #hero (designed from sketch)
- .greytitle (pre-defined untouched)
- .pageitem (pre-defined customized)

In Figure 8–11 and in the preceding list, we can see how we used some pre-defined framework structures with just a few customizations, while we needed to add a few more structures designed from scratch.

Resources for Coding

Unfortunately, there are only a few HTML5-compliant editors on the market. Table 8–11 indicates one of the HTML5 editors used in this chapter and a valid freeware alternative.

Here are the official resources for the three web standards presented in this chapter. If you are new to one or more of these technologies, I recommend you continue to build your web standard foundations using the following official sources.

Table 8–11. *Tools Used for Designing iPhone and iPad User Interfaces.*

Name	Type	URL	Operating System
SSEdit Pro	Application	http://seeditmaxi.cachefly.net/	OSX
Espresso	Application	http://macrabbit.com/espresso/	OSX
Coda	Application	www.panic.com/coda/	OSX
Smultron	Application	http://smultron.sourceforge.net/	OSX
Notepad++	Application	http://notepad-plus-plus.org/	Win
BlueFish	Application	http://bluefish.openoffice.nl/	Linux

Summary

In this chapter, we introduced the fundamental characteristics of a WebApp. First, using some examples, we saw how to set up a development environment, and then we introduced typical web application characteristics.

We presented the most important native iOS applications for a WebApp and how to interact with its services, presenting all the steps necessary for emulating a native-like environment.

We introduced the touch event paradigm and how to use single- and multi-touch events for emulating a traditional mouse browsing session. We also saw more complex gesture events and how to prevent them in case we need to develop custom gesture handling for our WebApp.

Lastly, we saw a special type of gesture, the device orientation change, how to use it via JavaScript, and how to achieve something comparable via media query. We saw when and how to expand the framework for achieving functionality that is not defined and natively supported by the framework itself.

## Chapter 9

Native iOS Design Implementation

*"If everything seems under control . . .
you're not going fast enough!"*

—Mario Andretti

In the previous chapter, we laid out the main points of how to set up an iOS environment, and in this chapter, we see how to implement some of these same aspects in our "The Store" use case.

First we see how to implement the iPhone page model and WebApp mode using metatags. In the second part, we see step by step how to implement the native-like interface of our use case. Each new element is presented using a top-down approach, always showing the code used for implementing the element.

iPhone Page Model Implementation

In the first part of this book about design, we saw that because of the iPhone's display dimension, iPhone web pages are structured on a page model paradigm. On top of that, the first thing we need to set up in our WebApp is the page structure.

Implement the Native-Like Page Structure

The code in this chapter is written on top of the iWebKit 5.04 framework and implements the page structure of our "The Store" use case. For our use case, we also wrote some custom HTML and CSS code. We use a caption to mark custom CSS and Framework code and a bold text style to mark the relative HTML code.

```
<!DOCTYPE html>
<html lang="en">
```

```
<head>
<meta charset="utf-8">
<title>The Store (U.S.)</title>
<link href="css/style.css" rel="stylesheet" media="screen" type="text/css" />
<link href="css/iphone.css" rel="stylesheet" media="screen" type="text/css" />
<link href="startup-image.png" rel="apple-touch-startup-image" />
<link href="apple-touch-icon.png" rel="apple-touch-icon" />
<script type="text/javascript" src="javascript/functions.js"></script>
</head>
<body>

/* page content will be here */

</body>
</html>
```

Some SEO metatags are intentionally missing from the <head> of our web page because we want to remain focused on the subject of this chapter. We see how to optimize our code using the SEO technique in Chapter 10.

The single page structure is the foundation of all our future web pages. Now we need to continue implementing our "The Store" use case by beginning to add the design element that emulates the native look of iOS for iPhone.

iPhone Native Interface Emulation

The native interface emulation starts with the apple-mobile-web-app-capable metatag. Without this tag, all our future efforts will vanish because the web page will not match the iPhone display dimensions and will not be in the WebApp mode.

```
<!DOCTYPE html>
<html lang="en">
<head>
<meta charset="utf-8" />
<title>The Store (U.S.)</title>
<meta name="apple-mobile-web-app-capable" content="yes" />
<meta content="minimum-scale=1.0, width=device-width, maximum-scale=0.6667,É
 user-scalable=no" name="viewport" />
<link href="css/style.css" rel="stylesheet" media="screen" type="text/css" />
<link href="css/iphone.css" rel="stylesheet" media="screen" type="text/css" />
<link href="startup-image.png" rel="apple-touch-startup-image" />
<link href="apple-touch-icon.png" rel="apple-touch-icon" />
<script type="text/javascript" src="javascript/functions.js"></script>
</head>
<body>
<div id="topbar">
        <div id="title">The Store</div>
</div>

/* page content will be here */

</body>
</html>
```

The Top Bar Section

In the <body> section, we insert the native-like **Top Bar** using a <div id="topbar">.

… … …

```
<body>
<div id="topbar">
        <div id="title">The Store</div>
</div>

/* page content will be here */

</body>
```

… … …

Then in Listings 9–1 and 9–2 we override some of its iWebKit CSS framework default rules.

Listing 9–1. *iWebKit Framework Top Bar Section*

```
/* from framework style.css stylesheet */

#topbar {
        position: relative;
        left: 0;
        top: 0;
        width: auto;
        background: -webkit-gradient(linear, 0% 0%, 0% 100%, from(#cdd5df),É
 color-stop(3%, #b0bccd), color-stop(50%, #889bb3), color-stop(51%, #8195af),É
 color-stop(97%, #6d84a2), to(#2d3642));
        margin-bottom: 13px;
}

/* for max-width: 320px */
#topbar {
        height: 44px;
}

/* for min-width: 321px */
#topbar {
        height: 32px;
}
```

Listing 9–2. *Custom Top Bar Section*

```
/* from custom iphone.css stylesheet */

#topbar {
        height: 44px;
        background: -webkit-gradient(linear, 0% 0%, 0% 100%, from(#566E93),É
 to(#314F7B));
}
```

With these rules, we override the default background gradient value, and we fix the top bar height at 44 pixels in the portrait and landscape orientations, as shown in Figure 9–1.

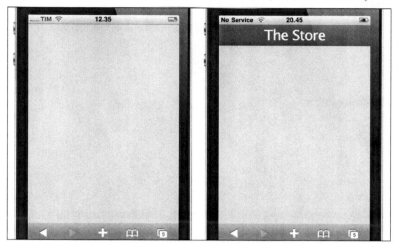

Figure 9–1. *"The Store" use case: the empty page (left) and the page title inside the Top Bar (right)*

The Page Title Element

Inside the Top Bar, we have the native-like **Page Title** added using a `<div id="title">` and customized. Listings 9–3 to 9–6 override a few other CSS rules from the default framework values:

… … …

```
<body>
<div id="topbar">
     <div id="title">The Store</div>
</div>

/* page content will be here */

</body>
```

… … …

Listing 9–3. *iWebKit Framework Page Style Element*

```
/* from framework style.css stylesheet */

#title {
        position: absolute;
        font-weight: bold;
        top: 0;
        left: 0;
        right: 0;
        padding: 0 10px;
        text-align: center;
        text-overflow: ellipsis;
        white-space: nowrap;
```

```
        overflow: hidden;
        color: #FFF;
        text-shadow: rgba(0,0,0,0.6) 0 -1px 0;
        }
```

Listing 9–4. *Custom Page Title Element*

```
/* from custom iphone.css stylesheet */

#title {
        color: #FFF;
        font-family: "Lucida Grande", Helvetica;
        font-size: 30px;
        text-shadow: #3B4C66 0 1px 0;
}
```

Listing 9–5. *iWebKit Framework Page Style Element*

```
/* from framework style.css stylesheet */

/* for max-width: 320px */
#title {
        line-height: 44px;
        height: 44px;
        font-size: 16pt;
}

/* for min-width: 321px */
#title {
        line-height: 32px;
        height: 32px;
        font-size: 13pt;
}
```

Listing 9–6. *Custom Page Title Element*

```
/* from custom iphone.css stylesheet */

#title {
        color: #FFF;
        font-family: "Lucida Grande", Helvetica;
        font-size: 30px;
        text-shadow: #3B4C66 0 1px 0;
}
```

Notice how we use the Helvetica font instead of the Myriad Pro as we did in the design phase. Myriad Pro is a commercial font and is not free to use.

> **NOTE:** Unlike the Helvetica font, Myriad Pro is not in the iOS Font Stack.
> If we want to use this font, in addition to buying it, we need to use the `@font-face` CSS3 property as shown in Chapter 7.

```
                        HEADING TAG EXERCISE
```

The iWebKit 5.04 framework doesn't use the HTML heading tags (for example, h1, h2, ... , h6) for makeup in the title section. The <h1> heading tag defines the most important title of the page whereas the <h6> heading tag defines the least important. At the end of the chapter, try to implement these tags.

- ▓ Use the <h1> tag instead of the standard <div> used by the iWebKit 5.0.4 framework.

- ▓ According to the text semantics, add other heading tags if necessary.

Repeat the same approach with the other page of "The Store" use case. You can download the use case source code from the Apress web site.

The Breadcrumb Bar

The second design element to add to the page structure is the **Breadcrumb Bar** and is added using <div id="breadcrumb"> as follows:

```
<head>
<meta charset="utf-8" />
<title>The Store (U.S.)</title>
<meta name="apple-mobile-web-app-capable" content="yes" />
<meta content="minimum-scale=1.0, width=device-width, maximum-scale=0.6667,É
 user-scalable=no" name="viewport" />
<link href="css/style.css" rel="stylesheet" media="screen" type="text/css" />
<link href="css/iphone.css" rel="stylesheet" media="screen" type="text/css" />
<link href="startup-image.png" rel="apple-touch-startup-image" />
<link href="apple-touch-icon.png" rel="apple-touch-icon" />
<script type="text/javascript" src="javascript/functions.js"></script>
</head>
<body>
<div id="topbar">
        <div id="title"> The Store</div>
</div>
<div id="breadcrumb">
        <a href="index.html"><img src="pics/breadcrumb_house.png" width="20" height="16"
/></a>
        <img src="pics/breadcrumb_arrow.png" width="22" height="16" />
        <a href="index.html"><img src="pics/breadcrumb_home.png" width="35" height="16"
/></a>
        <img src="pics/breadcrumb_arrow.png" width="22" height="16" />
        <a href="#"><img src="pics/breadcrumb_shop.png" width="32" height="16" /></a>
</div>

/* other page content will be here */

</body>
</html>
```

The breadcrumb contains three kinds of images: the house icon, the separator arrow, and the page name, as shown in Figure 9–2. In the last link, the href property doesn't have any value ("#") because it refers to the actual loaded page.

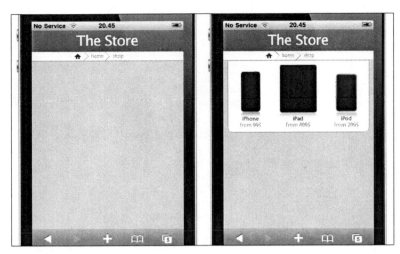

Figure 9–2. *"The Store" use case: the Breadcrumb Bar (left) and the Hero Content area (right)*

The breadcrumb is not a design structure offered by the iWebKit framework. Therefore, we didn't override any default value from the CSS stylesheet; instead, we developed from a sketch as shown in Listing 9–7.

Listing 9–7. *Custom Breadcrumb Bar*

```
/* from custom iphone.css stylesheet */

/* from custom iphone.css stylesheet */
#breadcrumb {
        background: #FFF;
        border-bottom: 1px solid #676767;
        font-family: "Lucida Grande", Helvetica;
        font-size: 11px;
        height: 16px;
        margin: -13px 0px 13px;
        text-align: center;
}
```

The Hero Content Area

Below the breadcrumb we have another design element developed from sketch, the **Hero Content** area. The Hero Content is added using a `<div id="hero">` element and contains three image links as in the following:

```
<head>
<meta charset="utf-8" />
<title> The Store (U.S.)</title>
<meta name="apple-mobile-web-app-capable" content="yes" />
<meta content="minimum-scale=1.0, width=device-width, maximum-scale=0.6667,É
 user-scalable=no" name="viewport" />
<script src="javascript/functions.js" type="text/javascript"></script>
<link href="css/style.css" rel="stylesheet" media="screen" type="text/css" />
<link href="css/iphone.css" rel="stylesheet" media="screen" type="text/css" />
<link href="startup-image.png" rel="apple-touch-startup-image" />
```

```
<link href="apple-touch-icon.png" rel="apple-touch-icon" />
<script type="text/javascript" src="javascript/functions.js"></script>

</head>
<body>
<div id="topbar">
        <div id="title"> The Store</div>
</div>
<div id="breadcrumb">
        <a href="index.html"><img src="pics/breadcrumb_house.png" width="20" height="16"
/></a>
        <img src="pics/breadcrumb_arrow.png" width="22" height="16" />
        <a href="index.html"><img src="pics/breadcrumb_home.png" width="35" height="16"
/></a>
        <img src="pics/breadcrumb_arrow.png" width="22" height="16" />
        <a href="#"><img src="pics/breadcrumb_shop.png" width="32" height="16" /></a>
</div>
<div id="hero">
        <a href="shop-iphone.html"><img src="pics/hero_iphone4.png"/></a>
        <a href="shop-ipad.html"><img src="pics/hero_ipad.png"/></a>
        <a href="shop-ipod.html"><img src="pics/hero_ipod.png"/></a>
</div>

/* other page content will be here */

</body>
</html>
```

The "The Store" use case often has three images with three different associated links to
increase the level of user experience giving him or her more options to jump from one
point to another in the sitemap. In addition, it's up to the developer to handle this
opportunity in a different way. In Listing 9–8, we can see the CSS stylesheet used to
design this element.

Listing 9–8. *Custom Content Hero Area*

```
/* from custom iphone.css stylesheet */


/* from custom iphone.css stylesheet */
#hero {
        border: 1px solid #676767;
        border-top: none;
        background: #FFF;
        font-family: "Lucida Grande", Helvetica;
        font-size: 12px;
        height: 150px;
        margin: -13px 10px 13px 10px;
        padding-top: 4px;
        text-align: center;
        -webkit-border-bottom-left-radius: 10px;
        -webkit-border-bottom-right-radius: 10px;
}
```

Now we approach the lower part of our web page dedicated to the content. On this specific page, the content is represented only by a menu, but on the other shop pages, use this section to add any sort of content.

```html
<head>
<meta charset="utf-8" />
<title>The Store (U.S.)</title>
<meta name="apple-mobile-web-app-capable" content="yes" />
<meta content="minimum-scale=1.0, width=device-width, maximum-scale=0.6667,
 user-scalable=no" name="viewport" />
<link href="css/style.css" rel="stylesheet" media="screen" type="text/css" />
<link href="css/iphone.css" rel="stylesheet" media="screen" type="text/css" />
<link href="startup-image.png" rel="apple-touch-startup-image" />
<link href="apple-touch-icon.png" rel="apple-touch-icon" />
<script type="text/javascript" src="javascript/functions.js"></script>
</head>
<body>
<div id="topbar">
        <div id="title"> The Store</div>
</div>
<div id="breadcrumb">
        <a href="index.html"><img src="pics/breadcrumb_house.png" width="20" height="16"
/></a>
        <img src="pics/breadcrumb_arrow.png" width="22" height="16" />
        <a href="index.html"><img src="pics/breadcrumb_home.png" width="35" height="16"
/></a>
        <img src="pics/breadcrumb_arrow.png" width="22" height="16" />
        <a href="#"><img src="pics/breadcrumb_shop.png" width="32" height="16" /></a>
</div>
<div id="hero">
        <a href="shop-iphone.html"><img src="pics/hero_iphone4.png"/></a>
        <a href="shop-ipad.html"><img src="pics/hero_ipad.png"/></a>
        <a href="shop-ipod.html"><img src="pics/hero_ipod.png"/></a>
</div>
<div id="content">
        <span class="graytitle">Browse Store</span>
        <ul class="pageitem">
                <li class="menu">
                        <a href="shop-mac.html">
                                <img src="pics/menu_mac.png" />
                                <span class="name">Shop Mac</span>
                                <span class="arrow"></span>
                        </a>
                </li>
                <li class="menu">
                        <a href="shop-ipod.html">
                                <img src="pics/menu_ipod.png" />
                                <span class="name">Shop iPod</span>
                                <span class="arrow"></span>
                        </a>
                </li>
                <li class="menu">
                        <a href="shop-iphone.html">
                                <img src="pics/menu_iphone.png" />
                                <span class="name">Shop iPhone</span>
```

```
                                        <span class="arrow"></span>
                                </a>
                        </li>
                        <li class="menu">
                                <a href="shop-ipad.html">
                                        <img src="pics/menu_ipad.png" />
                                        <span class="name">Shop iPad</span>
                                        <span class="arrow"></span>
                                </a>
                        </li>
                </ul>
        </div>

        /* other page content will be here */

</body>
</html>
```

The Menu Area

The **Menu** area is wrapped inside a `<div id="content">` and contains two main design elements: a title and a menu, as shown in Figure 9–3.

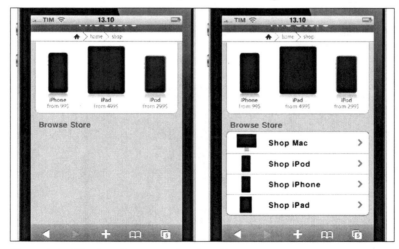

Figure 9–3. *"The Store" use case: the Menu Title (left) and the Edge-To-Edge Navigation (right)*

We insert the **Menu Title** using a `<div class="graytitle">`. This element is provided by the iWebKit framework and is styled by the CSS rules in Listing 9–9.

Listing 9–9. *The Menu Title Element*

```
/* from framework style.css stylesheet */


.graytitle {
        position: relative;
        font-weight: bold;
```

```
        font-size: 17px;
        right: 20px;
        left: 9px;
        color: #4C4C4C;
        text-shadow: #FFF 0 1px 0;
        padding: 1px 0 3px 8px;
}
```

Below the title we have the typical iPhone **Edge-to-Edge Navigation** wrapped inside a `<ul id="pageitem">`. This element is also provided by the iWebKit framework and is styled by the CSS rules in Listing 9–10:

Listing 9–10. *The Edge-to-Edge Navigation Area*

```
/* from framework style.css stylesheet */

.pageitem {
        -webkit-border-radius: 8px;
        background-color: #FFF;
        border: #878787 solid 1px;
        font-size: 12pt;
        overflow: hidden;
        padding: 0;
        position: relative;
        display: block;
        height: auto;
        width: auto;
        margin: 3px 9px 17px;
        list-style: none;
}
.pageitem li:first-child, .pageitem li.form:first-child {
        border-top: 0;
}
.pageitem li:first-child:hover, .pageitem li:first-child a {
        -webkit-border-top-left-radius: 8px;
        -webkit-border-top-right-radius: 8px;
}
.pageitem li:last-child:hover, .pageitem li:last-child a {
        -webkit-border-bottom-left-radius: 8px;
        -webkit-border-bottom-right-radius: 8px;
}
```

The list items of this unordered list are the single menu entries. Each entry is added using a `<li class="menu">` and is composed by three elements wrapped inside a link element, as shown in Figure 9–4.

Figure 9–4. *"The Store" use case: the Edge-to-Edge Menu Structure (left) and the Footer (right)*

Each link <a> element contains an image <img>, a text <span class="name">, and another
image inserted as a background image of a <span="arrow"> element. In the following, we
isolate the single menu entry code to better understand its structure. Each menu link
must have three images with the same image width in order to be consistent with the
menu layout.

… … …

```
<li class="menu">
        <a href="shop-iphone.html">
                <img src="pics/menu_iphone.png" />              /* icon   */
                <span class="name">Shop iPhone</span>      /* text */
                <span class="arrow"></span>                /* arrow */
        </a>
</li>
```

… … …

The Footer Section

The last design element in the page is the **Footer**. In our "The Store" use case, the
Footer is minimal and contains only the Apple logo. The **Footer** is added using a <div
id="footer"> and is styled by the CSS rules in Listing 9–11.

Listing 9–11. *The Footer Section*

```
/* from framework style.css stylesheet */

#footer {
        text-align: center;
        position: relative;
        margin: 20px 10px 0;
        height: auto;
        width: auto;
```

```
        bottom: 10px;
}
```

The following code shows the entire "The Store" use case page structure with the
Footer included.

```html
<!DOCTYPE html>
<html manifest="cache-iphone.manifest">

<head>
        <meta charset="utf-8" />
        <title>The Store (U.S.)</title>
        <meta name="apple-mobile-web-app-capable" content="yes" />
        <meta content="minimum-scale=1.0, width=device-width, maximum-scale=0.6667,É
         user-scalable=no" name="viewport" />
        <link href="css/style.css" rel="stylesheet" media="screen" type="text/css" />
        <link href="css/iphone.css" rel="stylesheet" media="screen" type="text/css" />
        <link href="startup-image.png" rel="apple-touch-startup-image" />
        <link href="apple-touch-icon.png" rel="apple-touch-icon" />
        <script type="text/javascript" src="javascript/functions.js"></script>
</head>
<body>
<div id="topbar">
        <div id="title"> The Store</div>
</div>
<div id="breadcrumb">
        <a href="index.html"><img src="pics/breadcrumb_house.png" width="20" height="16"
/></a>
        <img src="pics/breadcrumb_arrow.png" width="22" height="16" />
        <a href="index.html"><img src="pics/breadcrumb_home.png" width="35" height="16"
/></a>
        <img src="pics/breadcrumb_arrow.png" width="22" height="16" />
        <a href="#"><img src="pics/breadcrumb_shop.png" width="32" height="16" /></a>
</div>
<div id="hero">
        <a href="shop-iphone.html"><img src="pics/hero_iphone4.png"/></a>
        <a href="shop-ipad.html"><img src="pics/hero_ipad.png"/></a>
        <a href="shop-ipod.html"><img src="pics/hero_ipod.png"/></a>
</div>
<div id="content">
        <span class="graytitle">Browse Store</span>
        <ul class="pageitem">
                <li class="menu">
                        <a href="shop-mac.html">
                                <img src="pics/menu_mac.png" />
                                <span class="name">Shop Mac</span>
                                <span class="arrow"></span>
                        </a>
                </li>
                <li class="menu">
                        <a href="shop-ipod.html">
                                <img src="pics/menu_ipod.png" />
                                <span class="name">Shop iPod</span>
                                <span class="arrow"></span>
                        </a>
                </li>
                <li class="menu">
```

```
                            <a href="shop-iphone.html">
                                    <img src="pics/menu_iphone.png" />
                                    <span class="name">Shop iPhone</span>
                                    <span class="arrow"></span>
                            </a>
                    </li>
                    <li class="menu">
                            <a href="shop-ipad.html">
                                    <img src="pics/menu_ipad.png" />
                                    <span class="name">Shop iPad</span>
                                    <span class="arrow"></span>
                            </a>
                    </li>
            </ul>
    </div>

    <div id="footer">
            <img src="pics/footer_apple-logo.png"/>
    </div>
    </body>
    </html>
```

Summary

In the first part of the chapter, we saw how to implement the iPhone page model paradigm using the "The Store" use case.

In the second part of this chapter, we saw in practice how to emulate the native application interface in WebApp. We saw step by step the entire process of adding code after code for the fundamental design elements of our WebApps.

The entire code of our "The Store" use case is available on the Apress web site.

## Chapter 10

Optimizing iOS WebApps

"Perfection is achieved not when there is nothing more to add, but when there is nothing more to take away."

—Antoine de Saint-Exupéry

This chapter is about web optimization and search engine optimization (SEO). First we talk about iPhone and iPad compatibility, and then we show how to optimize the performance of a WebApp. We also suggest some rules for optimizing the code, reducing HTTP requests, and minimizing DOM access.

We then demonstrate how to compress a WebApp, optimize its usability, and make it capable of working offline. Finally we look at a mobile SEO approach to WebApps, analyzing first the anatomy of a search engine and then exploring how to implement a search engine oriented design. We also look at the principles behind the Google algorithm and some useful mobile SEO tools.

iPad and iPhone Compatibility

Beside the fact that the user experience is totally different between iPhone and iPad users, most of the concepts behind good optimization are common to both devices.

Some of these concepts are implemented in different ways in order to optimize specific aspects of the device, whereas others are equally applied in order to increase the level of user experience.

Performance Optimization

Optimizing the performance of our WebApp is not a development approach that we can perform only at the end of our project workflow. It is something that, exactly as for the test phase, is applied for the duration of the project. Obviously, at the end of the Development Phase we apply some optimization techniques to our WebApp, but it is most efficient to incorporate some good habits from the beginning in order to reduce mistakes and shorten the overall development time (See Figure 10–1).

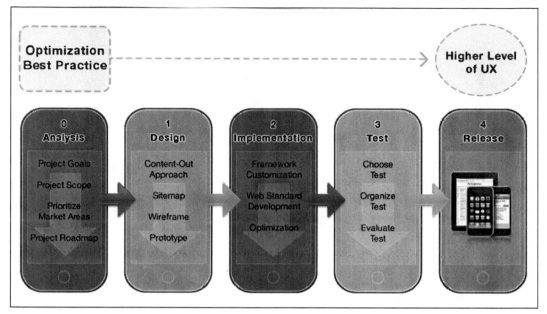

Figure 10–1. *Optimization best practice applied along the whole project workflow process*

When we optimize our web pages, it is important to know what can be optimized. For those who know the Vilfredo Pareto Principle, you also know that 80% of the consequences come from 20% of the causes, which means that it will be hard to get positive results without knowing exactly what to target with our optimization process.

Coming up we'll look at some of the best practices, presented as rules, in order to clearly present a pragmatic approach to a performance optimization process applicable to our WebApp.

Code Optimization

Code optimization is the first step of any type of optimization technique because everything is based on code—everything is coded in our web pages. Good code can save bandwidth, reduce rendering delay, and improve the page's readability and maintainability overtime.

The following are some best practices to keep in mind when writing any type of code in our WebApp.

Rule 1: Use Web Standards Complaint Code

Use HTML5, CSS3, and JavaScript compliant code. Besides clean HTML5 syntax, this also means inserting our style sheet in the <head> part of the page and (except the link to the iWebKit Framework) the JavaScript in the bottom of our web pages. This is because style sheets in the top of the page significantly speed up the loading time. On the other hand, insert the JavaScript in the bottom of the web page so the JavaScript code does not block HTTP requests. This is because when JavaScript is downloading, the browser will not start any other resource downloads, even if the resource is on a different hostname.

> **NOTE:** An alternative to this rule is to insert the Desktop-Mobile Redirect JavaScript code at the top of the page. We can do that because in this case it is more important to execute the script than render and load the web page.

This rule helps the parser work faster and helps reduce the overall rendering delay.

Rule 2: Write Slim Code

Write slim code. Remove unnecessary or redundant parts of the code and avoid using tab and space where it is not strictly necessary. Don't use CSS expressions if you can achieve the same result with other techniques. CSS rules are evaluated more frequently than we can imagine and can negatively affect the performance of our web page.

> **NOTE:** In our use-case, for illustration purposes, we overwrite many CSS rules in order to present both the original iWebKit Framework and our use-case custom code. In a real project, keep the number of overwritten CSS rules to a minimum.

Choose short and meaningful names for comments and CSS ID and class or JavaScript variables and functions. Don't hesitate to adopt xHTML5 syntax, if you like to write XHTML code, and combine CSS rules to a good level of factorization inside your style sheet. Use Gzip compression or minify HTML5, CSS, and JavaScript code, but always remember to store an uncompressed version for development purpose in the project.

This rule reduces the overall weight of our web page and, by default, the rendering and loading delays.

Rule 3: Reduce HTTP Requests

It is important to always keep one eye on the number of imported resources (images included). More files imported into our web page equals more rendering and loading latency from the browser. Minimizing the number of HTTP requests speeds up the web page loading time. With this in mind, it may be a good idea to consider adding HTTP caching to our web pages.

HTTP caching, also known as web cache, is based on good principles, but it is almost unusable in Apple Safari because of its specification limits. The following list summarizes some of the main limits of HTTP caching:

- **Single resource must be less than 15kB (non-compressed)**
  Web pages designed for iPhones should reduce the size of each
  component to 15kB (25kB before iOS3) or less for optimal caching
  behavior. The iPhone is able to cache 105 15kB components.
  Attempting to cache one more file results in removing an existing one
  from the cache.

- **Global cached resources must be less than 1.5MB**
  Although the iPhone is able to cache multiple components, the
  maximum cache limit for multiple components is around 1.5MB
  (500kB before iOS3). Maximum bytes available in the cache are
  around 105 * 15 = 1575kB.

- **Powering off the device clears the HTTP cache**
  If the user needs to force a hard reset, components in the cache will
  be lost. The reason is that, on the iPhone, Safari allocates memory
  from the system memory to create cached components but does not
  save the cached components in persistent storage.

- **Closing the tab clears the HTTP cache**
  Closing all tabs except the blank one and then closing Safari clears the
  cache.

We can see from a development point of view that this type of cache is unreliable
because it is cleared too often and can't cache the majority of the resources in a modern
web page. Even the most compressed JavaScript Framework or CSS are a struggle to
get under 15K, and none of the images used in almost every WebApp are under this
limit. The offline features provided by HTML5 are a better option for our goals, and we
introduce them later in this chapter.

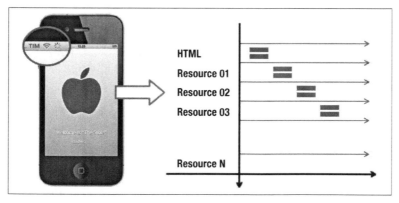

Figure 10–2. *WebApp resource requests according to the HTTP/1.1 protocol*

The best reason for following this rule, besides reducing the rendering time of our web
pages, is that the HTTP/1.1 protocol specifies that a browser can download only two
resources in parallel per hostname, as shown in Figure 10–2.

A workaround for this sort of bottleneck is to spread our external resources over multiple hostnames. Lastly we can't forget to avoid all HTTP redirects in our web pages. The HTTP redirect is accomplished using the 301 or 302 status code, and in both cases it adds a delay to the average page loading time, thereby decreasing the quality of user experience.

This rule reduces the loading time by reducing the communications delays between the client side and server side.

Rule 4: Combine CSS and JavaScript Files

This rule must take into account the project's complexity, but the basic idea is that we combine all our CSS rules and JavaScript code into one single file instead of having multiple files. This will reduce the HTTP header's weight and the latency of imported multiple resources in our web pages due to TCP slow starts, as shown in Figure 10–3.

A side effect of this approach is that we are forced to update larger files, even for small code updates; however, this is often a path that brings more positive effects than negative.

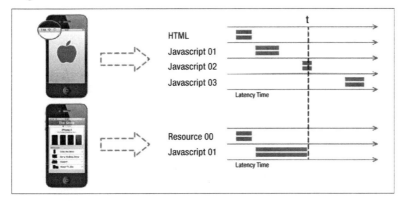

Figure 10–3. *Transfer latency time: comparison between single and multiple JavaScript files*

In our "The Store" use-case, the iWebKit JavaScript Framework Core and the CSS are all inside a single .js and .css file minified with an optimization program. We can keep the logical structure of our code in a development version (non-minified) of these files and subsequently add header and single comments to make the code maintenances and its feature updates easier. In the resource section at the end of this chapter, you will find some online minify resources.

Rule 5: Minimize DOM

In our project, the hard work is done by the framework, but we still need to write JavaScript code to accomplish some of the project requirements. In this case, the rule is simple: minimize the DOM access and the number of DOM objects.

This rule will reduce the web page loading time and user experience delays every time the web page runs a JavaScript.

Image Optimization

An important step in the Optimization Phase is image optimization. Image optimization is another example of a good habit that doesn't contain any great secret. Simply put, optimizing the images of our WebApp can dramatically improve the performance of our web pages by making them lighter and reducing loading delays.

The following are some best practices to keep in mind when we work on our WebApp's images.

Rule 6: Optimize Color Depth

After we design an image, we need to optimize its weight by exporting it using the right image format. If it's a photo, we need to use a good compression ratio in JPG format. If it's a user interface image, it is important to check the number of colors used. If we use fewer than 256 colors, we can export it in PNG8. In most cases, exporting in PNG8 renders a smaller image than exporting as a 256-color GIF. Using similar colors also helps to keep the color count and the image weight low.

We should also stress that exporting images using a graphic program like Adobe Photoshop, Fireworks, or Gimp will add unwanted metadata that will increase the image weight. We can see the metadata imposed on an image in Fireworks by accessing the Metadata Panel and browsing **File ➤ File Info (T)** or using ⌃⇧⌘F.

A workaround is to optimize our images using a program like PNGOut that will make them as slim as possible.

This rule reduces the web page loading time and increases the level of user experience.

Rule 7: Use CSS Sprites

The word "sprite" might remind you of the'80s, when people played all day with Commodore 64 or ZX Spectrum games. Because in computer science everything that is old sooner or later will become new again, web developers adopted the idea behind the old Sprite management and brought it to the CSS world. Look at the following Figure (10–4) for an example.

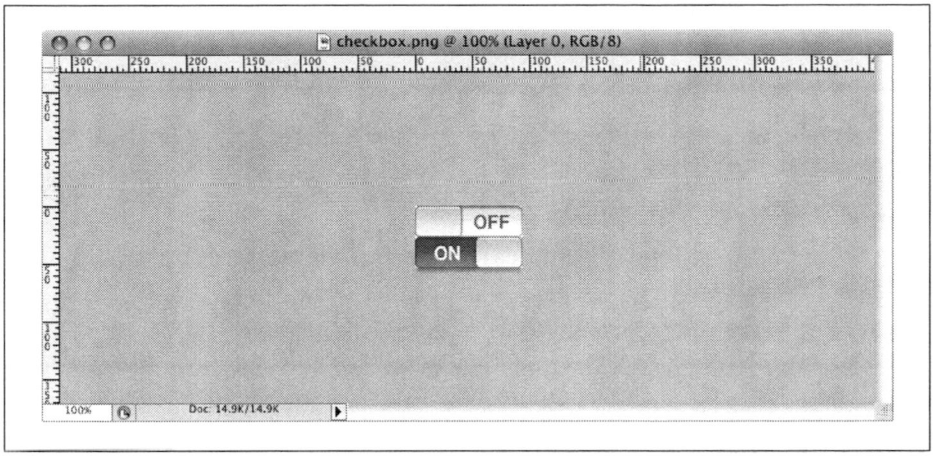

Figure 10–4. *The CSS Sprite techniques used for Design Checkbox in the iWebKit Framework*

To use the CSS Sprite technique, first we group two or more images into a single background image, then we set via CSS the single image width and height, and finally we adjust the background position using the CSS margin rule to display only the portion necessary. With this approach we can use a single background image and display several different graphics (single images) with it, thereby saving server requests and speeding up page load times.

```css
/* from framework style.css stylesheet */
input[type="checkbox"] {
  width: 94px;
  height: 27px;
  background: url('../images/checkbox.png');
  -webkit-appearance: none;
  border: 0;
  float: right;
  margin: 8px 4px 0 0;
}

input[type="checkbox"]:checked {
  background-position: 0 27px;
}
```

The CSS background rule shows every image from the coordinates 0px, 0px; this guarantees that if we set a height of 27px, the OFF state would be showed by default. In this case, the Sprite technique shows the ON state by using an offset of 27px, demonstrated by the second CSS rule.

If we use many images for our user interface, the CSS Sprite technique can help to reduce the global loading time of our web pages and avoid the typical white flash of the traditional rollover technique. Because the image loading time is larger than the rendering time, using a traditional image rollover technique creates a white flash every time the browser loads the rollover image for the first time.

SPRITE EXERCISE

In our "The Store" use-case, we design the Breadcrumb Bar using a few images. Implement the Sprite techniques to speed up the rendering time.

- Use a Sprite with all the Breadcrumb images.
- Group two or more Sprite Breadcrumb images and compare the rendering time with the single Sprite approach.

Compare the result and determine which approach is best for our specific use-case.

This rule reduces the web page loading time and the user experience delays every time the web page runs JavaScript.

Rule 8: Use CSS Rules Instead of Images

This rule may sound strange, but because the image optimization process aims to reduce the weight of images globally, use CSS rules every time it is possible instead of bitmap images.

CSS TEXT EXERCISE

In our "The Store" use-case, we design the Breadcrumb Bar using few images. Implement the CSS technique to speed up the rendering time even more.

- Use text instead of images for all the Breadcrumb links.
- Align the House Icon with the Breadcrumb text.

Compare the rendering time of both the Sprite and CSS approaches.

We need to use CSS rules for everything involved in our user interface and insert images only in rare cases. If we must use an image for a user interface element, it must have its color depth optimized. If we need to insert many images we need to insert these images into CSS Sprites. We should also use CSS rules for each small design detail such as borders, backgrounds, or gradients.

This rule reduces the web page loading time and user experience delays every time the web page runs a JavaScript.

Rule 9: Never Scale Images

Always use images with appropriate dimensions according to the device viewport or design element width and height. It is never a good idea to rely on Safari to scale an image for the right fit. The only exception to this rule is when we want to insert an image inside a single device WebApp (only for iPhone or iPad). In this case inserting an image with a width value of 100% will fit both the landscape (bigger) and portrait (smaller) orientations.

This rule reduces the web page loading time and user experience delays every time the web page runs a JavaScript. While it is important to follow this rule, remember that it is also important to specify the image width and height, as this will also help to reduce rendering times.

IMAGE OPTIMIZATION EXERCISE

All the images used in our "The Store" use-case are in PNG format. Try to determine when it is possible to optimize some of these images using another format like JPG or GIF. Don't forget that some formats don't support the Alpha Transparency.

Choose a graphic program and open some of the images used in the "The Store" use-case located in the directory "/images" and inside the directory "/pics".

- Export the images using a different format.
- Export the images using the same format with a different setting.

Compare the image weight and the image quality, and then see whether you can replace some of these images with optimized images.

Application Compressing

Safari supports GZIP compression (RFC 1952), so compressing some of the resources of our WebApp is often a good idea as this will result in an increase in the level of user experience. We can decide when to compress our HTML5 documents, CSS3 style sheets, or JavaScript code, whereas we don't want to compress images or PDF files because these are already compressed. Compressing images or PDF files adds CPU overhead and potentially increases the file size.

From the server side, in order to use GZIP-compressed resources in our WebApp, the server must be configured to provide compressed resources when requested. From the other side the client must be able support this type of files.

The Request/Respond process represented in Figure 10–4 can be resumed in the following three steps:

- **Client**

    Connect to the server

    Send a request with GZIP support: "accept-Encoding: gzip"

- **Server**

    Acknowledge GZIP support

    Compress resource with Gzip algorithm

Send GZIP-encoded resource: "content-Encoding: gzip"

■ **Client**

Receive GZIP-encoded resource

Decompress GZIP-encoded resource

Display (or use) the resource

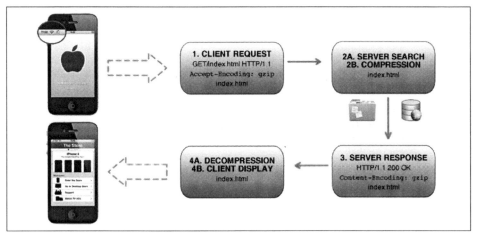

Figure 10–5. *The GZIP-compressed resource request: the HTTP/1.1 protocol in action*

The following code is an example of the header of a HTTP/1.1 request and response for a GZIP resource (also shown in Figure 10–5).

```
GET / HTTP/1.1
... ... ...
Accept-Encoding: gzip
... ... ...
```

After the server receives the client request, determine whether the requested resource is available in a compressed version. If yes, the server sends it to the client adding the following string to the response.

```
HTTP/1.1 200 OK
... ... ...
Content-Encoding: gzip
... ... ...
```

There is not a limit to the file that we can compress using GZIP, and this is the easiest way to achieve a significant reduction of the web page weight. The GZIP compression can reduce the weight by approximately 70%.

Despite that, and because perfection doesn't exist in this world, generally speaking GZIP compression has a few negative aspects.

- First we need to work with a browser that supports GZIP compression. In our context this is not an issue because Safari and WebKit-based browsers support GZip.

- Second, as previously stated, we can't compress images or PDF files because they are already compressed.

- Third, it is important to remember that because Safari needs to decompress these resources on-the-fly, in some cases this process can add CPU cycles and overhead to the application and eliminate the possible benefits. Perform a test in order to ensure that this overhead does not eliminate the possible benefits gained.

Usability Optimization

Usability is a fundamental necessity of our project, and it is always a good idea to test usability before arriving at the end of the project flow. Testing our work during a certain phase in the project flow can tell us whether we match the project requirement and give us a feedback on the achieved level of usability.

In Chapter 2, we saw that an error can be propagated through the project flow and how its cost increases along with its propagation. A good phase of testing eliminates, or at least mitigates, this cause-effect process.

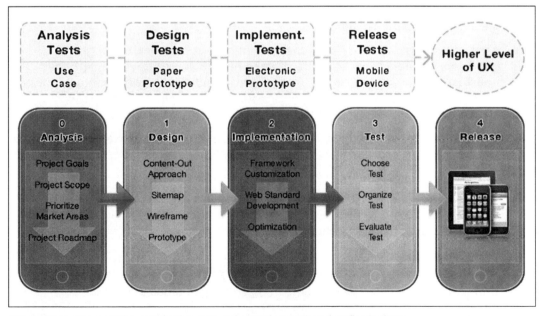

Figure 10–6. *The usability optimization: tests scheduled on each project flow's phase*

We can perform our usability optimization at different levels in every step of our project flow, and we can do it again at the end of the project flow before the final release of our WebApp. Following our diverse approach, we can schedule different types of tests according to the level of detail of the project. Figure 10–6 shows a type of approach that begins with the Paper Prototype Test and the Electronic Prototype Test and schedules a live test on a real mobile device for the Pre-Release Test Phase.

Compared to a simple web site, a WebApp needs a more accurate phase of testing, so we encourage you never to overlook this phase. Even if you work on a simple project, experience will tell you how hard or soft your project will need to be tested.

We have two types of usability tests depending on the subjects involved.

■ **Usability inspection**

Typically performed by an evaluator that is not the designer or the developer and has no involvement with the project. Usability inspection should be performed from the early phase of design. An example of usability inspection is the *Cognitive Walkthrough*, in which the evaluator simulates the user's problem-solving process for a specific task.

■ **Usability test**

Typically performed by the designer or the developer on a user. Usability tests are performed in the Design Phase, Implementation Phase, and Release Phase using different types of tests. An example of a usability test is the *Prototype Test* where the designer or developer tests the multiple user aspect of the design, including services and specific functions.

The Cognitive Walkthrough is an inexpensive form of test; however, although this approach is used more often in software development than web development, the Prototype Test is a valid option for our mobile design and development context. For this reason, we present the Prototype Tests in Chapter 11, in which we see in detail how to organize, perform, and evaluate the test.

For now it is important to introduce the anatomy of a usability test as well as a few more important concepts. A usability test, like a Prototype Test, is structured by the following steps:

1. **Choose testing environment.**
   We need to choose the test environment according to the type of prototype test we choose to perform and the project requirements.

2. **Create use-case.**
   We need to create a use-case that will define a task for the user that will verify one or more use-case requirements from the project requirements.

3. **Prepare test assets.**
   We need to prepare and re-use the assets that we will use to perform the test.

4. **Select users.**
   We need to choose the right user according to the use-case requirements.

5. **Perform test session.**
   We need to run the test to verify the use-case requirements.

6. **Debrief test.**
   We need to debrief the test with the user and with the observers.

7. **Evaluate test.**
   We need to evaluate the test according to the use-case requirements.

8. **Create findings and recommendations.**
   We need to provide findings and recommendations that will drive designers and developers to improve the project.

These eight steps require us to choose the users according to the application profile. However, we don't know how many users we need in order to gather reliable data for the test. We answer this question in the following section.

How Usability Problems Affect Users

We can define a problem as something that is difficult to deal with, solve, or overcome. Testing a project usually means finding something that can represent a problem for the user.

If we choose the "right" user for our use-case, even a single user test will give us reliable information to improve our project. However, no matter how "right" one user can be, their voice will still remain one in the crowd. The risk that a user performed a certain action by accident or was influenced by personal un-representative contexts is too high to create an entire test based on a single piece of user feedback.

The logical conclusion might be to add as many users as possible to discover as many problems as possible. While this approach may look like the right one, it is not. Those who have some probability and statistic knowledge know that there is a value that represents the best ratio between effort and result and that behind this value the result is minimal compared with the effort. For this reason, choosing a large group of users will not be the best approach to the problem.

It's best to choose a smaller group as a sample size to discover as many problems as possible. This path brings us to Jim Lewis, who published a study in 1982 that described how binomial distribution can be used to model the sample size. This study was supported by Robert Virzi in 1992. Virzi found that 80% of usability problems are found by the first four to five users and that severe problems are more likely to be discovered by the first few users.

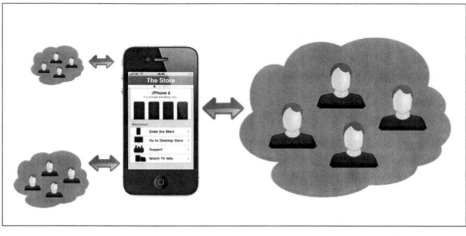

Figure 10–7. *Usability problems: different groups could discover different types of problems*

The problem of selecting a sample size seems to be solved because four to five users should be the right number for our test session. Even the Nielsen studies in early 1990s confirmed this size. Unfortunately, problems don't uniformly affect users, as Woolrych and Cockton showed in their studies in 2001. This means that a simple estimate of problem frequency with the binomial distribution is misleading.

For this reason, the best approach we can choose for a medium to large project is to set a few four-to-five user groups in order to represent different category of users, as shown in Figure 10–7, and discover as many problems as possible. In practice we need to perform a test with a group, fix the discovered problems, and then re-perform the test with another group. Probability and statistic studies on usability problems are long and complex, but by simplifying the conclusions (as in Figure 10–8) we can see that with an average number of 18 users we can discover 85% of the problems. This is supported by Jakob Nielsen and Thomas Landauer in their speech "A mathematical model of the finding of usability problems," at the Proceedings of ACM INTERCHI Conference (Amsterdam, The Netherlands).

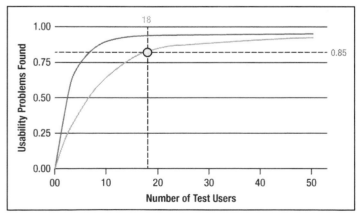

Figure 10–8. *Usability Problems Study: We need 18 users to discover the 85% of the usability problems.*

For a simple project, like a web site or a low-complex WebApp, we can rely on a single group of four to five users and fill the remaining gap by using our experience. We can also apply the cycle approach to the single group by testing the first three users, fixing the problems, and then testing the other two users. The data will not be as complete as in a multi-group approach, but the approach will be more agile and the feedback will still be useful.

Offline WebApp

In this book we always focus on emulating the native application environment and behavior with our web pages. It's obvious that our web pages are dependent on Internet access in order to provide any kind of service, but they are also dependent on the Internet in order to retrieve the various design elements of the web page itself.

Using the HTML5 Offline feature, we can address this issue by storing any type of resource inside the cache of our WebApp. The files that need to be cached are declared in a file called *Manifest File*. Once the files are cached, Safari looks for the Manifest File before beginning any server-side processing while avoiding downloading files previously downloaded and stored.

> **NOTE:** Safari evaluates the content of the Manifest File to determine whether or not to update it. The file date or any other attribute will not be evaluated as we used to see in an HTTP Conditional GET Request. If we want to force an update, we can do it via JavaScript.

The application cache persists between browser sessions, which means that a previously cached resource can be viewed or continue to work without any network support or if the iOS is in Airplane Mode.

The Manifest File

A manifest file is a simple text file hosted on the application's web server that lists all the static resources that need to be downloaded and cached by our WebApp. A Manifest File is composed by two main parts and one optional part:

- Cache Manifest Declaration
- Cache Manifest URL List
- Cache Types Declaration (not required)

The iWebKit framework doesn't use any Manifest File because from the 5.04 version it replaced most of its user interface images with a CSS3 approach. Despite that, from our use-case it is important to cache at least all the product's images and provide the users offline access to the catalogue.

The Cache Manifest file should begin with the uppercase prefix "CACHE MANIFEST." Below that we can define, always using an uppercase prefix, three (sub) section headers corresponding to three types of different behaviors according to the WebApp requirements:

■ **CACHE MANIFEST**
This is the Cache Manifest header.

■ **CACHE**
Resources are always loaded from the cache, even in online mode.

■ **NETWORK**
Resources are always loaded from the server, even if the file is listed under the CACHE header. This is an exception to the CACHE rule.

■ **FALLBACK**
Resources are used as replacements for other resources that fail to load or load incompletely.

If we list the resources right after the "CACHE MANIFEST" declaration header without specifying any of the three types of (sub) headers, the default CACHE type will be applied to all the listed resources. A typical cache manifest file looks like the following code:

```
CACHE MANIFEST
CACHE
# Comment on Cache Rule Files
file01
file02
fileN
NETORK
# Comment on Network Rule Files
file01
file02
fileN
FALLBACK
# Comment on Cache Rule Files
file01
file02
fileN
```

Below the header we can also insert comments using the prefix "#". This feature is often used to mark the cache version, modify the Manifest File, and force an update of the cache. The following code shows the Manifest File of our "The Store" use-case. If we need to cache an entire folder, like in "The Store" use-case, we can simply insert the absolute folder path and all the files will be added by default to the cache manifest whitelist.

```
CACHE MANIFEST
# WebApp Images inside the pic folder
http://www.thestore.com/images
# WebApp Images inside the images folder
http://www.thestore.com/images
```

In this code we use an absolute path, but a relative path is also allowed; it's totally up to you. After creating the Manifest File, we need to save it using the extension ".manifest".

For the "The Store" use-case, we use "cache-iphone.manifest" and we save in the application root directory.

The next step is to link the Manifest File in our web pages inside the <html> tag using the attribute manifest as shown in the following code:

```
<html manifest="cache-iphone.manifest">
```

The Manifest File must be served using the "text/cache-manifest" MIME type, so the last step is to add the "text/cache-manifest" content type inside an ".htaccess" file, which is in turn placed inside the web root directory. If it's not done in this order, Safari will not recognize the Manifest File.

```
AddType text/cache-manifest .manifest
```

Now everything is in place, but because our application looks to the resource list in the Manifest File to understand whether the manifest file needs to be updated or not, we need to use JavaScript if we want to force this update process.

> **NOTE:** We can make a change in the Manifest File by using a single comment line in the file. This generates an update from our WebApp the next time the Manifest File is checked. However the JavaScript approach is recommended because it provides more possibilities to the developer. If a failure occurs while downloading the manifest file (its parent file or a resource specified in the cache manifest file), the entire download/update process fails.

We can access the cache using the window.applicationCache JavaScript object and update it in three steps using the update() and swapCache() methods:

1. Test whether the (old) cache is ready to be updated.

2. Update the (new) cache.

3. Swap the old cache with the updated cache.

In Table 10–1 we can see the three items used for the cache update process.

Table 10–1. *The JavaScript object and the two JavaScript methods involved in the cache updated process*

Name	Description
window.applicationCache.status	Check whether the cache is ready to be updated
update()	Update the cache
swapCache()	Swap the old cache with the updated cache

When we check the applicationCache object using the status property, we observe different returns according to the cache status. Table 10–2 shows the possible value returned by the status property.

Table 10–2. *The values returned by the status property applied to the "applicationCache" object*

Name	Value	Description
window.applicationCache.UNCACHED	0	Cache is not available
window.applicationCache.IDLE	1	Cache is up to date
window.applicationCache.CHECKING	2	Manifest File checked for update
window.applicationCache.DOWNLOADING	3	Downloading the new cache
window.applicationCache.UPDATEREADY	4	New cache ready to be updated
window.applicationCache.OBSOLETE	5	Cache deleted because obsolete

Now we are ready to put everything into practice by writing an `if` statement to test the value of the status of the applicationCache object and, if ready, perform a cache update:

```
if (window.applicationCache.status == window.applicationCache.UPDATEREADY)
{
    applicationCache.update();
    applicationCache.swapCache();
}
```

At this point of the workflow our WebApp is almost ready for the Release Phase, but before we think about releasing it we need to take care of another important aspect of the optimization, an aspect that is based on the relationship between our WebApp and a search engine. We see how to work on this part in the next paragraph.

Mobile SEO

SEO is an important step of our project workflow. SEO is more fundamental for a web site than for a WebApp because compared to a web site, a WebApp rarely relies on search engine results to promote itself. Despite this fact, SEO should be behind every stage of a WebApp design as well.

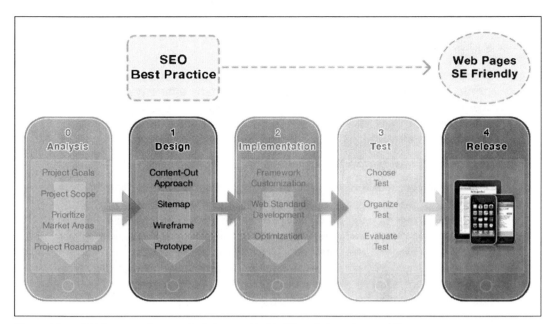

Figure 10–9. *SEO best practices applied along and behind the whole project workflow process*

The SEO Phase brings to the table some rules that are valuable for both web sites and WebApps. As we previously saw for accessibility, usability, and code or image optimization, optimizing our web pages for search engines is an approach that runs from the beginning to the end and behind our project workflow. Working on a complete SEO plan is beyond the scope of this book, but in the following sections we see some key points that make our web site rank higher and our WebApp friendlier to major search engines.

Anatomy of a Search Engine

There is much more behind the minimal user interface of a search engine like Google. Unfortunately we can't know every detail of how a search engine works because this is proprietary information. In spite of this fact, every search engine is composed of a few known parts that, in a general way, can help us to understand how they work.

▓ **Crawlers, Spiders, and Robots**

Crawlers, spiders, and robots are programs that crawl the web in search of web pages to index in a database. Google is an example of a crawler-based search engine, and its crawler scans the web collecting information about every URL.

▓ **User Interface (UI)**

User interface is where the user writes his query. The minimal user interface offered by Google is just one example of the front-end of every search engine.

Search Engine Database

Search engine databases contain multiple data points about each stored URL. These data could be arranged in many different ways and every search engine has its own way to accomplish this job. How every search engine arranges these types of data is a closely guarded secret; an example is the PageRank method used by Google.

◼ Search Engine Algorithm

Search Engine Algorithm is the heart of every search engine, which is the part that makes everything works. This algorithm evaluates one or more inputs (words inserted by the user in the search engine user interface) and generates an output and searches the database where URLs and keywords are stored. This algorithm, which can be catalogued as a Problem Solver Algorithm, is composed of multiple algorithms that analyze different web site parts. Every search engine has its own implementation of this algorithm.

◼ Search Engine Result Page (SERP)

The Search Engine Result Page, besides the search engine user interface, is the only part that is visible to the user. This page is a collection of links catalogued in a specific order by the Search Engine Algorithm.

In the following section, we see how to design and implement our web pages in order to be more search engine friendly.

Search Engine Oriented Design

Optimizing our web page for a search engine is important from the early phases of our project workflow. A search engine oriented design is a title that stands for an approach used during our Design Phase. Let's take a look at the steps of the Design Phase.

Domain Title

The first step of any SEO approach starts even before we can open our graphic program or code editor. Choosing the wrong domain can ruin all the future efforts to gain a good positioning on a search engine. Despite the crucial moment of this step, the solution is simple: insert the primary keyword in the domain name.

```
http://iphone.thestore.com      /* iPhone Third Level Domain Name */
```

This is an example of the hypothetic name of our "The Store" use-case. Inserting the primary keyword in the domain name guarantees that our WebApp will be stored using a word that will be used as primary keyword in the next steps of the SEO Optimization Phase.

Page Title

The HTML page title is one of the most important tags to optimize. The page title displays as the first line in the SERP, and it's the most meaningful source for our WebApp. A good title is short and includes the main keyword or keywords that identify our web page.

```
<title>The Store</title>                                /* Store Index
Page Title */
<title>The Store (U.S.)</title>                          /* US Home Page Title */
<title>The Store (U.S.) | Contact Us</title>        /* Contacts Page Title */
```

We must write a unique title for each page and every title must include the name of the WebApp. The code shows three examples for the "The Store" use-case.

Meta Tags

There was a time where meta tags were the holy grail of SEO, but nowadays the situation has changed due to the abuse of this type of tag from webmasters. An important tag to optimize is the description meta tag. A search engine like Google uses this tag to display a description of our web page as the second and third (if the text is long enough) line in the SERP. A good description tag includes our keyword (or keywords) and is informative. The following code is an example from the "The Store" use-case.

```
<meta name="description" content="Apple designs and creates iPod and iTunes,É
 Mac laptop and desktop computers, the OS X operating system, and theÉ
 revolutionary iPhone and iPad." />         /* Store Index Page Description Metatag */
```

Another important meta tag is the keyword tag; it's not fundamental but it's still important. As we can see from the following code, in our "The Store" use-case the choice is easy because a big brand like Apple needs only one keyword: Apple. In other projects, more than one keyword works fine; just don't abuse it.

```
<meta name="Keywords" content="Apple" />        /* Store Index Page Keywords Metatag */
```

Keywords must match the words and phrases that potential visitors will use when searching for your site.

Content

Content is important to optimize our web pages. In the end, what users are looking for is just a small piece of content to read. The point is that now we need to distinguish the case where the user lands on the Compatible page, on the iPad page, or on the iPhone page.

Generally, in a SEO content optimization, we need to use the keyword(s) specified in the keyword's metatag in a few strategic points of our web page:

- The page header (primary keyword)
- The page tagline (secondary keyword)

- The page content (primary and secondary keyword)
- The page links (primary keyword, only wherever is possible)

If we think in a Google-oriented way, it is important to use our keyword(s) in the upper part of our web page because it's the most important (meaningful) part for the crawlers. Because the iPad, and even more the iPhone, version has strictly prioritized contents, this can make our job both easier and harder.

Prioritized content can make our job easier because we assume that this type of content is based on important keywords and short meaningful paragraphs in order to deliver the message in the most direct and fastest way.

At the same time, prioritized content can make our job harder because sometimes the content is so short that it is practically impossible to organize in a meaningful way for both humans and crawlers.

Figure 10–10. *Search engine oriented design: an example of the use of the primary key "iPhone"*

The way to approach the situation is to stick with our prioritized content on our mobile version and play a little bit more with the content of the compatible version where we have more space and a chance to achieve good results.

The last thing we need to avoid is the pitfall of keyword stuffing. Keyword stuffing, simply put, is using a keyword too many times or forcing it in a paragraph with the sole purpose of increasing its usage. Don't use keywords if they don't make sense in context. This can lower the quality score of our webpage.

Links

A web page without links is like a lost island in the ocean; it is there, but almost no one knows that it exists or, if they do, how to reach it. The role of a link is to connect our web page with other relevant information, both internal and external to the web page itself. Another reason why links are so important is that links have a great value on the final weight of our WebApp SEO score. More precisely, inbound and outbound links have a "weight" whereas internal links serve only a better "crawl" of the site.

Google with its famous algorithm, developed by Larry Page and Sergey Bring in 1998 and patented by Stanford University, was the first to assign dynamic and different values to inbound and outbound links in a web page. The real specifics of the Google page rank algorithm are unknown because it is one of the closed secrets of the company; despite that, some details are known.

The Google PageRank Concept

The probability that a random user visits a web page is called its *PageRank*. The Google PageRank concept uses Google's global link structure to determine an individual page's value. The PageRank gives an approximation of a page's importance and quality.

The algorithm that implements this concept interprets a link from web page A to web page B as a vote, by web page A, for web page B. The Google PageRank Algorithm looks at more than the sheer volume of votes or links a page receives and analyzes the page that casts the vote. Votes cast by web pages that have high a PageRank value because they are themselves important or are favorably viewed as "established firms" in the Web community weigh more heavily and help to make other pages look established as well.

The Google PageRank Algorithm Concept

The PageRank value of web page A is given as follows:

$$PR(A) = (1-d) + d(PR(T1)/C(T1) + \ldots \ldots \ldots + PR(Tn)/C(Tn))$$

Here, the PageRank given by an outbound link equals the document's PageRank score PR(Ti) divided by the (normalized) number of outbound links C(Ti).

- **PR(A):** PageRank value of page A
- **PR(T1):** PageRank value of page 1 pointing to age A
- **C(T1):** Number of links off page 1, which points to page A
- **PR(Tn):** PageRank value of a page n pointing to page A
- **C(Tn):** Number of links off page n, which points to page A

- **d:** Dampening factor: The probability that, on each page, a random surfer will request another random page. Nominally this value is set to 0.85 and could be set between 0 and 1.

Let's assume a small universe of four web pages with the following relationship, as also shown in Figure 10–11.

- **Page A:** Doesn't link any page

- **Page B:** Link to page A and page C

- **Page C:** Link to page A

- **Page D:** Link to page A, page B, and page C

With a universe of four web pages, the initial approximation value of the PageRank would be evenly divided between these four web pages and is 0.25 (0.25 * 4 = 1). Assuming a damping factor of 0.85 for each page provides the following equation:

$$PR(A) = (1-d) + d(PR(B)/2 + PR(C)/1 + PR(D)/3)$$

$$PR(A) = (0.15) + 0.85(0.25/2 + 0.25/1 + 0.25/3)$$

$$PR(A) = (0.15) + 0.85(0.125 + 0.250 + 0.083)$$

$$PR(A) = (0.15) + 0.85(0.458)$$

$$PR(A) = (0.15) + 0.3893$$

$$PR(A) = 0.5393$$

In Figure 10–11 we can see the calculation of the PageRank value from our example using a mathematical notation.

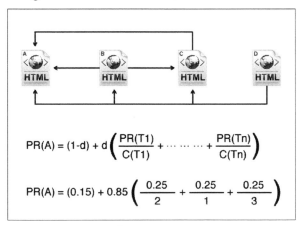

Figure 10–11. *The Google page rank algorithm: web page B, C, D add their PageRank value to web page A*

Figure 10–12 shows the same concept in which web page A receives a Page Rank value according to the PageRank value of each other web page that is linked to it.

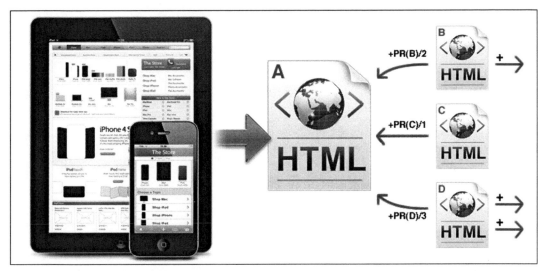

Figure 10–12. *The Google Page Rank Algorithm: web page B, C, D add their PageRank value to web page A*

Ingoing and outgoing links play an important role in the life of a WebApp, but links do much more than link other web pages. Links are also catalogued as internal and external. External links leave the web page and help the crawler to reach every page of your WebApp. In this case external links play the same role of a sitemap. That's why a sitemap is highly suggested in any web project. The same role is played by Breadcrumbs that link to many other (relevant) pages. On the other hand, an internal link is a link that, instead of pointing to a different web page, points to the web page itself.

Images

Search engines see web pages as text pages, which means that they don't understand images. Images have a fundamental role in our web sites and WebApps because as human beings we understand images much better than text. For this reason, we never avoid images in our projects.

The point here is to not rely on images when we need to give meaning to the web page. For example, don't insert important text messages in our images, such as calls-to-action or important titles. The role of the image is to support the content with a different, and possibly more powerful, series of symbols which readers can interpret.

Consider adding text messages as a companion to every image in a web page and an alt attribute to communicate with the crawler. Following the code is in the `<div>` that wraps the Hero Content in our "The Store" use-case home page.

```
<a href="#"><img src="pics/hero_iphone4.png" alt="The New iPhone4"/></a>
<a href="#"><img src="pics/hero_ipad.png" alt="The Revolutionary iPad"/></a>
<a href="#"><img src="pics/hero_ipod.png" alt="The New iPod Touch"/></a>
```

If we need to insert extra information about an element, we can choose to add the title attribute. We can also choose not to insert the alt attribute when the image doesn't have any relevant meaning for the crawler and thus the web page. An example of this is the following code from the images used as icons in the edge-to-edge menu. The following piece of code refers to only one menu entry.

```
<li class="menu"><a href="#">
<img src="pics/menu_mac.png" />
<span class="name">Shop Mac</span>
<span class="arrow"></span></a></li>
```

This image doesn't specify any `alt` attribute in the `<img>` tag. However, if you add a tag with a description, it will not be considered a mistake.

```
<li class="menu"><a href="#">
<img src="pics/menu_mac.png" alt="Shop Mac" />
<span class="name">Shop Mac</span>
<span class="arrow"></span></a></li>
```

That piece of code shows a suitable description for this example.

JavaScript Code

JavaScript helps us to build a better WebApp and to emulate the native-app look, but this doesn't mean that it is always SEO-friendly. The solution is to externalize our JavaScript code exactly as we did for the Framework Core used in our "The Store" use-case.

```
<script src="javascript/functions.js" type="text/javascript"></script>
```

Apart from rare cases, we need to import all our JavaScript code, wherever included, in order to make our web page more SEO-friendly. On the other hand, this will add loading latency to our web page, but as we have established, perfection doesn't belong in this world. In these cases we need to interpret the context and choose the right approach according to our project scope, goals, and dimension.

Mobile SEO Tools

Nowadays we have many tools to monitor our web pages, from WebApps like Google Analytics to a few native iOS applications. Google analytics is a fast an easy way to monitor traffic and have a clear idea about how our WebApp interacts with users.

Google Analytics was developed by Urchin in 2005 and has been publically available to users since 2006. The benefits that come from using a tool like Google Analytics are various. Google Analytics helps you determine exactly which is the most effective web page, understand the average amount of time spent browsing our web pages, or and even understand which visitor became an effective user. These and many other types of data are organized in textual and graphic reports that are easy to analyze.

Google Analytics

After registering a Google account, we are able to log in to the Google analytics page located at http://www.google.com/analytics. Once logged in, we are able to add our WebApp from the Google Analytics Control Panel in few steps.

At this point, it is important to create and add a Sitemap to our WebApp in order to be sure that every URL will be discovered by the Google's normal crawling process. The Sitemap can also be used to provide metadata to Google about specific types of content like images, videos, news, and so on.

The last step before the data from our project is collected by Google Analytics is to add a snippet of code from the Control Panel to all our web pages just before the head closing tag. Information is collected and visualized using a few different Dashboard views. We have a Dashboard where all the information is visualized together for a glance at all the information at once, but we can also switch minimizing information in a single view. Some of these views are as follows:

- Content Overview
- Pageview Display
- Visits View
- Bounce Rate View
- Traffic Sources View
- Referring Sites View
- Search Engine View

It is important to remember that data are not collected in real time, and the statistics aren't available until midnight PST of each day. Google Analytics also takes a few hours to fully update all the statistics entries. In case our web pages are able to generate more than a million page views per month, it is useful to remind you that besides the free service offered by Google Analytics, there exists a Premium version of the service available for larger sites.

Resource on Optimization and SEO

In Table 10–3 we have some of the tools used in this chapter to optimize our project. If you are new to one or more of these technologies, we recommend you to continue the project using the following service.

Table 10–3. *Tools Used for Optimization and SEO*

Name	Type	URL	Operative System
Minify CSS	WebApp	`http://www.minifyjavascript.com/`	OSX – Win - Linux
Minify CSS	WebApp	`http://www.minifycss.com/`	OSX – Win - Linux
SpriteMe	WebApp	`http://spriteme.org/`	OSX – Win - Linux
Yahoo SmushIt	WebApp	`http://www.smushit.com/`	OSX – Win - Linux
PNGOut	Application	`http://advsys.net/ken/utils.htm`	OSX – Win - Linux
Google Webmaster Tools	WebApp	`https://www.google.com/webmasters/tools/`	OSX – Win - Linux
Google Analytics	WebApp	`http://www.google.com/analytics/`	OSX – Win - Linux

Summary

In this chapter we worked on optimization. In the beginning of the chapter, we established the proper way to work on performance-oriented optimization by first explaining how to write and produce good images and then learning how to compress our WebApp.

In the second part of the chapter we worked on usability optimization and introduced two types of approaches and tests also standardized in UML (Unified Modeling Language). We also saw how problems really affect our users and how to choose the right user sample for our purposes.

The third part of the chapter dealt with offline applications, and we saw how to use the Manifest File to cache single or multiple files of our WebApp.

In the final section we worked on a search engine oriented optimization in which we first introduced the concept behind the Mobile SEO and then introduced the anatomy of a search engine. We ended by working on the part of our web pages that needs to be optimized to make it search engine friendly.

We also introduced the concept behind the famous Google algorithm and we saw how a tool like Google Analytics can help us to gather important information that can be used to plan the right mobile strategy and make important decisions on our WebApp.

## Chapter 11

Testing iOS WebApps

Be a yardstick of quality. Some people aren't used to an environment where excellence is expected.

—Steve Jobs

After seeing how to optimize our web application in the last chapter, we now approach the test phase. After an introduction about lifecycles and agile testing approaches, we will see how to organize a test, first creating a use-case and then the assets needed for testing it.

We will perform a test and then learn how to evaluate it using specific kinds of feedback, such as design or emotional feedback, and variables, such as the number of used touches, the number of mistakes, and the estimated time of arrival.

Web Development Lifecycles

In application development, we can apply two major types of lifecycles: the waterfall lifecycle and the iterative-incremental lifecycle. The *waterfall lifecycle* is defined as a sequential development model with clearly defined deliverables for every phase. In the waterfall lifecycle, there is minimal feedback from one phase to another.

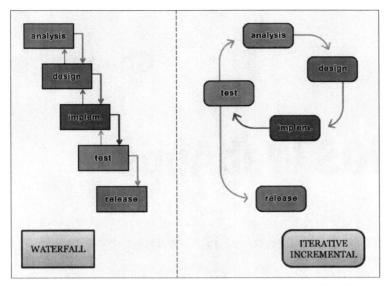

Figure 11–1. *The waterfall lifecycle (left) and the iterative-incremental lifecycle (right).*

The *iterative-incremental lifecycle* is defined through cycles (iterative) developed in a smaller portion of time (incremental). Compared to a waterfall lifecycle, an iterative-incremental lifecycle enables more flexibility in accommodating new requirements of change. Figure 11–1 presents a graphical comparison between a waterfall and an iterative-incremental lifecycle. In the next section, we will see how to approach the test phase at the end of the implementation phase.

Web Application Testing

In our simplified workflow, when we exit the development phase, we enter directly into the test phase. Particularly in iterative lifecycles, different levels of testing should occur at all stages of the process. As we now understand, different project flows can be implemented with different lifecycles according to project context and requirements.

As we will also learn, every project phase is overlapped by at least one other phase; this is also true for the test phase.

In our workflow, as shown in Figure 11–2, the test phase is performed after the implementation phase and before the release phase. It is used to conduct tests on performance, accessibility, usability, and more generally, on user experience.

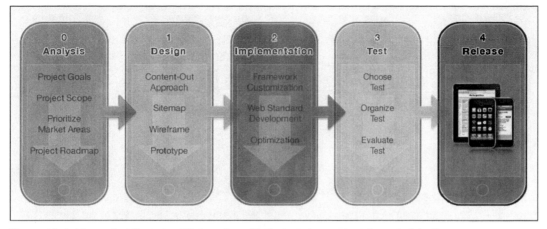

Figure 11–2. *The project flow: simplified version with the test phase only at the end of the flow.*

The testing approach depends on the nature of the web site or web application. Generally, in accordance with the specific moment in the project flow, we can choose different types of tests. In the next section, we will see agile approaches to tests, which are more comfortable for single developers or small development groups.

Agile Tests

In the first step of our project flow, we work with wireframes to implement an early version of our contents. From the wireframes, the next step is to create paper prototypes to get a better idea about both the content and layout of our future web pages.

The *paper prototype test* is the first level of useful testing to determine whether our design is correct in terms of user experience. This type of test is inexpensive because it can be prepared and performed by a single designer without any specific tools. Paper prototype tests can identify both user interface design and content-related problems.

A paper prototype test makes it easy to determine whether the user struggles with our interface by looking for a specific button or trying to orient him- or herself during a browsing session. Paper prototype tests can also show whether our content is in the right place and provides the right level of information to the user.

Paper prototype tests are performed in the design phase before moving on to the development phase (Figure 11–3). These tests are usually performed by the designer and are based on the same sketch used to define the web site or web application design.

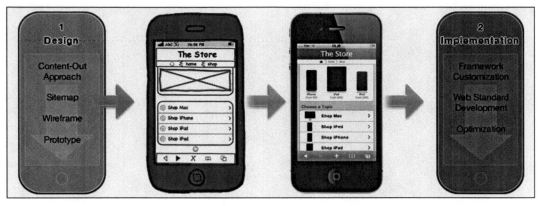

Figure 11-3. *The paper test performed between the design and the implementation phases of the flow.*

The second level of agile tests is the electronic prototype tests. These tests are performed by the designers as a final step in the design phase. Because each step often slightly overlaps the next, this type of test can be prepared by the designers and performed by the developers. Electronic prototypes can also be prepared and used by both the designer and the developer, allowing the designer introduce the work to the developer who will use the electronic prototypes as the starting point for his/her job.

If the electronic prototype runs on a mobile device, it offers virtually the same experience to the user and is reliable. It can also run on a desktop machine and provide a good level of feedback. The difference between a real mobile scenario and any other electronic prototype is the environment.

Figure 11-4. *A real environment can dramatically change the user experience (Image Miss HG).*

The environment can create significant differences in laboratory tests aiming to evaluate a real mobile experience (Figure 11-4). The best way to approach the problem is to perform preliminary paper prototype tests on the design, perform electronic prototype tests on the functions and services, and then develop an alpha version of the web site or web application to test in a real environment.

These types of tests are virtually free because paper and electronic prototypes have already been produced as a regular step in the design phase of the project workflow.

Heat Map Tests

Another type of test that is easy and inexpensive to set up and perform is the *heat map pseudo test*. We use the prefix "pseudo" because the real heat map test requires tools for eye-tracking that most development teams don't have (Figure 11–5).

As a workaround for this lack of technology, we can use one of the many online services (for example, Feng-GUI) offered by companies that use heuristic algorithms as a replacement for real eye-tracking. These heuristic algorithms are usually accurate and, along with their usability and accessibility, provide good feedback.

Typically, the process for using an online heat map service is standard and includes the following steps:

1. Register an account for the heat map service.

2. Insert the absolute path or upload a print-screen of the web page.

3. Download the heat map in an image format.

Some services are similar to Google analytics and offer a script to insert into web pages. While logged into our account, we can check the web page statistics and see the heat maps. This type of service should be considered accurate because we can analyze the web page over time with real users.

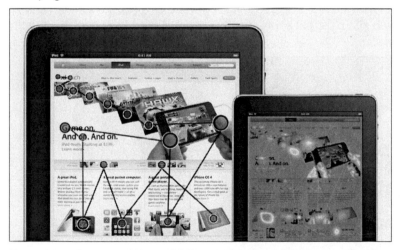

Figure 11–5. *The eye-tracking test (left) and the corresponding heat map (right).*

We introduced the heat maps technique in Chapter 4 to analyze reading patterns to show the basics of a good design and what can negatively influence the user experience. The point is that heat maps can reveal a design mistake and give early feedback during the design phase. By watching a heat map, we can determine if the user's attention might be hijacked by some unwanted design element. By using a heat map, we can test our design element hierarchy and check whether the reading pattern correctly follows the content.

We should also note that a heat map test is less informative in a small display context such as the iPhone, compared to the 9.7-inch context of an iPad. Despite this shortcoming, a heat map test still offers important information about our design to help prevent design-error propagation in the project flow.

Organizing a Test

Every detail of every test must be planned and organized in order to produce reliable feedback. The agile approach we chose is based on *artifact recycling,* allowing us to work on ideas and assets that we used for previous workflow phases. The artifact recycling approach contributes to keeping the preparation phase as lean as possible. In the following sections, we will see how to plan and create use-cases and how to perform a test.

Creating Use-Cases

The main thing to remember is that paper prototypes (shown in Figure 11–6) are design-oriented and work best in design tests, which means that they provide more reliable feedback on design details. Electronic prototypes can also give feedback on design details, but because they implement at specific levels of some or all of the functions and services offered by the web site or application, they are mostly used to collect feedback about functions and services.

Figure 11–6. *Developing paper views for use-cases (Image Resenfeld Media).*

The first step in the preparation phase is to create a use-case. When working on a web site or application, we can picture a browsing session with a specific user action path. Perhaps we want to test whether the contact page is easily reachable or whether a specific service is useful. Imagination and experience are your best friends in this phase.

Typically, textual use-cases are used in combination with use-case diagrams to better understand the project requirements in the analysis phase. In the test phase, this combination still offers the best results because the diagram can be seen as a graphic summary of the use-case, providing an idea of "who does what" and "who interacts with what," while the description provides a better understanding of the individual steps involved in the interaction between the actor (user) and the system (user interface, server, and so on).

Creating a Textual Use-Case

Now we are facing a fork in the road because designers and developers typically possess different background knowledge and use different tools. Not all designers know UML, whereas almost all developers know this useful modeling language; it is used in almost every object-oriented project.

For those who don't know UML, the textual use-case approach offers everything one needs to present and organize a test; familiarity with the tools offered by UML will definitely help in both the analysis and test phases of the project flow.

UML is beyond the scope of this book. However, in this chapter, we will present two ways to represent a use-case: textually and visually. In this section, we will present the textual way to represent a UML use-case, while in the next section we will do so visually, using diagrams.

> **NOTE:** UML stands for *Unified Modeling Language* and is a standardized, general-purpose modeling language used in software engineering. UML includes various types of visual models, but for our purposes, we present only two of them:
>
> ■ Textual use-case
>
> ■ Use-case diagram
>
> A simple book that can introduce you in simple terms to all the tools offered by the Unified Modeling Language is *UML Distilled*, by Mike Fowler.
>
> For more information, visit http://martinfowler.com/books.html.

When working with a team, we usually represent a use-case using both textual and graphic tools. If you work as a single designer or developer, you can choose which tool you prefer, assuming that you have every aspect and detail of your project clearly in mind.

The easiest and most intuitive way to create a use-case is the textual way. The first step is to write the header for your use-case, choosing the title that corresponds to the user's task, the level of detail, the actor, and the device used, which identifies the context. "The Main Successful Scenario" is the title of our use-case. The second step is to define the *scenario* by writing the body of our use-case in a numbered sequence of steps, where the *actor* (user) performs a number of actions to achieve his or her goals. Every step represents an interaction between the system (user interface, server, and so on) and the actor (user). The following is an example of a textual use-case taken from our Apple Store use-case.

Call the Apple Store Support

Level: Sea level (a.k.a. User goal level)

Actor: User

Device: iPhone

1. The user browses the menu by selecting the Support link.

2. The user browses the menu by selecting the Contact Us link.

3. The user browses the menu by selecting the "1-800-275-2273" link.

4. The device asks for confirmation of the call to the number "1-800-275-2273."

5. The user makes a call to Support.

In a use-case, there are five different levels of detail, shown from top to bottom in the following list:

1. Cloud level (Summary goal)

2. Kite level (Summary goal)

3. Sea level (User goal level)

4. Fish level (Sub-functional goal)

5. Clam level (Sub-functional goal)

We can work on a different level of detail by setting a different level, as shown in the following example:

Call Support

Level: Kite level

Actor: User

Device: iPhone

1. The user goes to the Contact page.

2. The user clicks the Support number.

3. The device asks for confirmation.

4. The user calls Support.

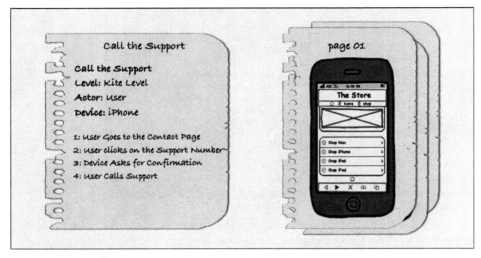

Figure 11–7. *The use-case: the textual use-case and its implementation on a paper prototype.*

In the first phase of our project flow, called *analysis*, the textual use-case was employed to identify the requirements of our project, but it can now be re-used in the test phase to compare the expected behavior from the textual use-case with the real user's behavior from the prototype test. Each entry in our textual use-case should match the actions performed by the user to complete the task. Figure 11–7 illustrates the use-case called "Call the Support."

Creating a Use-Case Diagram

A *use-case diagram* is a visual representation of the system boundary and its interactions with the external world. Those who interact with the system from the external world are the actors. An actor can be either a user or another system.

The system is represented by a square or rectangle that shows the system boundaries. Every use-case is represented as an oval that encloses the name of the use-case. The actor is represented by a stylized human, with an identity below it.

The use-case diagram uses a factorization approach, which means that a use-case can include another use-case, as shown in Figure 11–8. When a use-case includes another use-case, an arrow points to it, showing the word <<include>>.

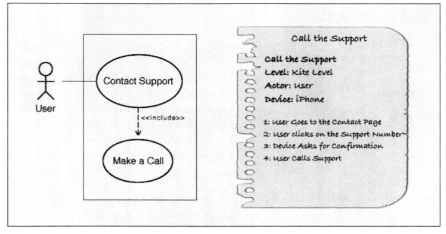

Figure 11–8. *Use-case: comparison between the diagram and the textual description.*

In our example, the Contact Support use-case includes another use-case called "Make a Call." If we refer to the Sea Level Detail of the textual description, the Contact Support use-case represents points 1 and 2, whereas the Make a Call use-case represents points 3, 4, and 5. In the Kite Level Detail, only point 1 belongs to the Contact Support use-case whereas points 2, 3, and 4 belong to the Make a Call use-case.

Use-case diagrams play a functional role in the test phase through organization and offering a visual reference to each test.

Creating the Assets

When the textual use-case and the use-case diagram are ready, we can begin to work on the test assets. We need to prepare two different types of assets: one type for the paper prototype and one type for the electronic prototype.

Paper Prototype

Paper prototypes are directly inspired by, or even recycled from, the paper prototype used in the design phase. Basically, we need to design a paper prototype for each step of our use-case, which means that paper prototypes and numbered points from the textual description have a one-to-one relationship, as illustrated in Figure 11–9.

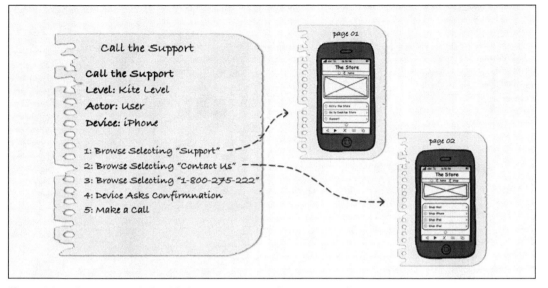

Figure 11–9. *One-to-one relationship between two textual use-case entries and two paper prototypes.*

Each paper prototype represents a view of a specific moment in the test in the same way a frame is a view of a specific moment in a movie clip. Paper prototypes always use some colors for reducing the gap in the brain between the perception of a simple piece of paper and a real image of a fully working device. A good approach is to use the Pantone Color Chart if you use a graphic program for choosing colors and design of your papers, or a Pantone pen if you use a handmade approach.

Electronic Prototype

Electronic prototypes are designed and developed as the last step before jumping into the implementation phase. As long as you haven't skipped this phase you should have an electronic prototype ready for the test phase.

Generally, an electronic prototype doesn't offer 100% of the functionality that the final release provides; the goal of this type of test is to perform checks in order to prevent errors and avoid their propagation in the implementation phase.

Nevertheless, in a web context, the electronic prototype is based on the same technology as the final release (HTML5, CSS3, and JavaScript), so this type of prototype is often very close to the final product that will be released (and is shown in Figure 11–10).

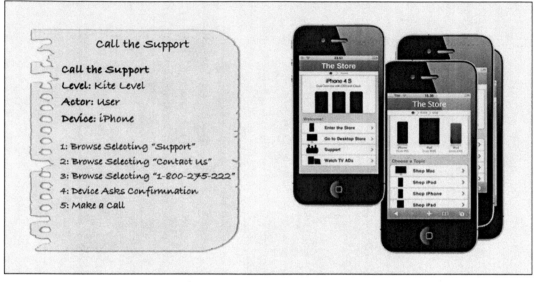

Figure 11–10. *The textual use-case (left) and the WebApp views (right).*

In Chapter 2, we suggested a framework plug-in to easily develop an electronic prototype of our project. Whatever approach we choose, the concept is always the same: create an HTML5, CSS3, and JavaScript model in order to be able to test a specific function or a specific service. According to the grade of functions and services offered by the electronic prototype, we can perform different grades of tests and have different grades of feedback.

Performing a Test

Once the assets are made, and assuming that the user is ready, we can start to perform the prototype tests. Any room with a table and two chairs is a perfect location for a paper prototype test.

Paper and electronic tests look different, the assets are different, the role of the tester in the test is different, and even the grade of feedback is different, yet the idea behind both types of tests is the same. Both could be categorized as *task-oriented tests*. We will see how the same idea drives these tests in the following sections.

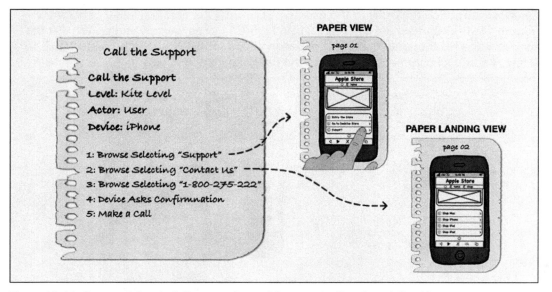

Figure 11–11. *Paper prototype test: the paper view and the paper landing view relationship.*

In these tests, the *paper view* is a physical paper page (an asset) while the *paper landing view* (another asset) is a link destination page. "Landing" is a relative prefix to increase the level of communication and better understand the context and relationship between two pages, which is useful when we need to analyze and discuss the results of the test.

Paper Prototype

The use-case that we need to perform with the user is represented by a *phrase* or an *order* that starts the use-case, and mentally leads the user through his actions. Referring to our Call Support use-case, a good phrase or order to start the test is Contact Support by Phone.

Call Support

Level: Sea level (a.k.a. User goal level)

Actor: User

Device: iPhone

Order: Contact the Support by Phone (for the user)

1. The user browses the menu by selecting the Support link.

2. The user browses the menu by selecting the Contact Us link.

3. The user browses the menu by selecting the "1-800-275-2273" link.

4. The device asks to confirm the call to the "1-800-275-2273" number.

5. The user makes a call to Support.

Once we introduce the order to the user, we show him the first and initial paper view (Figure 11–11), represented by "Page 01" in Figure 11–9 as we saw earlier. We ask the user to voice his thoughts during his experience and for every action he performs. The tester records all comments describing the user experience.

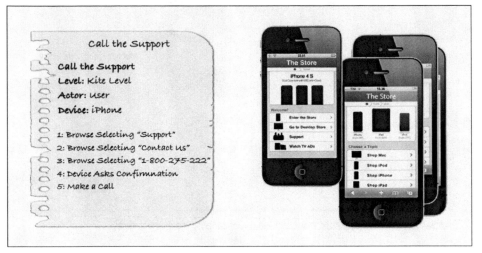

Figure 11–12. *Paper prototype test: the textual description used to drive the paper test.*

The user interacts with the paper prototype while the role of the tester is to replace the paper view with one relative to the user's action. In our example, if the user touches the Support link, the tester replaces the paper represented by Page 01 with the new landing paper view represented by Page 02, as in Figure 11–13.

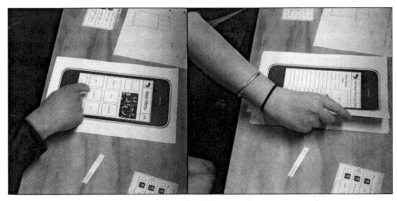

Figure 11–13. *Paper prototype test: tester changes the paper views (Image Samuel Mann).*

In the optimum case, the prototype test will finish when the user is able to achieve his task, and in the worst case, when he quits. In any case, the tester must record the user's experience, describing how the user achieved a task or why he failed.

Electronic Prototype

After learning as much as possible from the paper prototype tests, we are ready to perform the electronic variation called the *electronic prototype test* (see Figure 11–14). The test procedure remains the same; what changes is the level of user experience and the possibility for the tester to test functions and services that had not yet been implemented in the paper prototype test phase.

The electronic test can be performed using a desktop computer, which is the case if you use the Fireworks PlugIn. You will generally want to use a browser with a mobile user agent as a test environment.

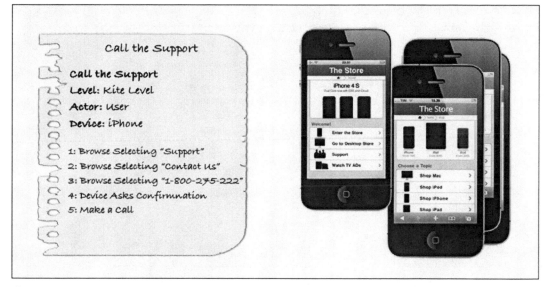

Figure 11–14. *Electronic prototype test: textual description used for driving the electronic test.*

Of course, because a web site or application typically shares the same technology used to develop electronic prototypes, a better version of this test could run directly inside the mobile device. In this case, we can have an electronic prototype that offers different levels of functionality or service from ~0% to ~100%.

An electronic prototype that is used only to test the design and level of feedback but provides almost none of the functions and services is comparable to a paper prototype. A prototype that provides most of the available functions and services produces a level of feedback comparable to the release version.

In both desktop and mobile versions of the electronic prototype test, the tester plays the same role that he played in the paper prototype test, except that he does not manually change the views during the test. The tester assigns the user certain tasks to accomplish while recording notes about the user's experience.

Evaluating a Test

Once all the prototype tests are complete, we need to work on our gathered data and feedback to evaluate the test and the project. It is important to remember that a test's feedback is only as reliable as the test model. This means that your prototype must simulate or represent the final release as much as possible.

The problem is that, in this context, where a short-circuit is obvious, we need to use prototype assets that look like the final release in order to get reliable feedback. However, we did perform prototype tests to understand how to design the final release and/or to verify that the actual design is correct before implementing the final release (see Figure 11–15). The bottom line is that a test is just a test, and reliability is based on tests performed on incomplete prototypes.

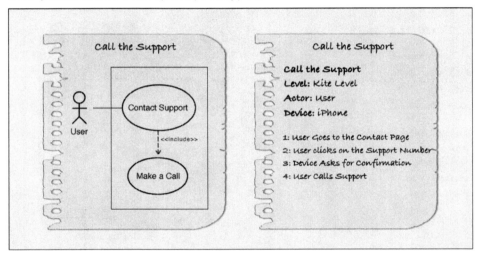

Figure 11–15. *Paper prototype test: two types of assets used by the tester to perform and evaluate the test.*

This fact is more apparent in a paper prototype test where paper seldom represents a real user interface and where poor color or details interact in different ways with the cognitive perception that is the foundation of every user's experience. These are things related to the visceral level of design—one of the three levels of design (along with behavioral and reflective) that Donald Norman explains in *Emotional Design*. Failure to create a link with the visceral level of design results in failure to anticipate the real user experience because it dismisses the level of effect, or emotional response, that a prototype can elicit in a user in a particular context.

> **NOTE:** Donald Norman is an academic in the field of cognitive science, design, and usability engineering and a co-founder and consultant with the Nielsen Norman Group.
>
> For more information, visit http://www.jnd.org/books.html.

In contrast, the electronic prototype shares the same technology with the final release, so the test and the feedback will be more accurate. The percentage of accuracy can change according to the number of functions and services implemented in the prototype.

Variables and Feedback to Evaluate

Generally speaking, a test can have a structure from very simple to very complex. Complex tests return rich and accurate feedback but also require resources and effort that are often beyond the scope of a small development team, let alone a single designer or developer.

Continuing with the agile approach, we use several variables and types of feedback in order to get a clear idea of what level of experience our design, functions, and services can trigger in the user's mind.

Number of Touches

The first variable to manage is the number of touches required by a user to accomplish a task. The number of touches is defined by the *shortest path tree* (SPT) from the starting point to the ending point of the content tree. The beginning point can be our home page or another page somewhere in the content tree for performing a more specific task. Figure 11–16 shows the steps necessary for the Call Support use-case. The path looks simple, but the simplified content tree represented by Figure 11–16 doesn't represent the internal links between web pages.

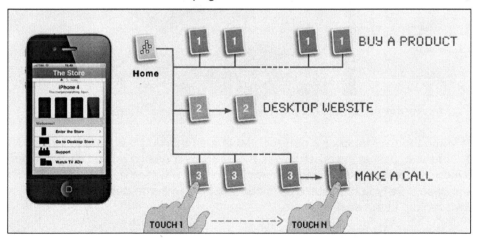

Figure 11–16. *The number of touches used to accomplish the Call the Support task.*

The SPT algorithm is used in other and more complex areas, but in our use-case the same concept is easily implemented by counting on the site map or content tree the number of touches needed to accomplish the task. The number of touches is reported by the tester in the use-case paper description as a reference.

Number of Mistakes

The second variable is the number of mistakes that the user makes while trying to accomplish his or her task. There are two categories of mistakes:

- **Touch error**. When the user touches the wrong link (Figure 11–17 left).

- **Touch misidentification**. When the user touches a non-touchable area (Figure 11–17 right).

When a user touches a wrong link, this means that he or she touched a link that brought him or her away from the ending point and that the link doesn't belong to the shortest path of the task. This type or mistake can either be the fault of the user or the design.

The tester needs to determine whether the design is correct and the user made a mistake triggered by the environment or some other cause, or whether the wrong design triggered the user's mistake.

Figure 11–17. *The types of user (touch) mistakes: wrong link (left) and non-touchable area (right).*

It is different when the user touches a non-touchable area thinking that he/she touched a link. In 99% of these cases, the mistake was triggered by a design error. Design errors could mean a context with a lack of user orientation, or just a wrong user interface design. In any case, this type of mistake calls our attention to some detail that we apparently overlooked in the design phase.

Estimated Time of Arrival

The third variable is the *estimated time of arrival* (ETA) (Figure 11–18), the time that the user needs in order to accomplish the task. The ETA is calculated against the tester, who knows the content tree and is able to pass the task.

Usually, the shortest path time is used as the lower-bound for the test, as taken by the experienced tester. The lower-bound defines the optimum, a standard that in practice is almost never matched by the user during a test. The closer the user is to this estimated time, the better he or she can accomplish the task and (presumably) the higher the level of user experience.

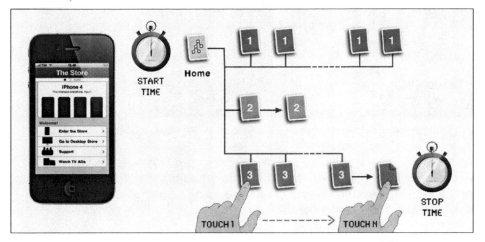

Figure 11–18. *Call Support use-case: calculating the estimated time of arrival (ETA).*

The ETA is reported in the use-case paper description as a reference for the tester.

Collecting Feedback

In addition to these three variables, there are three types of feedback that the tester can collect from the user's comments.

Design Feedback

The first type of feedback is *design feedback* about the quality of the user interface. In the design part of this book, we learned that, in the touch-oriented world, every part of the design is an interface that collects feedback about every design element. Figure 11–19 illustrates two different emotional feedbacks for the same user interface.

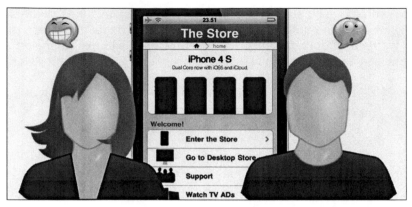

Figure 11–19. *Call Support use-case: two different design feedbacks for the same interface.*

Although this type of feedback can be useful in the paper prototype test to indicate the correctness of our design, it has more weight if gathered during the electronic prototype test because the implemented interface is almost the same as the release version and the information contains more useful details.

Expectation Feedback

The second type of feedback is *expectation feedback* about the design and service expectations of the user. This type of feedback is gathered every time the user lands on a web page that doesn't match his expectation or touches a link thinking that it represents a different service from the one implemented. Figure 11–20 shows what can happen when a user has a different mental representation of the landing page behind a link.

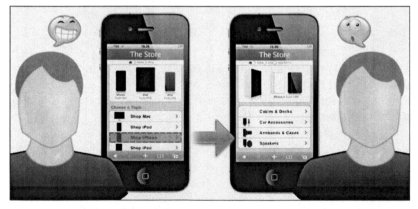

Figure 11–20. *Buy an iPhone Dock use-case: the expectation doesn't match the design in the landing page.*

The weight of this type of feedback is almost the same on both paper and electronic prototype tests. These tests are useful for understanding how semantically our design, functions, and services are represented in the user's mind and whether this meaning corresponds to our original plans.

Emotional Feedback

The last type of feedback is *emotional feedback* about the inner feelings of the user during the test session. This type of feedback has more weight for the electronic prototype test session and often isn't even gathered in the paper prototype test session.

Emotional feedback is triggered by two types of stimuli. One is *absolute* and triggered by colors, design elements, and everything involved in the identity of the project. In Figure 11–21, this stimulus is represented by the iPhone.

The other type of feedback is *relative* and involves the environment and the changes that this type of stimulus triggers in the user's inner world, as shown in Figure 11–21. The word "environment" refers to everything belonging to the physical world (except the mobile device) outside of the human user.

Figure 11–21. *Emotional feedback is triggered by two types of stimuli: absolute and relative.*

This type of feedback can give important information about the user's inner world during the test. This type of feeling is important as part of the global communication that comes from our web site or application. In order to test a relative stimulus, such as the environment, we need to implement an electronic prototype directly on the mobile device and go outside, allowing the user interface to join the real world.

Evaluation Techniques

Evaluating a test can be difficult, especially when working with a large amount of data and a wide-ranging project. We can apply statistical methods from a discipline called *descriptive statistics* in order to obtain reliable values. After performing a prototype test, we no longer need this type of approach, and an agile method can still provide reliable values without involving heavy calculations and complex mathematical skills.

Test Variable Evaluation

The simpler way to evaluate the variables involved in the prototype test is to count the number of occurrences of each variable and compare it to the number of occurrences in the actual test. In UML, the entity used to estimate (or represent) the expected value from a use-case test is called Oracle. In our test, the Oracle is represented by a set of variable values represented by natural numbers.

In our prototype tests, there are three natural numbers related to three types of variables: one for the number of touches, one for the number of mistakes, and one for the time of arrival.

The simplest method is to set a lower-bound for each variable that has to be matched in the test. Figure 11–22 shows a textual representation of the variable values in the use-case textual description. In our example, we set these values equal to the passed test (the user is four touches away from the Call the Support link), which means that the test will be either passed or failed.

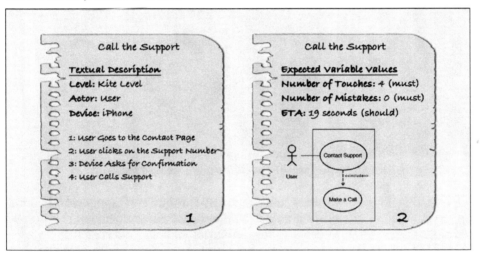

Figure 11–22. *A textual use-case with notes about the variable values.*

Once we set the minimum value for each variable, we need to set the *variable's modal operator* for the test. Variable modal operators set a verb for each variable showing how the expectation value should match. Generally, only a few modal operators are used. We use two for our purpose: "must" and "should."

The modal operator shows whether a variable's value *must* be matched or just *should* be matched in order to pass the test. We present only a simple example of a prototype test: for more complex projects and tests, it is a good idea to add a certain level of matching for each variable.

Our use-case test can be passed by performing only four touches, with no touch mistakes. The "should" attribute of the ETA variable says that the value of this variable is not a "must" for passing the test. In some cases, a more reliable result can be achieved by including some sub-set of passed cases, setting a percentage to match for each variable.

Test Feedback Evaluation

When working with variables, the most important thing is to know how to set them. After this difficult part is done, all that is left is to compare the data. This approach is more technical but doesn't require a great deal of skill or experience from the tester.

A completely different scenario is the feedback evaluation. This is because we will not have a number with which to compare and our experience will play a fundamental role. For this reason, we can introduce any experimental method or technique to evaluate the feedbacks, as long as we specify the procedure.

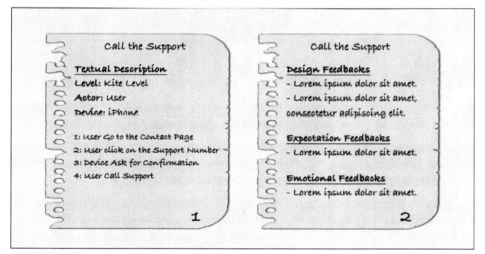

Figure 11–23. *The textual use-case with notes about the user feedbacks*

Collect the three types of feedback. Figure 11–23 shows an example of how we can note the user feedback. When everything is in place, we need to remember that every feedback has weight. The weight of a feedback is its inner value in relationship to the context. A user might report confusion with our interface, but the level of stress in a specific context might be the result of decreased cognitive resources, or these patterns might have been conditioned by another application or some ambient variables. For this reason, the tester's experience and practice are needed to gather reliable information from the user's feedback.

Resources on Testing

Table 11–1 provides some of the tools used in this chapter for testing our project.

Table 11–1. *Tools Used for Testing WebApp.*

Name	Type	URL	Operating System
Feng-Gui	WebApp	`http://www.feng-gui.com/`	OSX – Win - Linux
yUML	WebApp	`http://yuml.me/`	OSX – Win - Linux
Agilian	Application	`http://www.visual-paradigm.com/`	OSX - Win
OmniGraffle	Application	`http://www.omnigroup.com/`	OSX - iOS

Summary

In this chapter, we saw the importance of planning a testing phase and how this phase can be performed along the entire project flow—not just at the end of the process.

We began by showing how heat maps are a reliable source of feedback for the designer and developer. We then introduced paper and electronic prototypes. We saw how these two types of tests help the tester gather different types of feedback.

We discussed how to organize a test by applying artifact recycling from the previous steps of the process flow. We saw how to create a test and a use-case using different levels of detail. We used UML notations, introducing the use-case textual description and the use-case diagram.

We then saw how to perform a test with paper and electronic prototypes. We saw how to create and recycle the assets, and that the electronic prototype was performed in the early phase of design while the electronic prototype was performed at the end of the design phase before passing on to the implementation phase.

We also saw that the electronic prototype, because it shares the same technology with the web site or application, can be used to test the project outside the office in a real-world scenario.

Finally, we saw how to evaluate a test and the variables and types of feedback involved in this process. We presented three types of variables (number of touches, number of mistakes, and estimated time of arrival) and three types of feedback (design, expectation, and emotional feedback) used in the evaluation.

## Chapter 12

Maximizing the Market for iOS WebApps

Talent wins games, but teamwork and intelligence wins championships.

—Michael Jordan

In this chapter, you will learn how to promote a WebApp. You will see how using some specific approaches can help guarantee that the WebApp has good visibility, even before it's released on the net.

We will talk about Beta Tester invitations and about press releases; you will see the benefits of creating a web site for the WebApp and how to create awareness using video social networks, such as YouTube.

We will also show you how to submit the WebApp to the Apple WebApp Portal and what other options the net offers in addition to the official Apple portal. Finally, we will discuss monetizing your WebApp and which services you can use for doing so.

Use Your Mobile Strategy

Previously, in Chapter 2, we worked on a mobile strategy and discussed how this strategy is important in order to achieve goals and mitigate mistakes, ultimately creating a successful project. The keys to a winning marketing plan is knowing exactly what your Web application has to offer and the profile of your potential users. This is why the mobile strategy elaborated in the early phase of your project becomes crucial at this point.

Using the information gathered while developing your mobile strategy, you are able to better market your Web application, targeting a specific range of user profiles. Chapter 12 introduces some of the best approaches for doing this.

How to Promote Your WebApp

Assuming that your mobile strategy is on track and that you know the range of user profiles you want to target, you can consider how to promote your WebApp. As you will see in the following sections, various techniques can be used in order to reach a wider range of potential users.

These techniques can change according to the state of development of the Web applications. In the early phase of release, use Beta Invitations for both tests and introducing the Web application to a small number of important users. As shown in Figure 12–1, once the Web application is ready, you can design a web site to create an identity and/or create a YouTube channel where you can insert video tutorials about the most important features.

Figure 12–1. *A Wordpress theme to promote native and WebApps (source: image from Templatic).*

At this point, the Web application is ready to be released to the press on major Apple-oriented blogs and inserted in some major WebApp portals where you can gain visibility among potential users. Once the Web application is live on the major WebApp portals, it's time to use the viral nature of social networks to create positive hype around your Web application.

Use Beta Invitation Testers

The first step in your marketing plan begins even before the Web application is released. After the alpha tests are performed internally by the designers and developers, the Web application enters the beta test phase where real users test it in their own environments.

The Beta Invitation Phase involves a small group of users, chosen for their profile and potential connections with other important users. This kind of user is chosen because he/she represents a significant profile for testing the Web application; he/she also has important connections with potential users that are not reachable through other channels of communication.

In your Web application, it would be a good idea to create an account in advance for the Beta Tester and send this and other information to the user before he/she approaches the Web application. This will create a more comfortable environment for the tester and will help him contextualize all the services and functions, decreasing his learning curve.

A good choice for a Beta Tester could be a designer or a developer from another team, a user involved in a specific business who can spread the word about the Web application, or an important blogger or journalist. A testimonial to this strategy is Walter S. Mossberg, an American journalist and principal technology columnist for *The Wall Street Journal*, who always receives a version of the latest device from Apple before it is actually released to every Apple Store. In reality, the role Mossberg plays in the equation is more like a Beta Reviewer than a Beta Tester, but the concept behind the Apple strategy is the same.

Use Press Releases

The press is always the first link for all types of news, and digital news is no exception. It's important to distribute press releases regarding your launch to major Apple-oriented blogs on the net. You must be sure to provide a complete description and screenshots of crucial functions for your WebApp, making sure that details are not left in the hands of the blogger.

Create a WebApp Web Site

Creating a web site or Web application means spreading word of its identity over the Internet, being indexed by search engines, and representing a point of support for every potential user. Many designers and developers overlook this step in both native and Web application processes, which is a serious mistake. A web site is one of the best communication channels for every type of application.

When designing a web site, it is important that you keep the identity of your Web application and the primary user's target profile in mind so that you are not only pursuing your personal design tastes. In this phase, the choice of colors and the type of lines that will be used in the design are crucial. Creating an aggressive design for a primarily female Web application might work against you in your promotional campaign.

Figure 12–2. *The native application Twitterrific offers a good example of an application Web site.*

In Chapter 4, we discussed color psychology and the relationship between colors and users' moods. Along with the right choice of colors and lines, it is important that the web site includes the following sections:

- **Functionalities.** This is what the Web application can do for the user, stated clearly and directly. Functionalities can also be presented as a preview on the home page, as shown in Figure 12–2.

- **Version history.** It is important take note of all updates and new functions implemented in the Web application to create a background for the developers and a reference for the users.

- **Tutorials.** It is important that, on the web site, the user is able to find a tutorial, which will help him to use all the major functions and services implemented.

- **About.** When possible, it is important to give a clear representation of your team. Giving credit to the entire team will help your app look even more professional to your users.

- **Support.** It is important to offer support to the user for any issues that may arise regarding the services and functions implemented in the Web application. Providing good support is key for any team that wants to create return customers.

- **Social sharing options.** It is fundamental to provide a social sharing option in order to let the user spread the news about the Web application. From all the options available, the Twitter and Facebook sharing options are a must; it is also important to offer Facebook-like buttons.

■ **Community (optional).** It is important to provide a place where developers can meet each other, share, and grow together. This option is only for open source projects where developers work from different places without the opportunity to meet face to face.

■ **Blog (optional).** It is important to update the development status of the Web application. An active blog gives a positive image to the users, and acts as good support, helping to create return customers.

The best examples of application web sites are from those dedicated to native iOS applications because the need to sell behind a native iOS project brings native developers to adopt this technique before comparing web developers; a good example is provided by the Twitterrific app web site, as shown in Figure 12–2. The benefits are the same for both development approaches.

Finally, it is important to always implement an Add to Home Screen function for both iPad and iPhone users. This is considered a good practice to implement in every WebApp for two reasons. First, not all users bookmark pages, even if they perceive them as interesting; second, when adding to the home screen, a Web application is considered the last step in the native emulation process. Accessing a native-like WebApp without the possibility of launching it from the home screen dramatically decreases the user's native-like experience.

Use E-mail Marketing

After creating your App-promoting web site, it is a good idea to encourage your potential users to sign up for newsletters that deliver information about the status of your WebApp, introduce new features, or announce bug fixes.

Figure 12–3. *The native app "Shall I Buy" is a good example of e-mail marketing.*

Figure 12–3 shows a web site that implements this approach, which works to provide updates once the WebApp has exited the Beta Testing Phase and is available to all users online.

Create YouTube Video Tutorials

Video tutorials are a good way to offer support to users of your Web application, especially beginners; these tutorials simply and directly explain how to properly use the application's services and functions. YouTube videos can be embedded in your application web site's tutorial section. The YouTube channel has great visibility in a search engine such as Google.

In the past, many big names, such as Apple, had their own YouTube channels (see Figure 12–4). Recent channel features now enable users to customize channel styles and themes, offering the developer the opportunity to match a specific user identity.

Figure 12–4. *Apple's official YouTube channel on a desktop, iPad, and iPhone.*

Opening a YouTube channel is easy; it only takes a few minutes to register an account at http://www.youtube.com. You must remember to choose the right title, description, and tags when you use the upload video form. Good titles and tags are required in order to maximize the possibility of the video being indexed accurately on the Google search engine, making it easier for the user to view all important information at a glance.

The description under every video is composed of a three-line preview plus a (more info) link that shows the entire description content. In the three line preview, be sure to insert everything that is needed to describe the content of the video, going into detail only after the third line. This guarantees the highest possible level of user experience during his/her interaction with your videos.

Submit to Apple WebApp Portal

The Apple WebApp portal is the closest thing to the App Store for a web developer. This portal doesn't offer the same visibility to all the Web applications submitted as does the App Store using different channels, but it remains the best option for promoting any type of WebApp.

Exactly as in the world of the App Store, in order to submit a project, it is necessary to register a developer account with Apple. The difference here is that, in this case, even the free version will suffice for submission of a Web application to the portal.

Figure 12–5. *The official Apple WebApps portal on an iPad (left) and on an iPhone (right).*

From the Apple WebApp portal, as shown in Figure 12–5, click in the banner situated in the right sidebar titled "Submitting Applications." You will be redirected to the Apple Development Center at `http://developer.apple.com/devcenter/safari/` where, once logged in using your Apple ID, you will be able to access the Apple iPhone Web Application Form. At the end of the form, you can insert a 320 × 436 pixel application screenshot and a 128 ×128 pixel product application icon.

You can also manage your submissions from the Apple Development Center by updating or changing any type of information regarding your web applications.

Submit to Other WebApp Portals

The are several reasons why the use of the Apple Store WebApp portal is the best option for any web developer aiming to promote his or her application. First, the portal is an official source and is supervised by Apple personnel; second, it is well organized. The Apple WebApp portal is not the only way to go; other good options to promote your Web application are available.

OpenAppMkt, available at http://openappmkt.com/, is a WebApp portal in pure Apple style; it is well organized and offers several options, such as a sharing toolbar and a box for user reviews, that even the Apple portal doesn't offer. From a user standpoint, OpenAppMkt requires a free user account where a user inserts his e-mail information, which will be used to send the Web application directly to the developer's e-mail account.

Figure 12–6. *OpenAppMkt on an iPad.*

If you want to submit your Web application, you need to register a developer account. From the developer dashboard's sidebar, you can click the Submit New App button and fill in the form with all the Web application's information. You also need to provide an App icon, choose the correct category, and specify whether your Web application is designed for iPhone and/or iPad and its price.

OpenAppMkt is a great resource for a web developer, also providing revenue handling at an interest rate of 80–20%. This approach is similar to that used by the App Store. Figure 12–6 displays the Developer tab where you can upload your WebApp information.

Figure 12–7. *The Add to Home function of OpenAppMkt in action.*

Figure 12–7, shows that the OpenAppMkt has applied the best practice of inserting the reminder "Add to Home Screen" into the WebApp for both iPad and iPhone users, increasing the native-like experience.

Figure 12–8. *The eHub web site is a constantly updated resource for Web applications.*

Another good WebApp portal is eHub (see Figure 12–8), available at http://emilychang.com/ehub/. This portal hosts desktop projects as well as mobile Web applications and generates a large amount of Internet traffic.

Use the Virality of Social Networks

Building a web site is a fundamental step for the marketing plan of a Web application; adding a blog is also a good way to update users about bug fixes and new features. Social networks offer a perfect platform for various types of promotion, from personal to business.

Subscribing to a social network gives you the opportunity to post any type of update. It is even faster than a blog and gives you the opportunity to find and create new important relationships, as shown in Figure 12–9. In this respect, not all social networks are equal; for example, platforms such as Twitter and LinkedIn (which are able to import tweets inside a personal home page) are more business-oriented than Facebook. However, it is important to optimize any communication channel available.

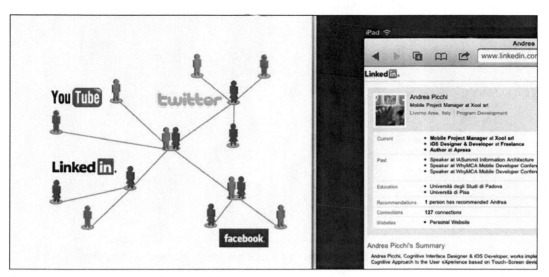

Figure 12-9. *An example of social network interconnection (source: image from Labrow Marketing).*

Speaking of general WebApp projects, the first step might be to create a LinkedIn account. LinkedIn (see Figure 12–9) is a business-oriented social network platform and is the best channel for creating important links with designers, developers, and professional teams around the world. A LinkedIn profile is complete and offers a great opportunity to show off your knowledge and past experience, also offering the ability to send invitations to your e-mail contacts and to import your Twitter Timeline and your SlideShare Presentations, while creating a powerful connection with many of your channels.

The second step might be to create a Twitter account. The account can be personal or dedicated to the Web application. Twitter is a creative micro-blogging social network platform. This means that, in addition to private users, many professional designers and developers use it to share news and updates on their projects. With its post limit of 140 characters, Twitter is perfect for short and fast project updates. Your personal Twitter home page can be customized by modifying the background image and the color palette of the theme to match any personal identity.

The third step might be to create a Facebook page for your WebApp. Facebook is the least business-oriented of these three networks because the percentage of people that use Facebook for professional purposes is minimal compared with Twitter and, especially, LinkedIn. Nevertheless, the smart use of Facebook might enable you to reach new potential users—those who are not already big WebApp users or who are returning customers. In this phase, it's also important to bear in mind that different projects have different requirements and priorities. Choose the right social network to reach your target user profile.

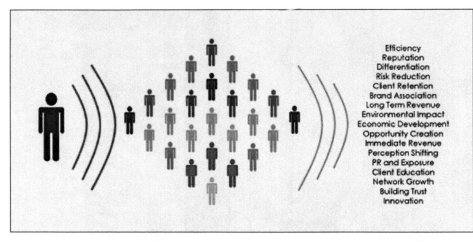

Figure 12–10. *The virality of distribution on social media networks (image Intersection Consulting).*

Monetizing a WebApp

It is not as easy to monetize a Web application as it is a native application because you can't rely on App Store support. The App Store assumes the responsibility of selling your native application. The application promotion is just a plus; the App Store offers good visibility of almost all Apps submitted to it. The music changes when it is necessary to raise income from a Web application that needs to be promoted from zero.

In addition to the opportunities offered by portals like OpenAppMkt, the two best ways to raise income are through Google AdSense and PayPal donations.

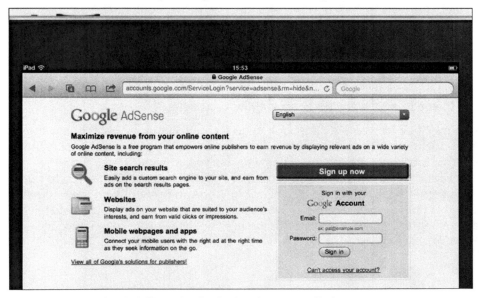

Figure 12–11. *The Google AdSense Service Registration page on iPad.*

Google AdSense offers the opportunity to insert and display targeted ads in your content and earn money from them. The service works on both mobile and desktop platforms, having a specific section for Web applications. After registering an account on Google AdSense, you need to add a snippet of code to your Web application, as in Google Analytics. Google AdSense also offers the ability to customize mobile ads to best match the look and feel of your Web application design.

PayPal is a well-known and widely used platform. You can use PayPal donations with your Web application in order to raise funds from it. In this case, it is a good idea to add the Donate button to both the application web site and the Web application. PayPal is an effective income generator if your Web application is a specific one and effectively solves user problems with its function or service.

Resources on WebApp Market

Table 12–1 lists the major WebApp portals and social networks for promoting any type of WebApp using the Internet. We have included the links to PayPal and AdSense for those interested in monetizing their project.

Table 12–1. *Tools Used to Design iPhone and iPad User Interfaces.*

Name	Type	URL
Apple WebDev Center	WebDev Portal	http://developer.apple.com/devcenter/safari/
Apple WebApps	WebApp Portal	http://www.apple.com/webapps/
OpenAppMkt	WebApp Portal	http://openappmkt.com/
Myijump	WebApp Portal	http://myijump.com/
eHub	WebApp Portal	http://emilychang.com/ehub/
WebApp TV	WebApp Portal	http://webapp.tv/
App Site	Showcase	http://www.appsites.com/
YouTube	Video Portal	http://www.youtube.com/
Twitter	Social Network	http://twitter.com/
Facebook	Social Network	http://www.facebook.com/
LinkdIn	Social Network	http://www.linkedin.com/
Google AdSense	WebApp	https://www.google.com/adsense
PayPal	WebApp	https://www.paypal.com/

Summary

This chapter discussed how to maximize the market for Web applications by showing that the Web application market is not comparable to the native app market because of the App Store paradigm.

In the first part of the chapter, we introduced how a mobile strategy developed in the early phase of a project can be useful for planning a promotional campaign and a marketing strategy for your projects.

In the second part of this chapter, we presented several approaches for achieving your marketing goals. We used (VIP) Beta Testers to both test and promote an application, and then we created a web site to introduce the Web application to search engines and to the Internet. After creating a web site, we created a YouTube channel to promote the application and provide video support to import video tutorials to the web site.

In the third part of this chapter, once the main structure around our Web application was built, we submitted it to the Apple WebApp portal as well as to other portals, such as the OpenAppMkt. We also saw how portals like OpenAppMkt can help us to raise income with the paradigm used with native applications in the App Store.

In the fourth part of this chapter, we used the virality of social networks to disseminate information about our Web application to specific types of users on LinkedIn and Twitter and to various types of potential users on Facebook.

In the last part of the chapter, we presented two methods for monetizing our Web application. The ADSense Service can provide developers with a good average income. We also saw how the PayPal Service works better with Web applications that solve important problems and generate a feeling of gratitude in the user, prompting him/her to make a donation.

## Chapter 13

Looking Beyond the Mobile Web to Ubiquitous Computing

... The people who are crazy enough to think they can change the world are the ones who do.

Steve Jobs

The Explosion of Mobile Devices, Wireless, and Cellular Communications

Delivering the keynote speech at an American Institute of Business event in Palm Springs in 2011, Google CEO Dr. Eric Schmidt provided some staggering predictions regarding mobile usage.

"Everything we've talked about and everything you're going to hear says, 'do mobile,'" Schmidt declared. "We look at the charts internally and it's happening faster than all of our predictions. This is the future, and everybody will adapt."

According to Schmidt, the CEO of one of the most revolutionary companies in the world, over the next few years, between 1.5 and 2 billion people will get connected. "This is a vision that includes everyone. It does not discriminate based on the amount of money you have, as long as you have some sort of mobile device," Schmidt continued.

These numbers seem enormous when compared with the predicted expansion of any other technology, but the fact is that according to a recent article by the ITU (the UN's International Telecommunication Agency), the growth of mobile usage has already eclipsed the Google CEO's lofty predictions. "With the world's population exceeding 6.8 billion, nearly one person in three surfs online," said Susan Teltscher, ITU's head of market information and statistics. Even President Barack Obama said that his plan to double the size of the broadcasting spectrum reserved for wireless devices is mostly aimed at addressing the growing mobile-device market.

New and upcoming mobile video applications will contribute to make up a large portion of the enormous traffic demand from mobile and media center devices. For instance, FaceTime on iPhone and iPad will dramatically impact network capabilities around the world.

According to the Cisco Global Mobile Data Traffic Forecast and recent Morgan Stanley reports, by 2015, nearly every human on Earth will have a mobile device, and tablet penetration will help raise the average mobile connection to 1.118 megabytes per month. The highest growth rates are in India, with 158 percent, and in the Middle East and Africa, with annual rates of 129 percent. This is followed by other countries and regions such as Latin America, Asia Pacific, South Africa, and Mexico.

Although home devices such as media centers and desktop computers in the near future will stay on existing networks, which will be improved as time goes on , mobile devices, such as smartphones and tablets, will have to wait to move to the upcoming 4G technologies, which they will need in order to efficiently run new video-based applications.

Next-Generation User Experience with Touchscreen and Multitouch Technology

The key term in the title of this section is "user experience." Multitouch technology brings to everyone—private users and professional developers alike—new benefits and opportunities. The impact of this type of technology has been so great that now we think of it as a revolution in the history of electronics. Figure 13–1 shows some examples of new application environments available on multitouch devices.

At first glance, the basis of this revolution seems to be multitouch-screen technology, but as you previously learned in this book, everything happens in the user's mind. From this point of view, a touchscreen is merely a trigger, not the event. The event is the change in the user's experience.

This improved level of user experience comes from the new multitouch paradigm, which the mobile user is able to utilize through the development of multitouch-screen technology. This advancement has fundamentally changed the relationship between the environment and the user. This is the evolutionary chain of the new multitouch user experience.

Figure 13–1. *New application environments available on multitouch-technology devices*

New Technology, New Usability, and New Opportunity

When the first iPhone was launched in 2007, the mobile community benefited from a device that was able to provide a new browsing experience. Before 2007, surfing the net from a cellular phone or any other mobile device wasn't nearly as pleasant as it is today. As a result, the mobile market began to grow with incredible speed, and even four years later, it's still growing rapidly.

In 2007, the only way to develop software for Apple's new device was to write web applications, but many countries weren't ready for this type of revolution. With the exception of the HTML5 cache feature, all web applications are, to some degree, dependent on Internet access, and many countries weren't able to offer inexpensive 24/7 contracts to satisfy users' new requirements, thereby limiting the device's enormous potential.

In 2008, Apple released its first SDK, and the second-generation iPhone. At the same time, the iPhone app store opened its doors to thousands and thousands of new native applications. These new applications brought new patterns for old tasks, offering a new and improved level of user experience. The enhanced usability of these native applications changed user habits and created brand new habits, taking the iPhone where no cellular or mobile device had been before.

The revolution had begun but was incomplete until 2010, when Apple introduced the iPad. The last barrier represented by the iPhone's small 3.5-inch display was finally overcome. The new 9.7-inch, multitouch display of the iPad boosted the level of user experience, setting a new standard for browsing the net. It was able to hit markets that the iPhone, because of its small display, had been unable to reach.

The iPad revolution is visible every day. Doctors, professors, lawyers, and musicians, as well as companies such as airline companies and car factories, have incorporated the new tablet into their daily activities or retail products, increasing the quality of their jobs and products and creating new types of activities.

The new and improved level of usability and user experience makes it possible—for the first time in the history of computers—to bring electronic devices to all categories of users, even those that had previously been unreachable. One category is children. For them, using a multitouch-based interface is more natural compared to using a mouse-based interface. This enables tablets to be used early on, for many types of school activities in which, for cognitive and logistical reasons, using a PC would be impractical, as shown in Figure 13–2.

Figure 13–2. *The new opportunities offered by a multitouch-technology device (image source: the LMUILA School of Education)*

Another new category is that of older users—people who have never used a PC before in their lives or who struggle to use one. I'm sure that you can come up with an example of a parent who has been unable to surf the net before getting his hands on an iPad and who immediately afterward started surfing with no problem. My mother was one such person. She had never been able to use a PC, and now she surfs the net like a geek, watching news channels on YouTube, checking weather forecasts, and reading the local newspaper.

However, the multitouch revolution is far from complete, and in keeping with this revolution, the next big step in this process will occur when these small mobile devices encourage the creation of larger touchscreen-based systems, ones that will ultimately enter our work and home environments. The computer-saturated future that we have become accustomed to seeing in sci-fi movies and television series is perhaps not so far away as we might think.

How the Multitouch-Screen Revolution Will Change Next-Generation Computing

The world is in the middle of a mobile network revolution. In this revolution, we can identify two distinct forces: smartphones and tablets. This conclusion might seem obvious, but its implications are deeper than you might think.

On one hand, mobile devices such as the iPhone changed the lifestyles of many users and introduced them to new ways of working or of simply accomplishing ordinary tasks. Smartphones, before any other device, were responsible for pushing the enormous network growth I talked about earlier, and these devices led one of the most exciting technology revolutions in computer history.

It's certainly true that some applications, such as YouTube, run perfectly on small displays, such as the iPhone's screen; other applications, such as Netflix, look much better on the iPad's 9.7-inch display. This, too, will contribute to the growth of broadband demand for video applications.

Larger-format video is not the only important feature of a tablet like the iPad. In addition to their bigger displays, tablets also have a touchscreen interface and portable capabilities. Before tablets, the only mobile objects capable of sending and receiving data from the Internet were laptops, and to use one was a different experience for the user.

Figure 13–3. *Crestron (left) and Savant (right) applications for home automation*

This new approach brought users numerous innovative applications, such as those shown in Figure 13–3. Many companies became familiar with tablets in order to integrate their functionalities into the company's projects. Developers working on products for the home were the first to realize the possibility of making their products compatible with the iPad. Media centers, home surveillance systems, and other types of remotely controlled systems are just a few examples of such products, and there will be even more such products in the future.

From Domestic to Ubiquitous Computing and Ambient Intelligence

Domestic and house automation are two aspects of a singular new type of connection between mobile devices and a user's environment, a connection that has resulted in what is called "ubiquitous computing." What exactly is ubiquitous computing?

In 1991, Marc Weiser, in his seminal paper "The Computer for the 21st Century"," noted that "The most profound technologies are those that disappear. They weave themselves into the fabric of everyday life until they are indistinguishable from it." That's the core concept behind ubiquitous computing.

The decade of the '80s was that of the microprocessor, symbolized by the personal computer. It was the decade when we actually built our computers. The decade of the '90s was that of networks and communication, the decade when people connected computers together. It was symbolized by the World Wide Web. The decade of the '00s was the decade when personal computers turned into small devices and became portable. It was symbolized first by the laptop and then by the smartphone. In the present decade, computers are everywhere, are connected everywhere, and are embedded everywhere. Every part of the world has become connected to the network, searchable through the network, and usable by the user. Figure 13–4 shows an example of ubiquitous computing. This project is called vrFlora and was presented at the UbiComp Conference. It shows an adaptive response suitable to a user's situation.

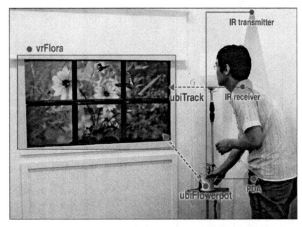

Figure 13–4. *The project vrFlora at the UbiComp conference (image source: Sejin Oh)*

The ubiquitous computing era arrived at the moment we realized that the computer had become invisible. In this era, people are no longer "users" in the strict meaning of the word but are "subjects." The user becomes a subject the moment that a person and computer switch from having a one-way relationship to having a two-way relationship. In other words, subjects are used by technology in the same way they use it themselves. A subject can walk down a street and interact with the touch interface of his or her smartphone connected to a GPS satellite; simultaneously, he or she can be watched by the video interface of a surveillance camera and be monitored through the sensor interface of a biometric system.

An example of a primitive implementation of ubiquitous computing can be seen in augmented-reality applications that can be run on both the iPhone and the iPad (see Figures 13–5 and 13–6). These AR applications have taken the first step toward a new paradigm of user experience, but the stream of data that they produce still flows in only one direction: from the object to the user.

Figure 13–5. *An implementation of augmented reality (image Earthmine)*

As computers become smaller and as their parallel processing increases exponentially, ubiquitous computing will bring about a new type of environment, one capable of interacting with a subject in both directions, sending and retrieving data and also implementing what is called "ambient intelligence." When the bridge between the World Wide Web and its users (subjects) is completed, the computing world will enter into a new era.

Today, we can do a lot with mobile devices, both smartphones and tablets, to build a little piece of that future. The web is the link between every device involved in the "ubiquitous paradigm," and this brings exciting opportunities for every designer and developer because the sky is the limit when it comes to ubiquitous computing.

Remember, "... the people who are crazy enough to think they can change the world are the ones who do."

Figure 13–6. *Objects in an environment are transformed into objects in an interface (image Fibre Design).*

Resources for Telecommunication and Ubiquitous Computing

In the following table, I list some resources where you can get more information about telecommunications, the actual growth of mobile markets, and new aspects of ubiquitous computing.

Table 13–1. *Resource on Mobile Technology*

Name	Type	URL
ITU	web site	http://www.itu.int/
Mobile Mix	web site	http://www.millennialmedia.com/
UbiComp	web site	http://www.ubicomp.org/
earthmine	web site	http://www.earthmine.com/

Summary

In this chapter, you saw what will come next in the mobile revolution and what ubiquitous computing will become. This is the next step in the evolution of combining new network capabilities and new mobile technologies.

First, you saw that the first mobile revolution is far from finished and that it still causes the mobile market and broadband demand to grow.

Next, you discovered how new touchscreen technologies will foster a new generation of usability and how this will bring new opportunities for both designers and developers.

You also read how the touchscreen revolution will change the next generation of computing and how domestic and ambient intelligence are part of the next evolutionary stage.

Finally, I analyzed how ubiquitous computing developed over the past decades, and I introduced the key concept of how the new ubiquitous computing paradigm will change the role of the user, transforming the way a user interacts with surrounding technologies and turning him or her into a system.

Index

R

T

CPSIA information can be obtained at www.ICGtesting.com
Printed in the USA
LVOW022334080112

262956LV00004B/1/P